Scott Foresman

Reader's and Writer's Notebook

Savvas Learning Company LLC, 15 East Midland Avenue, Paramus, NJ 07652

ISBN-13: 978-0-328-47667-1
ISBN-10: 0-328-47667-6
30 20
CC1

Readiness: My World

Unit 1: Animals, Tame and Wild

Unit 2: Communities

Unit 3: Changes

Unit 2: Communities

Unit 3: Changes

Unit 4: Treasures

Unit 5: Great Ideas

Name ____________________

Unit R Reading Log

Reading Time	Title and Author	What is it about?	How would you rate it?	Why?
From ____ to ____			Great OK Awful	
From ____ to ____			Great OK Awful	
From ____ to ____			Great OK Awful	
From ____ to ____			Great OK Awful	
From ____ to ____			Great OK Awful	

Name ______________________________

Unit 1 Reading Log

Reading Time	Title and Author	What is it about?	How would you rate it?	Why?
From _____ to _____			Great OK Awful	
From _____ to _____			Great OK Awful	
From _____ to _____			Great OK Awful	
From _____ to _____			Great OK Awful	
From _____ to _____			Great OK Awful	
From _____ to _____			Great OK Awful	

Name ______________________________

Unit 2 Reading Log

Reading Time	Title and Author	What is it about?	How would you rate it?	Why?
From _____ to _____			Great OK Awful	
From _____ to _____			Great OK Awful	
From _____ to _____			Great OK Awful	
From _____ to _____			Great OK Awful	
From _____ to _____			Great OK Awful	
From _____ to _____			Great OK Awful	

Name ______________________________

Unit 3 Reading Log

Reading Time	Title and Author	What is it about?	How would you rate it?	Why?
From _____ to _____			Great OK Awful	
From _____ to _____			Great OK Awful	
From _____ to _____			Great OK Awful	
From _____ to _____			Great OK Awful	
From _____ to _____			Great OK Awful	
From _____ to _____			Great OK Awful	

Name ______________________________

Unit 4 Reading Log

Reading Time	Title and Author	What is it about?	How would you rate it?	Why?
From _____ to _____			Great OK Awful	
From _____ to _____			Great OK Awful	
From _____ to _____			Great OK Awful	
From _____ to _____			Great OK Awful	
From _____ to _____			Great OK Awful	
From _____ to _____			Great OK Awful	

Name ______________________________

Unit 5 Reading Log

Reading Time	Title and Author	What is it about?	How would you rate it?	Why?
From ____ to ____			Great OK Awful	
From ____ to ____			Great OK Awful	
From ____ to ____			Great OK Awful	
From ____ to ____			Great OK Awful	
From ____ to ____			Great OK Awful	
From ____ to ____			Great OK Awful	

Name ____________________

Unit 4 Reading Log

Reading Time	Title and Author	What is it about?	How would you rate it?	Why?
From _____ to _____			Great OK Awful	
From _____ to _____			Great OK Awful	
From _____ to _____			Great OK Awful	
From _____ to _____			Great OK Awful	
From _____ to _____			Great OK Awful	
From _____ to _____			Great OK Awful	

Name ______________________________

Unit 5 Reading Log

Reading Time	Title and Author	What is it about?	How would you rate it?	Why?
From ____ to ____			Great OK Awful	
From ____ to ____			Great OK Awful	
From ____ to ____			Great OK Awful	
From ____ to ____			Great OK Awful	
From ____ to ____			Great OK Awful	
From ____ to ____			Great OK Awful	

Read Together

Name ______________________

Story Title ______________________

Author ______________________

A **picture walk** can help you learn about a story.

Look at the pictures in the story. What do you want to find out about the story?
Draw a picture of the thing or person you have a question about.

Who is the character in the story? **How** does the character feel or act? **Write**.

Read Together

Name ____________________

Story Title ____________________

Author ____________________

You can look at the pictures in a story and **predict** what might happen in the story.

You can **set a purpose** for reading by thinking about why you want to read this story.

Look at the pictures in the story.
What do you predict about the story?
Draw a picture about your prediction. **Write** a label about it.

Check your predictions. **Read** the part that tells in the story.
Write where the story takes place.

____

Read Together

Name ______________________

Story Title ______________________

Author ______________________

Circle the sentences that are true about realistic fiction.

It has animals that talk like people.

There are characters.

It has a setting.

It tells about things that could really happen.

Draw pictures to show what happens at the beginning, the middle, and end of the story.

Read Together

Name ____________________

Story Title ____________________

Author ____________________

You can **ask questions** about what you are going to read to better understand the story.

Look at the pictures in the story. What **questions** would you like to ask about the characters and events in the story? **Write**.

____

____

____

____

Circle each sentence that tells about realistic fiction.

It is a made up story that could happen in real life.

It is a story that could not happen.

There are one or more characters in the story.

It has a beginning, middle, and end.

Read Together

Name ______________________

Story Title ______________________

Author ______________________

Look at the pictures of the story. **Think** about what you know about the topic. **Write** a question about the story.

After reading, **reread** the part of the story that answers your question. Did you have to make any corrections to your question?

What happened in the story? **Draw** the problem or the solution.

Read Together

Name ________________________________

Story Title ________________________________

Author ________________________________

What do you think the characters in the story will see at the farmers market? **Draw** pictures and **write** labels.

Write a sentence in each box telling what happened in the story.

Beginning

Middle

End

Name ____________________

Story Title ____________________

Author ____________________

When you read, you should understand what and why things happen in the story.

Ask questions about the story before you read and then look for the answers in the story.

What would you do if you read a part of a story that did not make sense to you? **Write**.

Think about the story you just read. **Write** or **draw** what you did to understand the events in the story.

Name ______________________

Story Title ______________________

Author ______________________

A story can be a **fantasy**. This kind of story is made up.

Look at the pictures of the story. How do you know this is a fantasy? **Write**.

____

____

When you summarize a story, you tell the most important parts of the story in your own words.

Draw a picture to tell about an important event in the story.

Name ______________________________

Story Title ______________________________

Author ______________________________

Think about what you know about an ox. **Draw** a picture about how an ox can help on a farm. Write a sentence to tell about your picture.

When you **visualize** a story, you form pictures in your mind based on the details from the story.

Name ______________________

Story Title ______________________

Author ______________________

Draw a picture of a fox and a kit.

Draw a picture of what you think was the most important event in the story.

Name ______________________________

Story Title ______________________________

Author ______________________________

Look at the cover and the title of the story. Where do you think the story takes place? **Draw** the setting. **Explain** your drawing.

Think about the beginning, middle and end of the story. **Draw** a picture of the most important event in the story. Include the characters and setting of the story.

Name ______________________________

Story Title ______________________________

Author ______________________________

Underline the sentences that tell about literary nonfiction.

It tells information about real characters or places.

The characters are always animals.

It is a made up story.

It gives information about an event.

The events of the story happened in a certain order. **Draw** a picture of what the author saw at the animal park right after she saw the zebras. **Write** a label.

Name ______________________

Story Title ______________________

Author ______________________

Tell what you know about animal families. Then **look** at the pictures in the story.Predict what the story will be about and what might happen. **Write**.

Check your predictions. **Read** the part that tells in the story. Were your predictions correct? What was surprising and why? **Write**.

Name ______________________________

Story Title ______________________________

Author ______________________________

When you read, you should understand what and why things happen in the story.

Ask questions about the story before you read and then look for clues in the story.

Write some questions about the story to help you better understand the story when you read.

____

____

____

____

Look at the story again. What part did you not understand? **Write** what you did to understand that part of the story.

____

____

____

____

Name ______________________________

Story Title ______________________________

Author ______________________________

Underline the sentences that tell about expository text.

It is a made up story.

It gives facts and details.

It can be about real people, animals or places.

It is a story that should be acted out.

Write three facts you learned from reading the selection.

Name ______________________

Story Title ______________________

Author ______________________

What do you know about dinosaurs? **Write** about when and how dinosaurs lived.

Think about **what you knew** about dinosaurs before you read the story. Then use what you know and the clues in the text to **tell more** about dinosaurs. **Write** a list.

Name ______________________________

Story Title ______________________________

Author ______________________________

Draw a picture of an animal that lives in a forest.
Write a sentence about your picture.

____

____

Now **draw** your favorite forest animal. Tell the most important things about the animal. **Write** a caption.

____

____

Name ______________________________

Story Title ______________________________

Author ______________________________

You can **ask questions** about what you are going to read to better understand the story.

Look at the pictures in the text. What questions would you like to ask? **Write**.

Look for the answers to your questions in the text. **Write** the answers.

Name ______________________

Story Title ______________________

Author ______________________

Draw a picture of your favorite place to play.
Why is this your favorite place? **Write** a sentence.

Look at the picture you drew. **How** would you change it?
Add to your picture to show what you would change.

Name ______________________________

Story Title ______________________________

Author ______________________________

Circle the sentences that are true about an animal fantasy.

The characters are animals.

It is a story that could happen in real life.

The animals can talk.

The animals act like people.

Think about **what you knew** about animals before you read the story. **Draw** pictures to show the things you knew that helped you better understand the story.

Name ______________________________

Story Title ______________________________

Author ______________________________

Underline each sentence that is true about **expository text.**

It gives facts and details.

It tells about real people or animals.

The story may tell how make-believe characters act.

It is a play.

Think about something in the story that was hard to understand.
Write what you did to understand this part of the story.

Name ______________________

Story Title ______________________

Author ______________________

Draw a picture of a seed and a flower.
What can a gardener do to help the seed become a flower?
Write a sentence.

Draw a picture of Toad in his garden once it has bloomed.
How does Toad feel about his garden? **Write** a sentence.

Name ______________________

Story Title ______________________

Author ______________________

Circle the sentences that are true about literary nonfiction.

It teaches a lesson.

It describes events that happen in real life.

It gives information about real people or animals.

It tells about make-believe things.

Draw pictures of three things that happen in the life cycle of a butterfly. **Write** the number 1, 2, or 3 under each picture to show the order of the events.

Name ______________________________

Story Title ______________________________

Author ______________________________

Draw a picture of an animal getting ready for winter.
Write a label for the animal.
Then **write** a sentence telling what the animal is doing.

How is a play different from a story? **Write**.

Name ______________________________

Story Title ______________________________

Author ______________________________

What if something in the story you are about to read doesn't make sense?

Draw a picture of what you will do. **Write** a sentence about it.

Think about parts of the story that didn't make sense to you.

Draw what you did to help you understand what was happening.

Write a sentence about it.

Name ______________________________

Story Title ______________________________

Author ______________________________

Circle the sentences that are true about a fairy tale.

The characters are often princes or princesses.

The story takes place long ago.

The story tells information about real events.

The setting is in a make-believe land.

When you **visualize** a story, you form pictures in your mind based on the details from the story.

Draw a picture of Cinderella's dress or her coach. Write a label.

Name ______________________________

Story Title ______________________________

Author ______________________________

Draw a picture of a place you have visited on a trip.
Write a sentence about the thing you liked best about the place.

What did you learn from the story? **Write** two or three facts.

Name ______________________________

Story Title ______________________________

Author ______________________________

What questions do you have about life on a ranch?
Write your questions.

When you read, you should look for answers to your questions. Remember that sometimes a story will not answer every question.

Look at the questions you wrote before reading the story.
Write answers to as many questions as you can.

Name ______________________________

Story Title ______________________________

Author ______________________________

Draw a picture of your favorite thing from when you were a baby. **Why** was it your favorite? **Write** a sentence.

A **fiction story** has three parts. It has a beginning, a middle, and an end.

Think about the story you just read. **How** did knowing about the parts of a story help you understand what was happening? **Write** sentences to explain.

Name ___________________________

Story Title ___________________________

Author ___________________________

Look at the pictures in the story.
Write what you predict will happen in the story.

Think about why you want to read this story.
Write a purpose for reading it.

Check your prediction. **Read** the part in the story that tells what did happen.
Write a sentence telling if your prediction was correct or not.

Name ______________________

Story Title ______________________

Author ______________________

When you read, you should understand what and why things happen in the story. **Look for clues** in the pictures before you read and then read to find out what the clues mean.

What will you do if you don't understand what you read? **Write** a sentence.

You wrote what you would do if you didn't understand part of a story. **Reread** what you wrote above. If you did this, **write** how it helped you. If you did something else, **write** how that helped you.

Name ______________________

Story Title ______________________

Author ______________________

Draw pictures of people taking care of their pets. How do you think the pets feel about their owners? **Write** a sentence.

When you **summarize** a story, you tell the most important parts of the story in your own words.

Summarize the story you just read. **Write** two or three sentences.

Name ______________________________

Story Title ______________________________

Author ______________________________

What is informational fiction? **Write.**

Did you find parts of the story that were hard to understand?
Write what you used or would use to better understand the story.

Name ______________________________

Story Title ______________________________

Author ______________________________

Tell about machines that you have seen.
Where did you see those machines?
What jobs do they do? Then draw a picture of a machine you use often.

Summarize the story you just read. **Write** three sentences.

Name ______________________________

Story Title ______________________________

Author ______________________________

What is a biography? **Circle** the words that make the sentences true.

A biography is a ______ story. made-up true

A biography gives ______ about a person's life. facts jokes

A biography tells about a ______ person. magic real

You can think about how a **text is organized** to better understand what you are reading. Sequence is one way a text can be organized.

Write three events from Alexander Graham Bell's life. **Write** the events in the order in which they happened.

Name ______________________________

Story Title ______________________________

Author ______________________________

Think about what you know about gardens.
What are some things that grow in gardens?
Write sentences to tell what you know.

Write what you learned about how people help their communities by reading this story.

Name ______________________________

Book Talk Tips

- Talk about a book you like.
- Use a loud, clear voice.
- Look at your classmates.
- Don't tell how it ends!

Directions When you talk about a book, answer these questions.

1. What is the title of the book?
2. Who is the author?
3. What kind of book is it?
4. What other book has the author written?
5. Tell what you liked the best.
6. Tell why they should read the book.

Read Together

Name ____________________

Before Writing

- Think about ideas with a friend.
- Ask questions to help your friend pick a good topic.

Tips for Conferencing

- Read your friend's paper out loud. Listen for what you like.
- Tell your friend three things you like. Say: "I like how you ____."
- Read your friend's paper out loud again. Listen for what you do not understand.
- Ask your friend two questions that you have.

It might help to think about the:

- Title
- Beginning
- Ending
- Words that were used
- Use of verbs, nouns, adjectives or adverbs

Read Together

Name ______________________________

Title of Writing ______________________________

Directions Answer these questions about what you wrote.

1. What are the two things that are best about this?

____

____

2. What is one thing you could have done better?

____

3. Do you like what you wrote? Why or why not?

____

____

Name ______________________________

Mm

Say the word for each picture.
Write m on the line if the word has the same first sound as .

1. ________	2. ________
3. ________	4. ________
5. ________	6. ________
7. ________	8. ________

School + Home **Home Activity** Your child has reviewed words that start with *m*. Help your child think of other words with /m/ as in *map*.

Name ______________________________

Draw your favorite character from a story you know.
Tell what the character is doing.
Tell how the character feels.

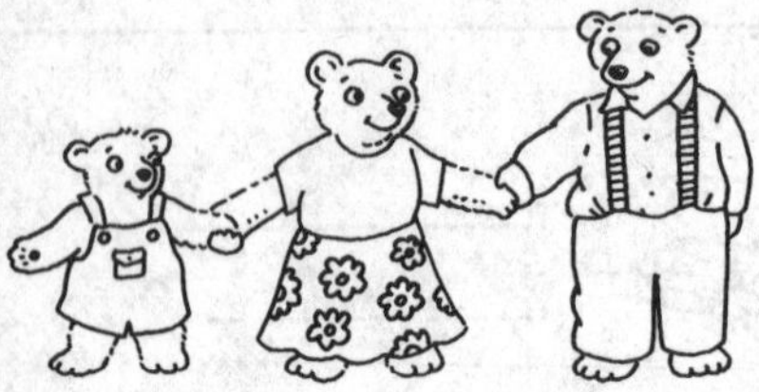

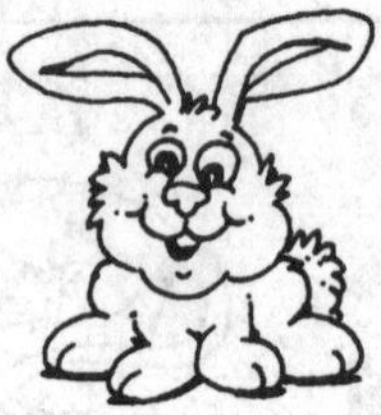

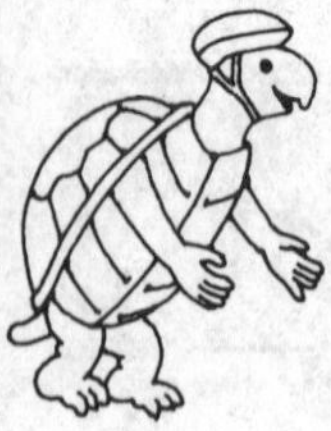

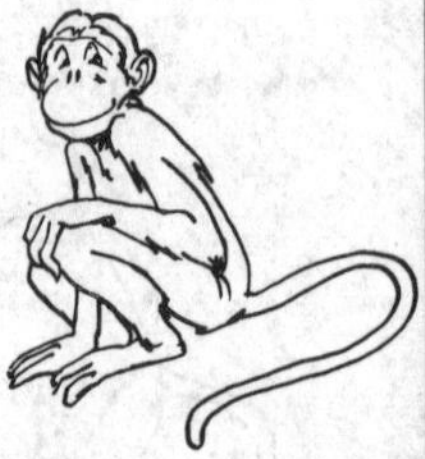

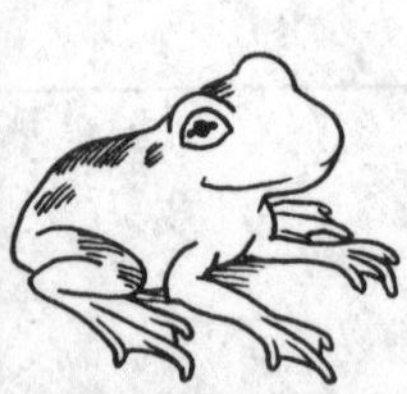

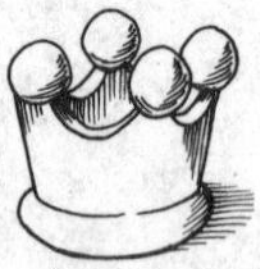

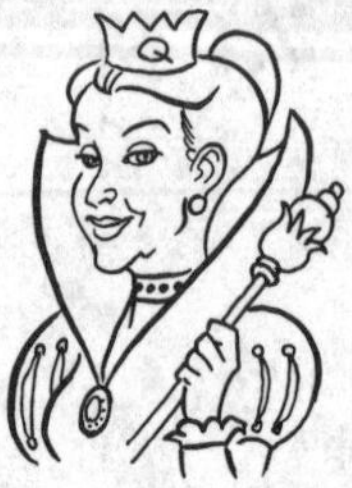

Home Activity Your child learned that characters in a story can be people or animals. As you read together, have your child tell you what he or she knows about the characters in stories.

Name ______________________________

Trace and **write** the letters. Make sure you write your letters the correct size.

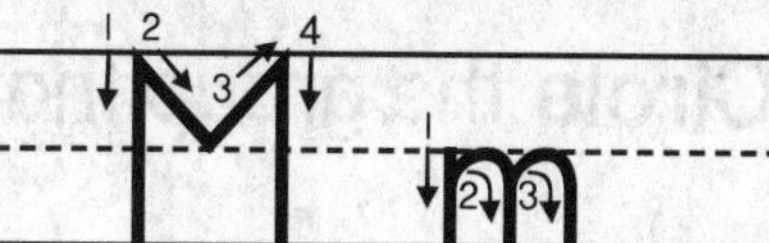

Home Activity Your child practiced writing *M* and *m*. Say names and words that begin with *M* and *m* and have your child write the correct letter each time you say a name or word.

Name ________________________________

Circle the group that could be a real word.

1. mat p2n 123 s3m 546

2. 237 e8b 476 ti9 pan

3. 530 213 63b Sam pp2

4. 760 tap m22 310 614

Look at the first group of letters. **Circle** the group of letters that is in the same order as the first group.

5. pan pan nap pna

6. cap tap cap pta

7. mat map abt mat

8. bag bad bag dma

Home Activity Your child identified groups of letters and compared the sequence of letters in words or letter groups such as *pan*, *nap*, and *pna*. Write some groups of numbers and some words. Have your child pick out the words.

Name ______________________

Ss

Say the word for each picture.

Write s on the line if the word has the same first sound as .

1. ______
2. ______
3. ______
4. ______
5. ______
6. ______
7. ______
8. ______

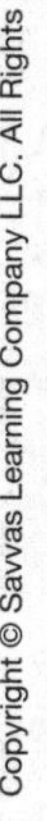

Home Activity Your child learned that some words begin with the letter *s*. Have your child find other words with /s/ as in *seal*.

Name ______________________________

Nouns: People, Animals, and Things

A **noun** names a person, an animal, or a thing.

The word **boy** names a person.

The word **cat** names an animal.

The word **bed** names a thing.

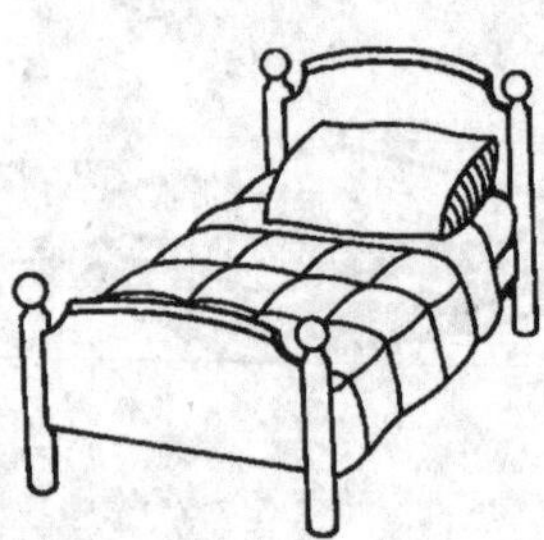

Circle the correct noun for each picture.
Say a sentence for each noun.

boy girl

car bus

pig dog

mom dad

Home Activity Your child learned about nouns that name people or things. Take turns with your child pointing to people and things in your home and saying the nouns that name them.

Name ______________________

Trace and **write** the letters. Make sure you write your letters the correct size.

S s

S

s

School + Home **Home Activity** Your child practiced writing *S* and *s*. Have your child cut out pictures from old magazines of objects that begin with *s* and paste them onto a sheet of paper and label each with the letter *s*.

Name ______________________

Circle the group that could be a real word.

1. 3576 bike t31m 1234 o471

2. road 2021 88bt 976a 54em

3. 2631 3142 987c mm32 pony

4. 4226 K310 look n325 7624

Look at the first group of letters. **Circle** the group of letters that is in the same order as the first group.

5. nap nap pna pan

6. tap pat tap apt

7. mad dam mad mda

8. pin nip pin imp

Home Activity Your child identified groups of letters and compared the sequence of letters in words or letter groups such as *pat, tap,* and *apt*. Write the letters of your child's name in different orders. Have your child identify the name with the letters in correct sequence.

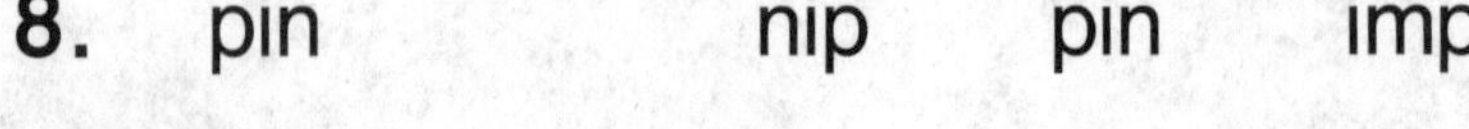

Name ______________________

Tt

Say the word for each picture.

Write t on the line if the word has the same first sound as  .

1. ______	2. ______
3. ______	4. ______
5. ______	6. ______
7. ______	8. ______

Home Activity Your child learned that some words begin with the letter *t*. Have your child find other words with /t/ as in *tiger*.

Name ______________________

Read the words in the box.
Pick a word to finish each sentence.
Write it on the line.
Read the sentence from left to right.

I see a green

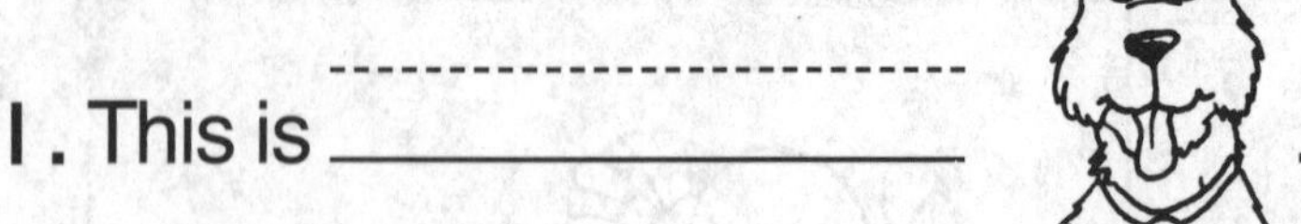

1. This is ________ .

2. We ________ a .

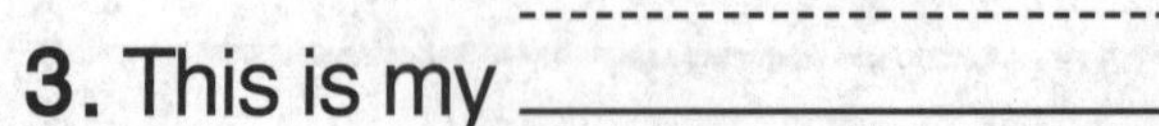

3. This is my ________ .

4. ________ am a .

School + Home **Home Activity** This week your child learned to identify and read the words *I*, *see*, *a*, and *green*. As you read with your child, encourage him or her to point out these words in print.

Name ______________________

Nouns: People, Animals, and Things

Tell about your room.
Finish the sentences.
Use words from the box or your own words.

a bed	a rug	a lamp	books	a cat

I have ______________________ in my room.

I have ______________________ in my room.

I have ______________________ in my room.

Find other nouns. **Say** a sentence for each noun.

Home Activity Your child learned how to use nouns for people and things in writing. Have your child write a sentence about people and things in another room in your home. Ask your child to identify the nouns in the sentence.

Name ______________________________

Trace and **write** the letters. Make sure you write your letters the correct size.

T t

T

t

School + Home

Home Activity Your child practiced writing *T* and *t*. Say names and words that begin with *T* and *t* and have your child write the correct letter each time you say a name or word.

Name ______________________________

Circle the group that could be a real word.

1. 5628 history s42p 12345 u572

2. 3023 science 66cv 786i 63fn

3. 6432 3543 786d number kk41

4. 2435 S221 woman m245 6734

Look at the first group of letters. **Circle** the group of letters that is in the same order as the first group.

5. pit pit tip pti

6. sag ags gas sag

7. nip imp nip pin

8. tip pit tpi tip

Home Activity Your child identified groups of letters and compared the sequence of letters in words or letter groups such as such as *pit, tip,* and *pti*. Make individual letter cards with the letters of your child's name. Ask your child to put the letters in correct sequence.

Name ______________________________

Aa

Say the word for each picture.
Write a on the line if the word has the same first sound as .

1. ______	2. ______
3. ______	4. ______
5. ______	6. ______

Say the word for each picture.
Write a on the line to complete the word.

7. 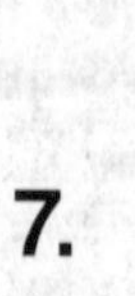  s __ t

8.  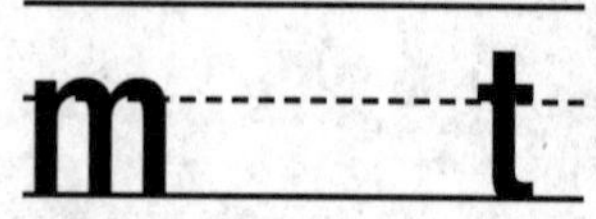 m __ t

Home Activity Your child learned about the short *a* vowel sound in words. Have your child find other words with /a/ at the beginning or in the middle, such as *apple* and *pat*.

Name ____________________________

Read Together

Read the story.
Draw the most important character from the story.

Blue Jay found some beautiful peacock feathers.

Blue Jay tied the feathers to his tail.

He thought he looked grand.

He strutted in front of the other jays.

The jays pulled out his peacock feathers.

Then they all flew away from Blue Jay.

Blue Jay knew then: No one likes a showoff.

Home Activity Your child read a fable (fiction) and identified the main character. Read a fiction story with your child. Have your child name the most important character (or characters) in the story. Ask your child to tell you what the character looks like and how the character acts.

Name ______________________________

Nouns: People, Animals, and Things

Mark the sentence that has a line under a noun that names a person, an animal, or a thing.

1. ◯ They <u>sat</u> on the bed.
   ◯ They sat <u>on</u> the bed.
   ◯ They sat on the <u>bed</u>.

2. ◯ She is with her <u>mom</u>.
   ◯ She <u>is</u> with her mom.
   ◯ She is <u>with</u> her mom.

3. ◯ He can read <u>a</u> book.
   ◯ He can read a <u>book</u>.
   ◯ He can <u>read</u> a book.

4. ◯ The boy <u>plays</u> with a pet.
   ◯ The boy plays <u>with</u> a pet.
   ◯ The boy plays with a <u>pet</u>.

Home Activity Your child prepared for taking tests on nouns for people or things. Read a story together. Have your child point out nouns that name people or things in the story.

Name ______________________________

Circle the front cover.

Place an X over the back cover.

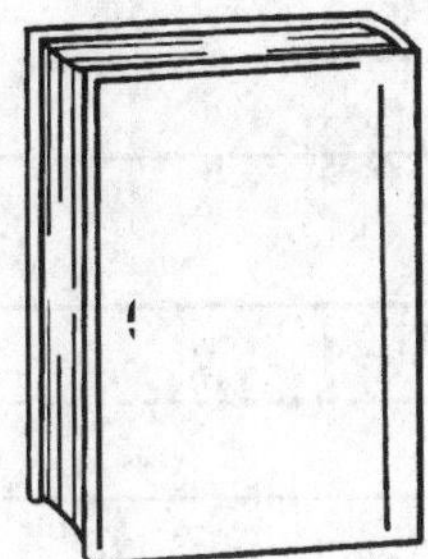

Circle the book that Sam wrote.

School + Home

Home Activity Your child learned to identify the front cover, back cover, and title page of a book. Have your child point out the front and back covers and title page of the next book you read together.

Name ______________________

Trace and **write** the letters. Make sure you write your letters the correct size.

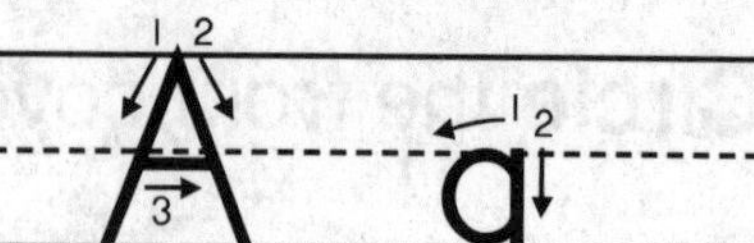

A

a

Copy the words. **Write** the letters from left to right.

Sam

Tam

mat

sat

am

at

as

Matt

Home Activity Your child practiced writing words with *Aa*. Have your child draw a picture of two of the words he or she wrote and label the pictures with the words.

Name ______________________________

Circle the group that could be a real word.

1. 9546 r2nf 23456 match t4ms

2. 6237 pancake e9bg 5769 oh77

3. girls 2531 9213 43cd jj33

4. 8762 2310 table n22p 5148

Look at the first group of letters. **Circle** the group of letters that is in the same order as the first group.

5. pot pot top opt

6. ten net ten ent

7. bat tab abt bat

8. sat tar sta sat

Home Activity Your child looked at the letter sequence in words and compared the sequence of letters in words or letter groups such as *pot, top,* and *opt*. Look at item 1 with your child. Have your child explain his answer.

Name ______________________

Read the words in the box.
Pick a word to finish each sentence.
Write it on the line.
Read the sentence from left to right.

I	see	a	green

1. ______ have a  .

2. The  is ______ .

3. I ______ the 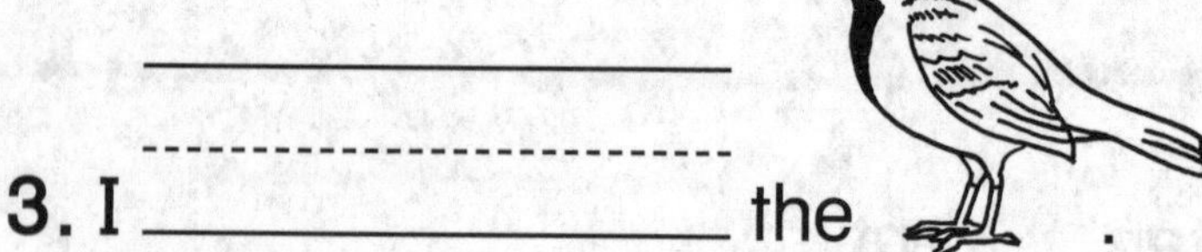 .

4. This is ______  .

Home Activity This week your child identified and read the words *I, see, a,* and *green.* Write each word on a card. Have your child read each word and then use it in a sentence.

Name ________________________________

Cc

Say the word for each picture.
Write c on the line if the word has the same first sound as .

1. ______	2. ______
3. ______	4. ______
5. ______	6. ______ 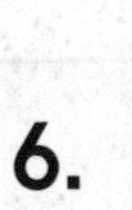 
7. ______	8. ______  

School + Home **Home Activity** Your child learned that some words begin with the letter *c*. Have your child find other words with /k/ as in *cat*.

Name ______________________________

Look at each set of pictures.
Circle the picture that shows a place.

1.	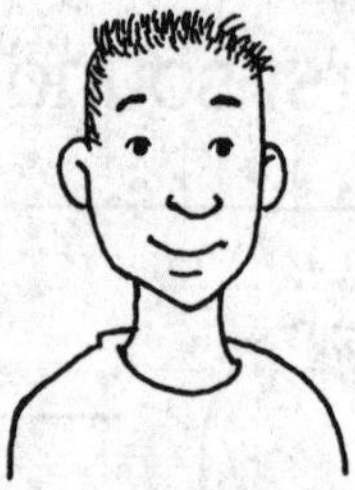	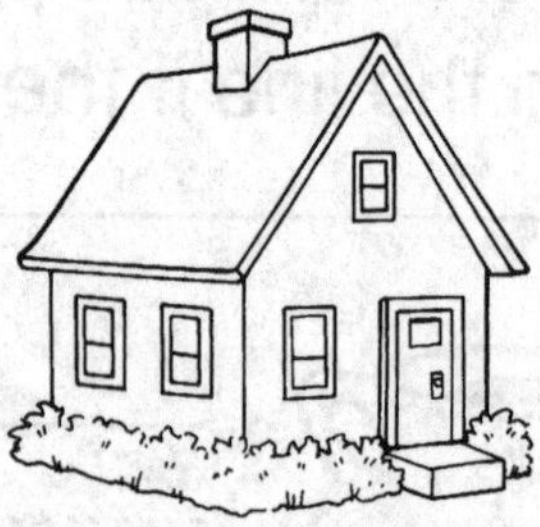
2.	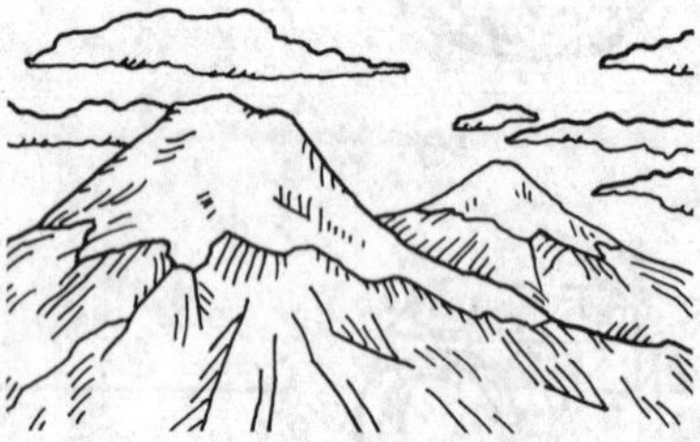	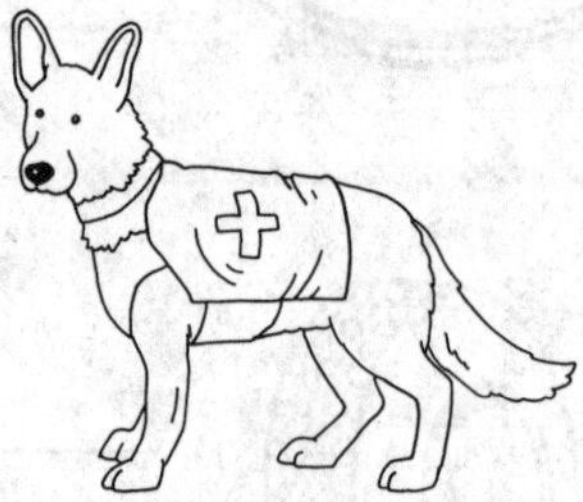
3.	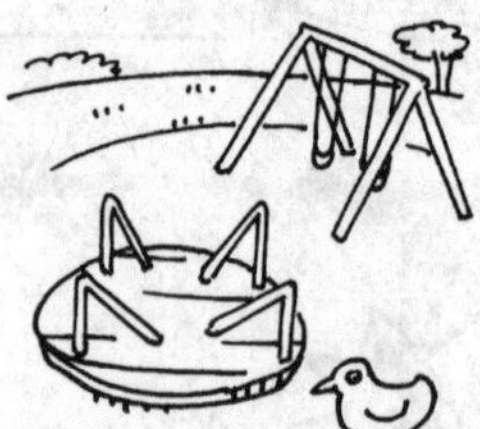	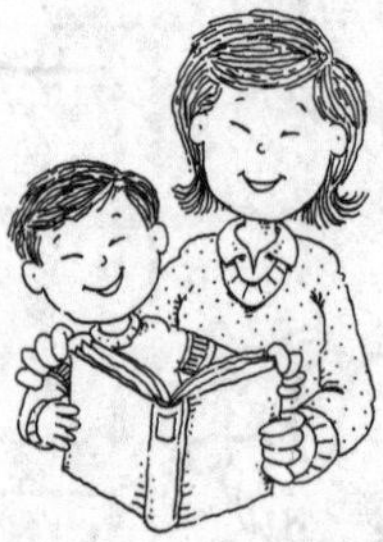
4.	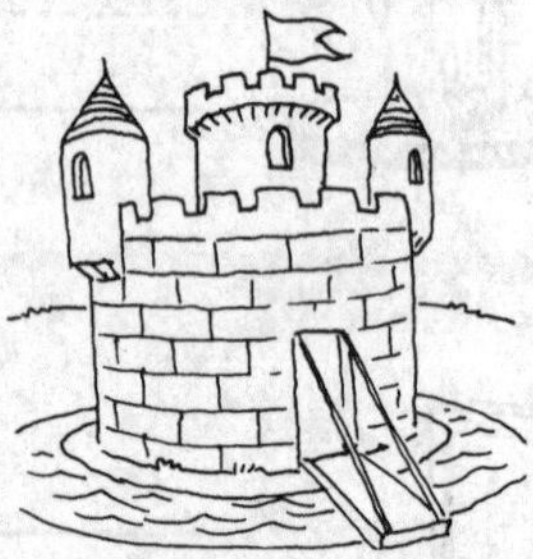	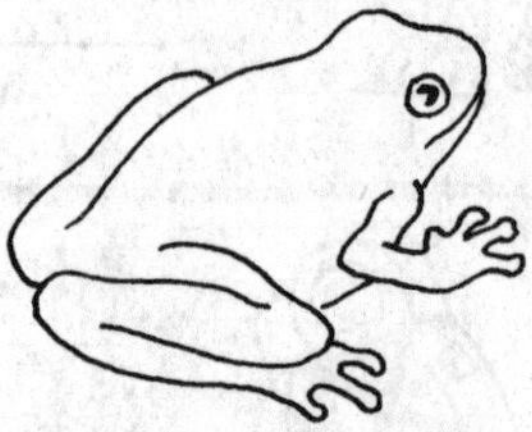
5.	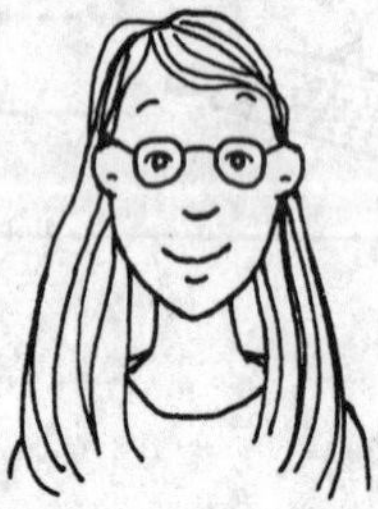	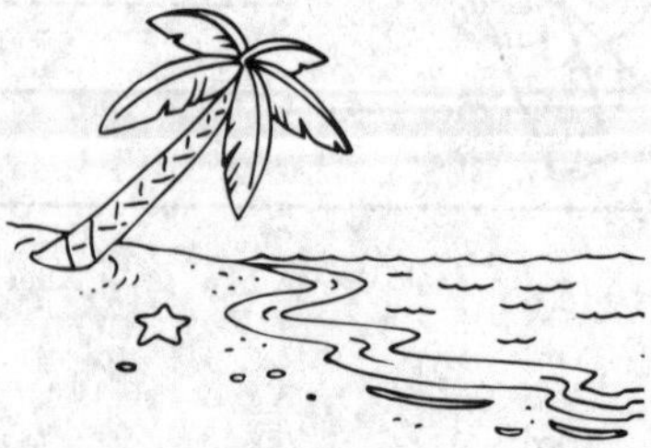

Home Activity Your child learned about places in a story. As you read together, have your child tell you what he or she knows about the setting of the story.

Name ______________________

Trace and **write** the letters. Make sure you write your letters the correct size.

C c

C

c

Copy the words. **Write** the letters from left to right.

Mac

sat

Cam

Tam

cat

tat

mat

Sam

School + Home

Home Activity Your child practiced writing words with *Cc*. Have your child choose two words from the box and write them on a separate piece of paper.

Name ______________________________

Look at the first group of letters. **Circle** the group of letters that is in the same order as the first group.

1. 
top

top pot opt

2. 
net

ten net ent

3. 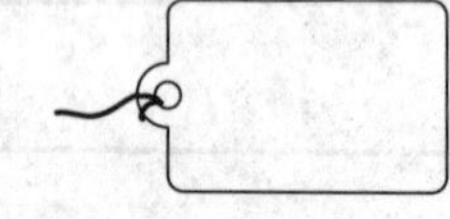
tag

got agt tag

4. 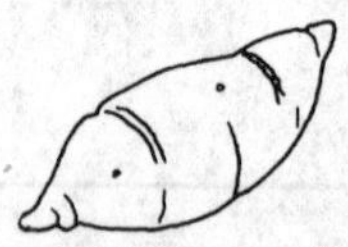
yam

yam may yma

5. 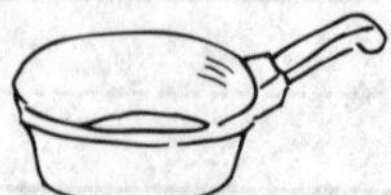
pan

nap pan npa

6. 
bag

bga gab bag

Home Activity Your child looked at the letter sequence in words and compared the sequence of letters in words or letter groups such as *top, pot,* and *opt*. Have your child identify the sequence of letters of each pictured word. Then say the word with your child.

Name ______________________________

Pp

Say the word for each picture.
Write p on the line if the word has the same first sound as .

1.	2.
3.	4.

Say the word for each picture.
Write p on the line if the word has the same ending sound as .

Home Activity Your child learned that some words begin and end with the letter *p*. Have your child find other words that begin and end with /p/.

Name ______________________________

Nouns: Places

A noun also names a place.

The word **school** names a place.

The word **store** names a place.

Draw a line from the noun to the correct picture.
Say a sentence for each noun.

1. zoo

2. park

3. lake

4. library

Home Activity Your child learned about nouns that name places. Have your child identify places in his or her neighborhood.

Name ______________________________

Trace and **write** the letters. Make sure you write your letters the correct size.

P p

P

p

Copy the words. **Write** the tall and small letters the correct size. **Write p** so that it falls below the line.

Pam

map

Pat

sap

tap

cap

Home Activity Your child practiced writing words with *Pp*. Say these words to your child: *Pennsylvania, Peter, Patrick, pickle, plum, pet.* Have your child write *P* or *p* to show how each word begins.

Name ______________________________

Trace the arrows.
Connect the word trains from left to right and top to bottom.

START:

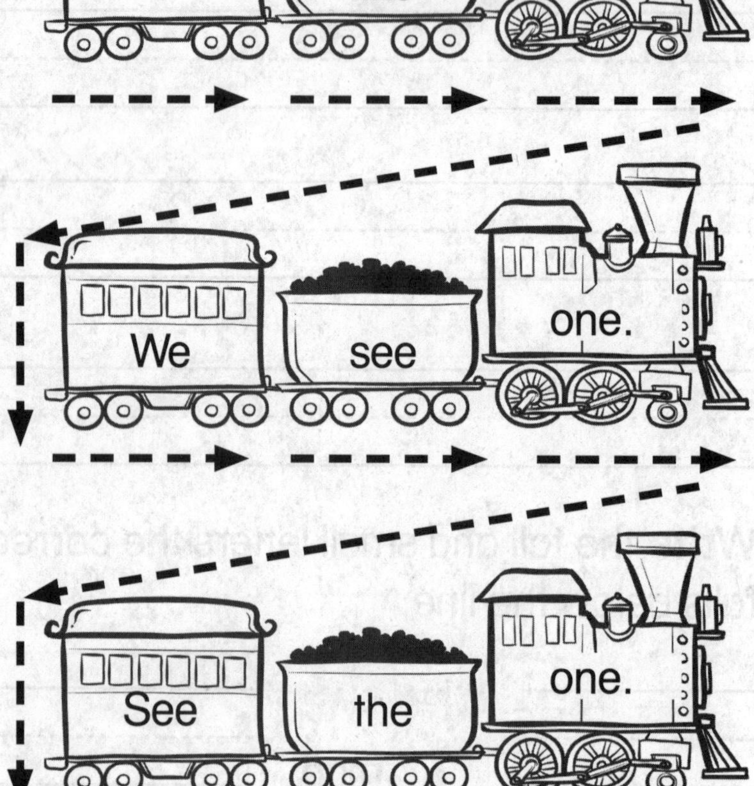

END

Home Activity Your child learned that reading is done from top to bottom, and from left to right with a return sweep. Show your child a page from a favorite book. Have him or her point to each word from left to right, then return to the beginning of the next line and move again from left to right.

Name ______________________

Nn

Say the word for each picture.
Write n on the line if the word has the same first sound as .

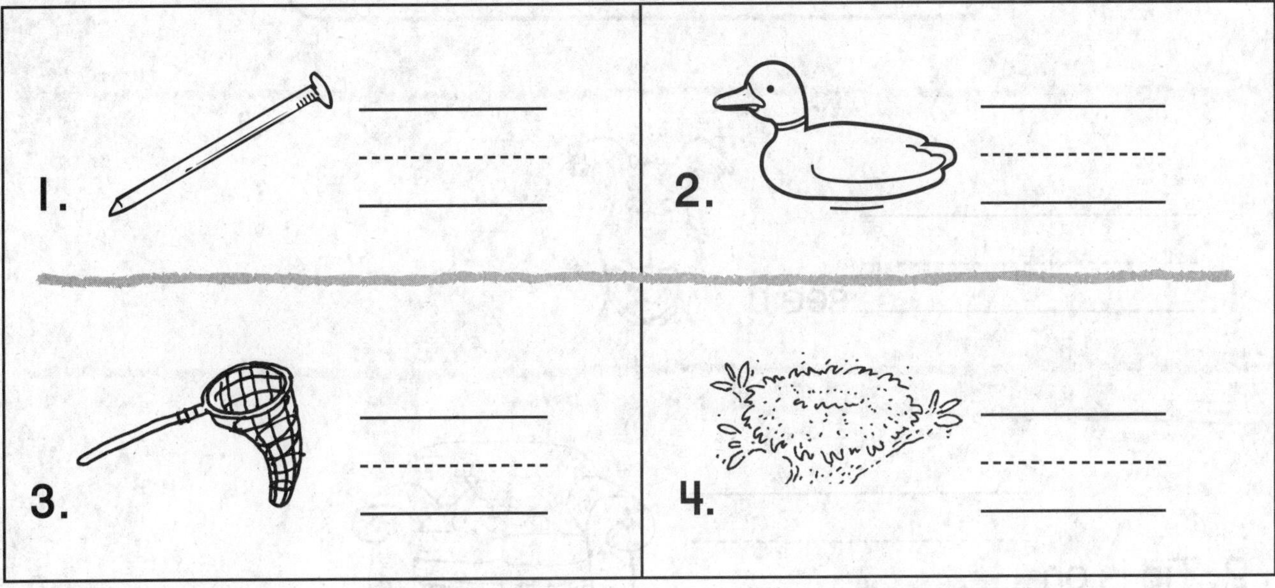

1. ____
2. ____
3. ____
4. ____

Say the word for each picture.
Write n on the line if the word has the same ending sound as .

5. ma____
6. ca____
7. ma____
8. ca____

Home Activity Your child learned that some words begin and end with the letter *n*. Have your child find other words that begin and end with /n/.

Name ______________________

Read the words in the box.
Pick a word to finish each sentence.
Write it on the line.

we	like	the	one

1. ______________ see a .

2. Tip is on ______________ .

3. I have ______________ .

4. I ______________ our .

School + Home

Home Activity This week your child identified and read the words *we, like, the,* and *one*. As you read with your child, encourage him or her to point out these words in print.

Name ____________________________

Nouns: Places

Tell about places you go with your family.
Finish the sentences.
Use words from the box or your own words.

store	playground	park	zoo

My family and I go to the ____________________.

My family and I go to the ____________________.

My family and I go to the ____________________.

Find other nouns. **Say** a sentence for each noun.

Home Activity Your child learned how to use nouns for places in writing. Have your child write two sentences that tell about a place he or she would like to go. Ask your child to identify the noun he or she used.

Name ______________________

Trace and **write** the letters. Make sure you write your letters the correct size.

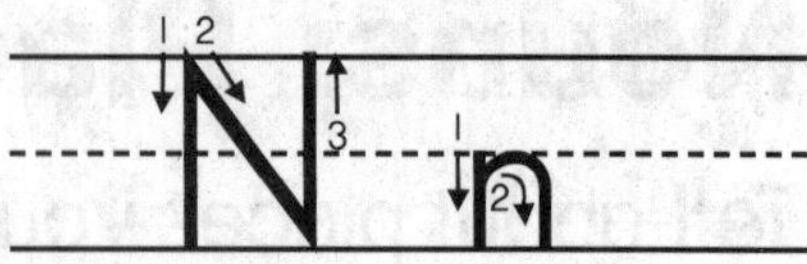

N

n

Copy the words. **Write** the letters from left to right.

Nan

nap

man

tan

Nat

can

pan

mat

Home Activity Your child practiced writing words with *Nn.* Have your child find all the words above that have an *N* or *n* in them and practice writing them one more time.

Name ______________________________

Trace the arrows.
Connect the word trains from left to right and top to bottom.

START: I like one.

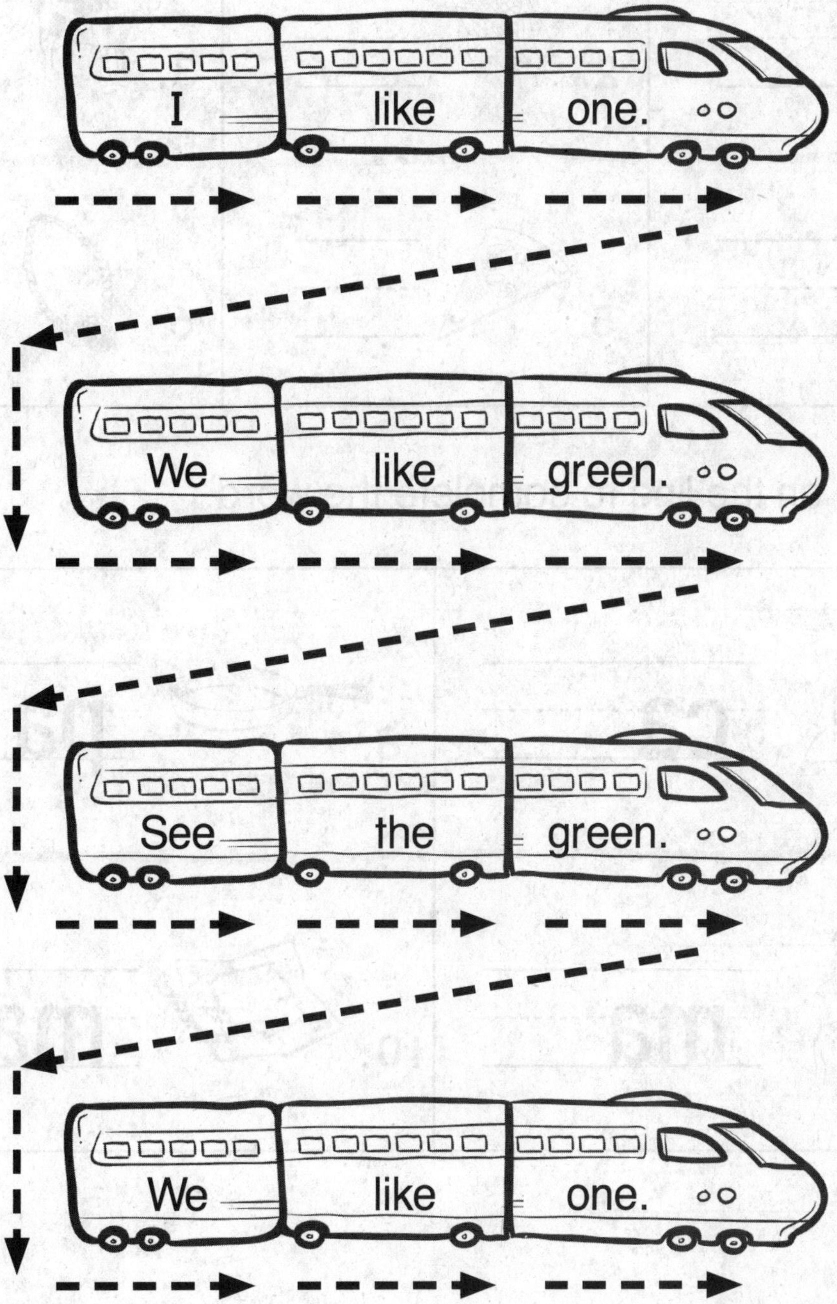

We like green.

See the green.

We like one. END

Home Activity Your child learned that reading is done from top to bottom, and from left to right with a return sweep. Show your child a page from a favorite book. Have him or her tell you where to start reading a sentence (left) and in which direction to read (to the right). Remind your child that reading starts at the top and goes to the bottom of the page.

Name ______________________________

Say the word for each picture.
Write the letter on the line that begins the word.

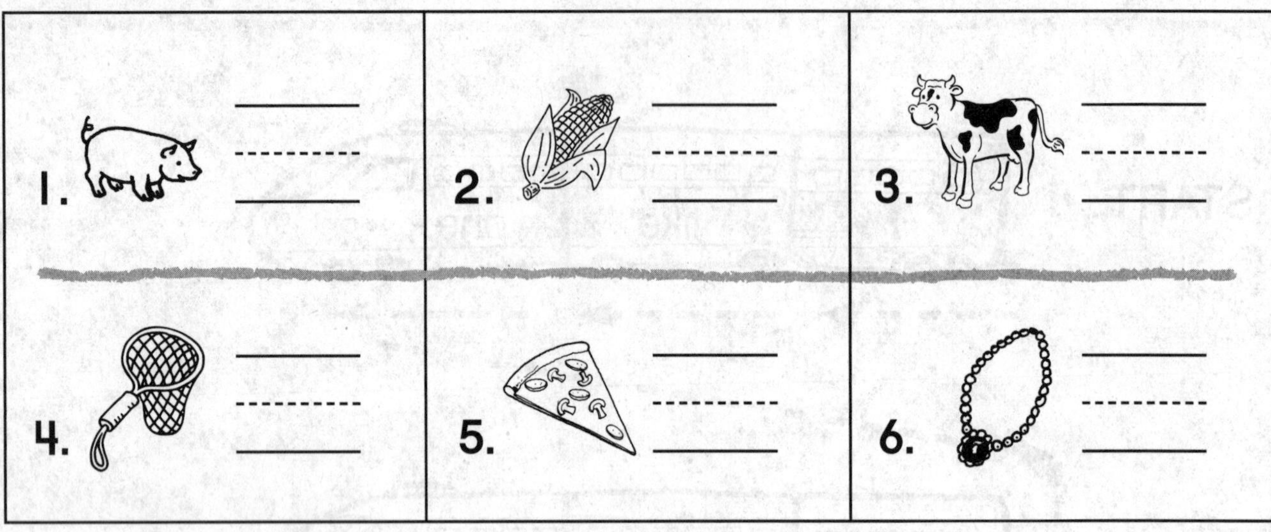

1. ____
2. ____
3. ____
4. ____
5. ____
6. ____

Write p or **n** on the line to complete the word.

7. ca__
8. pa__
9. ma__
10. ma__

School + Home **Home Activity** Your child reviewed words that begin with *c, n,* and *p* and reviewed words that end with *n* and *p*. Have your child find other words with /c/ as in *cat,* /p/ as in *pig,* and /n/ as in *nut.*

Name ______________________

Read Together

Read the story.
Draw a picture that shows where the story takes place.

Mei and Jake walk in the warm sand.

Waves splash their bare feet.

Mei and Jake decide to make a sand castle.

They make thick walls and tall towers.

The children stand up to look at their castle.

Suddenly a giant wave comes to shore!

Now the castle is gone.

Home Activity Your child read a story (fiction) and then identified where the story takes place (setting). Have your child name one or two favorite stories. Help your child identify the setting of each story.

Name ______________________________

Nouns: Places

Mark the noun for a place that completes the sentence.

1. We see animals at the _______.
   - ◯ zoo
   - ◯ fish
   - ◯ eat

2. Sam and Tam swim in the _______.
   - ◯ cat
   - ◯ dip
   - ◯ lake

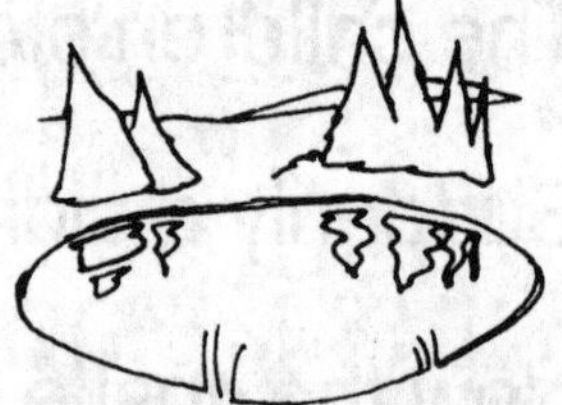

3. Tip can run in the _______.
   - ◯ park
   - ◯ man
   - ◯ pet

4. The _______ has a big yard.
   - ◯ call
   - ◯ baby
   - ◯ home

School + Home **Home Activity** Your child prepared for taking tests on nouns for places. Read a story together. Have your child point out the nouns that name places.

Name ______________________________

Animal Families

Contents

Use this **table of contents** from a social studies book to find information.

1. **Draw** a circle around the page numbers.

2. **Draw** a box around the chapter titles.

3. **Write** the name of Chapter 5.

____

4. **Write** the page number on which the chapter "Zebras and Foals" begins.

____

5. **Write** how many chapters are listed.

____

Home Activity Your child learned to use the table of contents in a book to find information. As you read together, point out the table of contents and encourage your child to help you find information such as the page number for a specific chapter.

Name ________________________

Copy the words. Make sure you write your tall and small letters the correct size. Remember **p** falls below the line.

Nan	________	pat	________
man	________	can	________
pan	________	mat	________
Sam	________	Mac	________
tan	________	map	________
cat	________	sap	________
Pam	________	Cam	________
tap	________	Ann	________
sat	________	cap	________

Home Activity Your child practiced writing words with *Aa, Mm, Ss, Tt, Cc, Pp,* and *Nn*. Have your child choose a word that begins with the letter *p* from the list and then write the word. Repeat for the letters *m, s, t, c,* and *n*.

Name ______________________________

Underline the name of the book.

Place an X over the book about Sam.

Circle the book that Nan wrote.

Draw a box around the book that Pam drew pictures for.

Home Activity Your child learned to use the information on a book cover and title page to figure out what the book is about. Point out the cover and title page of the next book you read together. Explain that the title tells what the book is about.

Name ______________________________

Read the words in the box.
Pick a word to finish each sentence.
Write it on the line.

we	**like**	**the**	**one**

1. Here is ____________ man.

2. I ____________ to run with my  .

3. I have ____________  too.

4. ____________ have a  and a  .

Home Activity This week your child identified and read the words *we, like, the,* and *one.* Write each word on a card. Have your child read each word and then use it in a sentence.

Name ___________________________

Ff

Say the word for each picture.

Write f on the line if the word has the same first sound as  .

1. ______	2. ______
3. ______	4. ______
5. ______	6. ______
7. ______	8. ______

Home Activity Your child learned that some words begin with the letter *f*. Have your child find other words with /f/ as in *fish.*

Name ___________________________

Look at the pictures.
Tell a story about the pictures.
Draw a picture to tell what happens next.

Home Activity Your child learned that the plot tells what happens in a story. Have your child tell you a story about the pictures on this page. Help your child by asking what happens in the beginning of the story, in the middle, and at the end.

Name ______________________

Trace and **write** the letters. Make sure you write your letters the correct size.

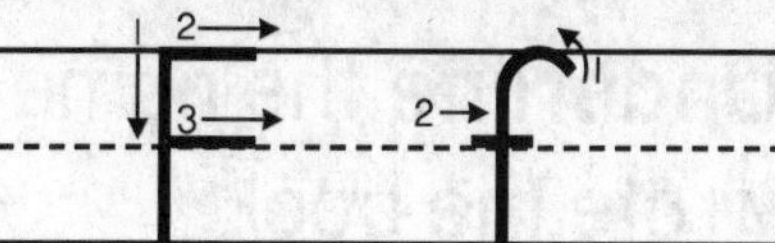

F

f

Copy the words. **Write** the letters the correct size.

Fam

fan

pat

sat

Ann

fat

nap

man

School + Home **Home Activity** Your child practiced writing words with *Ff.* Have your child choose two words from above that begin with *f* and practice writing the words again.

Name ______________________________

Underline the name of the person who wrote the book.
Circle the name of the person who drew the pictures.

Circle the book that Kim Fin wrote.

Place an X over the book about Tam.

Home Activity Your child learned to use the information on a book cover and title page to figure out what the book is about. Your child also learned to look for the name of the author and illustrator of a book. Discuss illustrations in a favorite book with your child.

Name ______________________

Bb

Say the word for each picture.

Write b on the line if the word has the same first sound as 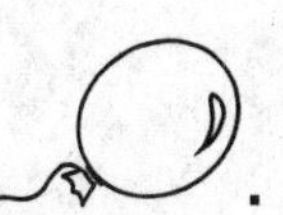.

1. ______	2. ______
3. ______	4. ______
5. ______	6. ______

Write two words that rhyme with **nab.**

7. t______

8. c______

School + Home

Home Activity Your child learned that some words begin and end with the letter *b*. Have your child find other words with /b/ as in *balloon*.

Name ______________________________

Verbs

A **verb** names an action. It tells what a person or thing does.

The dog **eats. Eats** is the verb.

Circle the verb in each sentence.

1. Sam and Tip run in the yard.
2. The cat hit the bag.
3. They play with the bag.
4. The cat fit in a bag.
5. Tam hid in the bag.

Find other verbs. **Say** a sentence for each verb.

Home Activity Your child learned about verbs. Have your child think of a verb and then pantomime the action.

Name ______________________

Trace and **write** the letters. Make sure you write your letters the correct size.

B b

B

b

Copy the words. Sit and hold your paper the correct way.

Bab ______ nab ______

bat ______ ban ______

Tab ______ cab ______

bam ______ fat ______

Home Activity Your child practiced writing words with *Bb.* Have your child choose a word from above with *B* and a word with *b* and practice writing each three times as neatly as possible.

Name ____________________________

Underline the title of the book.

Circle who wrote the book.

Circle the book that Peg Bud wrote.
Draw a box around the book that Ken Fox drew the pictures for.

Home Activity Your child learned to use the information on a book cover and title page to figure out what the book is about. Your child also learned to look for the name of the author and illustrator of a book. On a book your child enjoys, point out the cover and title page. Point to the name of the author and read it aloud.

Name ___________________________

Gg

Say the word for each picture.
Write g on the line if the word has the same first sound as .

1. ________	2. ________
3. ________	4. ________

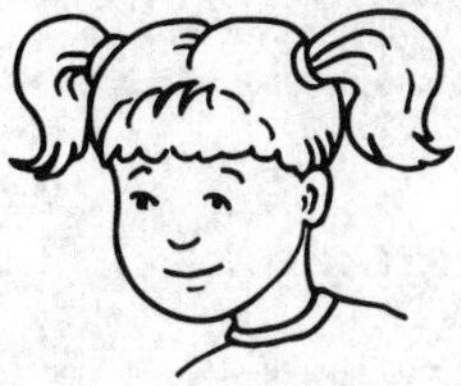

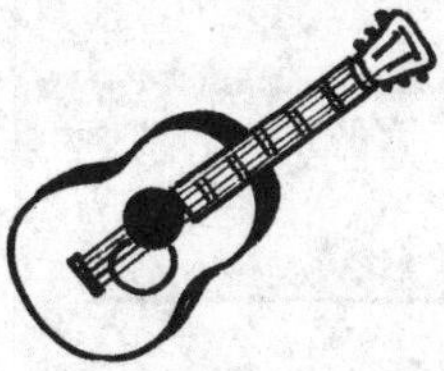

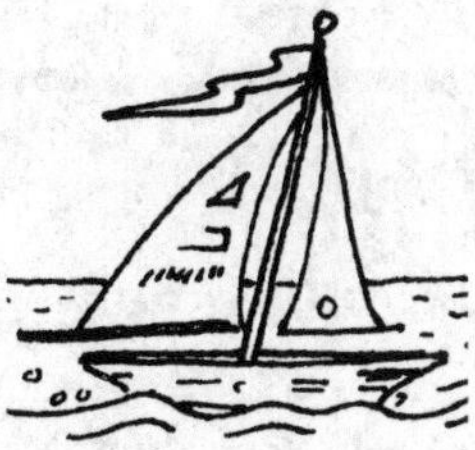

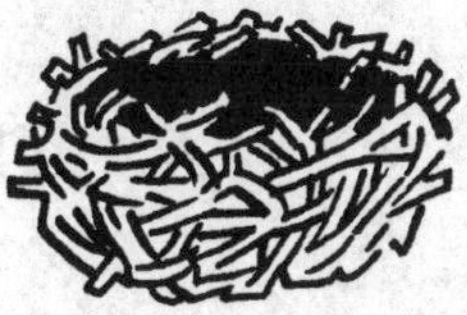

Write four words that rhyme with **gag**.

5. s________	6. n________
7. t________	8. b________

Home Activity Your child has learned that some words begin and end with the letter *g*. Have your child find other words with /g/ as in *goat*. Work with your child to make words that rhyme with *gag*.

Name ______________________

Read the words in the box.
Pick a word to finish each sentence.
Write it on the line.

do	look	you	was	yellow

1. Tip ______________ sad.

2. ______________ in the .

3. ______________ you see the ?

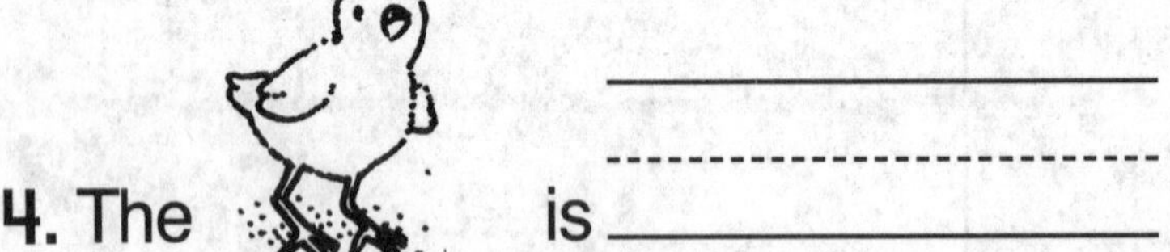

4. The is ______________.

5. ______________ can hold the .

Home Activity This week your child identified and read the words *do, look, you, was,* and *yellow*. As you read with your child, encourage him or her to point out these words in print.

Name ___________________________

Verbs

Tell about things you do in the yard.
Finish the sentences.
Use words from the box or your own words.

ride a bike	run	play catch	jump rope

I ______________________________ in the yard.

I ______________________________ in the yard.

I ______________________________ in the yard.

Say a sentence to tell what you like to do.

Home Activity Your child learned how to use verbs in writing. Have your child write two sentences that tell about what he or she does after school. Ask your child to identify the verbs in the sentences.

Name ___________________________

Trace and **write** the letters. Make sure you write your letters the correct size.

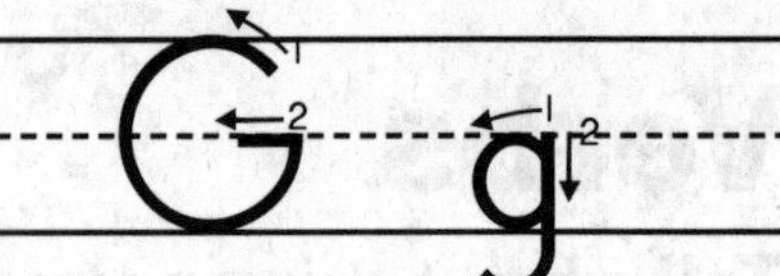

G

g

Copy the words.

Gam

nag

bag

gas

tag

gab

Did you write the letter **g** so that it falls below the line each time?

Yes **No**

Home Activity Your child practiced writing words with *Gg*. Say the following words: *Gus, Gary, Gwen, girl, give, get.* Have your child write *G* or *g* to show how each word begins.

Name ______________________________

a b c d e f g h i j k l m n o p q r s t u v w x y z

Circle the letter that comes first in the alphabet.

1. s t a	2. c p n	3. f b g
4. n a g	5. s f p	6. t g n

Write the letters in alphabetical order.

7. m a s	8. t c p	9. n f b g
10. t g n	11. s c f	12. n a p f

School + Home

Home Activity Your child learned to put letters in alphabetical order. Write three different letters on index cards, one letter on each card. Have your child put the letters in alphabetical order.

Name ______________________

Ii

Say the word for each picture.
Write i on the line if the word has the same first sound as  .

1. ____

2. ____

3. ____

4. ____

Say the word for each picture.
Write i on the line if the word has the same middle sound as  .

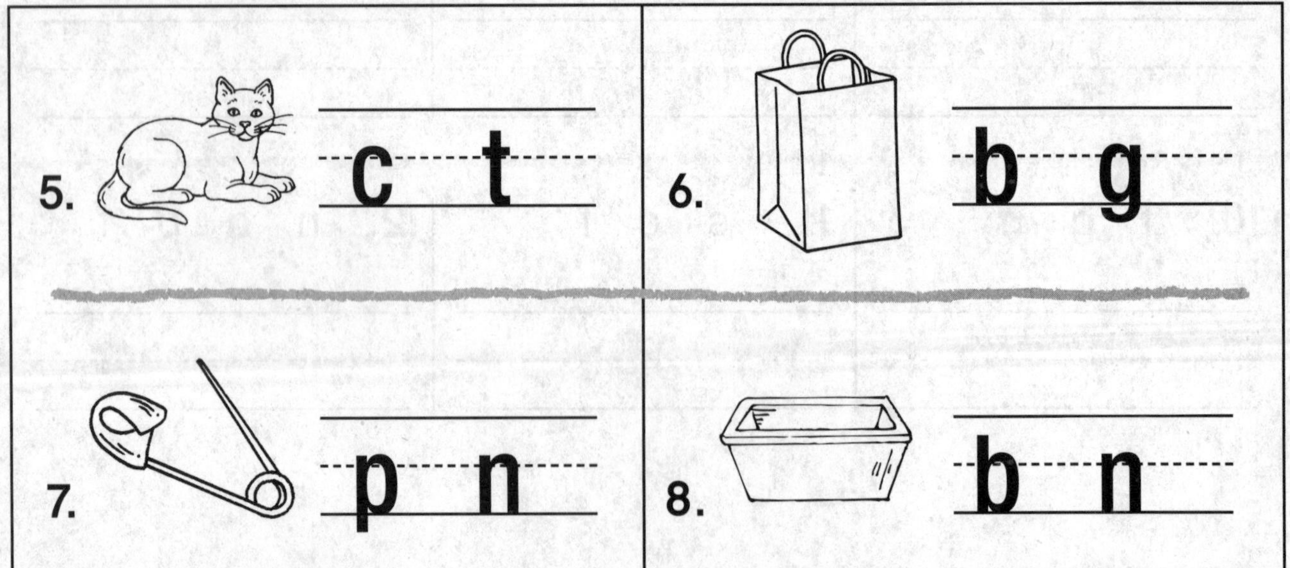

Home Activity Your child learned that some words have the short *i* sound. Have your child find other words with /i/ at the beginning or in the middle, such as *ink* and *sit*.

Read Together

Name ______________________________

Read the story.
Circle the picture that shows what happened next.

Maria put on her baseball uniform.

Dad helped Maria find her baseball cap.

Then Maria and Dad got in the car.

Dad drove to the baseball field.

Maria ran over to her team, the Hawks.

The coach told Maria to pick up a bat.

Home Activity Your child read a story and then identified the events that happen, or the plot, in the story. Read a fiction story with your child and have your child tell you the important events in the story.

Name ____________________________________

Verbs

Mark the sentence that has a line under the verb.

1. ◯ Sam jumps in the bag.
   ◯ Sam jumps in the bag.
   ◯ Sam jumps in the bag.

2. ◯ She can tap the bag.
   ◯ She can tap the bag.
   ◯ She can tap the bag.

3. ◯ She can see the hat.
   ◯ She can see the hat.
   ◯ She can see the hat.

4. ◯ He can play here.
   ◯ He can play here.
   ◯ He can play here.

School + Home

Home Activity Your child prepared for taking tests on verbs. Read a story together. Have your child point out the verbs in the story.

Name ___________________________

Read each question. **Circle** the correct answer.

1. This sign tells you how fast to go.

2. This sign tells you not to go.

3. What does this sign mean?

eat here   do not speed   stop

4. What does this sign mean?

police   library   hospital

5. Which sign would help you if you were sick?

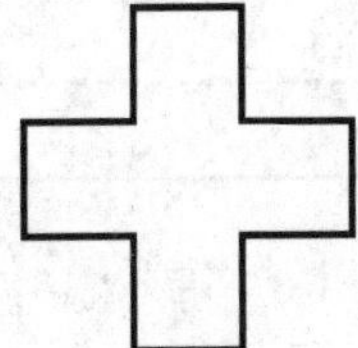

Home Activity Your child learned the meanings of many different signs. Take a walk in the neighborhood and point out the different signs you see on the road or street. See how many of the signs your child can explain.

Name ______________________________

Trace and **write** the letters. Make sure you write your letters the correct size.

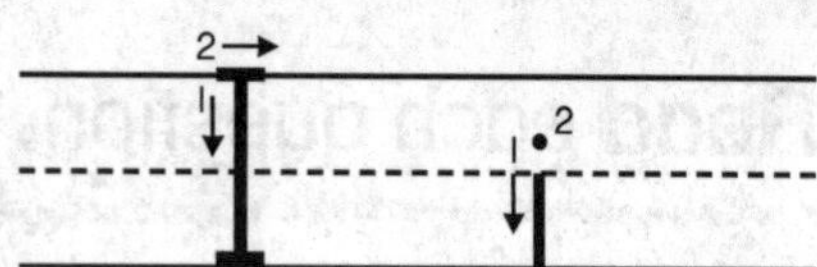

I

i

Copy the words. Write the tall and small letters the correct size. Write **p** and **g** so that they fall below the line.

If

sit

pan

tap

pig

big

Home Activity Your child practiced writing words with *Ii*. Have your child think of words that rhyme with *pig*. Then help your child write two of the rhyming words: *big, dig, fig, rig, wig.*

Name ______________________________

a b c d e f g h i j k l m n o p q r s t u v w x y z

Circle the letter that comes first in the alphabet.

1. s t i

2. a p n

3. f c g

4. g s f

5. n i p

6. t g n

Write the letters in alphabetical order.

7. b a g

8. p c i

9. g f b

10. p a s

11. n c i

12. t f b

School + Home

Home Activity Your child learned to put letters in alphabetical order. Write three different letters on index cards, one letter on each card. Have your child put the letters in alphabetical order, and then write them in order.

Name ______________________

Read the words in the box.
Pick a word to finish each sentence.
Write it on the line.

do	look	you	was	yellow

1. This  is ______________ .

2. Can ______________ see the  ?

3. ______________ at that big 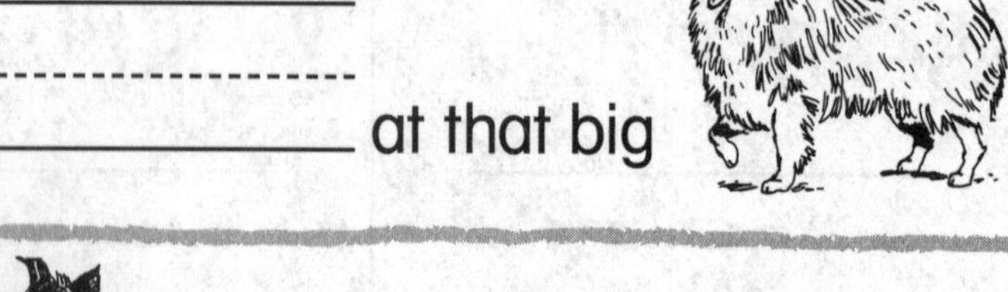 !

4. The ______________ in the bag!

5. ______________ you like my ?

Home Activity This week your child learned to read the words *do, look, you, was,* and *yellow*. Write each word on a card. Have your child read each word and then use it in a sentence.

Name ________________________________

Dd

Say the word for each picture.
Write d on the line if the word has the same first sound as .

1. ________	2. ________
3. ________	4. ________

Say the word for each picture.
Write d on the line if the word has the same ending sound as .

5. ________	6. ________
7. ________	8. ________

Home Activity Your child learned that some words begin and end with the letter *d*. Have your child find other words that begin and end with /d/.

Name ______________________________

Circle the make-believe pictures.
Draw a box around the real pictures.

1.

2.

3.

4.

5.

6.

School + Home **Home Activity** Your child looked at pictures to tell which may be real and which may be make-believe. Have your child draw a picture of something that is make-believe and then draw a picture of something that is real.

Name ______________________

Trace and **write** the letters. Make sure you write your letters the correct size.

D d

D

d

Copy the words. **Write** the letters the correct size.

Dan

Dad

dip

dig

fad

bad

pad

Sid

Home Activity Your child practiced writing words with *Dd*. Have your child choose a word from above with *D* and a word with *d* and then write the words as neatly as possible.

Name ___________________________

Circle the title of the book.
Underline the author of the book.
Draw a box around the illustrator of the book.

Circle the book that Bess Dell wrote.
Draw a box around the book that Tom Lock illustrated.

Home Activity Your child learned to use the information on a book cover and title page to figure out what the book is about. Your child also learned to look for the name of the author and illustrator of a book. On a book your child enjoys, point out the cover and title page. Point to the name of the illustrator and read it aloud. Discuss the illustrations and invite your child to express an opinion about the illustrator.

Name ______________________________

L l

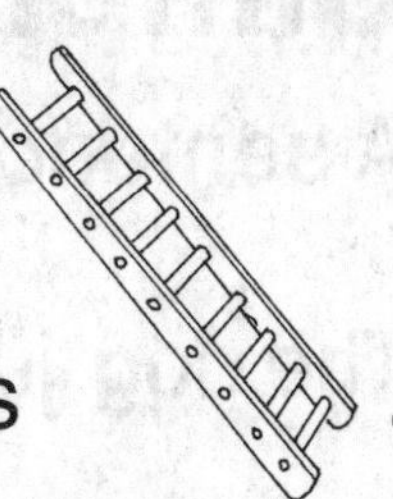

Say the word for each picture.
Write l on the line if the word has the same first sound as .

1. 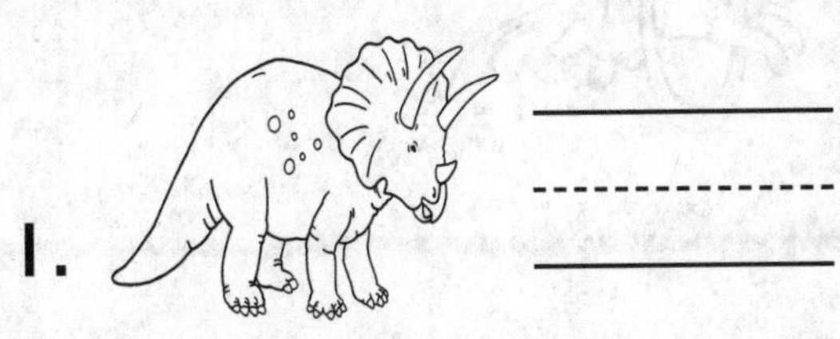 ______	2.  ______
3.   ______	4. 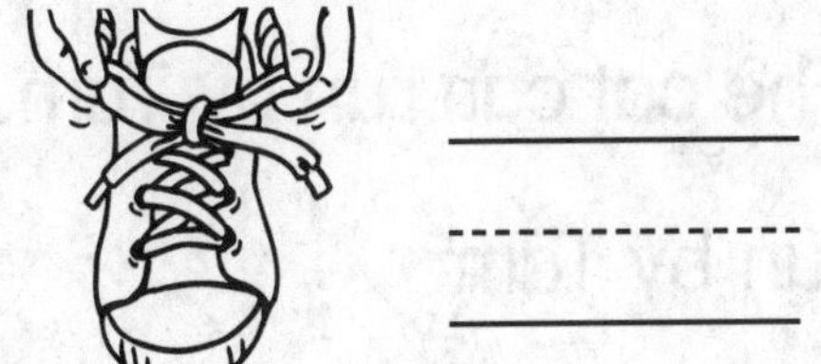 ______
5.  ______	6. 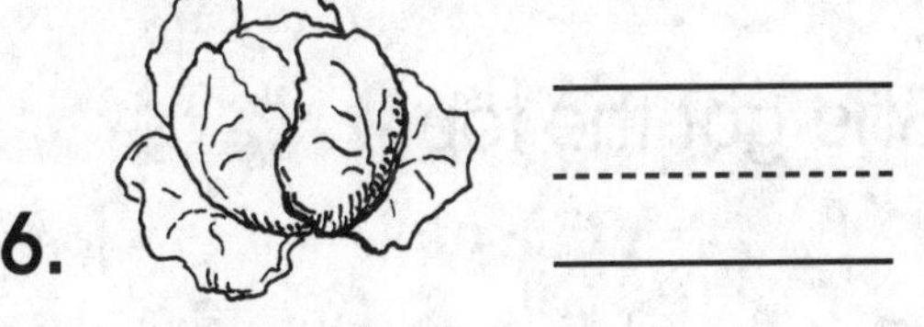 ______

Write two words that rhyme with **pill**.

7. ______________ 8. ______________

Home Activity Your child learned that some words begin with the letter *l*. Have your child find other words with /l/ as in *ladder*.

Name ______________________________

Simple Sentences

A **sentence** has a noun and a verb. It tells who did what.

The **dog jumps**.

Dog is a noun.

Jumps is a verb.

Find the sentence. **Circle** the sentence.

1. The cat can run by Tam.

   run by Tam

2. got the top

   She got the top.

3. The doll is on the mat.

   the doll

4. The cat sat on the mat.

   the mat

Home Activity Your child learned about simple sentences. Have your child find things in your house to make sentences about. Have your child identify the parts of his or her sentences.

Name ______________________

Trace and **write** the letters. Make sure you write your letters the correct size.

L l

L

l

Copy the words. Sit and hold your paper the correct way.

Lin

Cal

lid

lad

pill

lip

lab

mill

Home Activity Your child practiced writing *Ll*. Say names and words that begin with *L* or *l* and have your child write the correct letter each time you say a name or word.

Name ______________________________

a b c d e f g h i j k l m n o p q r s t u v w x y z

Circle the letter that comes first in the alphabet.

1. a l t	**2.** i p n	**3.** f d g
4. t h l	**5.** s n p	**6.** d c g

Write the letters in alphabetical order.

7. m b s	**8.** t d p	**9.** t f b
10. p w n	**11.** f c i	**12.** i f b g

Home Activity Your child learned to sequence the letters of the alphabet. Write three different letters in random order. Have your child write the letters in alphabetical order.

Name ____________________

Hh

Say the word for each picture.
Write h on the line if the word has the same first sound as  .

1. ______	2. ______
3. ______	4. ______
5. ______	6. ______
7. ______	8. ______

School + Home **Home Activity** Your child learned that some words begin with the letter *h*. Have your child find other words with /h/ as in *helicopter.*

Name ______________________________

Read the words in the box.
Pick a word to finish each sentence.
Write it on the line. **Remember** to begin a sentence with a capital letter.

are	have	they	that	two

1. ________________ are playing in the  .

2. Look at ________________ white .

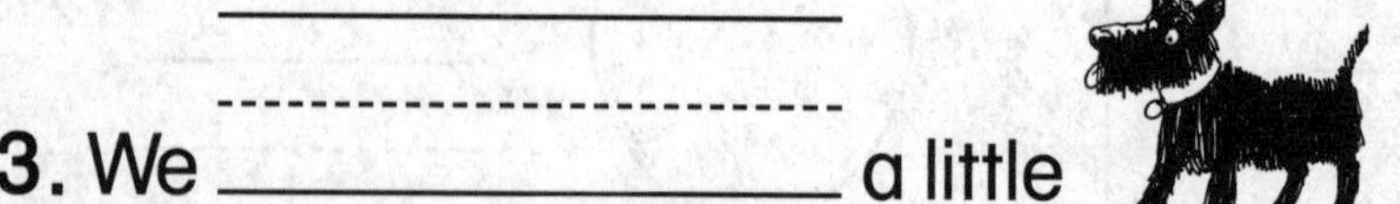

3. We ________________ a little .

4. My ________________ went home.

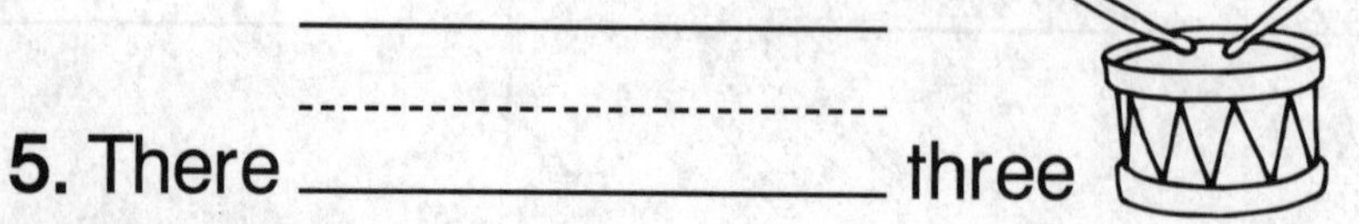

5. There ________________ three .

Home Activity This week your child identified and read the words *are, have, they, that*, and *two*. As you read with your child, encourage him or her to point out these words in print.

Name ____________________

Simple Sentences

Tell a story about what you like to play with.
Finish the sentence. **Use** words from the box.
Write a sentence of your own.

a doll	a ball	a toy car	games	a top

I like to play with ____________________.

I like to play with ____________________.

____

____

Say other sentences using the toys.

Home Activity Your child learned how to use simple sentences in writing. Have your child write two sentences that tell how he or she can help clean up a mess.

Name ____________________

Trace and **write** the letters. Make sure you write your letters the correct size.

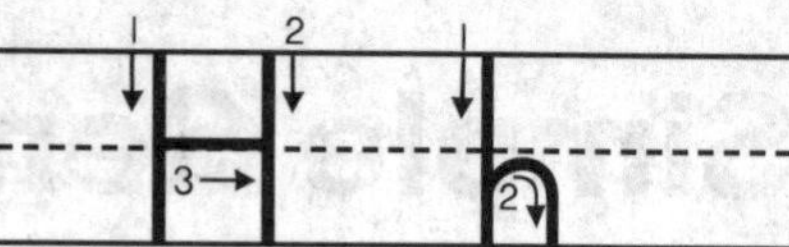

Copy the words.

Halt

his

Han

hat

hip

hand

Did you remember the crossbar on the letter **H**?  **Yes** **No**

Home Activity Your child practiced writing words with *Hh*. Say the following words: *Hal, Hank, Harry, have, him, hit.* Have your child write *H* or *h* to show how each word begins.

Name ______________________

a b c d e f g h i j k l m n o p q r s t u v w x y z

Circle the letter that comes first in the alphabet.

1. i t h	2. d p n	3. s b g
4. t f m	5. s p t	6. n g l

Write the letters in alphabetical order.

7. b d g	8. n f l	9. c b p
10. v h s	11. m f o	12. t m bi

School + Home

Home Activity Your child learned to put words in alphabetical order. Say two different letters in random order. Have your child write the letters in alphabetical order.

Name ______________________

Oo

Say the word for each picture.
Write o on the line if the word has the same first sound as .

1.

2.

3.

4.

Say the word for each picture.
Write o on the line if the word has the same middle sound as ●.

Home Activity Your child learned about the short *o* vowel sound in words. Have your child find other words with /o/ at the beginning or in the middle, such as *octopus* and *box*.

Read Together

Name ______________________________

Read the story. **Circle** the make-believe pictures.
Draw a box around the real pictures.

My friend lives on a farm.

I like to visit the farm.

I help my friend feed the chickens.

We let the cows out of the barn.

One day we pick corn.

There is a lot of work to do on a farm.

1.

2.

3.

4.

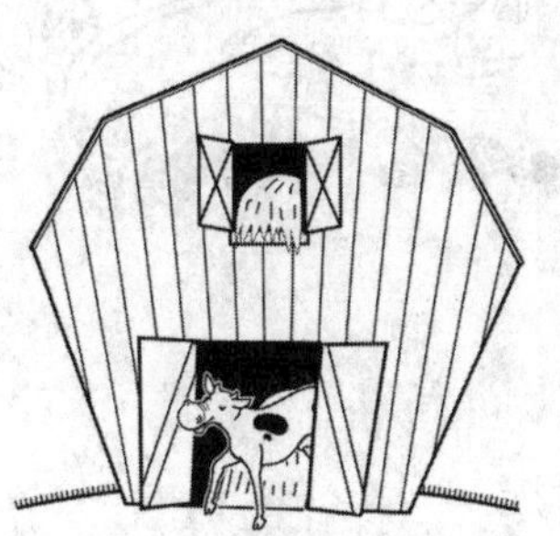

5.

6.

Home Activity Your child read a story and then identified pictures of real things and make-believe things. Remind your child that some stories could really happen and some stories are make believe. Have your child draw a picture of a real pig and a make-believe pig.

Name ____________________

Simple Sentences

Mark the group of words that is a sentence.

1. ○ look at that green
   ○ that green top
   ○ Look at that green top.

2. ○ The dog will jump.
   ○ will jump
   ○ the dog

3. ○ cat can do
   ○ look what the cat
   ○ Look what the cat can do.

4. ○ Mom can see the
   ○ Mom can see the bag.
   ○ the bag

Home Activity Your child prepared for taking tests on simple sentences. Read a story together. Have your child point out the parts of the sentences.

Name ________________________________

Circle the traffic symbols in each row.

1.

SPEED
LIMIT
25

2.

Place an X on the symbols that are found on the map.

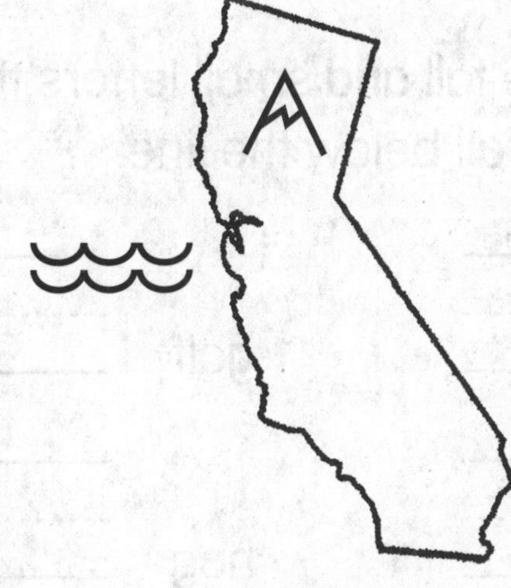

3.

Home Activity Your child has learned to identify traffic and map symbols. Point out traffic symbols when on the road together. Point out map symbols when you look at maps together.

Name ____________________

Trace and **write** the letters. Make sure you write your letters the correct size.

O o

O

o

Copy the words. **Write** the tall and small letters the correct size. Write **p** and **g** so that they fall below the line.

On golf

dog hog

pot hop

Home Activity Your child practiced writing *Oo*. Say names and words that begin with *O* (*Otto, Oscar, Otis*) and *o* (*only, octopus, ostrich, olive*) and have your child write the correct letter each time you say a name or word.

Name ______________________________

a b c d e f g h i j k l m n o p q r s t u v w x y z

Circle the letter that comes first in the alphabet.

1. o t d	2. i p n	3. s f l
4. g s f	5. s o p	6. t h n

Write the letters in alphabetical order.

7. p o l t	8. t b i a	9. r h v a
10. m u s z	11. g j d c	12. s n a o

School + Home

Home Activity Your child learned to put words in alphabetical order. Say three different letters in random order. Have your child write the letters in alphabetical order.

Name ______________________

Read the words in the box.
Pick a word to finish each sentence.
Write it on the line.

are	have	they	that	two

1. I like ____________ pretty  .

2. The  ____________ all black.

3. Stella has ____________ big  .

4. Jan and Pete ____________ funny  .

5. When will ____________ go to the  ?

School + Home **Home Activity** This week your child identified and read the words *are, have, they, that,* and *two*. As you read with your child, encourage him or her to point out these words in print.

Name ______________________________

Rr

Say the word for each picture.
Write r on the line if the word has the same first sound as  .

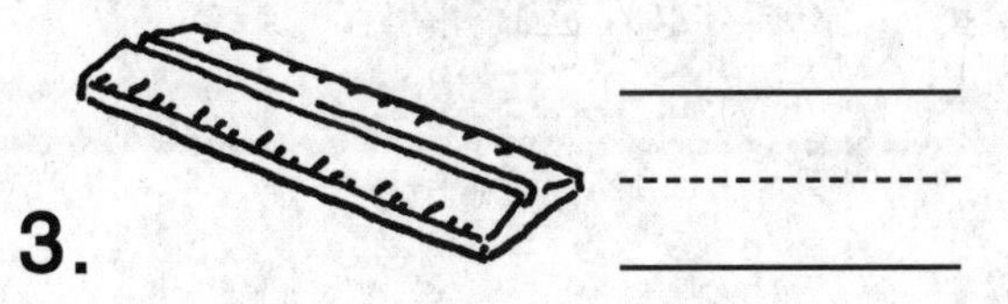
1. ______

2. ______

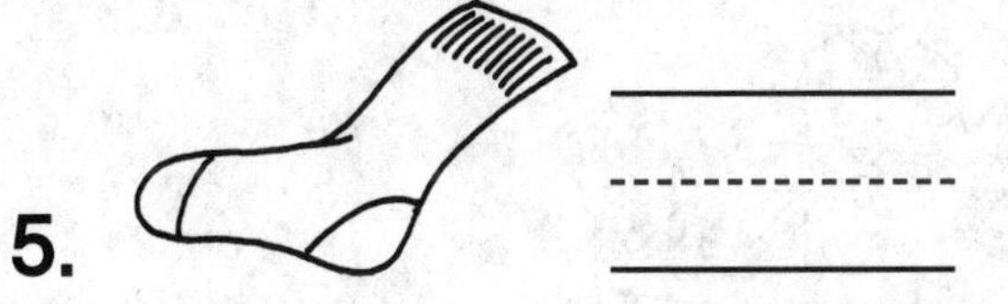
3. ______

4. ______

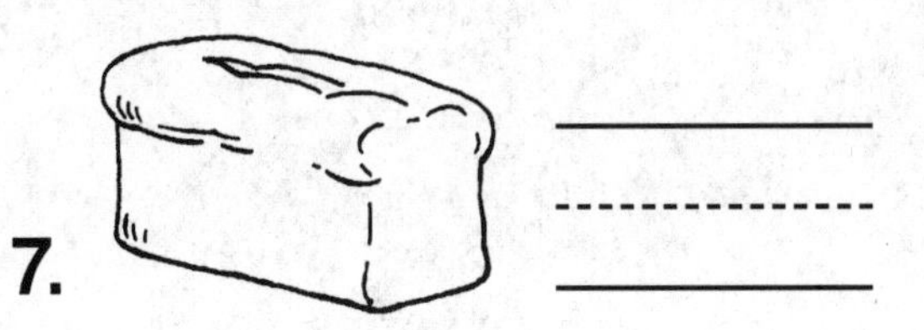
5. ______

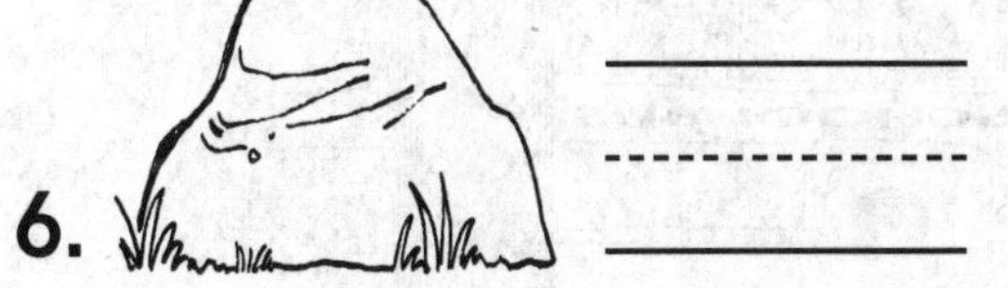
6. ______

7. ______

8. ______

School + Home

Home Activity Your child learned that some words begin with the letter *r*. Have your child find other words that begin with /r/ as in *rocket*.

Name ___________________________

Look at the pictures.

Circle the picture to show what happens next.

Look at the pictures.

Draw a picture of what could happen next.

School + Home **Home Activity** Your child has learned to identify plot, or the events that happen, in a story. When you read a story with your child, have your child retell the important events in the story.

Name ____________________

Trace and **write** the letters. Make sure you write your letters the correct size.

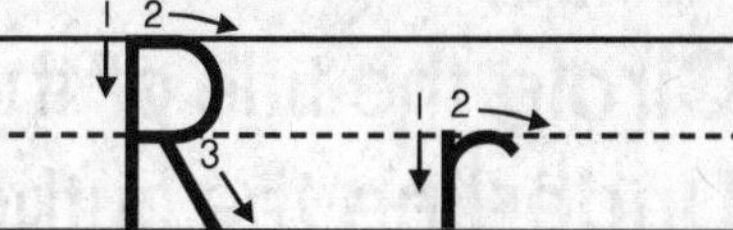

R

r

Copy the words. Write the letters the correct size.

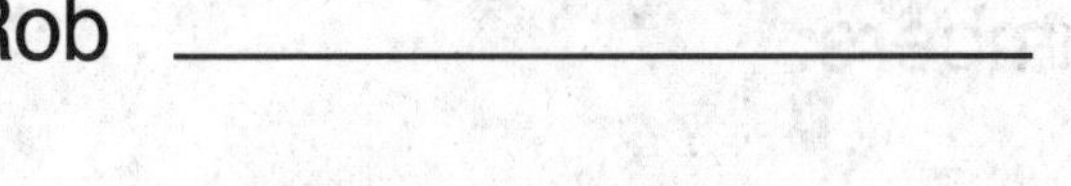

Rob

rat

Ron

rod

ran

rib

rip

rig

School + Home

Home Activity Your child practiced writing words with *Rr*. Have your child choose one word with *R* and one word with *r* from above, and practice writing the words one more time.

Name ______________________________

Circle the title of the book.
Underline the author of the book.
Draw a box around the illustrator of the book.

Contents

1. **Draw** a circle around the page numbers.

2. **Put** a box around the chapter titles.

3. **Write** the page number where the chapter about fish begins.

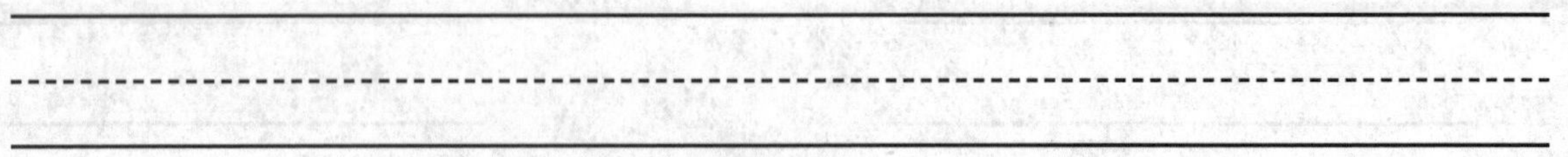

Home Activity Your child learned to use the title, author's name, illustrator's name and the table of contents in a nonfiction book to find information. As you read together, point out the table of contents and encourage your child to help you find information such as the page number for a specific chapter.

Name ______________________________

Jj Ww

Say the word for each picture.
Write j on the line if the word has the same first sound as .
Write w on the line if the word has the same first sound as .

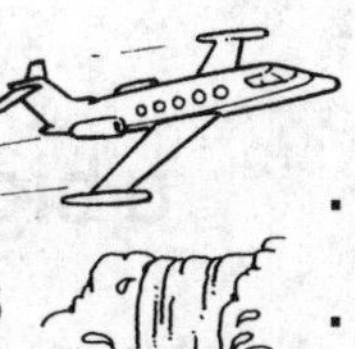

1. ________

2. ________

3. ________

4. ________

5. ________

6. ________

7. ________

8. ________

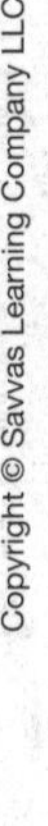

Home Activity Your child learned that some words begin with the letter *w* and some words begin with the letter *j*. Have your child find other words that begin with /w/ as in *waterfall* and /j/ as in *jet*.

Name ______________________________

Adjectives

An **adjective** tells about a person, place, or thing.

a **big** book

Read the sentence.
Circle the adjective.

1. Sam sees the yellow bus.

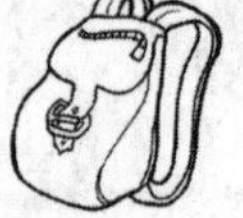

2. Sam has a big bag.

3. He met fun friends.

4. We read new books.

5. Jill can play with the red ball.

Say each word you circled in a sentence.

Home Activity Your child learned about adjectives. Have your child choose objects from home and use an adjective to describe each one.

Name ___________________________

Trace and **write** the letters.
Make sure you write your letters
the correct size.

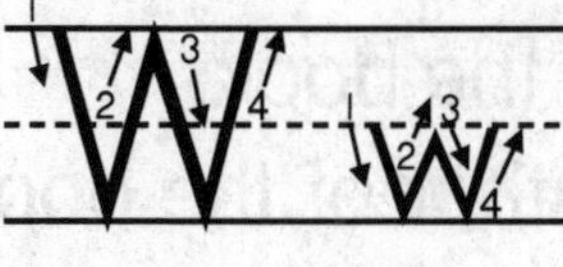

W

w

J

j

School + Home

Home Activity Your child practiced writing letters *Ww* and *Jj*. Have your child practice writing all four letters three more times. Make sure he or she writes the *j* so that it has a dot above it and falls below the line.

Name ___________________________

Circle the title of the book.
Underline the author of the book.
Draw a box around the illustrator of the book.

Contents

1. **Draw** a circle around the page numbers.

2. **Put** a box around the chapter titles.

3. **Write** the page number where the chapter about Ants That Dig begins. ___________________

Home Activity Your child learned to use the title, author's name, illustrator's name and the table of contents in a nonfiction book to find information. Point out the information on the cover and the table of contents in an interesting book. Encourage your child to count the number of chapters, find the page number for a specific chapter, and turn to that page.

Name ______________________

Kk

Say the word for each picture.
Write k on the line if the word has the same first sound as  .

1. ______	2. ______
3. ______	4. ______
5. ______	6. ______

Pick a word to finish each sentence.
Write the word on the line.

Kim **kiss** **kit**

7. Sam will ______________ Mom.

8. ______________ will hit the rim with the  .

Home Activity Your child learned that some words begin with the letter *k*. Have your child find other words that begin with /k/ as in *kitten*.

Name ______________________

Read the words in the box.
Pick a word to finish each sentence.
Write it on the line. **Remember** to begin each sentence with a capital letter.

he	is	to	with	three

1. She __________ on the  .

2. Bill came __________  .

3. We have __________ books.

4. My  are __________ me.

5. __________ has a cat.

Home Activity This week your child identified and read the words *he, is, to, with,* and *three*. As you read with your child, encourage him or her to point out these words in print.

Name ______________________________

Adjectives

Tell about your room at school.
Finish the sentences. **Use** words from the box.
Write a sentence of your own.

big	small	nice	new

The room is ______________________________.

The room is ______________________________.

____.

Say other sentences using the adjectives in the box.

Home Activity Your child learned how to use adjectives in writing. Have your child write two sentences that describe his or her favorite toy. Ask your child to identify the adjectives in the sentences.

Name ______________________________

Trace and **write** the letters. Make sure you write your letters the correct size.

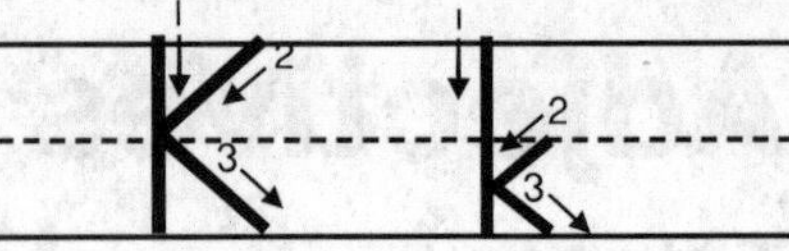

K

k

Copy the words.

Kip

kid

tack

sock

kiss

Kim

Did you write each **K** and **k** the correct size? 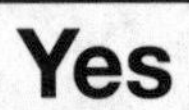 **Yes** **No**

Home Activity Your child practiced writing words with *Kk*. Say the following words: *Kim, Karen, Kevin, kite, kitchen, kitten.* Have your child write *K* or *k* to show how each word begins.

Name ________________________________

a b c d e f g h i j k l m n o p q r s t u v w x y z

Circle the letter that comes first in the alphabet.

1. w j e	2. k i r	3. s c l
4. o n h	5. f n m	6. p d g

Write the letters in alphabetical order.

7. y p e s	8. g i f a	9. t x m b
10. q o m r	11. t n l o	12. e a d b

Home Activity Your child learned to sequence letters of the alphabet. Say four different letters in random order. Have your child write the letters in alphabetical order. Then give your child five letter cards and have him or her put them in alphabetical order.

Name ______________________

Ee

Say the word for each picture.
Write e on the line if the word has the same first sound as .

1. ______	2. ______
3. ______	4. ______

Say the word for each picture.
Write e on the line if the word has the same middle sound as .

5. ______	6. ______
7. ______	8. ______

Home Activity Your child learned that some words have the short *e* sound. Have your child find other words with /e/ at the beginning or in the middle, such as *elephant* and *bell*.

Read Together

Name ______________________

Read the story.
Write 1, 2, 3 on the lines to tell what happens in the beginning, middle, and end.

Lucy plays outside with her puppy.
She wears a big, straw sunhat.
The wind blows the hat off Lucy's head.
So Mom sews ribbons to the hat.
Mom ties the ribbons under Lucy's chin.
Now Lucy's hat stays on.

______

______

______

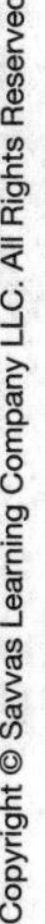

Home Activity Your child read a story and then identified the order of events that happen in a story. This story has a problem and solution. Reread the story with your child. Have your child tell you the problem in the story and how the problem is solved.

Name ______________________________

Adjectives

Mark the sentence that has a line under the adjective.

1. ○ Sam can hop on the big bus.
   ○ Sam can hop on the big bus.
   ○ Sam can hop on the big bus.

2. ○ She is a happy girl.
   ○ She is a happy girl.
   ○ She is a happy girl.

3. ○ We can read a short book.
   ○ We can read a short book.
   ○ We can read a short book.

4. ○ She will eat hot food.
   ○ She will eat hot food.
   ○ She will eat hot food.

Choose other adjectives. **Say** a sentence for each adjective.

Home Activity Your child prepared for taking tests on adjectives. Read a story together. Have your child identify the adjectives in the story.

Name ______________________________

Look at the calendar. **Read** the questions.
Circle the answers.

1. What day comes after Monday?

Sunday Tuesday Thursday

2. What day comes after Thursday?

Wednesday Saturday Friday

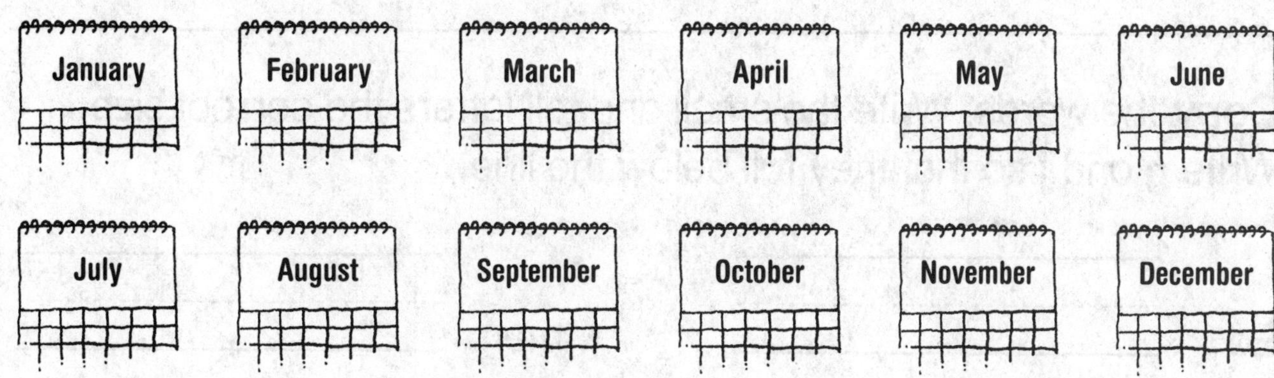

3. What month comes after March?

April May December

4. What month comes after June?

August July October

Home Activity Your child has learned how a calendar shows the order of the days and months. Look at calendars with your child. Have him or her point out the order of the days, weeks, and months.

Name ______________________________

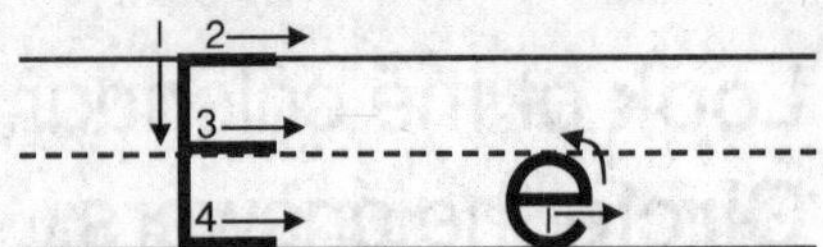

Trace and **write** the letters. Make sure you write your letters the correct size.

E

e

Copy the words. Write the small and tall letters the correct size. Write **g** and **j** so that they fall below the line.

Ed

men

get

egg

jet

beg

Home Activity Your child practiced writing words with *Ee*. Have your child copy the sentence and draw a picture to fill in the blank: *Ed has a pet*________.

Name ______________________________

Read each group of words.
Circle the group of words that is a sentence.

1. sat fat the a is
   Sam can see a cat.
   Sam a mad is I

2. The cat is fat.
   cat Tam is the
   Snap tap cat the

3. He cat the on bat
   He is on the mat.
   mat cat is in nap

4. Tip is with Tam.
   cat see Tip can
   Tam is hat mat

5. Egg hen the with is this
   egg the with is this hen.
   The hen is with this egg.

6. egg chick a is in the
   A chick is in the egg.
   chick A egg in is the

School + Home **Home Activity** Your child learned to recognize sentences. Write groups of simple words that are sentences and groups of words that are not. Ask your child to identify the sentences and explain his or her choices.

Name ____________________

Read the words in the box.
Pick a word to finish each sentence.
Write it on the line.

he	is	to	with	three

1. Basketball ____________ fun.

2. The ____________ squirrels are eating 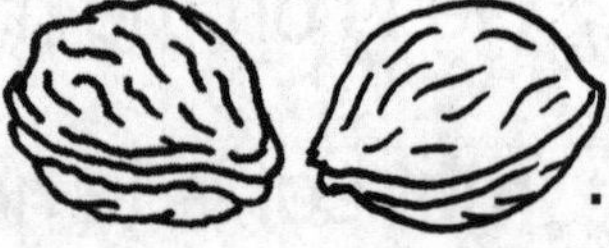.

3. Sam likes to play  ____________ Pat.

4. We can go ____________ the party Saturday.

5. When will ____________ move to his new house?

Home Activity This week your child identified and read the words *he, is, to, with,* and *three*. As you read with your child, encourage him or her to point out these words in print.

Name ______________________________

Vv

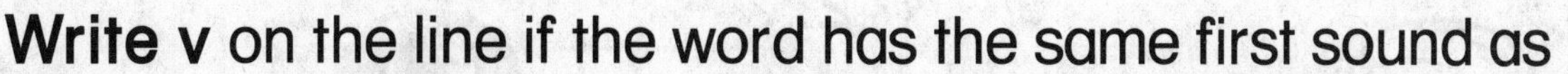

Say the word for each picture.
Write v on the line if the word has the same first sound as .

1. ________

2. ________

3. ________

4. ________

5. ________

6. ________

Write V or **v** to make a word.

7. ____at

8. ____ic

9. ____al

10. ____an

Home Activity Your child learned that some words begin with the letter *v*. Have your child find other words with /v/ as in *volcano*.

Name ____________________

Circle the make-believe pictures.
Draw a box around the real pictures.

1.

2.

3.

4.

5.

6.

Home Activity Your child looked at pictures to tell which may be real and which may be make-believe. With your child, look at a book about how real people and animals live.

Name ______________________

Trace and **write** the letters. Make sure you write your letters the correct size.

V v

V

v

Copy the words. Write the letters the correct size.

Val

vent

Vin

vat

vest

van

vast

Vic

Home Activity Your child practiced writing words with *Vv*. Have your child choose a word that begins with *V* and a word that begins with *v* from above, and practice writing each word two more times.

Name ______________________

Read each group of words.
Find and **copy** the complete sentence.

1. The cat ran.
   is my hat
   had been to

____

2. Kim can win.
   run Kim to see
   my van is a

____

3. A big jet is.
   Pam can pat the cat.
   on mat we see cat on

____

4. My top is in
   The lad is sad.
   Is sad the lad

____

Home Activity Your child learned to recognize sentences and features such as capitalization and end punctuation. Have your child circle the capital letter in each sentence on this page.

Name ______________________

Yy Zz

Say the word for each picture.
Write y on the line if the word has the same first sound as yo-yo.
Write z on the line if the word has the same first sound as zebra.

1. ______	2. ______
3. ______	4. ______
5. ______	6. ______
7. ______	8. ______

Home Activity Your child learned that some words begin with *y* and some words begin with *z*. Have your child find other words that begin with /y/ as in *yo-yo* and /z/ as in *zebra*.

Name ______________________________

Sentences

A **sentence** tells a complete idea.
It begins with a capital letter.
Many sentences end with a period.

noun ↑

The wet dog runs.

↓ adjective ↓ verb

Find the sentence.

Underline the sentence.

1. The girl will get the one with fuzz.
   the one with fuzz
2. the fun park
   They can go to the fun park.
3. Here is where they sell good fruit.
   good fruit
4. wet up here
   You can get wet up here.
5. I can see the big rainbow.
   big rainbow

Home Activity Your child learned about expanding sentences. Say a simple sentence to your child and have him or her add a word to the sentence.

Name ________________________________

Trace and **write** the letters. Make sure you write your letters the correct size.

Y y Z z

Y

y

Z

z

Home Activity Your child practiced writing *Yy* and *Zz*. Have your child practice writing all four letters three more times each.

Name ________________________________

Read each group of words.
Find and **copy** the complete sentence.

1. pup Ned is a
Ned and Ted
Ned is a pup.

____

2. a is dog this
This dog is a
This is a dog.

____

3. Tim dog is for this
This dog is for Tim.
dog this Tim for is

____

4. The dog nap and will Tim
The dog and Tim nap.
Tim nap dog The and will

____

Home Activity Your child learned to recognize sentences and features such as end punctuation. Find sentences and other groups of words in a flyer, periodical, or used worksheet. Ask your child to identify the sentences and circle the end punctuation.

Name ______________________________

Uu

Say the name of the picture.
Write u on the line if the word has the same first sound as  .

1. ______

2. ______

3. ______

4. ______

Say the name of the picture.
Write u on the line if the word has the same middle sound as  .

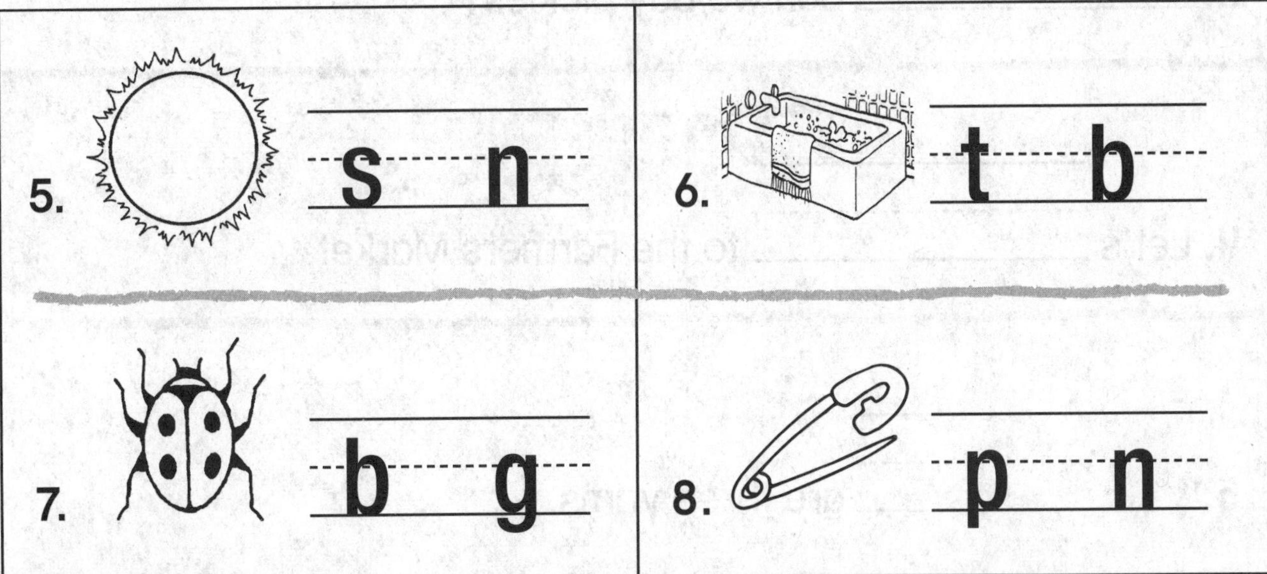

Home Activity Your child learned about the short *u* vowel sound in words. Have your child find other words that have the same sound as /u/ at the beginning or in the middle, such as *umbrella* and *rug*.

Name ______________________

Read the words in the box.
Pick a word to finish each sentence. **Write** it on the line.
Remember to begin a sentence with a capital letter.

where	here	for	me	go

1. The  is for ______________ .

2. We are waiting ______________ the rain to stop.

3. ______________ can we buy pickles?

4. Let's ______________ to the Farmers Market.

5. ______________ are three yams.

Home Activity This week your child identified and read the words *where, here, for, me,* and *go*. As you read with your child, encourage him or her to point out these words in print.

Name ______________________

Sentences

Tell about what you get at a store.

Use words from the box or words of your own.

food	toys	books	games

Say other sentences about things in a store.

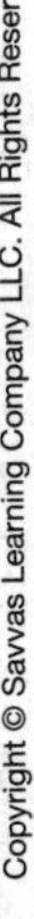

Home Activity Your child learned how to expand sentences in writing. Have your child add adjectives to the sentences he or she wrote.

Name ______________________________

Trace and **write** the letters. Make sure you write your letters the correct size.

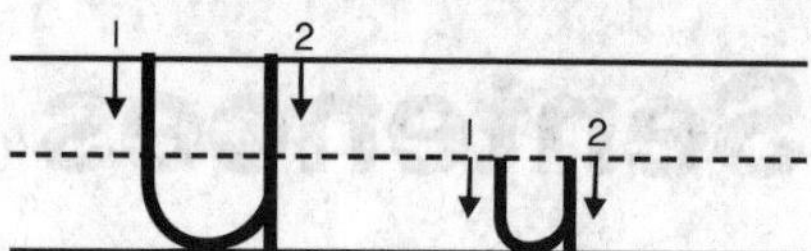

U

u

Copy the words.

Uncle

junk

just

dull

hug

sun

Did you write each **U** and **u** the correct size? **Yes** **No**

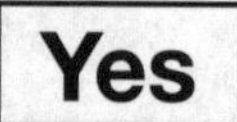

Home Activity Your child practiced writing words with *Uu*. Read the following sentence to your child: *It is fun to run in the sun.* Have your child copy the sentence as neatly as he or she can.

Name ______________________________

Read each group of words.
Find and **copy** the complete sentence.

1.	2.
pup sit and Tom The pup can sit. Tom the pup sit	A pup can run. The fat pup fat on fat pup beg can

Finish each sentence. **Write** a word and a [.]

3. I like ______________________________

4. We see a ______________________________

5. Tom fed the ______________________________

6. Sam is with ______________________________

7. Tam can go ______________________________

8. Tip has a yellow ______________________________

Home Activity Your child learned to recognize sentences and features such as capitalization and end punctuation, and then use these features to complete sentences. Point to sentences in a newspaper or magazine. Have your child identify the features of a sentence. Then have your child find complete sentences.

Name ______________________________

Qq

Say the word for each picture.
Write q on the line if the word has the same first sound as 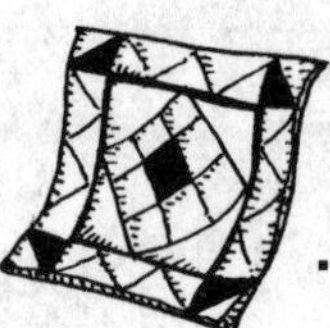 .

1. ______	2. ______
3. ______	4. ______
5. ______	6. ______

Write qu to make a word.

7. ______ilt

8. ______it

9. ______iz

10. ______ick

Home Activity Your child learned that some words begin with the letter *q*. Have your child find other words that begin with /kw/ as in *quilt*.

Read Together

Name ___________________________

Read the story.
Look at each pair of pictures.
Circle the one that shows something real.

My class went to a museum.

Butterflies were flying around in a special room.

In another room, we learned about horses.

There were models and pictures of horses.

We saw the bones of a huge dinosaur.

That was my favorite part of the museum.

1. 

2. 

3. 

4. 

5. 

6. 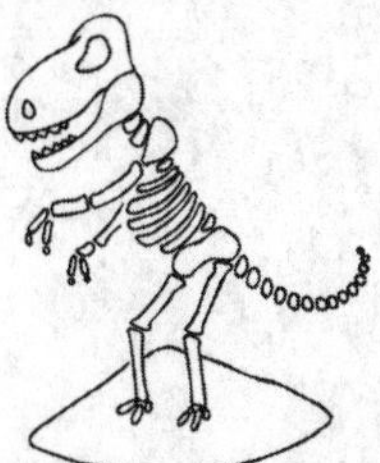

Home Activity Your child read a story that could really happen. Then your child identified which of two pictures shows something real. Talk about a place you and your child have gone to, such as a zoo, park, or fair. Have your child name things that were real at that place.

Name ______________________

Sentences

Mark the word that completes the sentence.

1. Zak can ______ a big yam.
   - ◯ girl
   - ◯ fuzz
   - ◯ sell

2. We go for a ______ run.
   - ◯ Sam
   - ◯ long
   - ◯ quit

3. They can go here to get ______.
   - ◯ mop
   - ◯ run
   - ◯ fruit

4. They can ______ up at the rainbow.
   - ◯ look
   - ◯ big
   - ◯ zoo

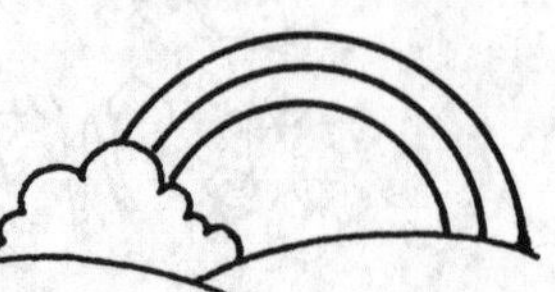

Home Activity Your child prepared for taking tests on expanding sentences. Name a family member and have your child say two sentences about that person. Tell your child to include a noun, a verb, and an adjective in each sentence.

Name ___________________________

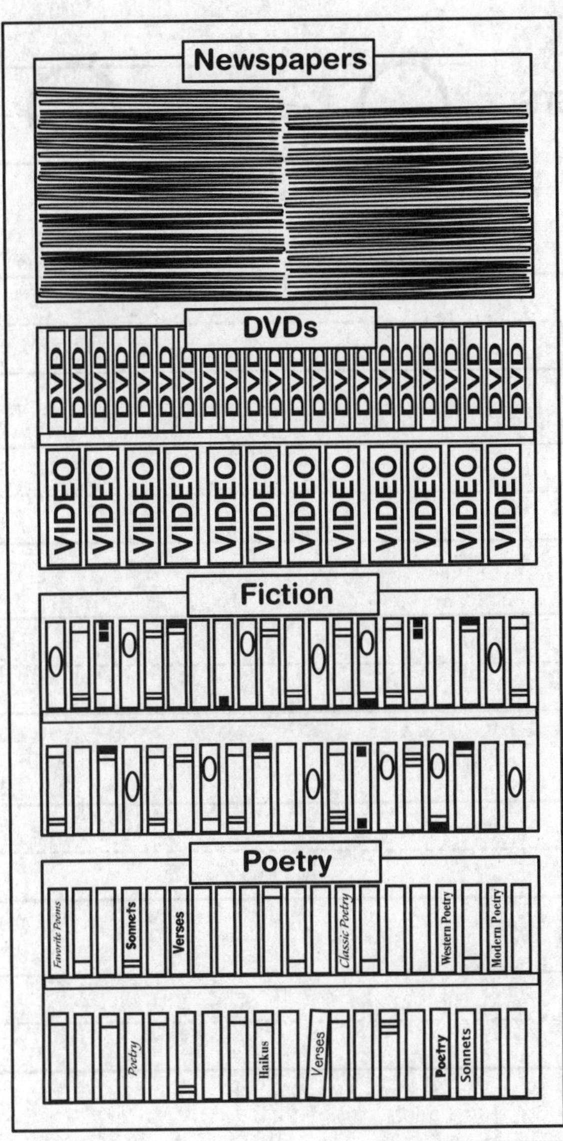

1. **Circle** the shelf with .

2. **Draw** a box around the shelf with .

3. **Draw** an X over the computer.

4. **Draw** an arrow to the shelf with books of poems.

5. **Underline** the shelf with DVDs.

Home Activity Your child learned to find resources in the library. Visit your local library with your child and help him or her find the storybooks, poems, newspapers, signs, and labels.

Name ______________________________

Trace and **write** the letters.
Make sure you write your letters the correct size.

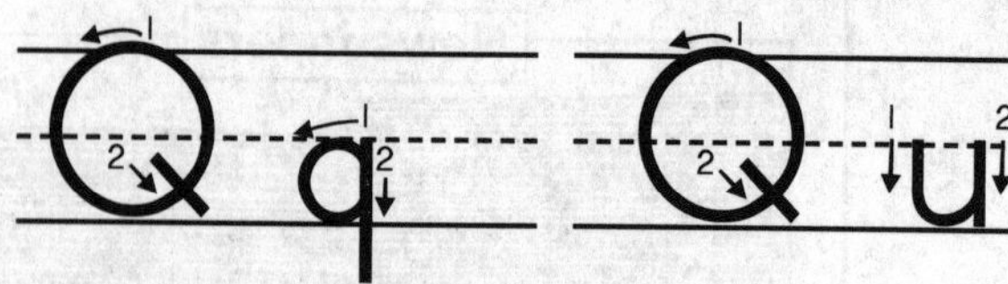

Q

q

Qu

qu

Home Activity Your child practiced writing *Qu* and *qu*. Have your child practice writing this sentence: *Quin quit his quest.*

Name ______________________________

Read each group of words.
Find and **copy** the complete sentence.

1. ham the Ben is for
The ham is for Ben.
Ben ham is the for

____

2. I see a big yam.
A yam I see big
See yam big I a

____

Finish each sentence. **Write** a word and a [.]

3. Dad can ______________________________

4. The hat is ______________________________

5. They have to ______________________________

6. A cat is on ______________________________

7. Kit and Tip see ______________________________

8. I see a green ______________________________

Home Activity Your child learned to recognize sentences and features such as capitalization and end punctuation, and then use these features to complete sentences. Read the sentences that your child completed. Discuss the features of each sentence. Ask if each sentence makes sense.

Name ______________________________

Read the words in the box.
Pick a word to finish each sentence.
Write it on the line.

where	here	for	me	go

1. Viv asked if Tim could come ____________ for a visit.

2. The rainbow may ____________ away.

3. I know ____________ you live.

4. Bill can come with ____________ to the game.

5. She bought vegetables ____________ Jan.

Home Activity This week your child identified and read the words *where, here, for, me,* and *go*. As you read with your child, encourage him or her to point out these words in print.

Name ______________________

Say the word for each picture.
Write a on the line if you hear the **short a** sound.

c<u>a</u>t

1. 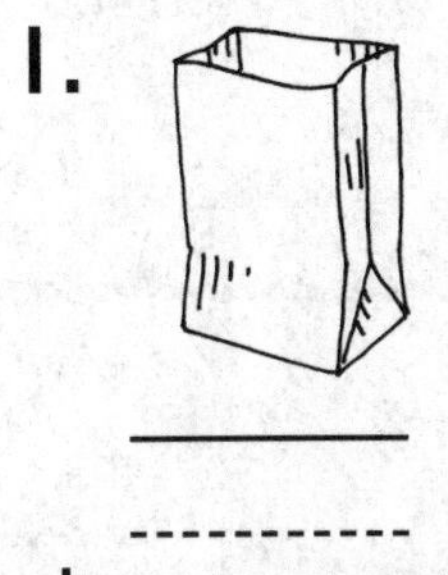

b ____ g

2. 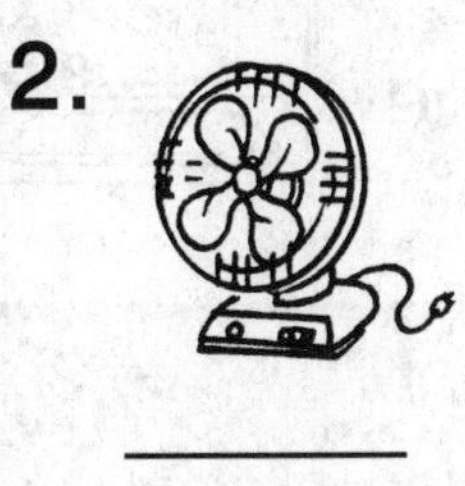

f ____ n

3. 

m ____ p

4. 

m ____ p

5. 

c ____ n

6. 

m ____ n

7. 

p ____ g

8. 

v ____ n

Write a word for each picture.

9. 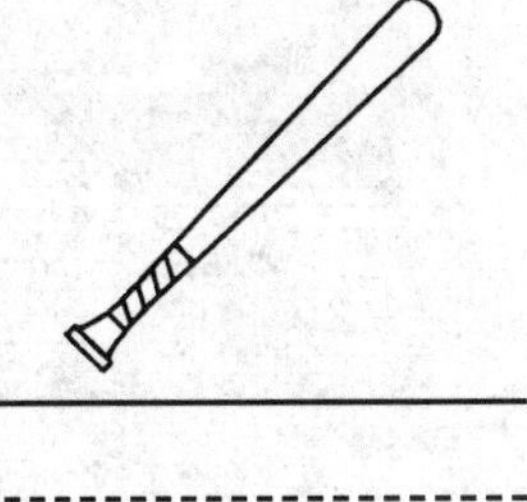

____

10. 

____

Home Activity Your child has reviewed words with the short *a* sound heard in *cat*. Work with your child to make words that rhyme with *cat* and *man*.

Name ______________________________

Read the words in the box.
Pick a word to finish each sentence.
Write it on the line.

my	on	way	in	come

1. We go that ________________ to the  .

2. The can ________________ to me.

3. This is ________________ .

4. The 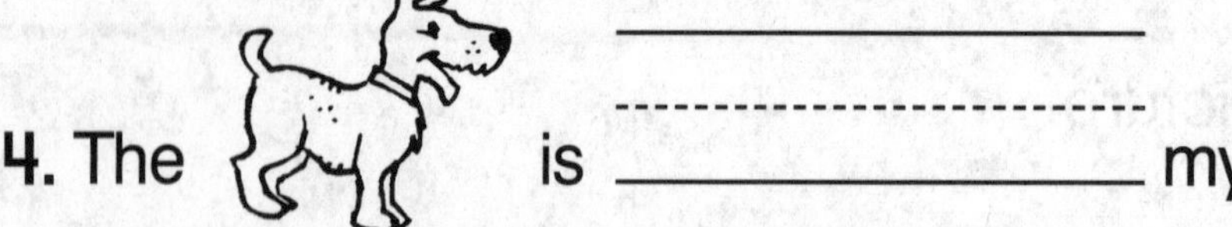 is ________________ my  .

5. The 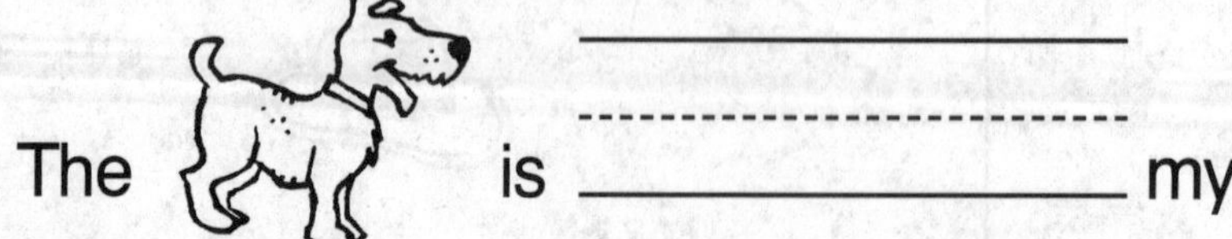 is ________________ my  .

School + Home **Home Activity** This week your child identified and read the words *in, on, my, way,* and *come*. Write each word on a card. Have your child read each word and then use it in a sentence.

Name ______________________________

Look at the pictures.

Circle a word to finish each sentence of the story.

1. Sam has a cat.
The cat had a _____. nap tag

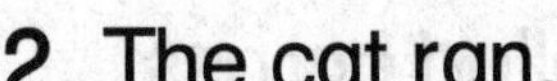

2. The cat ran.
Sam is _____. lap sad

3. The cat is in the jam.
Sam is _____. bad mad

4. The cat ran.
The cat is _____. bad sad

Circle the picture to finish the sentence.

5. The story takes place in a _____.

Home Activity Your child identified characters' actions and feelings. Reread the story with your child. Talk about why Sam felt the way he did.

Name ______________________________

Writing • Story

Pooky the Cat

Pooky is our cat. He is silly. He plays with everything.

Today, Mom dropped a pen. The pen fell on the floor.

Pooky ran to the pen. He hit the pen. The pen rolled across the floor. Pooky chased the pen. He hit it again. It rolled away.

"Silly Pooky!" said Mom. "He thinks the pen is a toy!"

Key Features of a Story

- The story has characters and tells what they do.
- It is made of sentences.

Name ______________________

Say the word for each picture.

Write ck on the line if the word has the same ending sound as 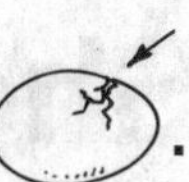.

1. 

ta ______

2. 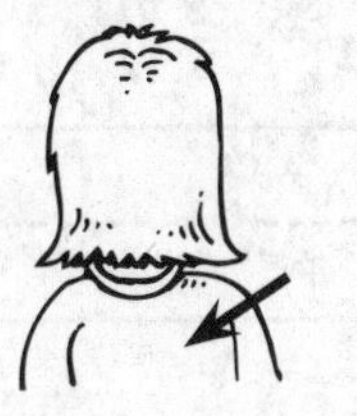

ba ______

3. 

fa ______

4. 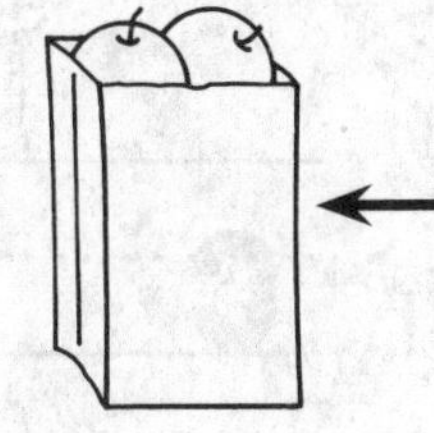

sa ______

5. 

ha ______

6. 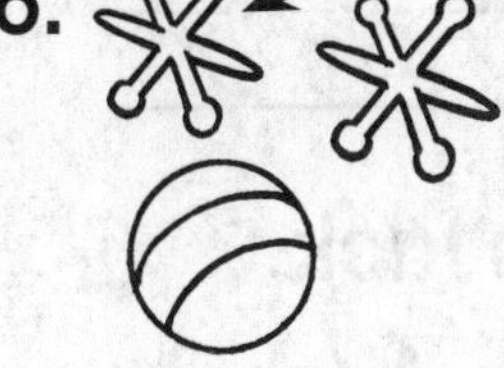

ja ______

7. 

pa ______

8. 

ca ______

Write two words that have the same ending sound as [backpack picture].

______________________ ______________________

School + Home

Home Activity Your child practiced reading and creating words that end in *ck*. Help your child write words that rhyme with *sack*.

Name ______________________

Short *a* Words

Spelling Words

- at
- can
- cat
- back
- dad
- am
- bat
- mad
- ran
- sack

Write two list words that rhyme with **pan**.

1. c______ 2. r______

Write two list words that rhyme with **sad**.

3. m______ 4. d______

Write two list words that rhyme with **tack**.

5. b______ 6. s______

Write two list words that rhyme with **hat**.

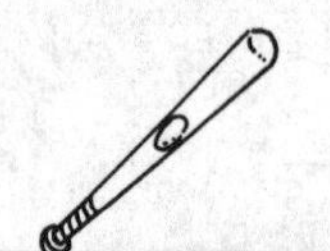

7. c______ 8. b______

Write the missing words. **am at**

9. Look ______ me. 10. I ______ on a box.

Home Activity Your child wrote words with the short *a* vowel sound. Point to a picture on this page and have your child spell the word.

Name ____________________

Sentences

A **sentence** is a group of words that tells a complete idea. It begins with a capital letter. Many sentences end with a period **(.)**.

The cat is on a mat. ← This is a sentence.
on a mat ← This is not a sentence.

Find the sentence. **Write** the sentence.

1. Jim has a pet. has a pet

2. His pet His pet is a cat.

3. The cat The cat runs away.

4. Jim looks for his pet. for his pet

5. with Jim We go with Jim.

Home Activity Your child learned about sentences. Name an animal your child knows. Have your child say two sentences about the animal.

Name ______________________________

Story Chart

Title ______________________________

Characters

Beginning

↓

Middle

↓

End of Story

Home Activity Your child is learning to write a little story. Ask your child what stories are like.

Name ______________________

A a

Copy the words. Write the letters the correct size.

Ann ______________ nap ______________

tap ______________ ham ______________

cap ______________ ran ______________

jab ______________ yak ______________

wag ______________ sad ______________

rag ______________ pal ______________

sat ______________ Pam ______________

Did you write all of your letters the correct size? 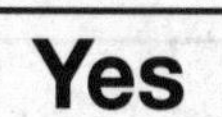 Yes  No

Home Activity Your child practiced writing words with *A* and *a* and the short *a* sound. Have your child draw a picture of two of the words he or she wrote and label the pictures with the words.

Name ____________________

Read each question. **Write** the correct answer.

a frog a bird a fish

1. Who is Ted? ____________________

in a nest on the ground in a chair

2. Where does Ted sleep? ____________________

3. Which book is about pet doctors?

____

4. Which book could help you learn about feeding your pet?

____

5. Other than books, where else could you look to learn more about birds?

____

Home Activity Your child learned how to select books based on their titles or key words. Together with your child, make a list of topics you may enjoy reading about. Then, if possible, go to the library and choose some age-appropriate books based on your topics of interest.

Dad had the bag at the van.

Jack ran back!

Decodable Story *Jack and Dad Pack*
Target Skill Short *a,* Final *-ck*

Name ______________________

Jack and Dad Pack

Short a			Final *–ck*	High-Frequency Words
at	cap	ran	Jack	I
bag	Dad	sat	back	said
and	had	van	sack	the
bat	hat		pack	look
can	map			

Jack and Dad sat.

"I can pack the bag," said Dad.

"I can pack the sack," said Jack.

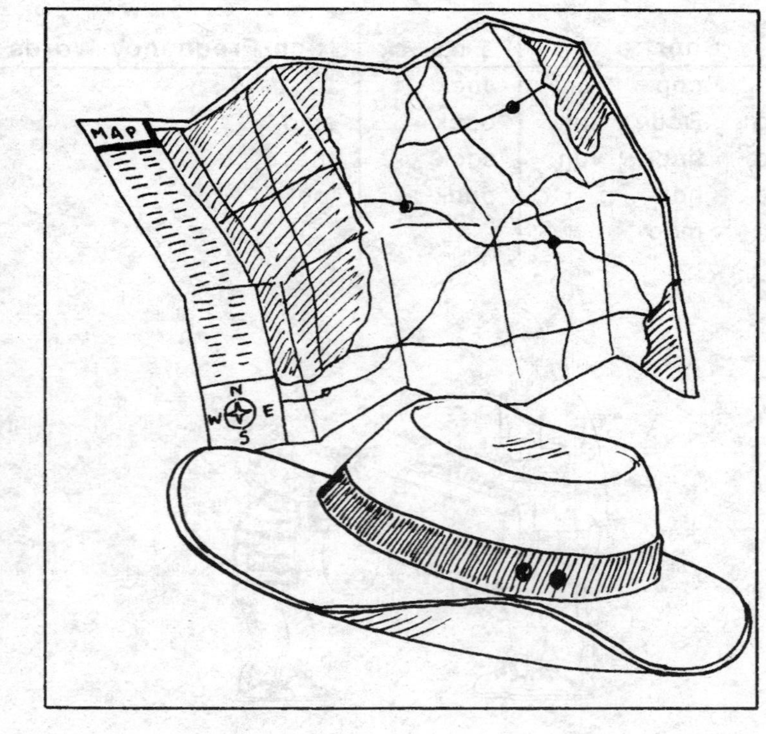

"I can pack the map," said Dad.

"I can pack the hat."

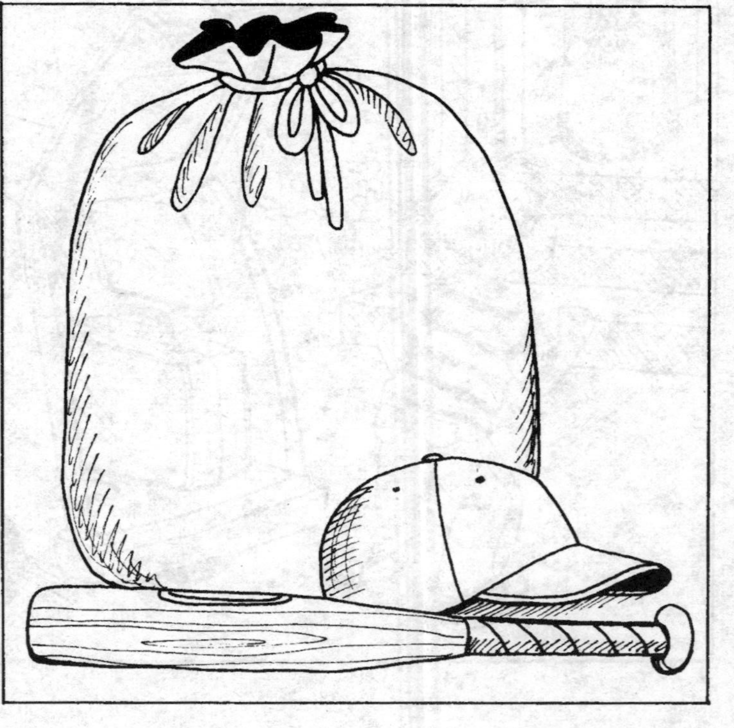

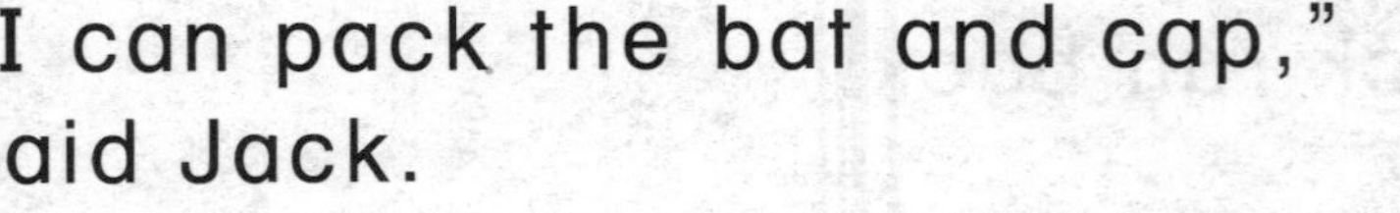

"I can pack the bat and cap," said Jack.

"Look at the sack!" said Dad.

Name ______________________

Short *a* Words

Find a list word to finish the sentence.
Write it on the line.

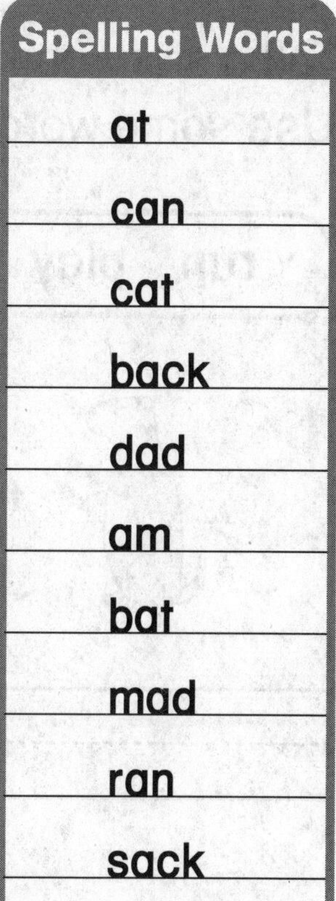

1. The bug ______________ hop.

2. I ______________ sad.

3. His ______________ has a van.

4. The dog ______________ .

5. I ______________ the ball.

6. Look ______________ the fox.

7. I fed my ______________ .

8. Put the can in the ______________ .

9. I know the ______________ to go.

10. I want to ______________ with you.

High-Frequency Words

way

come

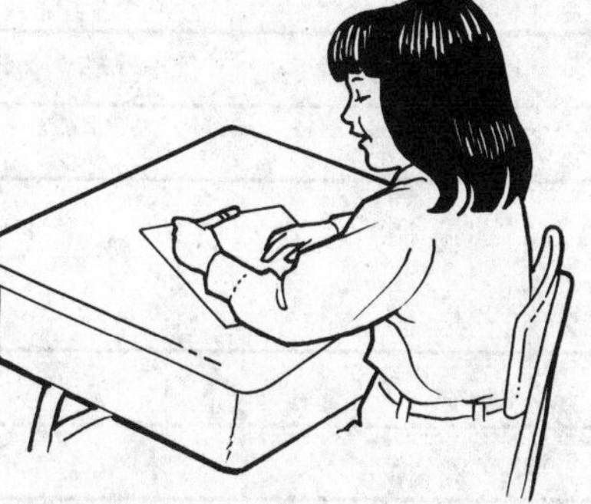

Home Activity Your child wrote spelling words to complete sentences. Help your child make up a new sentence for each spelling word.

Name ______________________

Sentences

Tell a story about when you did something with a pet.
Use some words from the box in your sentences.

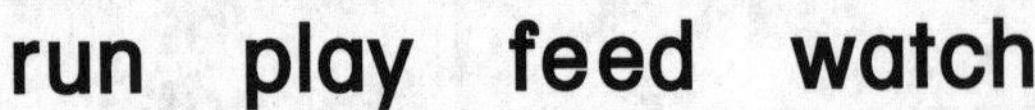

run	play	feed	watch

Home Activity Your child learned how to use sentences in writing. Have your child write two sentences that tell about a pet your family has had.

Name ______________________________

Short *a* Words

Circle the word that names the picture.

Spelling Words
at
can
cat
back
dad
am
bat
mad
ran
sack

1. sack / can / cat

2. cat / bat / dad

3.  back / sack / bat

4. dad / ran / mad

5.  can / bat / ran

6.  can / ran / cat

Say the words. **Circle** the two words that are the same.
Write the word.

7.	can	at	at	am	7. ________
8.	back	sack	at	back	8. ________
9.	ran	am	can	am	9. ________
10.	ran	mad	mad	dad	10. ________

Home Activity Your child has been learning to spell words with short *a*. To review what your child has learned, take turns thinking of and spelling simple words with short *a*.

Name ______________________________

Sentences

Mark the group of words that is a sentence.

1. ◯ Ron gets a pet today.
   ◯ a pet today
   ◯ gets a pet

2. ◯ a big cat
   ◯ The pet is a big cat.
   ◯ the pet

3. ◯ plays with his
   ◯ with his cat
   ◯ Ron plays with his cat.

4. ◯ He rolls the ball to the cat.
   ◯ ball to the cat
   ◯ rolls the ball to

5. ◯ hits the ball
   ◯ the ball back
   ◯ The cat hits the ball back.

6. ◯ and the cat like
   ◯ Ron and the cat like the game.
   ◯ Ron and the cat

Home Activity Your child prepared for taking tests on sentences. Read a story together. Have your child point out sentences in the story.

Name ________________________________

Say the word for each picture.
Write i on the line if you hear the **short i** sound.

pig

1. 

k ______ ck

2. h ______ ll

3. 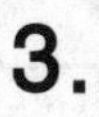

t ______ ck

4. 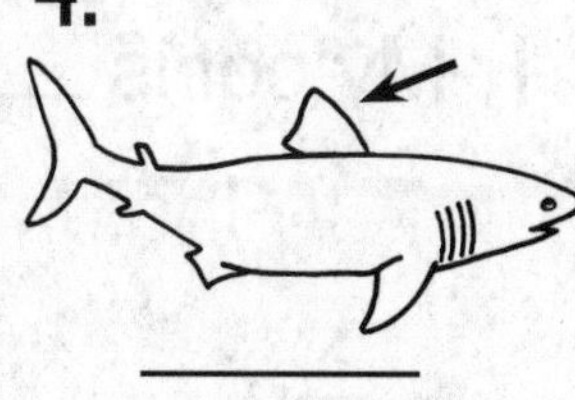

f ______ n

5. 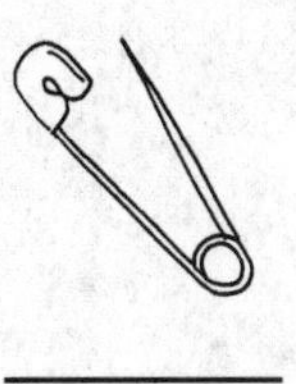

p ______ n

6. 

d ______ g

7. 

w ______ g

8. 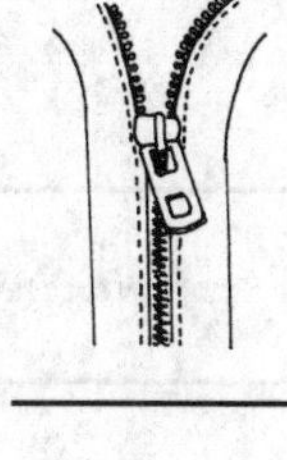

z ______ p

Circle the word to finish each sentence. **Write** it on the line.

9. I ______________ go.

will wall

10. Sam ______________ the mat.

hip hid

Home Activity Your child practiced creating words with the short *i* sound heard in *pig*. Help your child make up fun rhymes using short *i* words, such as *The big pig in the wig can dig and do a jig.*

Name ______________________________

Read the words in the box. **Pick** a word to finish each sentence. **Write** it on the line. **Remember** to use a capital letter at the beginning of a sentence.

up	take	she	what

1. My cat is ______________ .

2. You can ______________ two.

3. ______________ has a pack.

4. ______________ can Nan fix?

Home Activity This week your child identified and read the words *up, take, she,* and *what*. As you read with your child, encourage him or her to point out these words in print.

Name ______________________________

Read the story.
Circle the answer to each question about the story.

Jill and Meg play with a  .

They hit the  .

They pop the  !

Jill and Meg are sad.

But Dad has a  for them.

Jill and Meg play with the .

---

1. What happens first?

Jill and Meg play with a  .

Jill and Meg are sad.

2. What happens that is sad?

Jill and Meg kick the  .

Jill and Meg pop the  .

3. What happens so Jill and Meg are not sad?

Dad has a   for Jill and Meg.

Dad has a doll for Jill and Meg.

4. What happens last?

Jill and Meg hit the 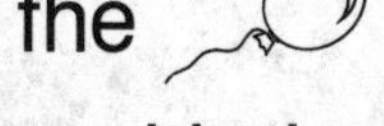.

Jill and Meg play with the .

Home Activity Your child identified the plot, or what happens in a story, and the problem and solution in a story. Read a short fairy tale and have your child identify a problem and solution.

Name ______________________________

Writing • Fantasy Story

Wise Owl

One day, Janey visited her friend, Wise Owl. He was sad.

"The animals come to ask me questions," he said. "Now I have a question. Whom should I ask?"

"I can help you," said Janey.

"I miss my brother and sister," Wise Owl said. "But my brother lives in the east. My sister lives in the west. I do not know where to go. What should I do?"

"Ask them to visit you!" said Janey.

Wise Owl smiled. "Thank you for your help," he said.

Key Features of a Fantasy Story

- Characters and events are made up.
- Characters do things that real people and animals cannot do.

Name ____________________

Say the word for each picture.
Write x on the line if the word has the same ending sound as **ax**.

ax 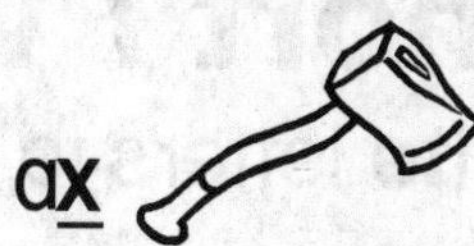

1. 6

si ____

2. 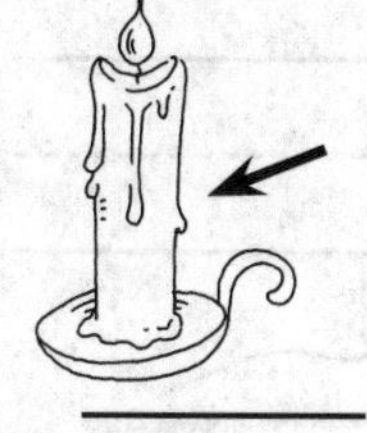

wa ____

3. 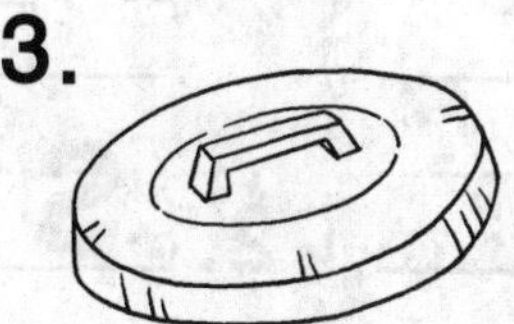

li ____

4. 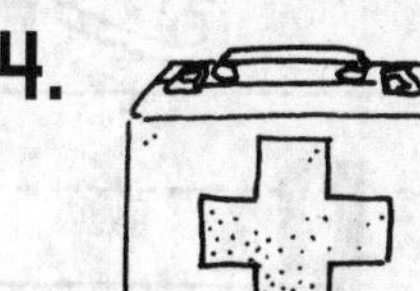

ki ____

5. 

bo ____

6. 

mi ____

7.

si ____

8. 

fi ____

Write two words that have the same ending sound as **6**.

____________________ ____________________

Read the sentence below. **Underline** the words that have the same ending sound as **ax**.

He saw six wax cats.

Home Activity Your child practiced creating words that end with *x*. Write *six, mix,* and *fix* on cards. Have your child choose a card, read the word, and use it in a sentence.

Name ____________________

Short *i* Words

Write letters to finish the word.

Spelling Words
in
it
did
sit
six
fix
lip
mix
pin
wig

1. p ______

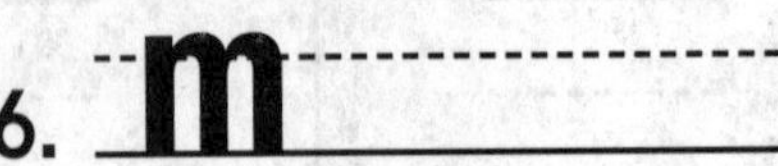

2. s ______

3. w ______

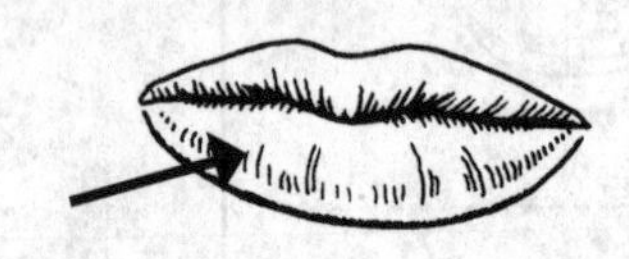

4. l ______

5. s ______

6. m ______

7. f ______

8. i ______

Write the missing words. it did

9. I hit ______.

10. Yes, I ______.

Home Activity Your child spelled words with the short *i* vowel sound. Point to a picture on this page and have your child spell the word.

Name ______________________________

Subjects of Sentences

A sentence has a **naming part.** It names a person, place, animal, or thing. The naming part tells who or what the sentence is about.

Pat sees a pig.

naming part

The pig is big.
↑
naming part

Write the naming part of each sentence.

1. My pig is sick.

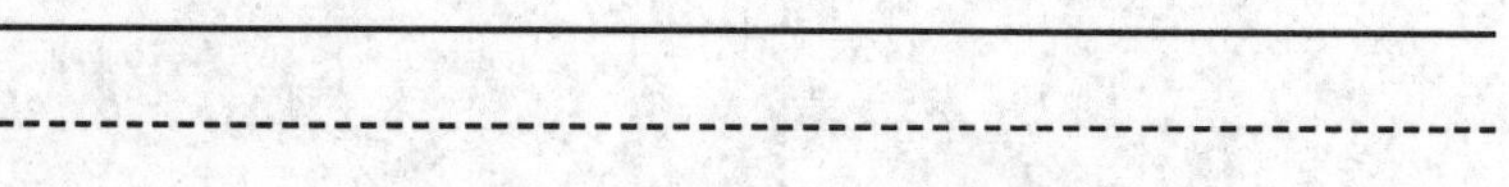

2. A vet can help the pig.

3. We go to the vet.

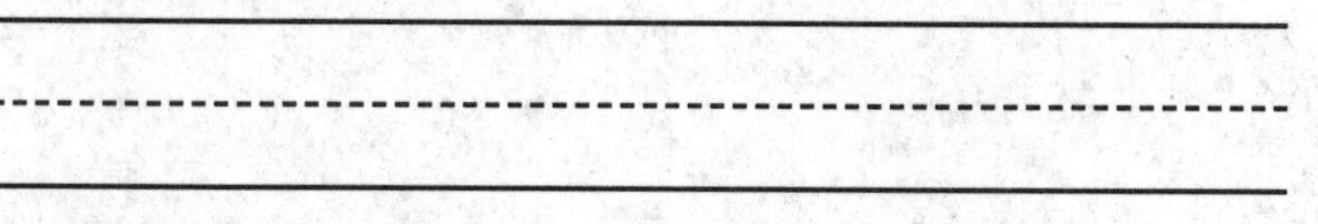

4. The pig feels better.

____

5. My dad thanks the vet.

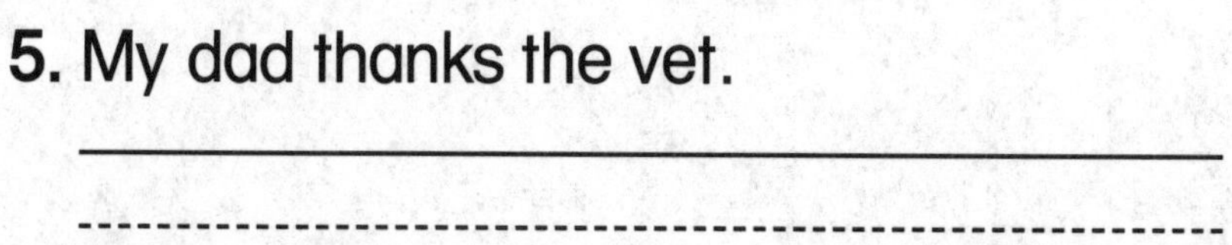

Home Activity Your child learned about the naming parts of sentences. Read a story together. Point to several sentences. Ask your child to identify the naming part of each sentence.

Name ______________________________

Story Chart

Title ____

Characters

Beginning

↓

Middle

↓

End of Story

Home Activity Your child planned a story. Share a brief story, and have your child tell what happens at the beginning.

Name ______________________

Trace and **write** the letters. Make sure you write your letters the correct size.

X

x

Copy the words. Leave the correct space between letters.

X-ray ______________ six ______________

pig ______________ Ina ______________

mix ______________ rip ______________

Did you leave the correct space between your letters?  

Home Activity Your child practiced writing words with *Ii* and *Xx*. Have your child practice writing each of these letters five more times.

Name ______________________________

Read each question. **Circle** the correct answer.

1. What would you use to read a story about a frog?

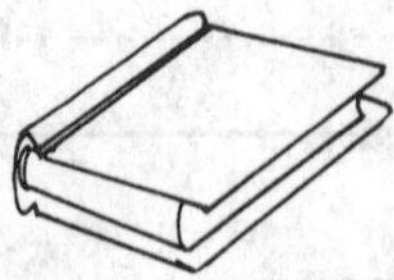

2. What would you use to find the meaning of **vet**?

3. What would you use to find more about what vets do?

4. What would you use to find out what time the zoo opens?

5. What would you use to watch a show about animals?

Home Activity Your child learned about sources that are available at a library or media center. Together with your child make a list of some of the sources found at a library. If possible, go to the library together and see how many of these sources you can find.

Jill can pick the bat.

Jill is quick!

Jill will win.

Decodable Story *Jill Can!*
Target Skill Short *i*, Consonant *x*/ks/

Jill Can!

Short i			Consonant *x* /ks/	High-Frequency Words
pick	zip	fit	six	is
quick	pin	sit	fix	the
Jill	rip	win		with
will	lid			

Jill is six.

Jill can zip.

Jill can pin the rip.

Jill can fix the lid.

The lid will fit.

Jill can pat the cat.

The cat will sit with Jill.

Name ________________________________

Short *i* Words

Spelling Words					High-Frequency Words
in	it	did	sit	six	she
fix	lip	mix	pin	wig	take

Circle a word to finish the sentence. **Write** the word.

1. He is fix six pin . ____________
2. I bit my lip did sit . ____________
3. Put sit it fix in the box. ____________
4. Can she in wig fix it? ____________
5. You can sit lip six here. ____________
6. His did wig in is red. ____________
7. They pin six did not go. ____________
8. Help me find a pin sit in . ____________
9. I will did pin take the book. ____________
10. Can did she pin mix it? ____________

Home Activity Your child wrote spelling words to complete sentences. Read a sentence, say the spelling word, and ask your child to spell the word. Continue with other sentences.

Name ______________________

Subjects of Sentences

Complete each sentence with a naming part.

1. ______________________ is my favorite color.

2. ______________________ is my favorite food.

3. ______________________ is my favorite day.

Tell about things you like to do. **Write** your sentences.

____

____

____

____

____

____

____

____

Home Activity Your child learned how to use naming parts of sentences in writing. Ask your child to underline the naming parts of the sentences he or she wrote on the page.

Name ______________________

Short *i* Words

Write the missing letters. Then write the words.

1. [ ] t ______________________

2. f [ ] [ ] ______________________

3. [ ] n ______________________

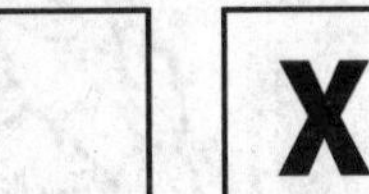

4. S [ ] X ______________________

Spelling Words
in
it
did
sit
six
fix
lip
mix
pin
wig

Write a list word that rhymes with each word.

5. pig ______________________

6. hip ______________________

7. lid ______________________

8. tin ______________________

9. fit ______________________

10. six ______________________

Home Activity Your child has been learning to spell words with short *i*. To review, draw some circles. Have your child write a short *i* word in each circle.

Name ______________________________

Subjects of Sentences

Mark the sentence that has a line under the naming part.

1. ○ My mom is a vet.
   ○ My mom is a vet.
   ○ My mom is a vet.

2. ○ She helps sick animals.
   ○ She helps sick animals.
   ○ She helps sick animals.

3. ○ That dog cut its leg.
   ○ That dog cut its leg.
   ○ That dog cut its leg.

4. ○ This cat hurt its paw.
   ○ This cat hurt its paw.
   ○ This cat hurt its paw.

5. ○ A vet will fix them.
   ○ A vet will fix them.
   ○ A vet will fix them.

6. ○ The animals like my mom.
   ○ The animals like my mom.
   ○ The animals like my mom.

Home Activity Your child prepared for taking tests on the naming parts of sentences. Write simple sentences about your family, such as these: *Anne is your sister. Your mother works at a bank.* Ask your child to circle each naming part.

Name ______________________________

Say the word for each picture.
Circle the picture if the word has the **short o** sound you hear in **top.**

top

1. 
2. 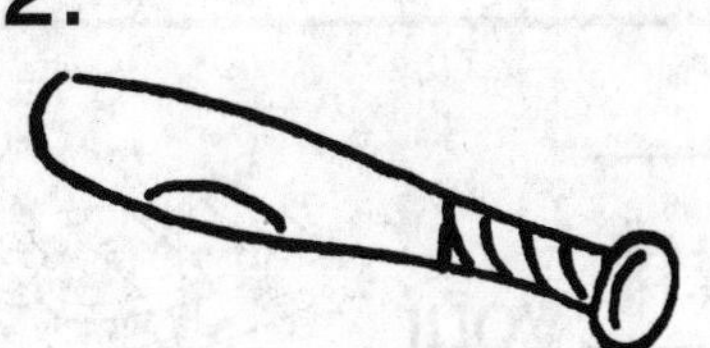
3. 
4. 
5. 
6. 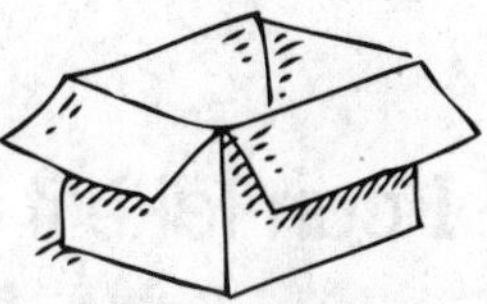
7. 

8. 
9. 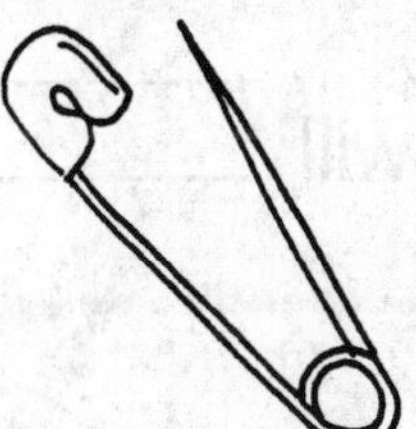
10. 
11. 
12. 
13. 
14. 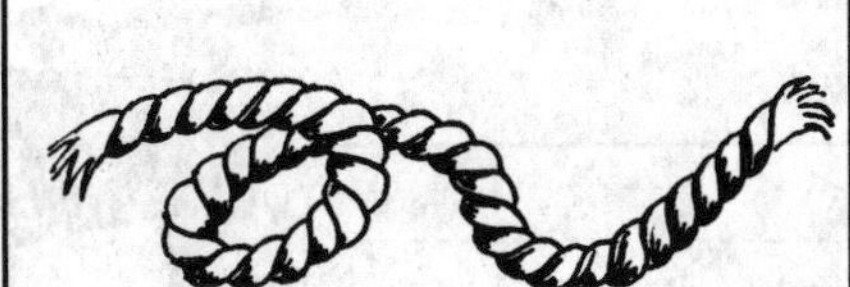
15. 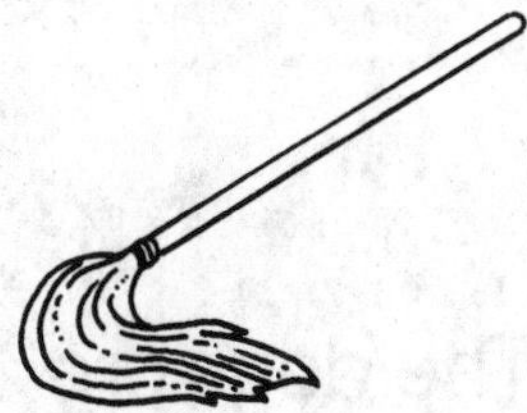

Home Activity Your child practiced creating words with the short *o* sound heard in *top*. Encourage your child to use the short *o* words pictured above in sentences.

Name ______________________

Read the words in the box.
Pick a word to finish each sentence.
Write it on the line.

blue	from	help	little	get	use

1. Can I ______________ your ?

2. I can take it ______________ you.

3. I will ______________ a .

4. My dogs ______________ you go.

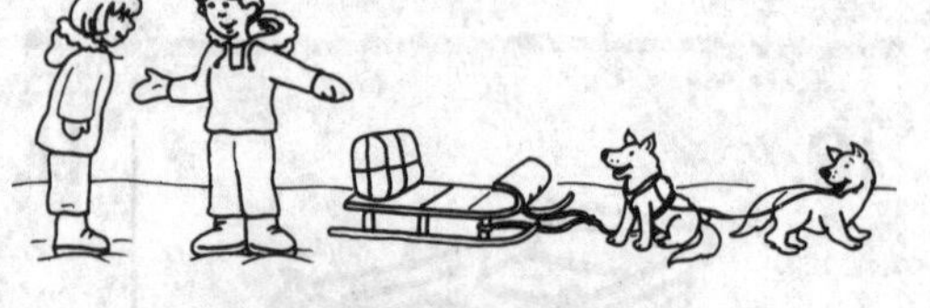

5. I see a big ______________ ox!

6. The dogs are ______________.

Home Activity This week your child identified and read the words *get, blue, from, help, little,* and *use*. Encourage your child to find these words in everyday print.

Name ______________________________

Look at each pair of pictures.
Circle the pictures that show characters in settings that make sense. **Think** about what they are doing.

1.

2.

3.

Draw a picture of a character from a story doing something.
Show how he or she feels.

4.

School + Home

Home Activity Your child learned about characters and places in a story. As you read together, have your child tell you what he or she knows about the characters and settings in the stories.

Name ___________________________

Writing • Short Poem

Kitty

Kitty's eyes are big and green.
She stretches, yawns, and licks her paws clean.

Key Features of a Short Poem

- A short poem has words written in lines that may rhyme.
- It can describe something or can express feelings.

Name ______________________

Circle a word to match each picture.

pan<u>s</u>

1. 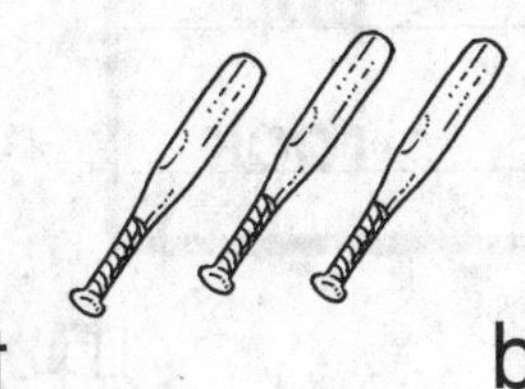

bat bats

2. 

mop mops

3. 

rock rocks

4. 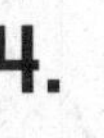   

pig pigs

5. 

top tops

6. 

cap caps

7. 

kit kits

8. 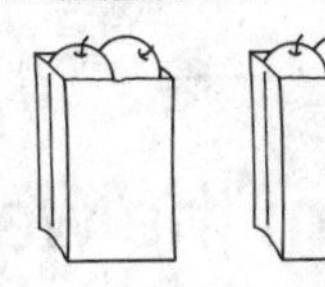

sack sacks

Write a sentence for each word.

9. **cats** ______________________

10. **wigs** ______________________

Home Activity Your child identified singular and plural nouns. Have your child name items around the house. Point out the use of -*s* at the end of many plural words, such as *books, apples,* and *bowls.*

Name ______________________

Short *o* Words

Spelling Words				
Mom	hot	hop	pot	pop
ox	lock	mop	got	rock

Write a word that rhymes.

1. **sock** on a ______
2. **hot** ______
3. **box** on an ______

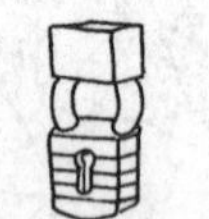

4. **block** on a ______
5. **top** by a ______
6. **Tom** and ______

Draw a line from the word to its shape.
Write the word in the shape.

hot

mop

pop

got

7. 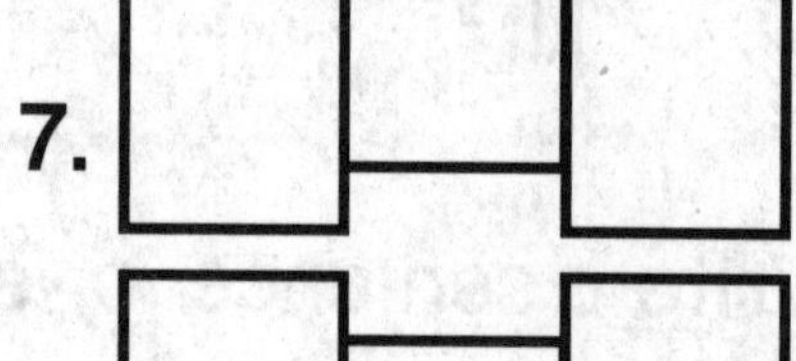

8. 

9. 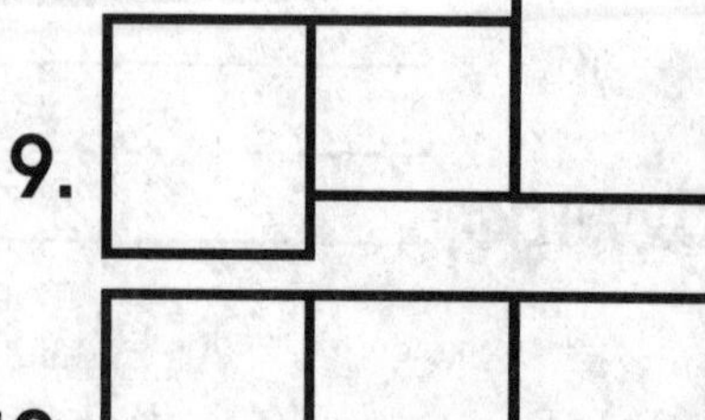

10. 

Home Activity Your child spelled words with the short *o* vowel sound. Help your child spell each word and then think of a rhyming word.

Name ____________________

Predicates of Sentences

A sentence has an **action part.** It tells what a person or thing does.

The ox **helps.**

action part

He **pulls the wagon.**

↑

action part

Write the action part of each sentence.

1. The cow gives milk.

2. Pop milks the cow.

3. The hen lays eggs.

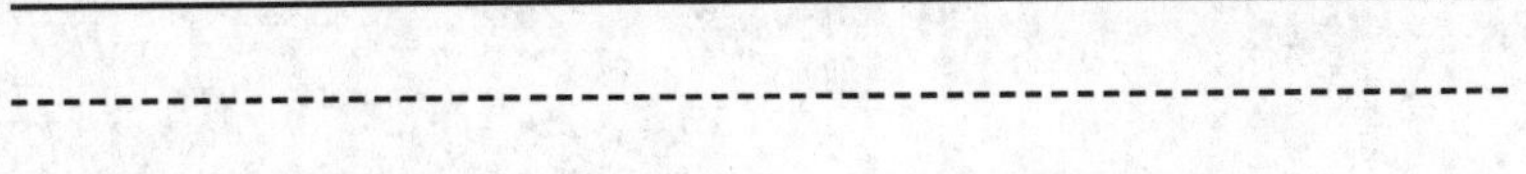

4. Mom gets the eggs.

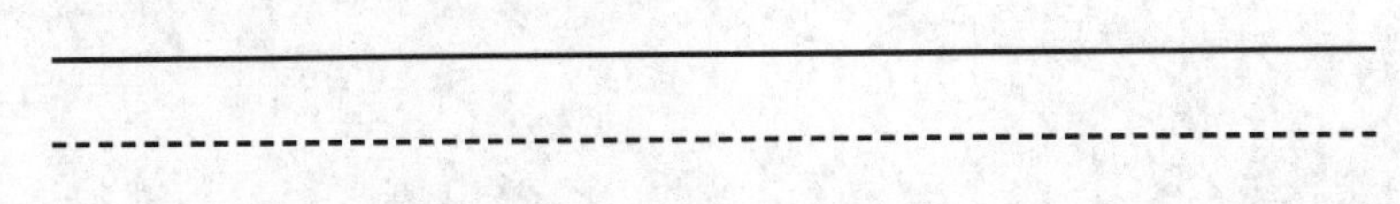

5. The cat chases mice.

Home Activity Your child learned about the action parts of sentences. Read a story together. Point to several sentences. Ask your child to identify the action part of each sentence.

Name ______________________________

Web

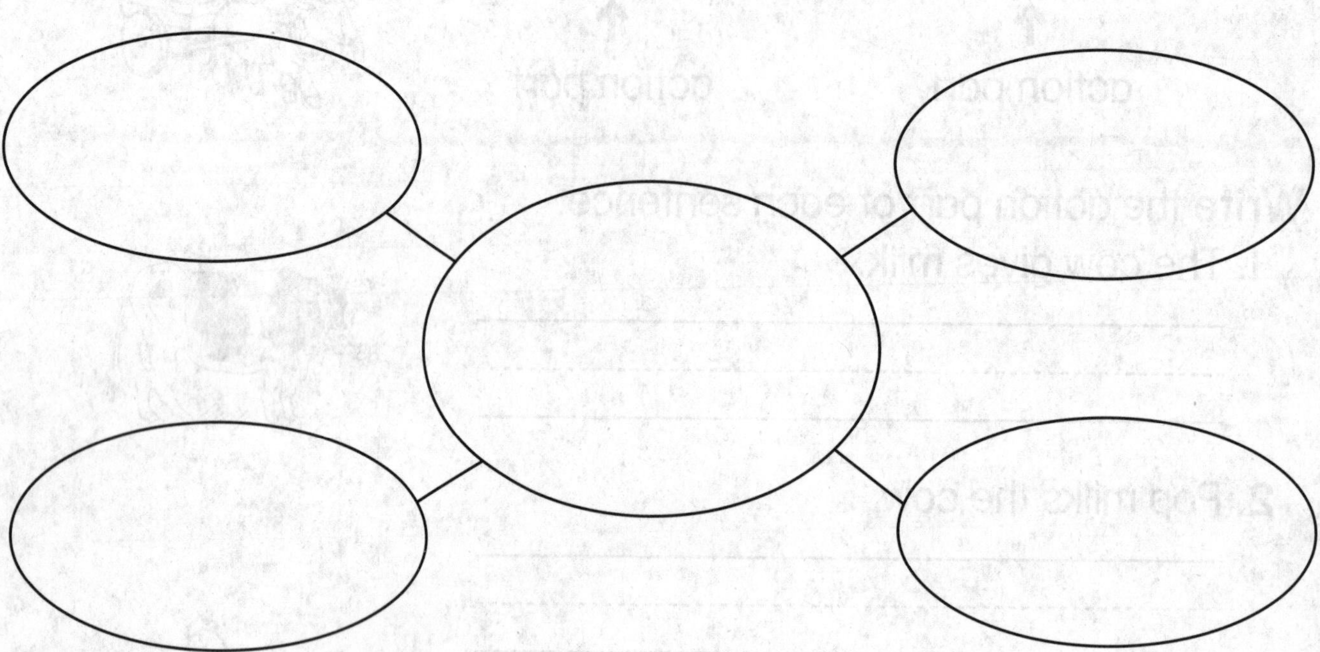

Home Activity Your child is learning about writing a short poem. Talk with him or her about words that rhyme.

Name ______________________

O o

Copy the words. Write the letters from left to right.

Oz	______	job	______
pot	______	hot	______
box	______	not	______
mom	______	got	______
cob	______	sob	______
doll	______	rod	______
log	______	fox	______

Did you write the letters from left to right? 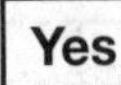 Yes 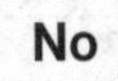 No

Home Activity Your child practiced writing words with *O* and *o* and the short *o* sound. Have your child choose two words from above and write the words three more times.

Name ___________________________

How do animals help people?

1. Use the picture to think about a topic. **Write** two topic ideas.

2. Circle your favorite topic.

3. Think about what else you want to know about your topic. **Write** three questions.

Home Activity Your child generated topic ideas for a picture and then formulated questions to research. Discuss topics that your child is interested in and, if possible, look up information about one of the topics.

A fox is not in the box.

The fox is on top!

Decodable Story *What Is In the Box?*
Target Skills Skills Short *o*, Plural *-s* + Consonant *s/z/*

Name ______________________

What Is In the Box?

Short *o*		Plural *-s* + Consonant *s/z/*	High-Frequency Words	
box	not	rocks	are	**go**
fox	on	socks	in	**is**
got	top	**mops**	the	**what**
Dot				

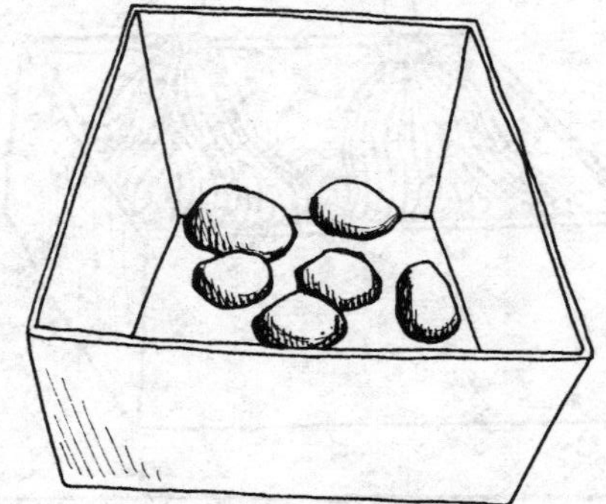

Are rocks in the box?

Six rocks are in the box.

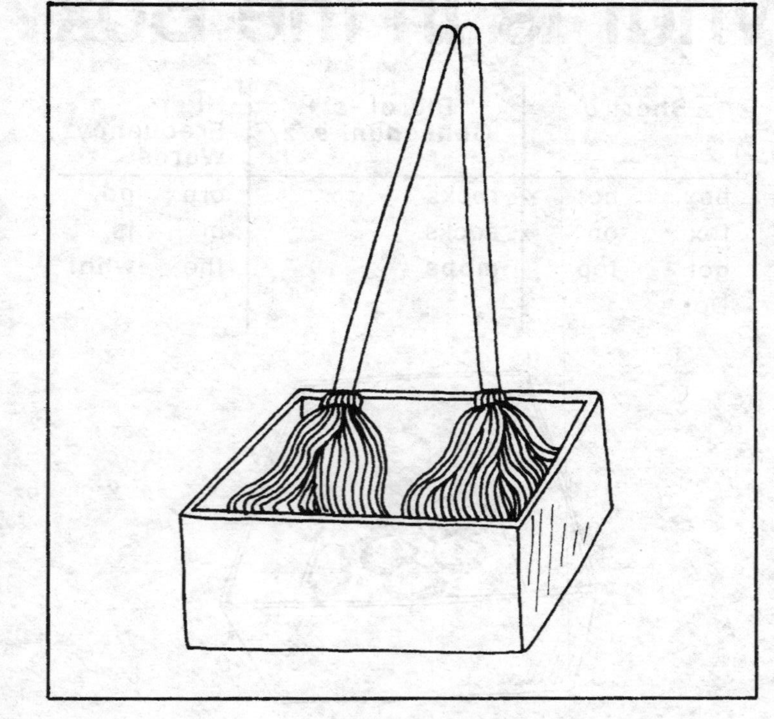

Are mops in the box?

The mops are in the box.

Dot got the socks.

The socks can go in the box.

Name ______________________

Short *o* Words

Find a list word to finish the sentence.
Write it on the line.

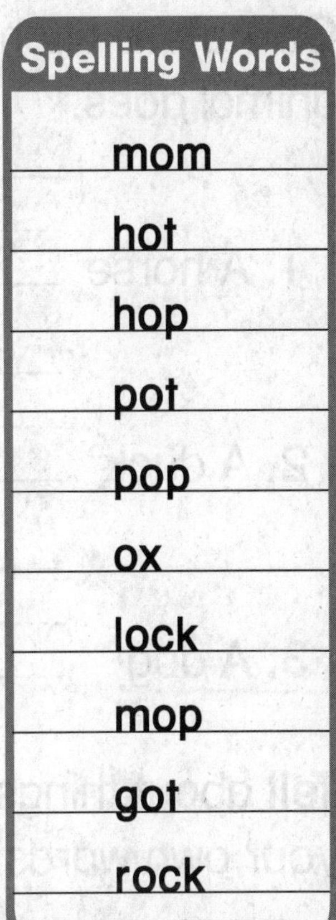

1. Fill the ______________ .
2. She is my ______________ .
3. I will ______________ up the mess.
4. Frogs can ______________ .
5. The sun is ______________ .
6. He is my ______________ .
7. Put a ______________ on his van.
8. I ______________ wet.
9. I will ______________ my top.
10. Can you ______________ me now?

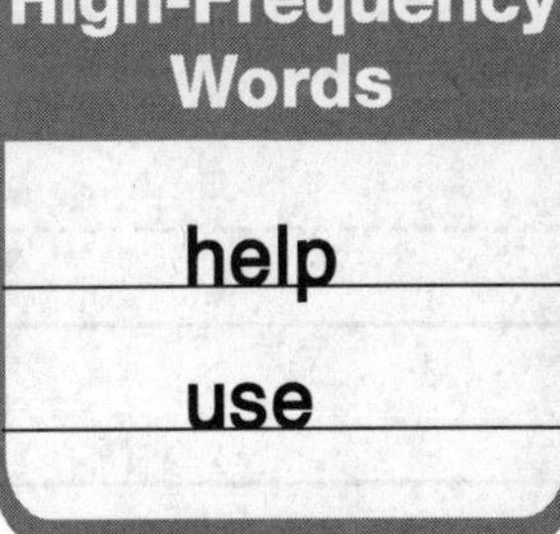

Home Activity Your child wrote spelling words to complete sentences. Have your child make up and write new sentences for several of the words.

Name ______________________________

Predicates of Sentences

Complete each sentence. **Write** an action part. **Tell** what the animal does.

1. A horse ______________________________.

2. A duck ______________________________.

3. A dog ______________________________.

Tell about things that other animals do. **Use** words from the box or your own words. **Write** your sentences.

swims	jumps	hops	runs

____

____

____

____

Home Activity Your child learned how to use action parts of sentences in writing. Ask your child to underline the action parts of the sentences he or she wrote on the page.

Name ______________________________

Short *o* Words

Write the words in the puzzle.

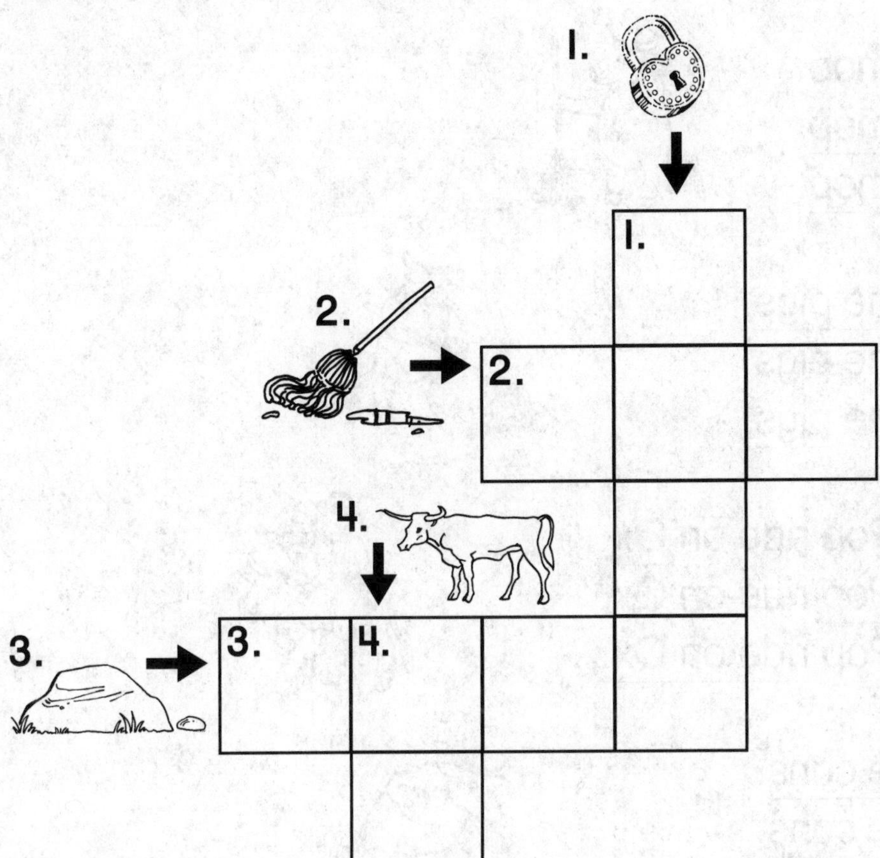

Spelling Words
mom
hot
hop
pot
pop
ox
lock
mop
got
rock

Connect the matching hearts.

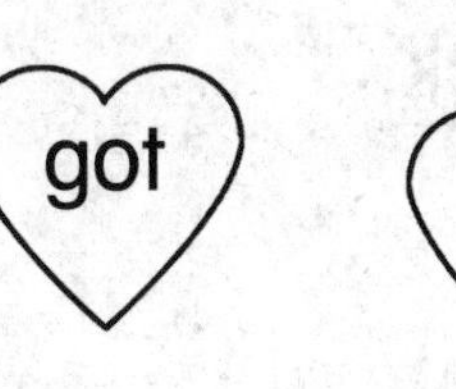

hop

Home Activity Your child has been learning to spell words with short *o*. Have your child think of and write words that rhyme with *spot* or *stop*.

Name ________________________________

Predicates of Sentences

Mark the sentence that has a line under the action part.

1. ◯ Ox gets a mop.
   ◯ Ox gets a mop.
   ◯ Ox gets a mop.

2. ◯ He mops the pigs.
   ◯ He mops the pigs.
   ◯ He mops the pigs.

3. ◯ Mom and Pop ride on Ox.
   ◯ Mom and Pop ride on Ox.
   ◯ Mom and Pop ride on Ox.

4. ◯ Ox gets the cans.
   ◯ Ox gets the cans.
   ◯ Ox gets the cans.

5. ◯ He packs the sack.
   ◯ He packs the sack.
   ◯ He packs the sack.

6. ◯ They take a nap.
   ◯ They take a nap.
   ◯ They take a nap.

Home Activity Your child prepared for taking tests on the action parts of sentences. Write simple sentences about your family, such as these: *Bill plays football. Your sister feeds the baby.* Ask your child to circle each action part.

Name ______________________________

Add -s to each word.
Write the new word on the line.

1. hop ____________	2. sit ____________

3. see ____________	4. pat ____________	5. help ____________

Use the words you wrote to finish the sentences.
Write the words on the lines.

6. Jack ________________ a big dog.

7. Jack ________________ the dog.

8. Jack ________________ on a rock.

9. The dog ________________ Jack.

10. The dog ________________ on Jack.

Home Activity Your child added *-s* to verbs. Have your child write the verbs *see, fan, nap, dig, sit, hop, jog,* and *mop,* and add an *-s* to each verb. Have your child pick a verb and use it in a sentence about you, such as *Mommy hops*. Then act out the sentence.

Name ___________________________

Read the words in the box.
Pick a word to finish each sentence.
Write it on the line. **Remember** to begin a sentence with a capital letter.

eat	four	five	her	this	too

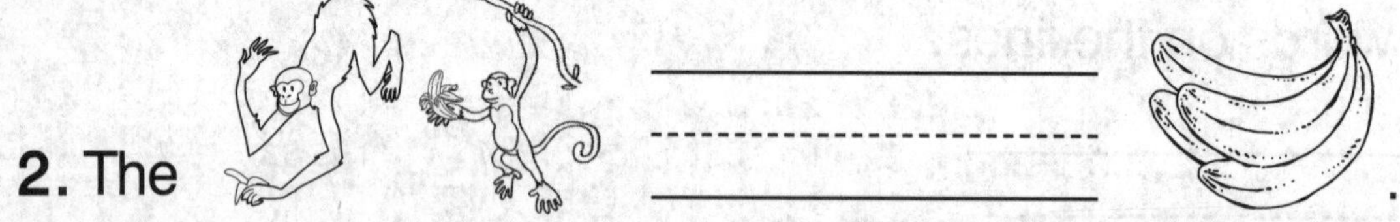

1. We see ______________ .

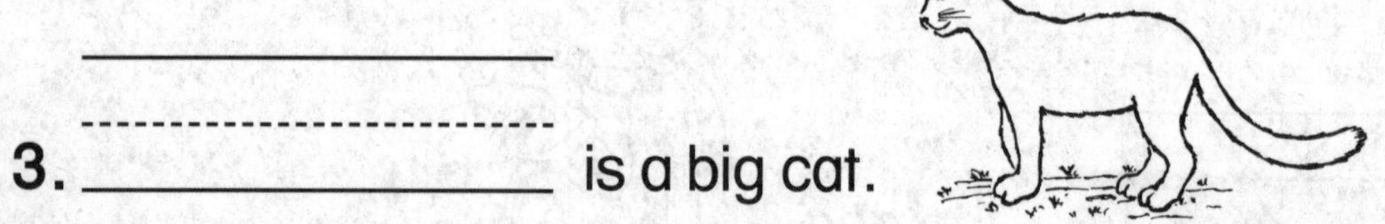

2. The ______________ .

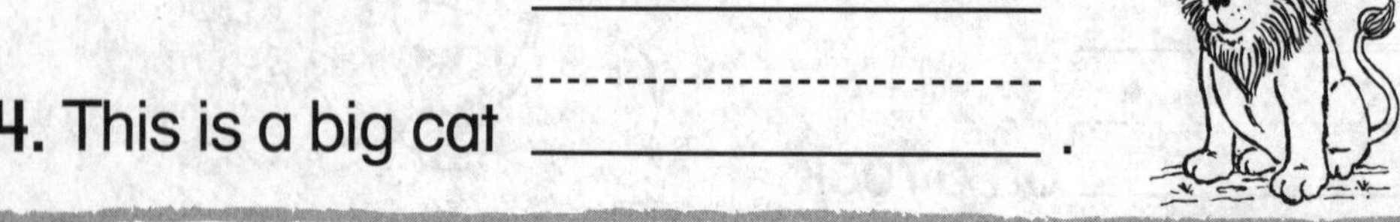

3. ______________ is a big cat.

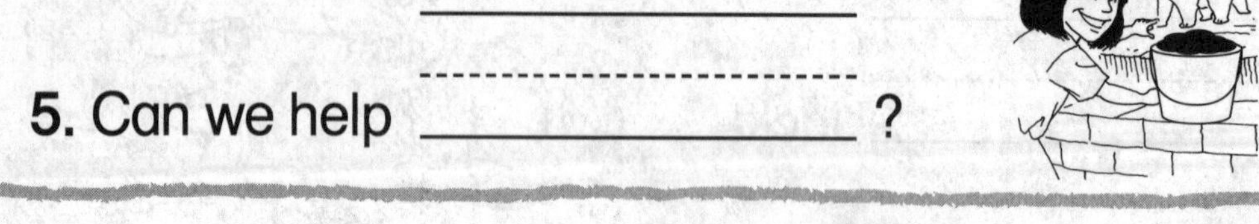

4. This is a big cat ______________ .

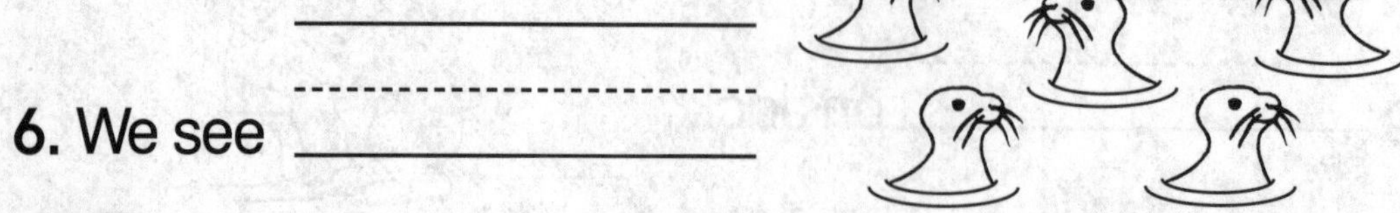

5. Can we help ______________ ?

6. We see ______________ .

Home Activity This week your child identified and read the words *eat, four, five, her, too,* and *this*. Look through books to find these words in print and have your child read them aloud.

Name ______________________________

Read each story.
Circle the sentence that tells best what the story is about.
Underline a detail that tells about the main idea.
Then **write** the topic of the story.

---

1. Dan has a cat.
The cat is tan.
The cat is fat.
Dan has a fat, tan cat.

2. **Topic:** ______________

cat mop

---

3. Whales are big animals.
Whales have big tails.
Whales have big fins.
Whales eat a lot.

4. **Topic:** ______________

fins whales

Write the name of a story you have read.
Draw a picture that shows what the story is about.

5. ______________________________

School + Home

Home Activity Your child learned about the main idea and details of a story. As you read stories together, have your child tell you the main idea.

Name ______________________________

Writing • Personal Narrative

The Loon

Last summer my family camped next to a lake. I liked waking up outside. Then I swam all day long!

One morning my dad took me to the lake. "Look!" he said. I saw a beautiful black bird floating on the lake.

"It is a loon," Dad said. "Loons can stay underwater a long time. They can dive deep and swim far. Watch!"

The loon dived underwater. We watched and waited. A minute later, we saw the loon again. I was amazed! It was so far away. We could hardly see it.

"If the loon comes again tomorrow, let's use our binoculars to watch," Dad said. I couldn't wait!

Key Features of a Personal Narrative

- The narrative tells a story about a real event in the author's life.
- It tells how the author feels about the event or gives the author's opinion.

Name ______________________

Add -ing to each word.
Write the new word on the line.

1. help ____________ 2. look ____________

3. fix ____________ 4. lick ____________ 5. play ____________

Use the words you wrote to finish the sentences.
Write the words on the lines.

6. Jan is ____________ at the cats.

7. Jan is ____________ the cats.

8. The cats are ____________ with the can.

9. The big cat is ____________ the little cat.

10. Jan is ____________ the lock.

Home Activity Your child added *-ing* to verbs. Have your child write the verbs *lick, rock, kick, eat,* and *mix* on slips of paper. Then have your child add *-ing* to each verb. Have your child pick a slip of paper and act out the word for you to guess.

Name ______________________________

Inflected Ending *-s*

Write list words to finish the sentences.

- nap
- naps
- sit
- sits
- win
- wins
- fit
- fits
- hit
- hits

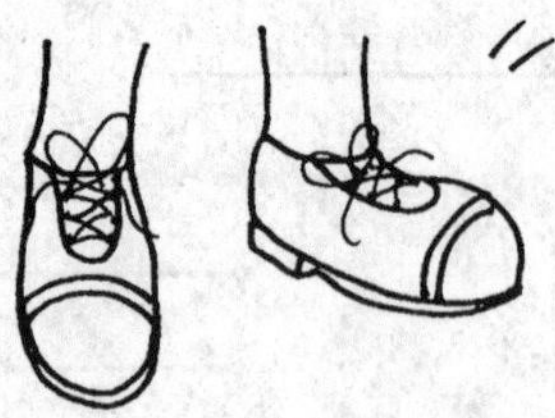

1. They ______________ . **2.** It ______________ .

3. They ______________ . **4.** He ______________ .

5. They ______________ in bed. **6.** He ______________ in bed.

7. They ______________ on mats. **8.** She ______________ on a mat.

9. They ______________ the race. **10.** He ______________ the race.

Home Activity Your child spelled pairs of words with and without the *-s* ending. Point to a word on this page and have your child spell the other word in the pair.

Name ___________________________

Declarative Sentences

A **telling sentence** tells something. It is a **declarative sentence**. It begins with a **capital letter**. It usually ends with a **period (.)**.

The fox has a kit.
The kit naps.

Find the sentence. **Underline** the sentence.

1. The children see a fox.
   the children see a fox

2. they see the kit
   They see the kit.

3. The kit can run.
   the kit can run

4. the fox and kit play
   The fox and kit play.

5. fox naps on the rocks
   Fox naps on the rocks.

Home Activity Your child learned about telling sentences. Read a story together. Have your child point to sentences in the story and name the capital letter at the beginning and the period at the end.

Name ______________________

Story Chart

Title ______________________

Beginning

↓

Middle

↓

End of Story

Home Activity Your child can plan to write about real events. Share a memory about an event such as a time you saw animals at a zoo.

Name ____________________

N n   G g

Copy the words. Slant all of the letters the same way.

Gus	____________	acting	____________
Nan	____________	fixing	____________
singing	____________	mixing	____________
Gil	____________	bumping	____________
ringing	____________	telling	____________
adding	____________	packing	____________
passing	____________	kicking	____________

Do all of your letters slant the same way? 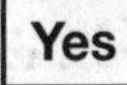 Yes 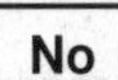 No

Home Activity Your child practiced writing words with *Nn* and *Gg* and words ending in *-ing*. Name a word from the chart, point to it, and have your child copy it on a separate sheet of paper. Continue with other words.

Name ______________________________

Look at the chart. **Answer** the questions.

Adult Animals	Baby Animals
bear	cub
deer	fawn
elephant	calf

1. The topic of Lee's report is "Animals." Will this chart help?

____

2. Is there enough information in the chart for Lee to write about "Animals"?

____

3. Lee wants to revise his topic. Use Lee's chart to choose the topic.

   Animals and Their Babies

   Big Animals

4. Why is that a better topic for Lee?

____

Home Activity Your child learned how review and revise a topic. Ask your child to choose a topic that is of interest to him or her. Have him or her list some facts about the topic. Then using a reference source, read about the topic and ask your child to revise the facts based on your research.

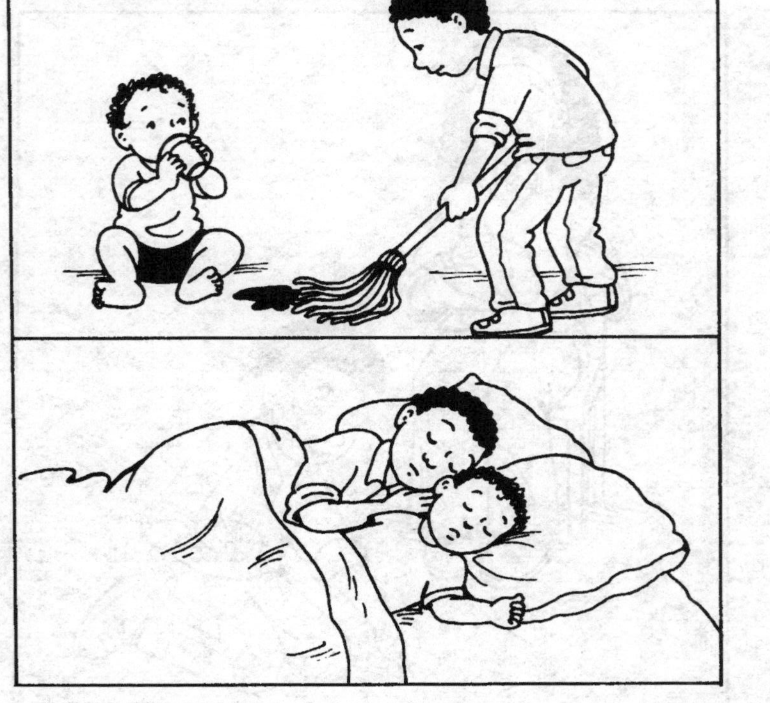

Kit sits and sips.

Rob mops up.

Kit naps. Rob naps, too!

Decodable Story *Rob*
Target Skills Inflected ending -*s*, Inflected ending -*ing*

Name ____________________

Rob

Inflected ending -*s*		**Inflected ending -*ing***	**High-Frequency Words**	
fills	sips	mixing	do	the
digs	mops	tossing	of	up
picks	naps	fixing	is	too
sits				

Rob will do lots of jobs.

Mom is mixing in the pot.

Rob fills the pan.

Dad digs the rocks.

Rob is tossing the rocks in the box.

Tam is fixing the rip in the cap.

Rob picks up the pins.

Name ______________________

Inflected Ending *-s*

Write list words to finish the sentences.

1. The pups ______________.
2. The pup ______________.
3. The pups ______________.

4. The pup ______________.

5. I can ______________ the game.
6. She ______________ all the games.
7. The wind ______________ the flag.
8. He can ______________ the ball.
9. Will the hat fit her ______________?
10. My mitt fits ______________.

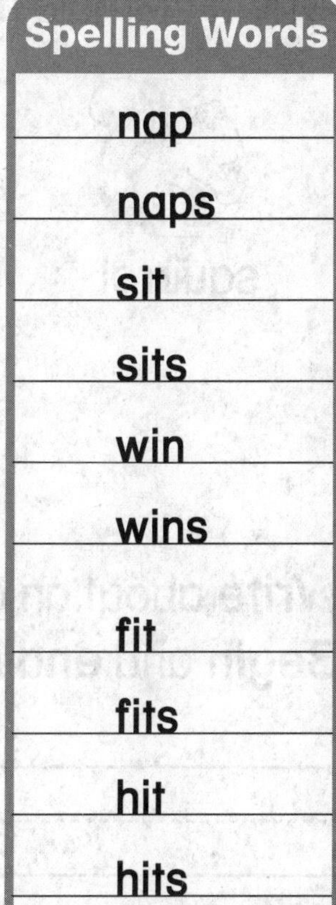

Spelling Words
nap
naps
sit
sits
win
wins
fit
fits
hit
hits

High-Frequency Words
her
too

Home Activity Your child wrote spelling words to complete sentences. Have your child circle the list words that end in *-s*.

Name ____________________

Declarative Sentences

Which animals have you seen?

Write about an animal you have seen.
Begin and **end** each sentence correctly.

Home Activity Your child learned how to use telling sentences when writing. Take turns with your child saying sentences that describe the animals on the page.

Name ______________________

Inflected Ending *-s*

Draw a line to help Kit find her mitt.
Follow the words that rhyme with **Kit**.
Circle the words. **Write** the words.

Spelling Words
nap
naps
sit
sits
win
wins
fit
fits
hit
hits

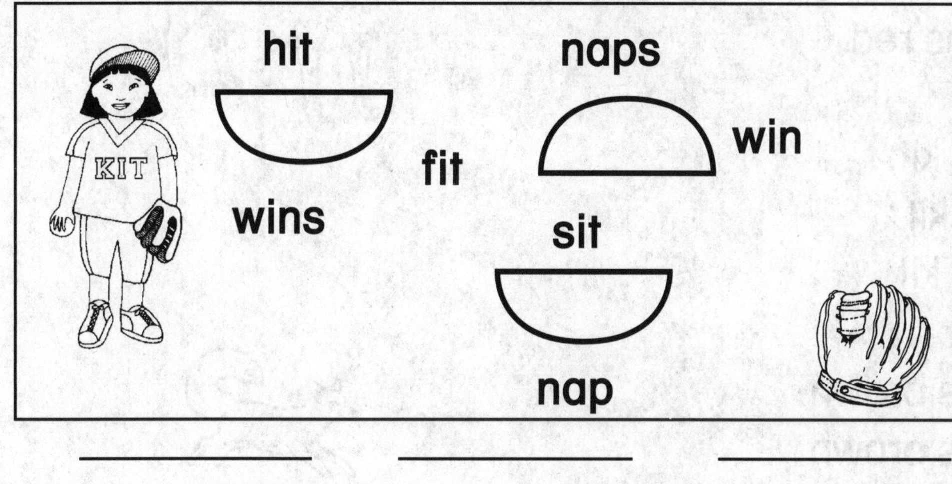

1. ____________ 2. ____________ 3. ____________

Write these words in ABC order.

nap wins sits

4. ____________ 5. ____________ 6. ____________

Write these words in ABC order.

win hits naps fits

7. ____________ 8. ____________

9. ____________ 10. ____________

Home Activity Your child has been learning to spell words that end in *-s*. Help your child look on food boxes and cans for words that end in *-s*.

Name ______________________________

Declarative Sentences

Find the sentence. **Mark** the sentence.

1. ○ the fox is red.
   ○ The fox is red.
   ○ the fox is red

2. ○ It has a kit.
   ○ it has a kit.
   ○ It has a kit

3. ○ the kit is brown.
   ○ the kit is brown
   ○ The kit is brown.

4. ○ The man has a pan.
   ○ the man has a pan.
   ○ The man has a pan

5. ○ the pan is tan
   ○ the pan is tan.
   ○ The pan is tan.

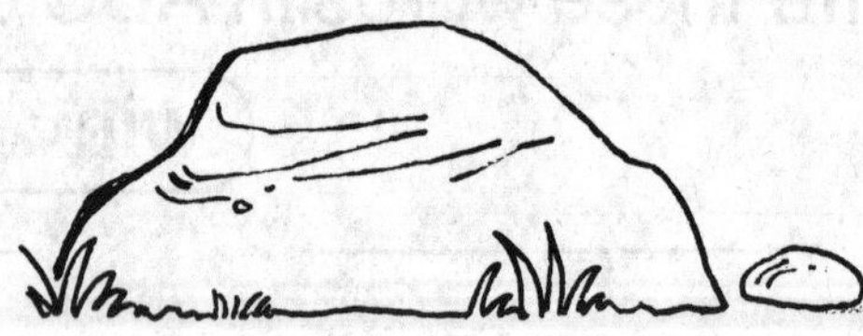

6. ○ the kit sits on the rocks.
   ○ The kit sits on the rocks.
   ○ the kit sits on the rocks

Home Activity Your child prepared for taking tests on telling sentences. Name a familiar animal. Have your child say a sentence that tells about the animal.

Name ______________________________

Circle the word for each picture.

we̲b 

1. 

mitt men man

2. 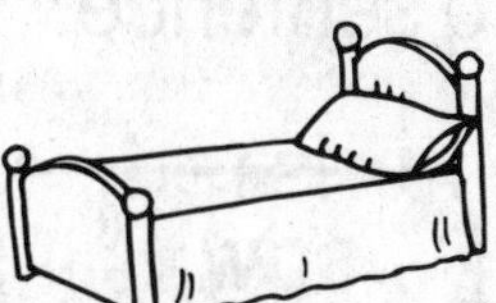

bed bid bad

3. 

pen pan pin

4. 

tin tan ten

5. 

jam jet jog

6. 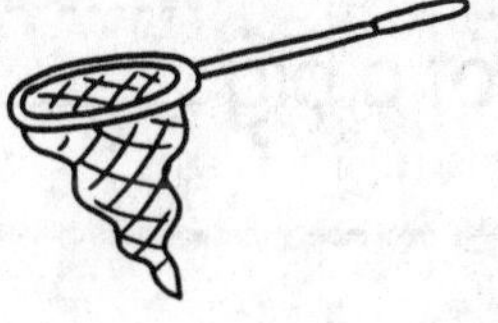

net not nip

Circle the word the completes each sentence.

7. The fat ____________________ sits on my lap.

hen hat

8. I like my short ____________________ hat.

rid red

Home Activity Your child practiced reading words with the short *e* sound heard in *web*. Work with your child to make words that rhyme with *pet* or *bell*.

Name ______________________

Read the words in the box.
Pick a word to finish each sentence.
Write it on the line. **Remember** to use a capital letter at the beginning of a sentence.

saw	small	tree	your

1. We __________ a tree.

2. It was not a big __________.

3. Do you like this __________ tree?

4. __________ tree is not wet.

Home Activity This week your child identified and read the words *saw, small, tree,* and *your.* Make flashcards with one word on each card. Mix them up and have your child read the words.

Name ____________________

Read each story.
Circle the sentence that tells best what the story is about.
Underline a detail that tells about the main idea.
Then **follow** the directions.

1. Ben has a hen.
The hen is red.
The hen is fat.
Ben has a fat, red hen.

2. What is the topic of the story? **Write.**

____

red hen

3. Kim is a kid.
Brad is a kid.
Kim likes to play.
Brad likes to play.
Kim and Brad like to play.

4. **Write** your own main idea for the story.

____

____

5. The bird has a nest in the tree.
The bird is big.
The nest is small.
The tree is tall.

6. **Write** your own main idea for the story.

____

____

Home Activity Your child learned about the main idea and details of a story. As you read stories together, have your child tell you the main idea, or the most important point of the story.

Name ______________________________

Writing • Realistic Story

Little Squirrels

Luis and Lisa were playing at Lisa's house. They were running around and around.

"You are just like little squirrels!" Lisa's mom said. "The house is not for running! Go outside!"

Luis and Lisa went outside. "Why did your mom say that we are like squirrels?" Luis asked.

There was a big oak tree in the yard. Luis and Lisa sat under it. They watched the squirrels. The squirrels ran up the tree. The squirrels ran down the tree.

"Maybe we are like squirrels because we run so much!" Lisa said.

Key Features of a Realistic Story

- The characters, events, and setting seem real.
- Characters do things that really can happen.

Name ______________________________

Pick letters from the box to finish each word.
Write the letters on the line.

<u>sw</u>im

bl cl cr dr fl fr gr sl sm st

1. ________ ag
2. ________ ock
3. ________ ap
4. ________ ess
5. ________ ab
6. ________ og
7. ________ ell
8. ________ ed
9. ________ ep
10. ________ in

Home Activity Your child practiced creating words with initial blends *(flag, dress, sled)*. Help your child make up silly sentences that each contain words beginning with just one blend, such as *Freddy frog likes French fries.*

Name ______________________

Short *e* Words

Spelling Words				
bed	men	red	step	ten
net	leg	jet	sled	wet

Write three list words that rhyme with **pet**.

1. ____________ 2. ____________ 3. ____________

Write three list words that rhyme with **Ted**.

4. ____________ 5. ____________ 6. ____________

Write the missing word.

leg
step
men
ten

7. Let's make two ____________ out of snow.

8. We need ____________ buttons.

9. Do not ____________ on his hat.

10. Does he need a ____________ ?

Home Activity Your child spelled words with the short *e* vowel sound. Have your child draw and label some of the words.

Name ______________________

Interrogative Sentences

A **question** is an asking sentence. It is an **interrogative sentence.** It begins with a **capital letter.** It ends with a **question mark (?).**

What will we see**?**
Is that a nest**?**

Put a ✓ by each question.

1. Who lives in the nest? ______
   A bird lives in the nest. ______

2. The big bird is red. ______
   Is the big bird red? ______

3. Can the big bird help? ______
   The big bird can help. ______

4. I can get the eggs. ______
   Can you get the eggs? ______

5. Where is the egg? ______
   The egg is in the nest. ______

Home Activity Your child learned about questions. Read a story together. Have your child find any questions in the story and name the capital letter at the beginning and the punctuation mark at the end.

Name ______________________________

Story Chart

Title ______________________________

Characters

Setting

Beginning

↓

Middle

↓

End of Story

Home Activity Your child is learning about realistic stories. Have him or her describe a real place.

Name ___________________________

E e

Copy the words. Write the letters the correct size.

Emma ____________ red ____________

set ____________ ten ____________

leg ____________ vest ____________

bed ____________ hen ____________

fell ____________ jet ____________

net ____________ den ____________

hem ____________ get ____________

Did you write all of your letters the correct size? Yes No

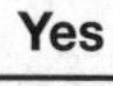

Home Activity Your child practiced writing words with *E* and *e* and the short *e* sound. Have your child write as many words with *E* or *e* that he or she can think of that are not on this page. You can use the words from above to help your child write rhyming words.

Name ______________________________

Look at the lists.
Follow the directions and **answer** the questions.

Wild Animals	Pets
bear	cat
fox	dog
frog	fish
lion	frog
tiger	hamster

1. **Think** of two more wild animals. **Write** the animal names.

2. **Think** of two more pets. **Write** the animal names.

3. **Circle** the animal that you would like to know more about. **Share** your choice with the class.

4. **Think** about what else you want to know about your animal. **Write** two questions.

Home Activity Your child learned how to identify topics and ask questions about a topic. Ask your child to make up another question about one of the topics above.

"Pick up the blocks," Mom yells.

"Peg will help!"

Decodable Story *The Blocks*
Target Skills Short *e*, Initial consonant blends

The Blocks

Short *e*		Initial consonant blends	High Frequency Words
Meg	bed	blocks	the
gets	fell	black	a
ten	Peg	step	up
red	mess	stack	help
sets	yells		

Meg gets ten blocks.

Meg has red blocks.

Meg has black blocks.

Meg sets the blocks on the step.

Meg will stack the blocks on the bed.

The blocks fell.

Peg got Mom.

"Meg has a mess!"

Name ______________________

Short e Words

Spelling Words									
bed	men	red	step	ten	net	leg	jet	sled	wet

Choose a word to finish the sentence.
Fill in the circle. **Write** the word.

1. I made the ○ **bed** ○ **men** ○ **leg** . ______
2. Do not get me ○ **step** ○ **wet** ○ **net** ! ______
3. Her sock was ○ **sled** ○ **jet** ○ **red** . ______
4. Kick with your ○ **ten** ○ **net** ○ **leg** . ______
5. Kim has a ○ **red** ○ **sled** ○ **wet** . ______
6. A fish is in the ○ **net** ○ **ten** ○ **step** . ______
7. Sit on the ○ **ten** ○ **step** ○ **red** . ______
8. I will count to ○ **ten** ○ **jet** ○ **sled** . ______

Write the words and complete the sentence.

9. I ______ ______ sled.

High-Frequency Words
saw
your

Home Activity Your child wrote spelling words to complete sentences. Help your child find other spelling words that make sense in the sentences. For example, sentence 1 could read "I made the **net**."

Name ________________________

Interrogative Sentences

Finish the question. **Write** an animal name.

a bird

a cat

a dog

an elephant

an ostrich

What does ________________________ look like?

Read the sentence. **Change** the words to make a question. **Write** the question.

The bird is red.

Home Activity Your child learned how to use questions when writing. Say a sentence about one of the animals on the page, such as *The elephant is big*. Have your child write your sentence as a question: *Is the elephant big?*

Name ______________________________

Short *e* Words

Spelling Words

- bed
- men
- red
- step
- ten
- net
- leg
- jet
- sled
- wet

Write the words.

1. ____________ 2. ____________

3. ____________ 4. ____________

Circle the word that matches. **Write** it.

5.	bed	bed	red	____________
6.	men	wet	men	____________
7.	ten	net	ten	____________
8.	sled	step	sled	____________
9.	red	red	sled	____________
10.	wet	net	wet	____________

Home Activity Your child has been learning to spell words with short *e*. Have your child think of and write words that rhyme with *set* or *fed*.

Name ____________________

Interrogative Sentences

Find the question. **Mark** the question.

1. ◯ The nest big is.
   ◯ is the nest big?
   ◯ Is the nest big?

2. ◯ Do birds live here?
   ◯ Birds do live here.
   ◯ do birds live here?

3. ◯ can you see the nest?
   ◯ You can see the nest.
   ◯ Can you see the nest?

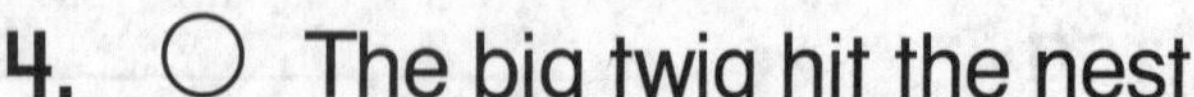

4. ◯ The big twig hit the nest.
   ◯ Will the big twig hit the nest?
   ◯ will the big twig hit the nest?

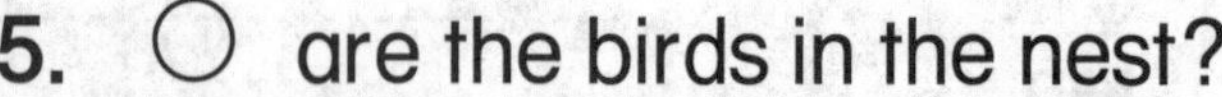

5. ◯ are the birds in the nest?
   ◯ Are the birds in the nest?
   ◯ The birds in the nest are.

6. ◯ Do you see eggs in the nest?
   ◯ do you see eggs in the nest?
   ◯ You do see eggs in the nest.

Home Activity Your child prepared for taking tests on questions. Together listen to a conversation or an interview on TV. Each time your child hears a question, have him or her say "Question!"

Name ____________________

Say the word for each picture.
Write u on the line if you hear the **short u** sound.

pup

1. b ___ g
2. d ___ ck
3. b ___ s
4. h ___ g
5. b ___ x
6. dr ___ m
7. s ___ n
8. sl ___ d

Write a sentence for each word.

9. mud ____________________

10. plum ____________________

Home Activity Your child identified and created words with the short *u* sound heard in *pup*. Work with your child to write words that rhyme with *rug*.

Name ___________________________

Read the words in the box.
Pick a word to finish each sentence.
Write it on the line.

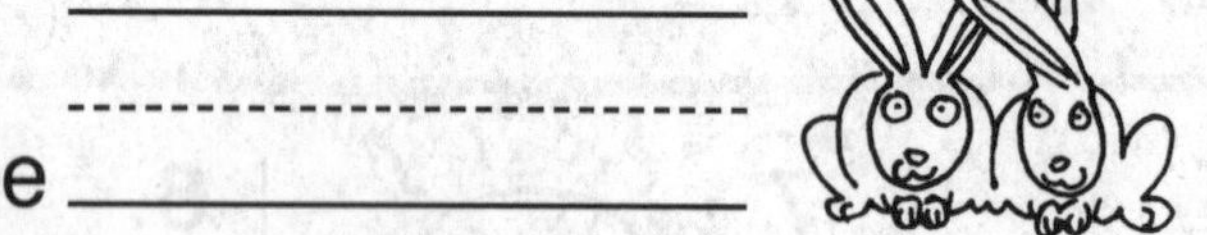

1. This is a ______________ for [rabbits] .

2. We see ______________ [rabbits] .

3. Do you see ______________ ?

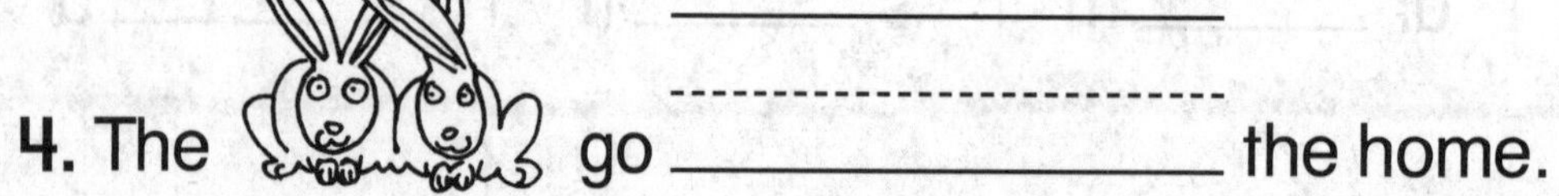

4. The [rabbits] go ______________ the home.

Draw a picture of you going into your home.

5.

Home Activity Your child identified and read the words *home, into, many,* and *them.* Invite your child to use the words to describe life in his or her home.

Name ___________________________

Look at the picture that shows what happened.
Circle the picture that shows why it happened.

1. 

2. 

3. 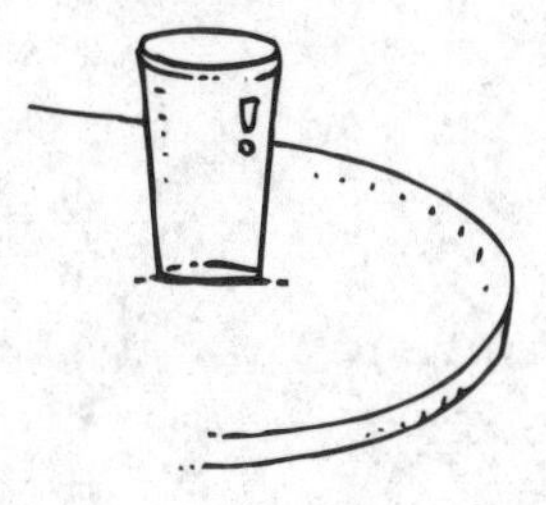

Read the two story sentences. **Circle** the one that tells what happens.

4. Val is tan. The pup ran.

5. Sam is sick. Sam naps in bed.

Home Activity Your child learned about cause (why something happens) and effect (what happens). Look for cause and effect with your child. For example, you might point out that when the temperature drops in the fall, frost forms.

Name ______________________________

Writing Prompt: Write a composition about an animal you like.

Rabbits

I like rabbits. My mom and I watch rabbits in our yard. We see them in the evening. They eat and play at night. They rest during the day.

Rabbits eat plants. We try to keep them away from our garden.

Rabbits stand very still. They do not want us to see them! If I go too near to a rabbit, it hops away.

I learn a lot by watching rabbits.

Name ______________________

Say the word for each picture.
Circle the letters that finish each word.
Write the letters on the line.

ne<u>st</u>

nd nt

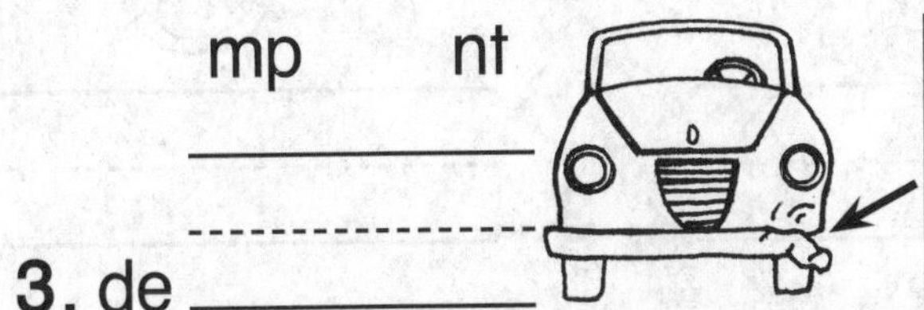

1. po ______

nt mp

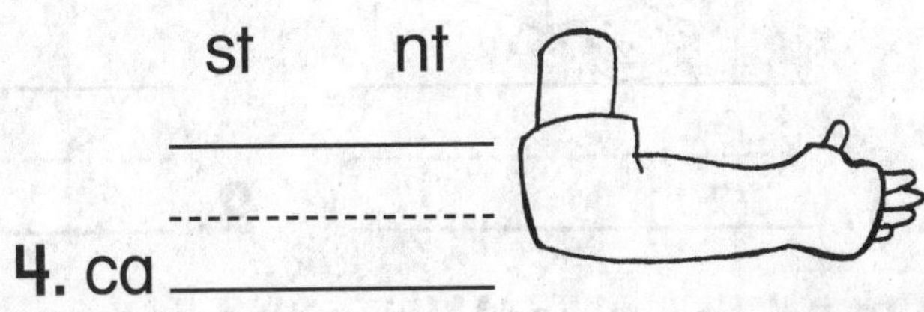

2. ju ______

mp nt

3. de ______

st nt

4. ca ______

st mp

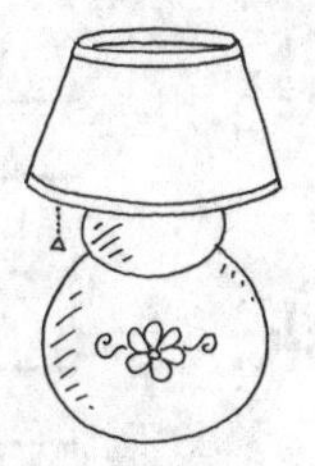

5. la ______

nt nd

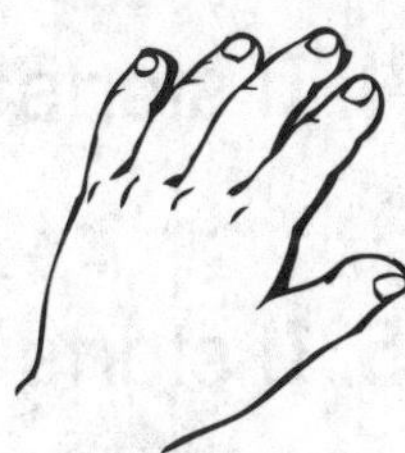

6. ha ______

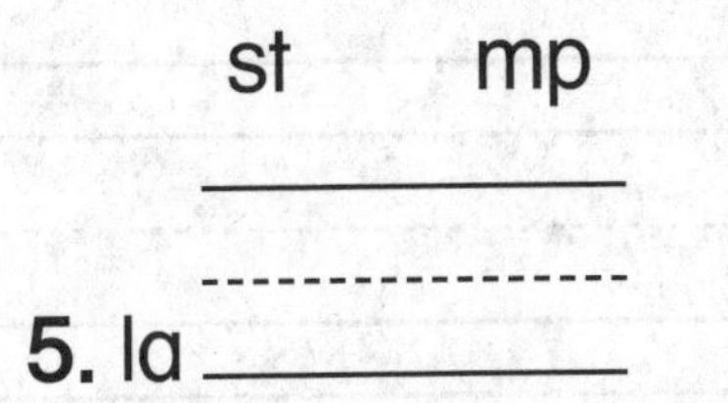

st nt

7. ve ______

nt mp

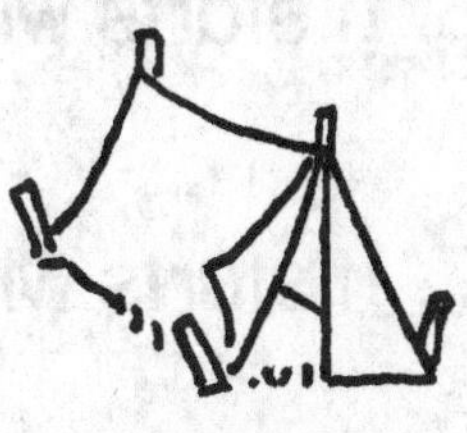

8. te ______

nt st

9. fi ______

mp st

10. sta ______

Home Activity Your child created words using final consonant blends such as *mp, nd, nt,* and *st*. Have your child make up sentences using words from this page.

Name ______________________

Short *u* Words with Final Consonant Blends

Spelling Words				
just	dust	must	hunt	crust
bump	jump	trust	lump	dusk

Write a list word to name the picture.

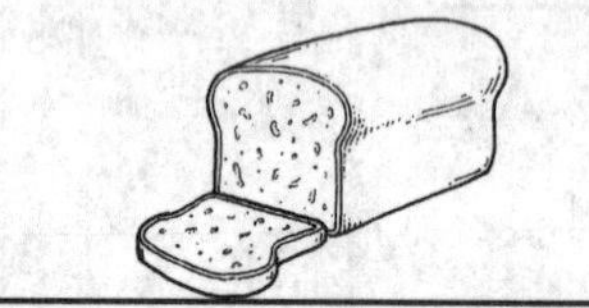

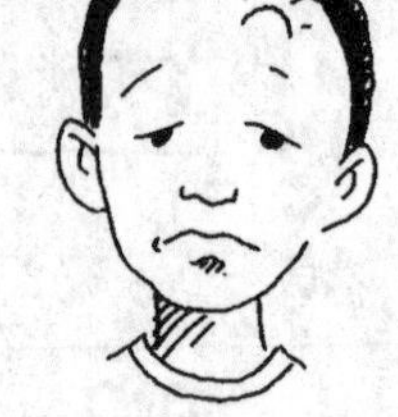

1. ______________ 2. ______________ 3. ______________

Read the clue. **Write** the list word.

4. It starts with **j**. It rhymes with **must**. ______________

5. It starts with **d**. It rhymes with **husk**. ______________

6. It starts with **h**. It rhymes with **stunt**. ______________

7. It starts with **m**. It rhymes with **just**. ______________

8. It starts with **d**. It rhymes with **bust**. ______________

9. It starts with **tr**. It rhymes with **dust**. ______________

10. It starts with **b**. It rhymes with **pump**. ______________

Home Activity Your child wrote words with the short *u* vowel sound. Take turns with your child making up clues and then guessing and spelling the word.

Name ______________________________

Exclamatory Sentences

An **exclamatory sentence** is a sentence that shows strong feeling. It begins with a **capital letter**. It ends with an **exclamation mark (!)**.

The animal is big!

Underline each sentence that is an exclamation.

1. That hippo is funny!

2. It looks mad!

3. Where does it live?

4. It can live in the mud.

5. Now the hippo is happy!

6. I like the hippo.

Home Activity Your child learned about exclamations. Have your child read each exclamation on this page with strong feeling. Then take turns with your child saying exclamations of your own.

Name ______________________________

Composition

Top-Score Response

Focus/Ideas	A good composition tells about one topic.
Organization	A good composition tells important ideas in an order that makes sense.
Voice	A good composition tells about the topic in a way that is interesting.
Word Choice	A good composition uses clear words.
Sentences	A good composition is written in complete sentences.
Conventions	A good composition has sentences that are punctuated correctly.

Home Activity Your child can begin to learn about writing on writing tests. Ask how writing a composition about a topic such as real animals is different from making up a story.

Name ______________________________

Q q   U u

Copy the words. Leave the correct space between each letter.

Quin	tub
Uta	sun
quick	quiz
bus	duck
quit	hug
fun	mug
quack	jug

Did you leave the correct space between each letter? Yes No

Home Activity Your child practiced writing words with *Qq* and *Uu* and words with short *u* sound. Have your child copy this sentence as neatly as possible: *Quin and Uta quickly run to the bus.*

Name ______________________________

Use the picture to choose and revise a topic.

1. **Name** three animals you see. **Circle** the animal you would like to know more about.

2. What more would you like to know about this animal? **Write** two questions.

3. Use your questions. **Write** your new topic. Ask for help if needed.

Home Activity Your child learned how to answer questions about a topic. Encourage your child to ask questions about the topic "Preparing a Family Meal." After the questions are answered, ask your child if he or she wants to reword the topic.

Bud got the sums.

Bud did his best.

Bud did well!

Decodable Story The Test
Target Skills Short *u*, Final Consonant Blends

Name ______________________

The Test

Short u		Final Consonant Blends	High-Frequency Words	
Huff	fun	test	the	said
Bud	stuck	must	a	is
sum	sums	best		

"The class will get a test," said Miss Huff.

"The class will add."

I + I. Bud gets the sum.

3 + 3. The sum is six.

The test is fun!

5 + 5. Bud is stuck.

Bud must get the sum.

The sum is ten.

Name ______________________

Short *u* Words with Final Consonant Blends

Spelling Words				
just	dust	must	hunt	crust
bump	jump	trust	lump	dusk

Write a list word to name the picture.

1. It is ____________ .
2. I see the ____________ .
3. I ____________ you.
4. I ____________ want to run.
5. I ____________ for an egg.
6. Mom eats a ____________ .
7. I ____________ into the car.
8. My arm has a ____________ .
9. The car hits a ____________ .
10. We ____________ go on the bus.

Home Activity Your child wrote spelling words to complete a story. Help your child use some of the words in a story about his or her day.

Name ______________________

Exclamatory Sentences

What animal would you like to have?
Write about the animal.
Use an exclamation to show how you felt.

a zebra

an elephant

a lion

an ostrich

a hippo

Read the question. **Change** the words to make an exclamation.
Write the exclamation.

Is the pet big?

Home Activity Your child learned how to use exclamations in writing. Name an object in the room and a word that describes the object *(lamp/bright; sofa/big; pillow/soft; rug/dark).* Have your child write exclamations using the word pairs *(The lamp is too bright! That pillow is so soft!).*

Name ________________________________

Short *u* Words with Final Consonant Blends

Write the words in the puzzle.

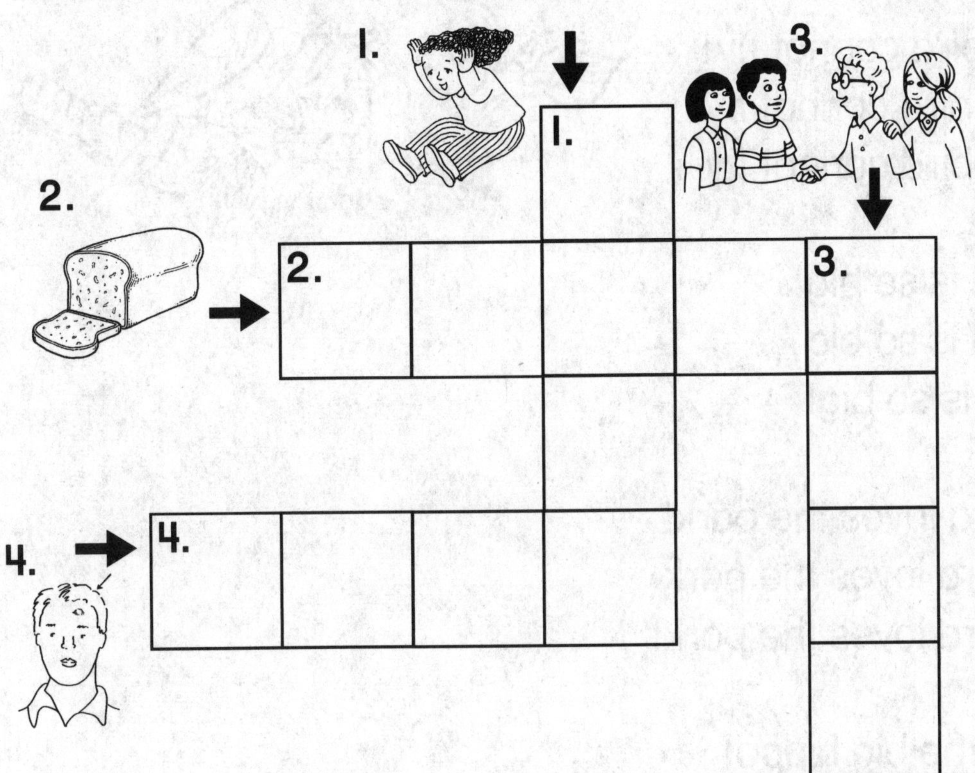

Spelling Words
just
bump
dust
jump
must
trust
hunt
lump
crust
dusk

Write the missing words.

bump dusk must just

5. Do not ______________ it.

6. I ______________ get the ball.

7. I ______________ want to play.

8. It is ______________ now.

Home Activity Your child has been learning to spell words with short *u*. Help your child find words with short u in library books or schoolbooks.

Name ______________________________

Exclamatory Sentences

Mark the correct exclamation.

1. ◯ the big bird cannot fly!
   ◯ The big bird cannot fly!
   ◯ The big bird cannot fly

2. ◯ The bird is so big!
   ◯ The bird is so big
   ◯ the bird is so big!

3. ◯ the zebra loves the park!
   ◯ The zebra loves the park
   ◯ The zebra loves the park!

4. ◯ Look at the big hippo!
   ◯ Look at the big hippo
   ◯ Look at the big hippo?

5. ◯ The zebra is fast
   ◯ The zebra is fast!
   ◯ the zebra is fast

6. ◯ Oh no, the bird fell
   ◯ oh no, the bird fell!
   ◯ Oh no, the bird fell!

Home Activity Your child prepared for taking tests on exclamations. Together read a favorite book. Have your child point out the exclamations and tell how he or she knew they were exclamations.

Name ______________________________

Say the word for each picture.
Write sh or **th** to finish each word.

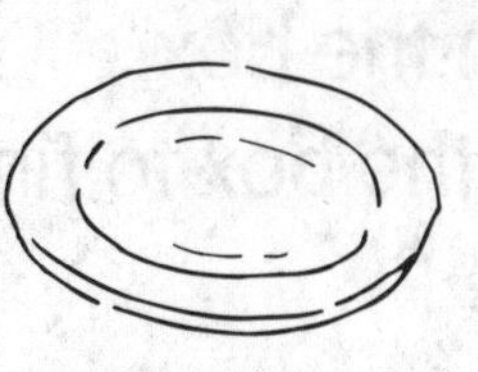

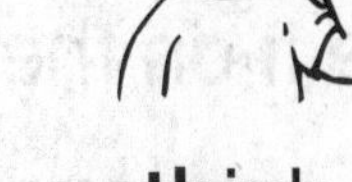

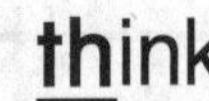

di**sh** **th**ink

1. 

_____ op

2. 
fi _____

3. _____ in

4. 
_____ ell

5. ba _____

6. 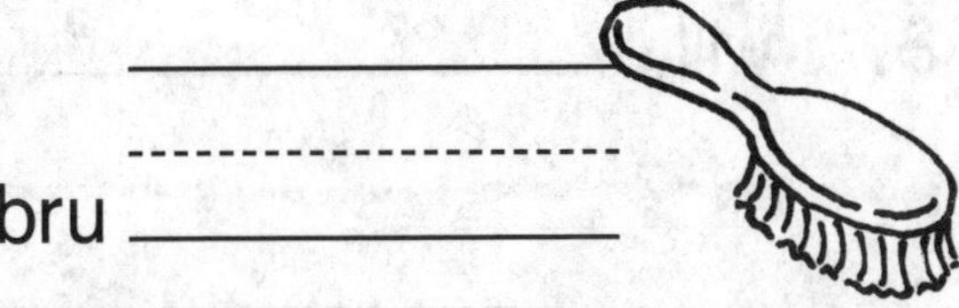
bru _____

Circle a word to finish each sentence. **Write** the word.

path math

7. She walked on the bike _____________.

drip ship

8. I saw the _____________ from the beach.

Home Activity Your child added the digraphs *sh* and *th* (two letters that together stand for one sound) to complete words. Have your child copy the words that contain *sh* from this page and use as many of those words as possible in one sentence. Repeat using the *th* words.

Name ______________________

Read the words in the box.
Pick a word from the box to finish each sentence.
Write it on the line.

catch	good	no	put	said	want

1. Dad and Bob ______________ to fish.

2. "You can ______________ it here," Dad said.

3. "I will," ______________ Bob.

4. Bob has ______________ fish yet.

5. Bob can ______________ that fish!

6. It is a ______________ fish.

Home Activity Your child identified and read the words *catch, good, no, put, said,* and *want.* As you read with your child, encourage him or her to point out these words in print.

Name ______________________________

Read the story.
Follow the directions.

Ted sees a nest fall from a tree.

It has three blue eggs in it.

Ted picks up the nest.

Ted sets the nest back in the tree.

---

1. **Write** a sentence that tells what happens at the beginning of the story.

____

____

2. **Write** a sentence that tells what happens in the middle of the story.

____

3. **Draw** a picture that shows what happens at the end of the story. Then **act out** what happened in the story.

Home Activity Your child learned about the order in which things happen in a story. Reread this story with your child. Ask your child to tell you what might happen next in the story.

Name ______________________________

Writing • Friendly Letter

Dear Uncle Karl,

My favorite thing is fishing. I want you to go with me. We can go to the pond down the road. Then we will catch a bunch of fish. It will be really exciting! I hope you can go with me.

Your niece,
Lynn

Key Features of a Friendly Letter

- It begins with a greeting and ends with a closing.
- It often tells how the writer feels or gives the writer's opinion.
- It can tell ideas in time order, or sequence.

Name ______________________________

Circle a word to finish each sentence.
Write it on the line.

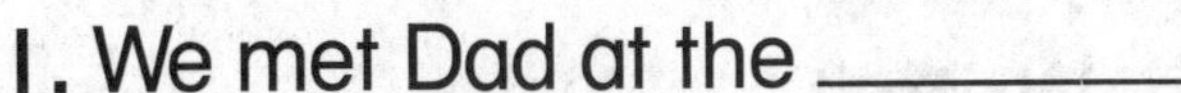

mall   mill

1. We met Dad at the ______________.

well   walk

2. We take a ______________ and talk.

tell   tall

3. Dad got a ______________ bag.

all   ill

4. We ______________ go in.

smell   small

5. I am too ______________ to see!

Home Activity Your child practiced reading words with the vowel sound heard in *ball* and *walk*. Work with your child to write a list of words that rhyme with *ball*.

Name ______________________

Words with *sh, th*

Spelling Words				
ship	fish	then	shut	with
rush	shell	shop	trash	thin

Find a list word to name the picture. **Write** it.

1. ______________

2. ______________

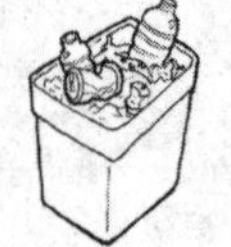

3. ______________

4. ______________

5. ______________

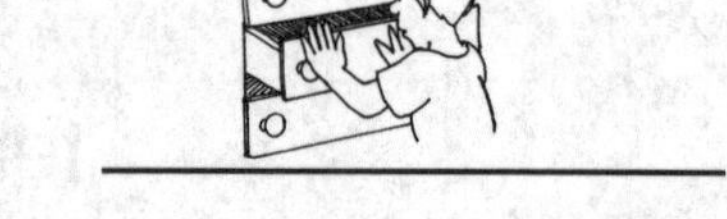

6. ______________

Unscramble the word. **Write** the word.

s h u r

7. ______________

i t h w

8. ______________

n e t h

9. ______________

n t h i

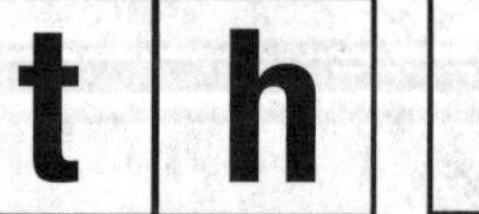

10. ______________

Home Activity Your child wrote words with the *sh* or *th* sound. Say a list word. Ask if it has *sh* or *th*. Have your child spell the word.

Name ______________________________

Common Nouns

A **noun** names a person, a place, an animal, or a thing.

The word **man** names a person.

The word **park** names a place.

The word **fish** names an animal.

The word **net** names a thing.

Write the noun for each picture. **Say** a sentence for each noun.

Person

girl boy

1. ______________________

Place

city pond

2. ______________________

Animal

cat rabbit

3. ______________________

Thing

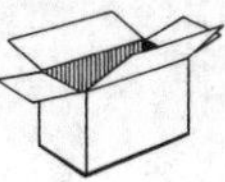

box pan

4. ______________________

Home Activity Your child learned about nouns. Read a story together. Have your child point to nouns in the story and tell whether they name people, places, animals, or things.

Name ____________________

Letter Format

Dear ____________________,

____

____

____

____

____

____________________,

____

Home Activity Your child is learning about writing letters. Help him or her plan a letter to a relative or family friend.

Name ______________________________

Ss Hh

Copy the words. Write the letters the correct size.

Shem	____________	shack	____________
Hal	____________	dish	____________
shop	____________	rash	____________
fish	____________	mush	____________
wish	____________	cash	____________
shut	____________	Hank	____________
ship	____________	rush	____________

Did you write all of your letters the correct size? 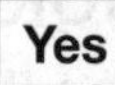

No

Home Activity Your child practiced writing words with *Ss* and *Hh* and short vowels. Have your child choose two words from the chart and write the words three more times.

Name ______________________________

See the USA

Contents

Use this **table of contents** from a travel book to find information.

1. **Draw** a circle around the page numbers.

2. **Put** a box around the chapter titles.

3. **Write** the name of the last chapter.

____

4. **Write** the page number on which the chapter "Beaches, Beaches, Beaches" begins.

5. **Write** the total number of chapters in *See the USA*.

____

Home Activity Your child learned to use the table of contents in a storybook to find information. As you read together, point out the table of contents and encourage your child to help you find information such as the page number for a specific chapter.

Miss Smith talks with Ned.

“Do not fill the land with trash!”

Decodable Story Cans
Target Skills Consonant Digraphs, Vowel Sound in *ball* and *walk*

Name ______________________

Cans

Consonant Digraphs		Vowel Sound in *ball* and *walk*	High-Frequency Words
shed	cash	all	she
trash	Smith	walk	the
crush	with	talks	to
smash	then		do

Miss Smith has cans.

She will not fill the trash with cans.

Miss Smith will walk to the shed.

She will crush and smash the cans.

Miss Smith will fill all the bins with cans.

Then she will get cash.

Name ______________________

Words with *sh, th*

Find a list word or high-frequency word to finish the sentence.
Write it on the line.

Spelling Words
ship
fish
then
shut
with
rush
shell
shop
trash
thin

High-Frequency Words
want
good

1. I will ______________ home.
2. Will you feed my ______________?
3. Come ______________ me.
4. Dad did a ______________ job.
5. Put the paper in the ______________ can.
6. This egg has a brown ______________.
7. Do not ______________ the door.
8. I ______________ to buy a new cap.
9. She came on a ______________.
10. That dog is ______________.

Home Activity Your child wrote spelling words and high-frequency words to complete sentences. Ask your child to write a sentence using two or more of the words.

Name ___________________________

Common Nouns

Write about things you do with your family.
Use words from the box or words of your own.

mom	dad	brother
grandma	grandpa	sister

Choose other nouns. **Say** a sentence for each noun.

Home Activity Your child learned how to use nouns in writing. Write sentences about family members, such as *Your sister has brown hair. Your mother loves flowers.* Have your child circle the nouns in the sentences.

Name ______________________________

Words with *sh, th*

Read the clue. **Write** a list word.

It rhymes with 

1. ____________

It rhymes with 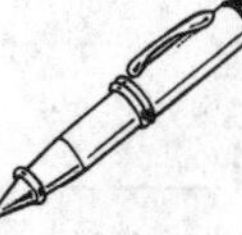

2. ____________

It rhymes with 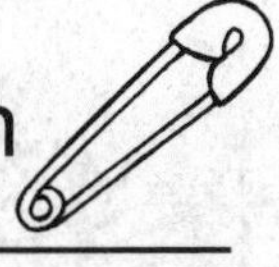

3. ____________

It rhymes with 

4. ____________

Spelling Words
ship
fish
then
shut
with
rush
shell
shop
trash
thin

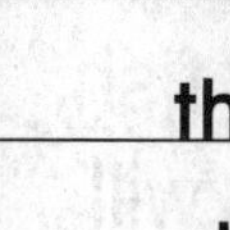

Find a list word in each row of letters.
Circle it. **Write** it.

r u s h t e 5. ____________

t s h u t r 6. ____________

s h o p t h 7. ____________

s t r a s h 8. ____________

w i f i s h 9. ____________

r w i t h s 10. ____________

fish
shut
trash
rush
shop
with

Home Activity Your child has been learning to spell words with *sh* and *th*. Have your child circle *sh* and *th* in the spelling words.

Name ______________________________

Common Nouns

Mark the noun that completes the sentence.

1. Max wants a ____.
   - ◯ eat
   - ◯ fish
   - ◯ will

2. The ____ has a pond.
   - ◯ in
   - ◯ sit
   - ◯ park

3. Max got a red ____.
   - ◯ ball
   - ◯ talk
   - ◯ this

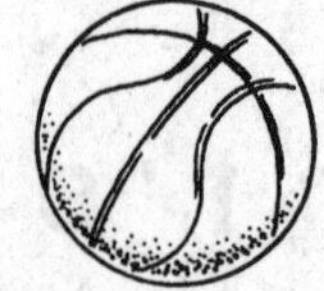

4. A ____ is in the net.
   - ◯ call
   - ◯ and
   - ◯ shell

5. The ____ gave them a fish.
   - ◯ fat
   - ◯ woman
   - ◯ that

Home Activity Your child prepared for taking tests on nouns. Together read a simple piece of mail, such as an ad. Have your child circle the nouns in the article.

Name ______________________________

Circle the word for each picture.

cake

1. 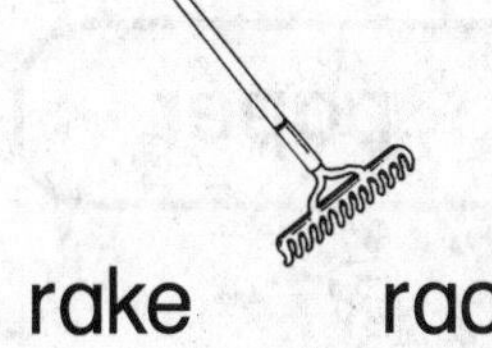 rake rack	2.  snack snake	3.  frog frame
4.  can cane	5.  cape cap	6.  plane plan

Choose a word to finish each sentence. **Write** the word on the line.

lake lock

7. I like to swim in the ______________.

plant plate

8. Please put the food on the ______________.

gum game

9. Will you play this ______________ with me?

gate skate

10. I can ______________ fast.

Home Activity Your child practiced reading words with the long *a* sound spelled *a _ e,* such as *cake.* Work with your child to write a list of words that rhyme with *cake*. Repeat with *cave.*

Name ______________________

Read the words in the box.
Pick a word to finish each sentence.
Write it on the line.

be	could	horse	of	old	paper

1. Dad gave me a ______________ .

2. She was not ______________ .

3. She ______________ run and jump.

4. I put her name on a ______________ .

5. I can make the horse the color ______________ a fox.

6. We will ______________ pals!

Home Activity Your child identified and read the words *be, of, could, horse, old,* and *paper*. Write these words on small pieces of paper or self-stick notes. Tape them on a mirror or desk for your child to practice every day.

Name ______________________________

Look at the first picture that shows what happened.
Circle the picture that shows why it happened.

1.  

2. 

3.   

4.   

Look at the picture that shows what happened.
Draw a picture that shows why it happened.

5. 

Home Activity Your child learned about cause (why something happens) and effect (what happens). Call your child's attention to causes and effects by asking questions such as: *What happened?* (effect) *Why did it happen?* (cause)

Name ______________________________

Writing • Brief Composition

Group Time

Every day we have group time. I work with José and Kim. We help each other with math. Sometimes we change papers. We talk about stories. We answer questions. Then we share with the class.

Key Features of a Brief Composition

- It tells interesting facts.
- It tells about one topic.

Name ______________________

Circle the word for each picture.
Write it on the line.

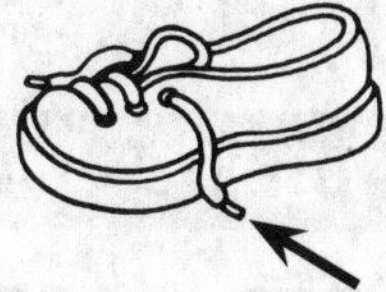

lace

age

1. 
face fake
____

2. 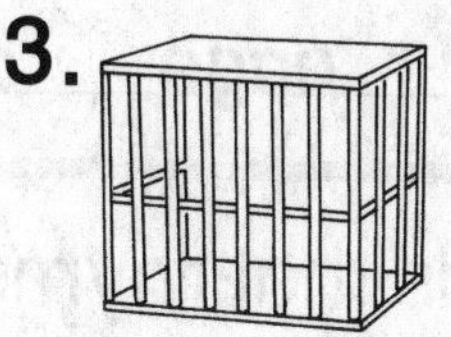
rake race
____

3. 
cave cage
____

4. wag wage
____

5. speck space
____

6. 
stage stake
____

7. 
track trace
____

8. pace page
____

Circle the word to finish each sentence. **Write** the word.

lace brake

9. I tripped on my ______________.

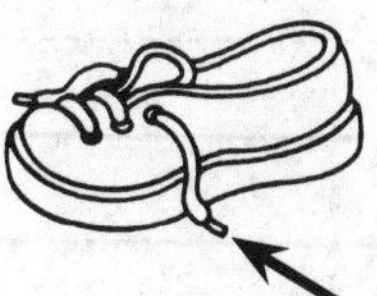

page cage

10. My pet bird lives in a ______________.

Home Activity Your child practiced reading and writing words that have the sound that *c* stands for in *lace* and the sound that *g* stands for in *age*. Ask your child to write a list of words that rhyme with *lace* and a list of words that rhyme with *age*.

Name ______________________

Words with Long *a*

Spelling Words				
face	made	age	safe	take
make	cage	cake	late	name

Write three list words that rhyme with **rake**.

1. ____________ 2. ____________ 3. ____________

Write two list words that rhyme with **page**.

4. ____________ 5. ____________

Write the missing word.

safe face name late made

6. Her ____________ is Bo.

7. Bo ____________ a dog.

8. Her ____________ is happy.

9. Is that ball ____________?

10. Can we stay ____________?

Home Activity Your child wrote words with the long *a* sound. Help your child think of words that rhyme with the spelling words.

Name ______________________________

Proper Nouns

Special names for people, places, animals, and things are called **proper nouns.** Proper nouns begin with capital letters.

Meg Rose Pond Rex Tell Tower

Look at each picture. **Write** the proper name on the line.
Say a sentence for each proper noun.

Beth

1. This girl is ______________________.

Hall School

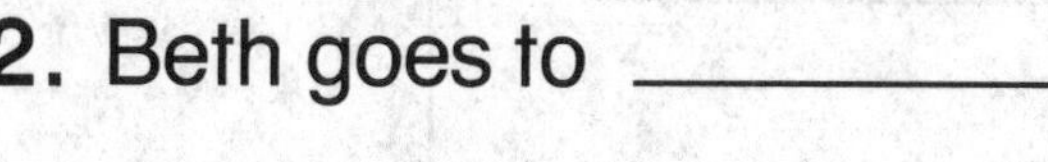

2. Beth goes to ______________________.

Post Road

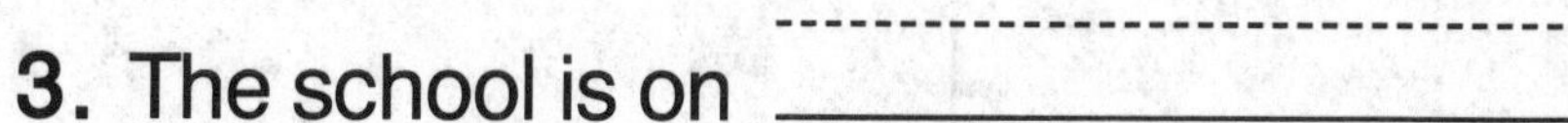

3. The school is on ______________________.

Coco

4. The class pet is ______________________.

Home Activity Your child learned about proper nouns. Read a story together. Have your child point to proper nouns in the story.

Name ______________________________

Idea Web

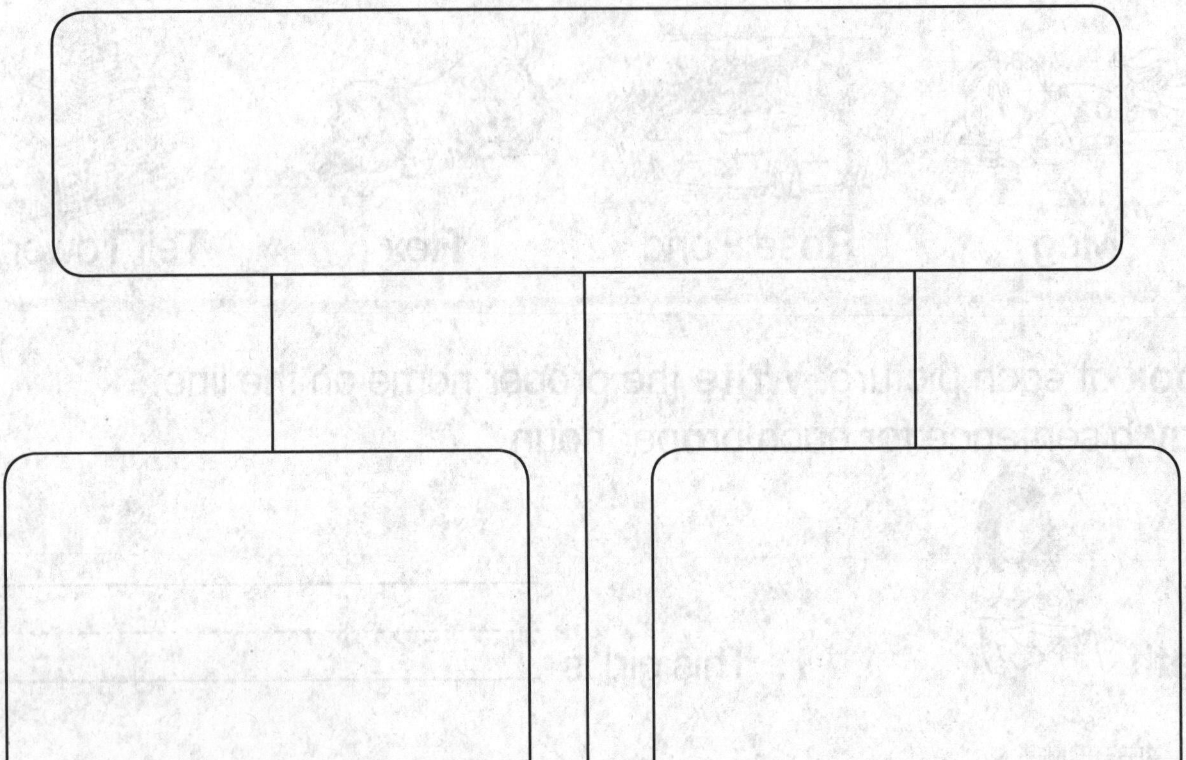

Home Activity Your child has thought of ideas for writing about how children work together. Share ideas about how people do things together at home.

Name ______________________

P p

Copy the words. Leave the correct space between the letters.

Page ______ wage ______

pace ______ lace ______

pave ______ race ______

tape ______ shade ______

cape ______ pale ______

cage ______ pane ______

face ______ rage ______

Did you leave the correct space between your letters? Yes No

School + Home

Home Activity Your child practiced writing words with *P* and *p*. Have your child find two pairs of rhyming words in the list above and write the words two more times as neatly as possible.

Name ______________________________

custodian – a person who helps keep buildings clean and safe

librarian – a person trained to work in a library

teacher – a person who helps people learn

---

1. Circle the school helper you would like to know more about.

2. What would you like to know? Write three interview questions.

____

____

____

3. Ask your interview questions. Write one thing you learned.

____

4. Then act out your interview to share your results with the class.

Home Activity Your child learned how to interview. Have your child make a list of family members or friends that he or she would like to interview. Help your child come up with some interesting questions for the interview.

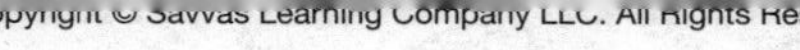

Jake takes the fast lane.

See Jake dash past the gate.

Jake is fast for his age!

Decodable Story *The Race*
Target Skills Long *a: a_e*, Consonants *c/s/, g/j/*

The Race

Long *a: a_e*			Consonants *c /s/* and *g /j/*	High-Frequency Words	
Jake	gate	lane	race	I	see
lake	late	shape	pace	the	is
cake	skates	shade	place	of	for
takes	waves		age		
ate	came		Page		

Jake waves at Page. "I am in shape!"

"I will win the race at the lake."

Page waves at Jake.

"I came late. I ate lots of cake.

I will get last place."

Page walks in the shade.

She is not fast.

"I wish I had skates!"

Name ______________________________

Words with Long *a*

Spelling Words				
face	made	age	safe	take
make	cage	cake	late	name

High-Frequency Words
could
old

Circle a word to finish the sentence. **Write** the word.

1. I love **cake** **late** **make**! ______________
2. Have a **face** **safe** **name** trip. ______________
3. I **made** **age** **cake** it. ______________
4. What is your **made** **late** **name**? ______________
5. His **age** **face** **make** got red. ______________
6. What is in the **cage** **age** **face**? ______________
7. She won't tell her **cake** **late** **age**. ______________
8. Let's **safe** **made** **make** a kite. ______________
9. I **could** **cage** **cake** stay up late. ______________
10. That is an **age** **old** **take** **cage**. ______________

Home Activity Your child used spelling words to complete sentences. Have your child identify and write as many spelling words as possible to finish this sentence: *This is my*_____.

Name ______________________________

Proper Nouns

Finish each sentence with a proper noun.

My teacher is ______________________________.
(name of your teacher)

My school is ______________________________.
(name of your school)

Write the names of three children in your class.

______________ ______________ ______________

Tell something about each child.

____

____

____

Home Activity Your child learned how to use proper nouns in writing. Write sentences about people that you and your child know, such as *Steve is a friend. Maria is our cousin.* Have your child circle the proper nouns in the sentences.

Name ______________________________

Words with Long *a*

Spelling Words				
face	made	age	safe	take
make	cage	cake	late	name

Use this code. **Write** the words.

▲	★	♥	●	⬟	◆	■	∩	⌂	▼	▶
a	c	d	e	f	g	k	m	n	s	t

▲◆●

1. ____________

⌂▲★●

2. ____________

∩▲■●

3. ____________

★▲■●

4. ____________

∩▲♥●

5. ____________

★▲◆●

6. ____________

▼▲⬟●

7. ____________

⌂▲∩●

8. ____________

▶▲■●

9. ____________

Write the missing letters. **Write** the word.

10. l ___ t ___ ____________

Home Activity Your child has been learning to spell words with long *a*. Ask your child to explain how all the list words are alike. (All have long *a*, and all end in *a*-consonant-*e*.)

Name ______________________________

Proper Nouns

Mark the sentence that uses the proper noun correctly.

1. ◯ This boy is jake.
   ◯ This boy is Jake.
   ◯ This boy is JAKE.

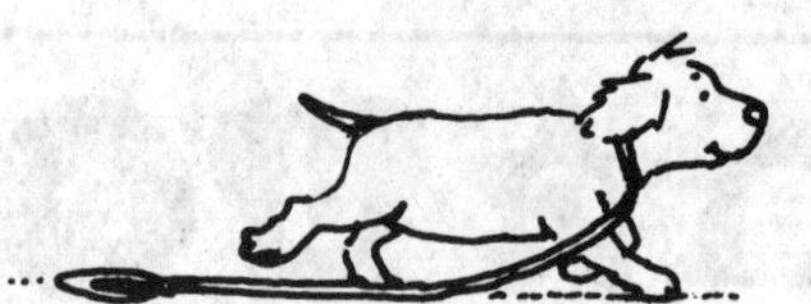

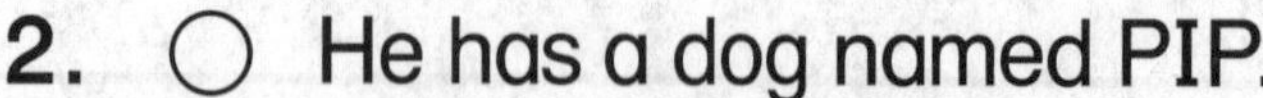

2. ◯ He has a dog named PIP.
   ◯ He has a dog named pip.
   ◯ He has a dog named Pip.

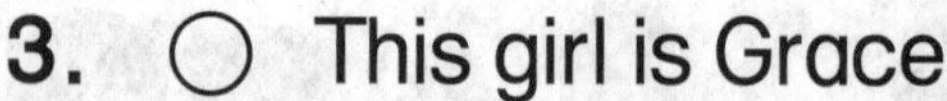

3. ◯ This girl is Grace.
   ◯ This girl is GRACE.
   ◯ This girl is grace.

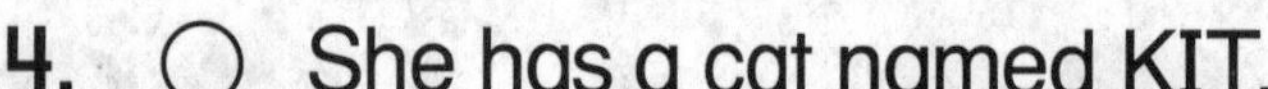

4. ◯ She has a cat named KIT.
   ◯ She has a cat named kit.
   ◯ She has a cat named Kit.

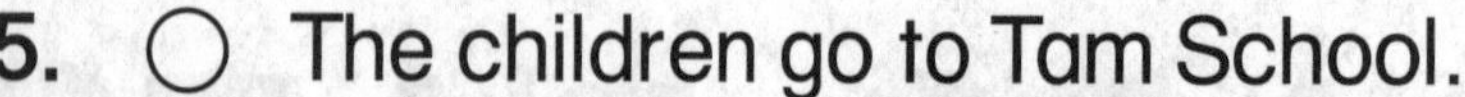

5. ◯ The children go to Tam School.
   ◯ The children go to tam School.
   ◯ The children go to Tam school.

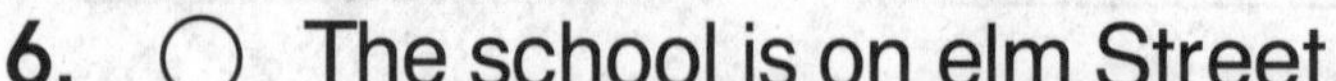

6. ◯ The school is on elm Street.
   ◯ The school is on Elm Street.
   ◯ The school is on Elm street.

Home Activity Your child prepared for taking tests on proper nouns. Together read a short newspaper or magazine article. Have your child circle the proper nouns in the article.

Name ______________________________

Circle the word for each picture.

9 ni̲ne

1. 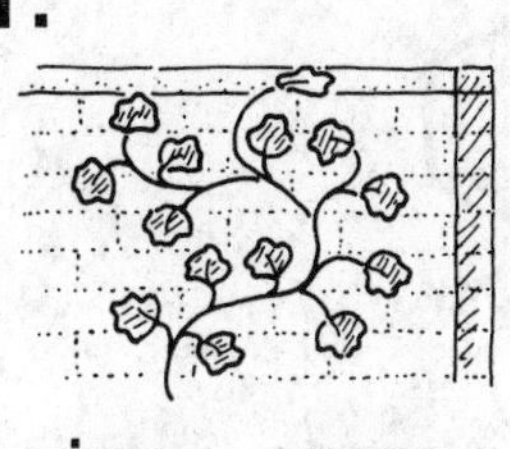
vine vane

2. 
mane mice

3. 
wig wipe

4. 
bike bill

Say the name of each picture.
Write the letters to finish each word.

5. 

___ ___ ___ ___

6. 
___ ___ ___ ___ ___

7. 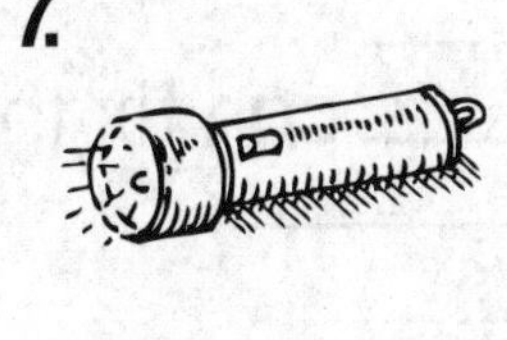
___ ___ ___ ___ ___

8. 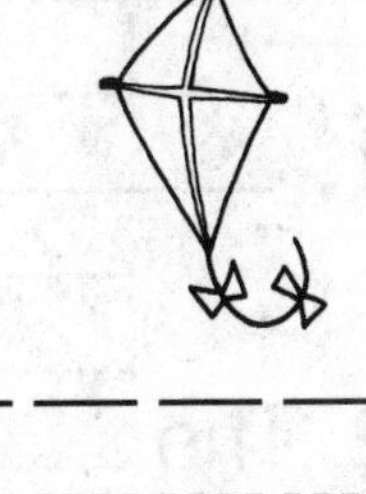
___ ___ ___ ___

Pick a word to finish each sentence. **Write** the word on the line.

slice price

9. I bought a ______________ of pizza.

bite rice

10. "Would you like a ______________?" I asked.

Home Activity Your child practiced reading words with the long *i* sound spelled *i _ e*, such as *nine*. Work with your child to write a list of words that rhyme with *nine*. Repeat with *hide*.

Name ______________________

Read the words in the box.
Pick a word to finish each sentence.
Write it on the line. **Remember** to use capital letters at the beginning of a sentence.

live out people who work

1. ______________ can fix this clock?

2. The ______________ in the shop can fix it.

3. They will ______________ on it.

4. Where does your dog ______________?

5. His home is ______________ here.

Home Activity Your child identified and read the words *live, out, people, who,* and *work*. Point to these words on the page. Have your child read each word and use it in a spoken sentence.

Name ______________________________

Look at this book.
Write or **circle** your answers.

Who Works at the Zoo?

ZOO

by Kim Green

1. Who is the author of this book? ____________________

2. What is the topic of this book?

people in the ocean   people at the zoo   people on a ship

3. Why do you think Kim wrote this book?

to make you laugh   to teach you tricks   to tell facts

Draw a picture that shows what this book is about.

4.

Home Activity Your child learned to tell what a book might be about by figuring out why it was written. As you read various materials with your child, ask what he or she thinks each is about and why the author wrote it.

Name ___________________________

Writing • Explanation

My Piano Teacher

Ms. Kindler teaches me to play piano. She shows me how to hold my fingers. She helps me read notes. She shows me the keys to press. She teaches me to play songs on the piano.

Key Features of an Explanation

- It tells about a person, idea, or thing.
- It helps people understand the topic.

Name ______________________

Circle the word for each picture.

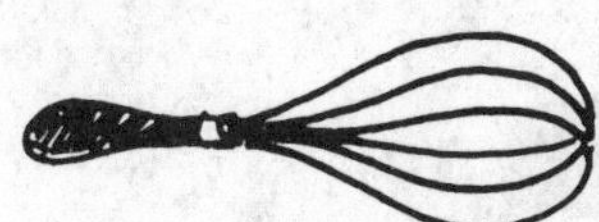 whisk  chick  itch

1. 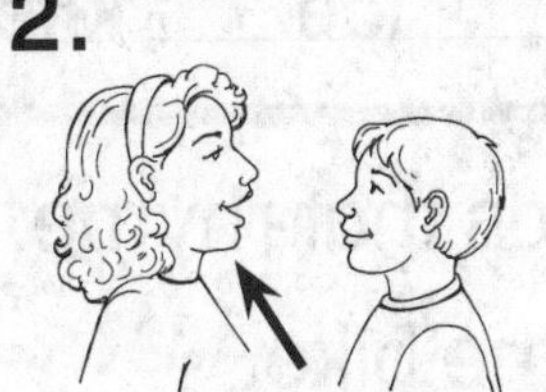
wall whale

2. 
shin chin

3. 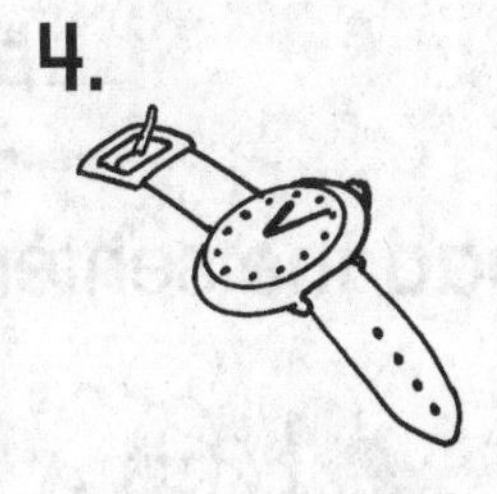
catch cats

4. wash watch

5. ship whip

6. chick check

7. 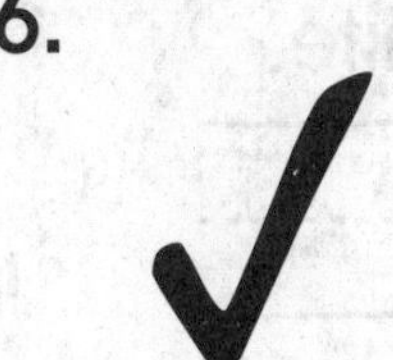
patch pass

8. 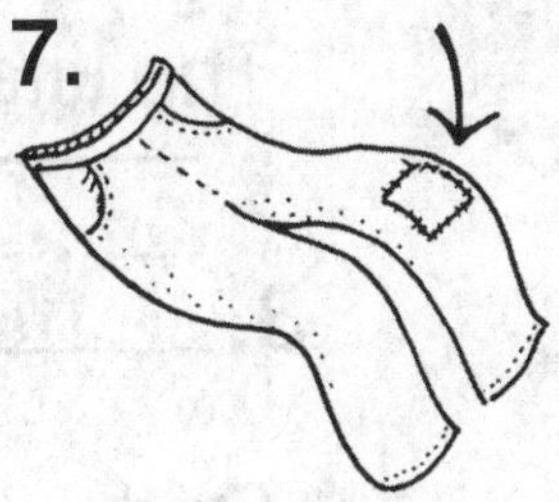 
limp chimp

Pick a word to finish each sentence. **Write** the word on the line.

graph grass

9. Henry made a mistake on his ______________.

what want

10. He did not know ______________ to do.

Home Activity Your child practiced reading words with digraphs *wh, ch,* and *tch* (letters that together stand for one sound). Have your child use each word above in a sentence.

Name ____________________

Words with Long *i*

Spelling Words				
like	ride	smile	time	white
bike	dime	hide	ice	kite

Read the sentence. **Write** the words that rhyme.

They like the bike.

1. ____________ 2. ____________

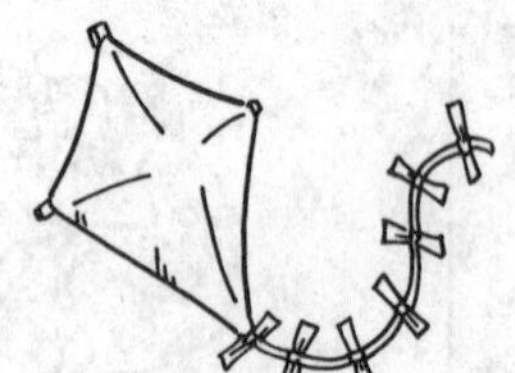

The kite is white.

3. ____________ 4. ____________

Dad will use a dime this time.

5. ____________ 6. ____________

Write the missing word.

ice
hide
ride
smile

7. The ____________ makes me cold.

8. Did you walk or ____________?

9. She has a big ____________ on her face.

10. The cat likes to ____________ from me.

Home Activity Your child wrote words with the long *i* sound. Take turns with your child making up sentences containing the words. Spell the words aloud.

Name ______________________

Special Titles

A **title** can come before the name of a person. A title begins with a capital letter. Titles can be abbreviations. Abbreviations end with a **period (.)**.

Doctor Silva

Mrs. Faber

Mr. Gray

Write the title and the name correctly on the line.

1. miss oda

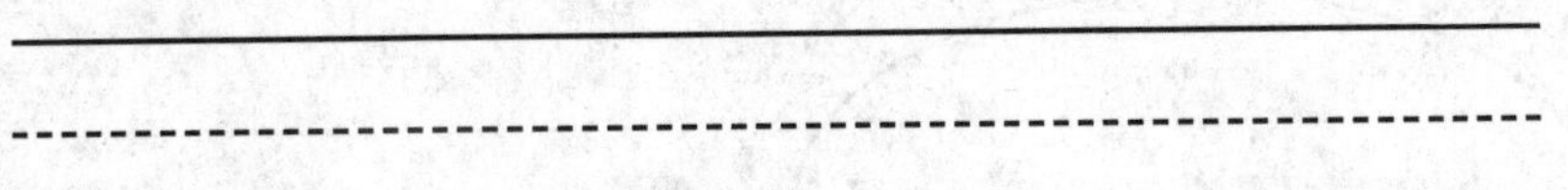

2. captain bartz

3. dr. hashmi

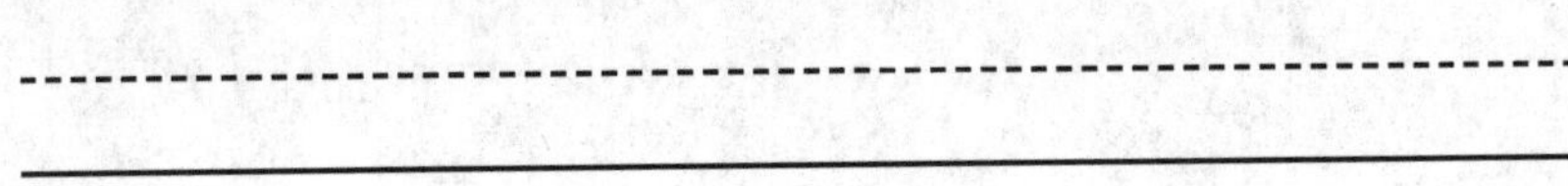

4. ms. ford

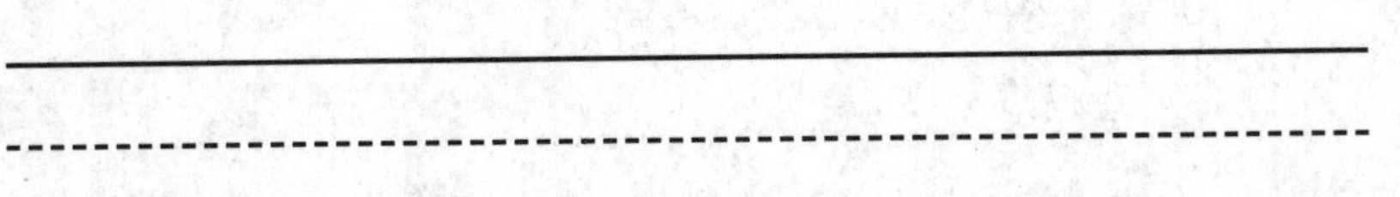

Home Activity Your child learned about special titles. Say the names and titles of adults your child knows, for example, *Dr. Kahn, Ms. Bell, Mr. Garcia.* Ask your child to identify and write the person's title.

Name ___________________________

Idea Web

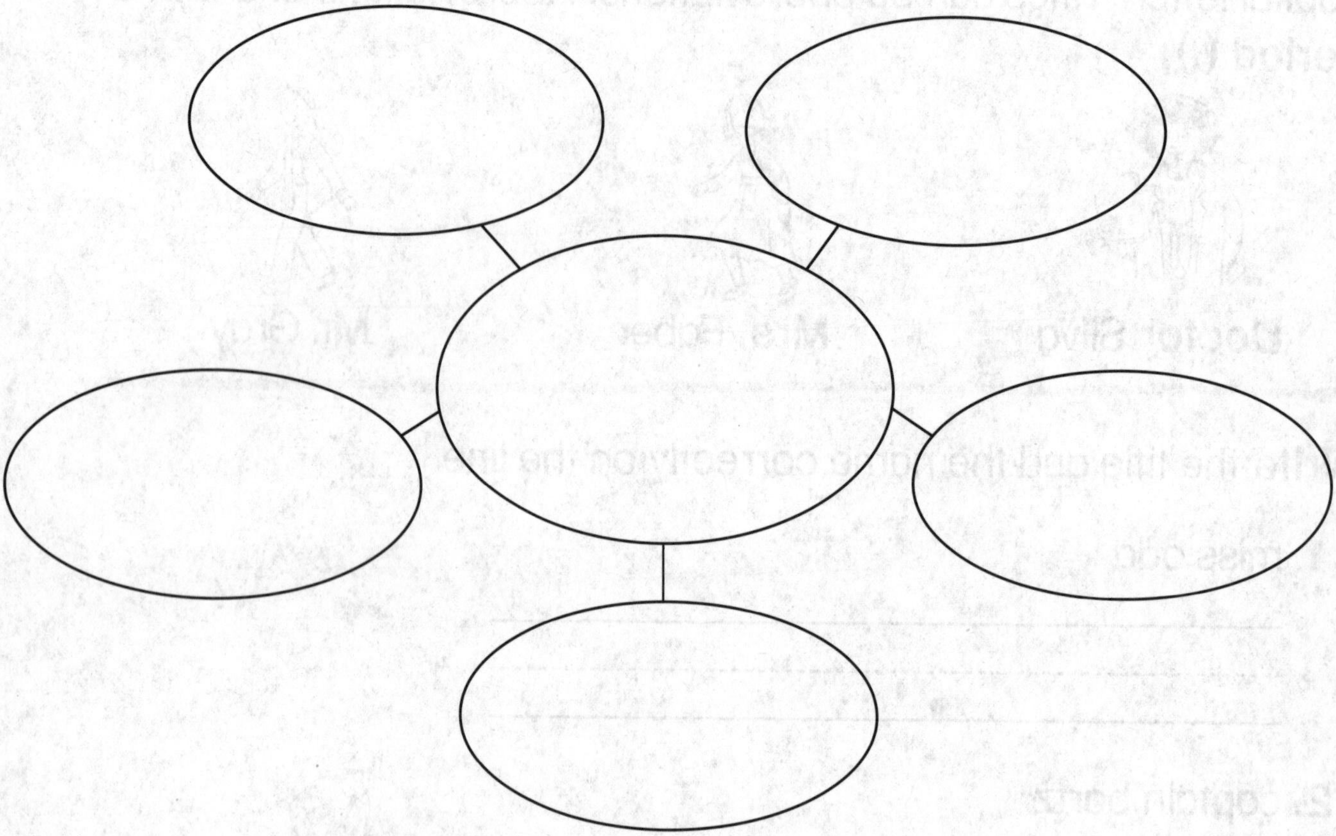

Home Activity Your child is learning about writing an explanation by telling what a teacher does. Talk with your child about jobs that people in a community do.

Name ______________________________

W w

Copy the words. Write the letters from left to right.

Wade

white

chime

whine

chin

while

chase

chop

when

whim

chill

which

whale

Will

Did you write your letters from left to right? 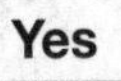 Yes 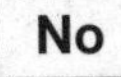 No

Home Activity Your child practiced writing words with *Ww*, *wh* and *ch*. Have your child choose three words from above and write the words one more time.

Name ________________________________

Look at the map.

1. **Circle** the school.

2. **Draw** a box around the bank.

3. **Underline** the park.

4. **Write** the number of houses on block C.

____

5. **Write** the number of cars on the map.

____

Home Activity Your child learned to use a map to gather information. Point out maps as you see them and challenge your child to point out places featured on the maps.

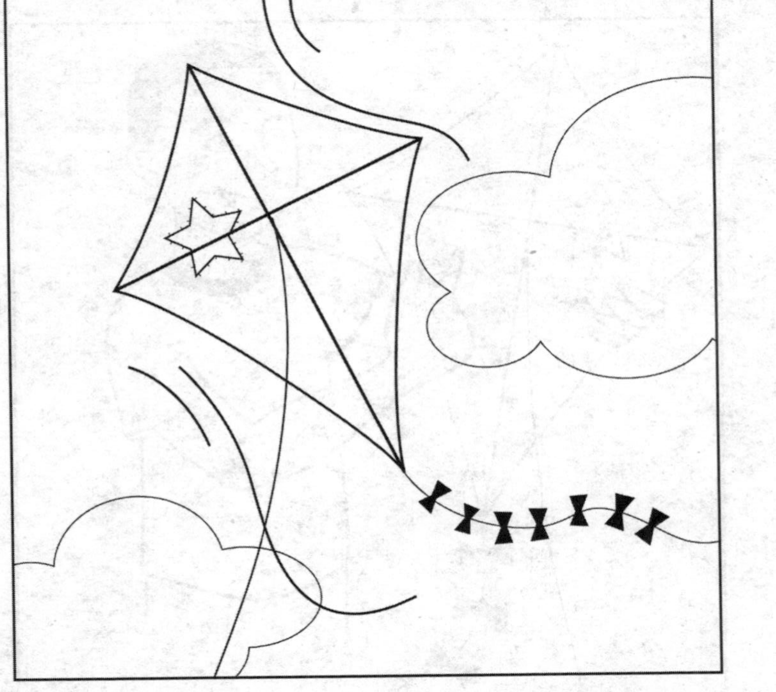

Ralph lets the kite go up.

It dips and dives.

"I like this kite!" Ralph tells Ann.

Decodable Story *The White Kite*
Target Skill Long *i: i_e*, Consonant Digraphs *wh, ch, tch, ph*

Name ____________________

The White Kite

Long *i: i_e*		Consonant Digraphs *wh, ch, tch, ph*	High-Frequency Words
kite	nice	white	the
quite	line	checks	I
mile	dives	patch	a
smiles	like	Ralph	is
			go

Ralph calls Ann on the cell.

"I made a white kite!"

Ann checks the kite.

"It is small. But it is quite nice!"

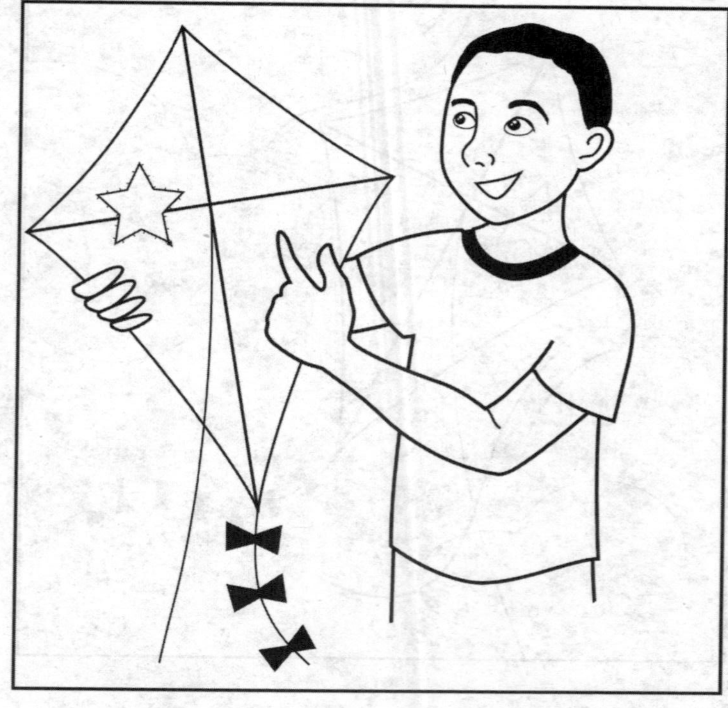

Ralph smiles.

"The kite has a patch and a line.

It will go up a mile!"

Name ______________________

Words with Long *i*

Spelling Words				
like	ride	smile	time	white
bike	dime	hide	ice	kite

High-Frequency Words
who
work

Choose a word to finish the sentence.
Fill in the circle. **Write** the word.

1. The glass is full of ○ **ice** ○ **bike** ○ **dime**. ______
2. Be at ○ **who** ○ **smile** ○ **work** on time. ______
3. Look at the ○ **kite** ○ **hide** ○ **like**! ______
4. It costs a ○ **white** ○ **dime** ○ **ice**. ______
5. ○ **Work** ○ **Bike** ○ **Who** is coming? ______
6. You can ride my ○ **bike** ○ **ice** ○ **time**. ______

Read the word. **Write** the list word that means the opposite.

7. black ______
8. show ______
9. walk ______
10. frown ______

Home Activity Your child used spelling words and high-frequency words to complete sentences. Have your child identify and write as many spelling words as possible to finish this sentence: *This is my* ______.

Name ______________________________

Special Titles

Tell about people who work in your community.
Use words from the box or your own words.
Use titles and names.

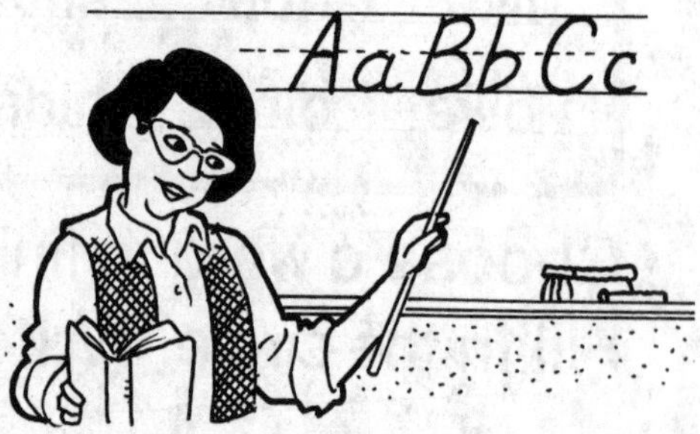

Aa Bb Cc

teacher	mail carrier	police officer
doctor	vet	librarian

Say other sentences about the people you chose.

Home Activity Your child learned how to use special titles in writing. Write these titles and names on paper: *mr jones, ms gold, dr novak*. Have your child explain what is wrong and write the titles and names correctly.

Name ___________________________

Words with Long *i*

Write the list words in the puzzle.

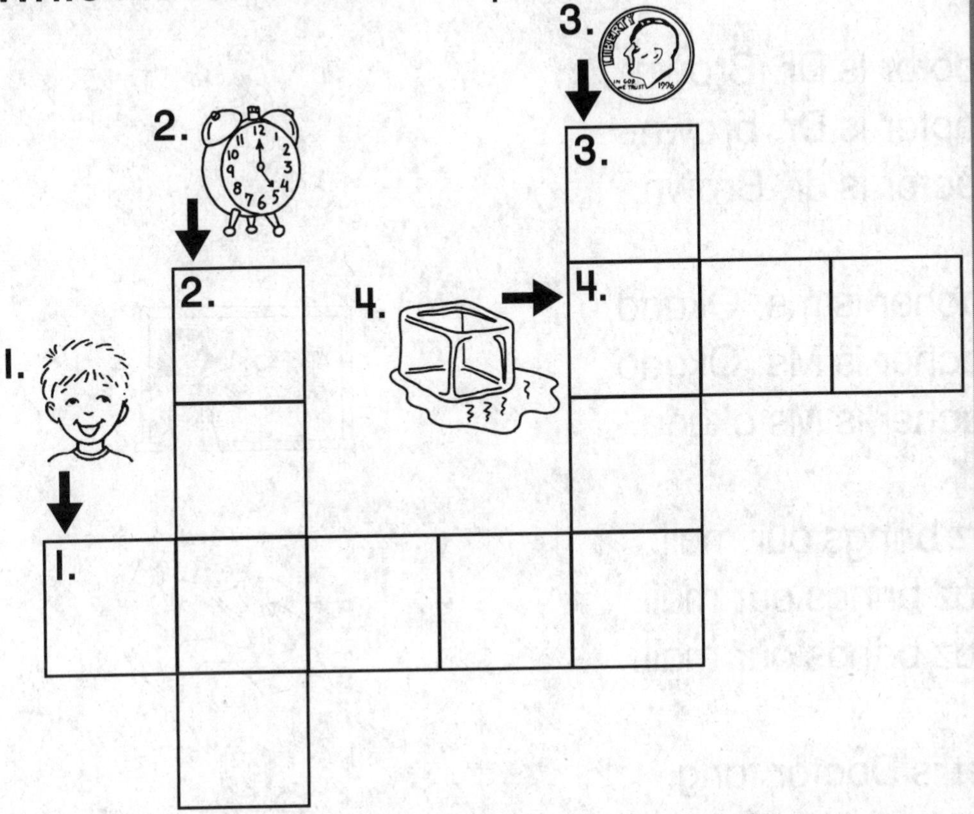

3.

2.

4.

1.

Spelling Words
like
ride
smile
time
white
bike
dime
hide
ice
kite

Draw lines to connect the words that rhyme. **Write** each word.

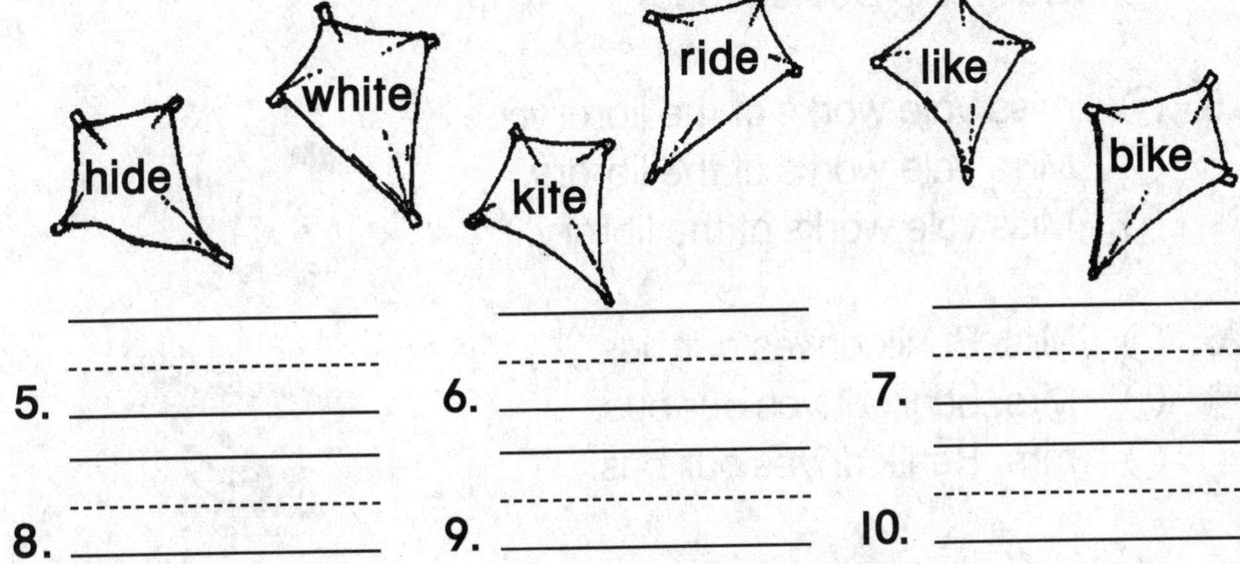

5. ___________ 6. ___________ 7. ___________

8. ___________ 9. ___________ 10. ___________

Home Activity Your child has been learning to spell words with long *i*. Draw large kite shapes. Have your child write long *i* words on them.

Name ______________________________

Special Titles

Mark the sentence that uses the title and name correctly.

1. ◯ Our doctor is Dr. Brown.
   ◯ Our doctor is Dr. brown.
   ◯ Our doctor is dr. Brown.

2. ◯ My teacher is ms. Okada.
   ◯ My teacher is Ms. Okada.
   ◯ My teacher is Ms okada.

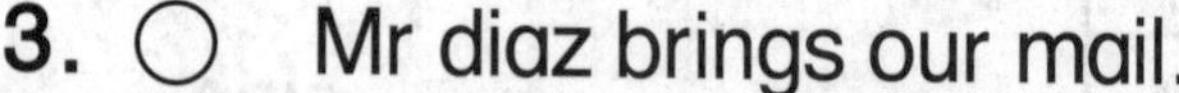

3. ◯ Mr diaz brings our mail.
   ◯ mr. Diaz brings our mail.
   ◯ Mr. Diaz brings our mail.

4. ◯ Our vet is Doctor tang.
   ◯ Our vet is doctor Tang.
   ◯ Our vet is Doctor Tang.

5. ◯ miss Vale works at the library.
   ◯ Miss Vale works at the library.
   ◯ Miss vale works at the library.

6. ◯ Mrs. Benik drives our bus.
   ◯ Mrs. benik drives our bus.
   ◯ mrs. Benik drives our bus.

Home Activity Your child prepared for taking tests on special titles. Together look through a newspaper or magazine. Have your child find and circle as many special titles as he or she can.

Name ______________________________

Write the letters to make a word in each sentence. Then read the story.

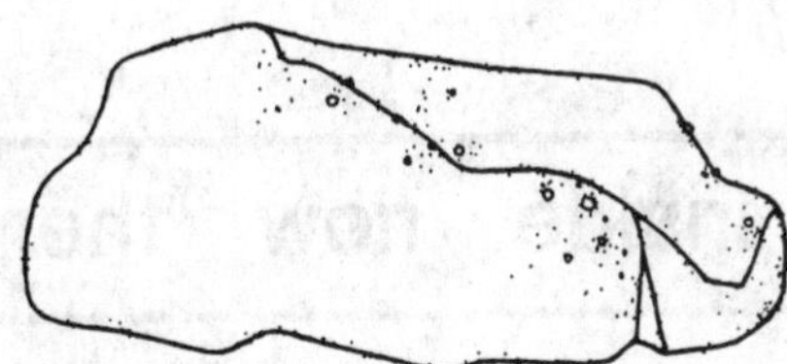

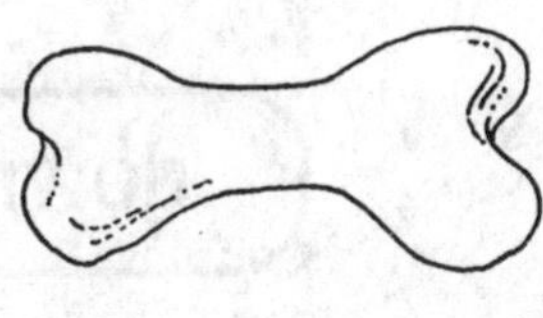

R ___ **s** ___ wanted to make soup. She didn't have a **b** ___ **n** ___ . So she put a big **st** ___ **n** ___ in the pot. She didn't have a **st** ___ **v** ___ . She made a fire outside her **h** ___ **m** ___. She hung the pot on a **p** ___ **l** ___ .

"I **h** ___ **p** ___ this will be good," Rose said.

Circle the words that have the same long o sound as  .

clove	bond	not	poke	stop	spoke
drop	lost	vote	son	color	told

Home Activity Your child practiced reading words with the long *o* sound spelled *o – e,* such as *rope*. Work with your child to write a list of words that rhyme with *bone*. Repeat with *joke*.

Name ________________________________

Read the words in the box.
Pick a word from the box to match each clue.
Write it on the line.

down	**inside**	**now**	**there**	**together**

1. not up

____

2. not here

____

3. not outside

____

4. not then

____

5. not one here and not one there

____

Home Activity Your child identified and read the words *down, inside, now, there,* and *together*. Read one word aloud. Have your child point to it and use it in a sentence. Repeat with the other words.

Name ______________________________

Write a number in each box to show the right order.
Then **act out** the story.

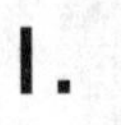
1. 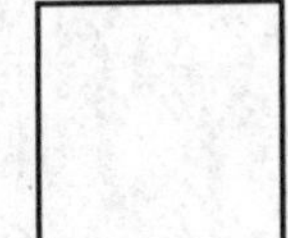

2. 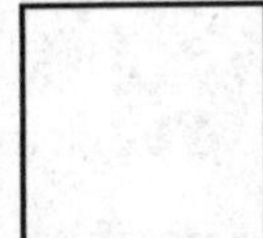

3. 

Look at each picture.
Draw what will happen next.

4. 

5. 

Home Activity Your child learned about the order in which things happen in a story. After you read a story with your child, have your child tell you what happened first, next, and last in the story.

Name ______________________________

Writing • Poem

Time for Spines

It is late Monday night.
I go out for a bite.
It is dark out there.
But I am not scared.
Down comes the owl.
I will just bow
And stick out my spines
Because I am a porcupine.

Key Features of a Poem

- It can describe an event.
- The lines may rhyme.

Name ______________________

Read each sentence.
Write the contraction for the underlined words.

I do not think I can do this. I **don't** think I can do this.

---

1. "I **can not** make a nest," said the little bird. ____________

2. "I will need help with the sticks," said the little bird. ____________

3. "I do not think I can help," said the frog. ____________

4. "You will need a big bird to help you," said the frog. ____________

5. "I am a big bird! I can help," said the big bird. ____________

Home Activity Your child combined words to form contractions ending with *n't, 'm,* and *'ll.* Say a contraction aloud. Have your child tell you the two words that were combined to make the contraction. Repeat with the other contractions.

Name ______________________

Words with Long *o*

Spelling Words				
home	hope	rose	woke	those
bone	hose	joke	rode	stone

Write a list word for each clue.

1. You use it to water the grass. ______
2. You live here. ______
3. It is a part of your body. ______
4. It makes you laugh. ______
5. It grows in a garden. ______
6. It hurts when it gets in your shoe. ______

Write the word that rhymes with each word.

those
woke
hope
rode

7. smoke ______
8. rope ______
9. nose ______
10. code ______

Home Activity Your child wrote words with long *o*. Work together to think of other long *o* words. Take turns making up clues for the new words and guessing them.

Name ______________________________

Proper Nouns: Days, Months, Holidays

Days of the week begin with capital letters.

Sunday Wednesday Saturday

Months of the year begin with capital letters.

February May October

Holidays begin with capital letters.

Fourth of July Memorial Day

Write the day, month, or holiday correctly on the line.

1. We learn about dinosaurs on monday.

____

2. On thursday a man tells us about dinosaurs.

____

3. In november we put on a play about dinosaurs.

____

4. The play tells about dinosaurs at thanksgiving!

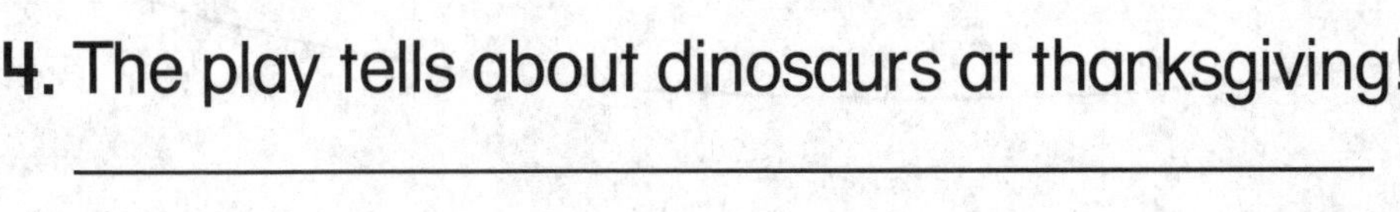

Home Activity Your child learned about days, months, and holidays. Say the names of a day, a month, and a holiday and help your child write each name. Be sure each name begins with a capital letter.

Name ___________________________

Sequence

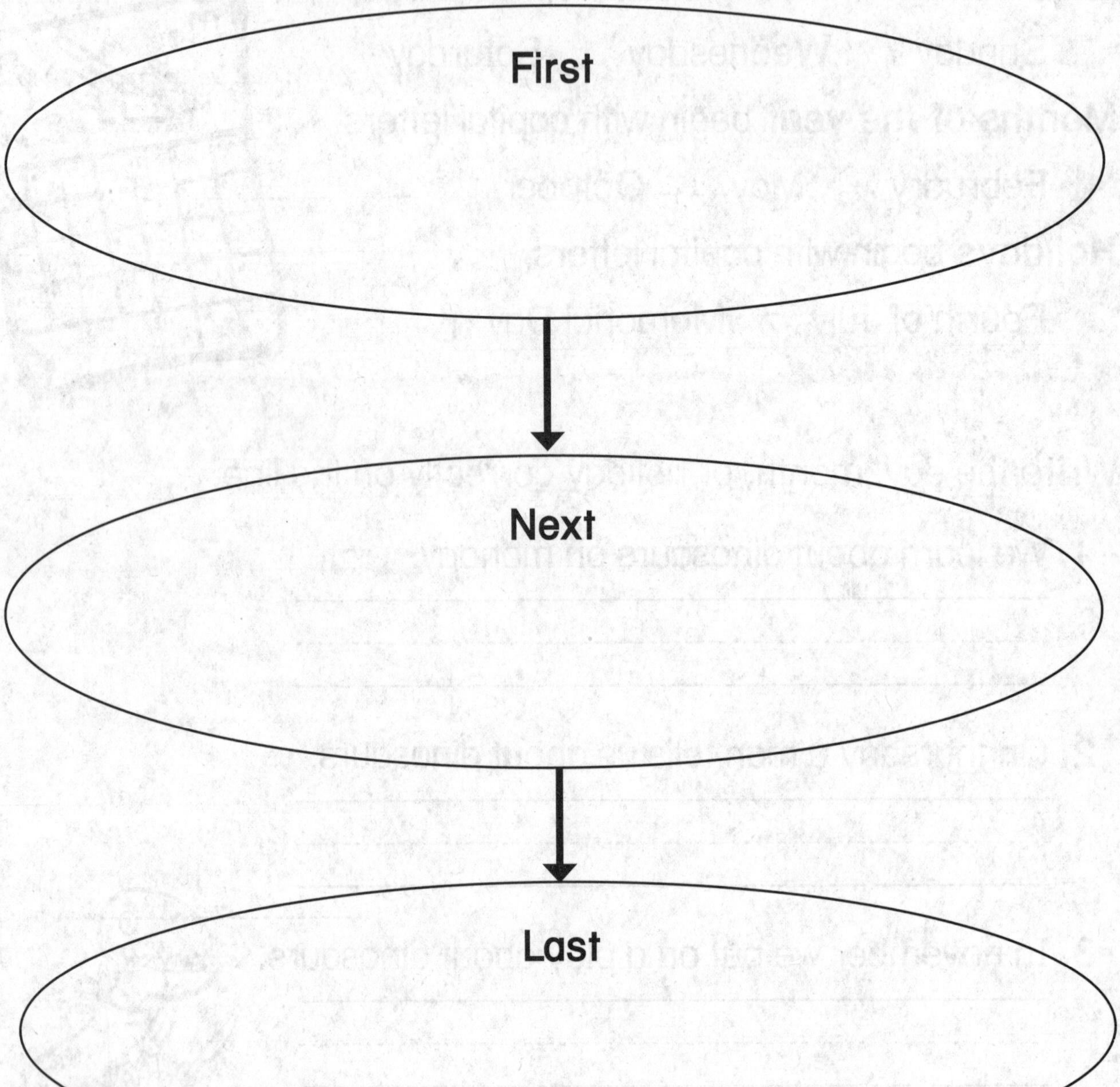

First

Next

Last

Home Activity Your child is writing a poem about an animal. Have your child describe an animal.

Name ______________________

T t

’t

An apostrophe takes the place of missing letters.

Copy the words. Slant all of your letters the same way.

isn’t ______________ you’ll ______________

can’t ______________ we’ll ______________

Tom ______________ they’ll ______________

don’t ______________ I’ll ______________

didn’t ______________ wasn’t ______________

I’m ______________ won’t ______________

Did you slant all of your letters the same way? Yes No

Home Activity Your child practiced writing words with *Tt* and contractions with *’t*. Say the following words and have your child look at the list and write the contraction for them: *can not (can’t); they will (they’ll); is not (isn’t); I am (I’m); can not (can’t).*

Name ______________________________

Read the newsletter. **Answer** the questions.

The Neighborhood

March

Kids Help!

by Pam Ride

Jill and Sam went for a walk. Mrs. Bell's pet cat was out! The kids could see the cat. They ran to it. They got the cat. Mrs. Bell said, "You are good kids!" She gave them a hug.

1. What is the name of the newsletter?

2. What is the story about?

3. What is the story about?

Home Activity Your child learned to use a newsletter to get information. As you look at newsletters, newspapers, or magazines, point out the different kinds of type, such as bold or italic text. Discuss why the text looks different from the surrounding type. Then have your child act out a piece of information they learned from researching newsletters, newspapers, or magazines.

I'm a ball that isn't in a game.

You'll see shapes and lines on me.

What am I? (I'm a globe!)

Decodable Story *What Am I?*
Target Skill Long *o: o_e*, Contractions *n't, 'm, 'll*

Name ____________________

What Am I?

Long *o: o_e*		Contractions *n't, 'm, 'll*		High-Frequency Words	
nose	rope	I'm	can't	a	what
hole	pole	you'll	isn't	I	me
bone	globe			see	

I'm on a face.

I can't see, but I can smell.

What am I? (I'm a nose!)

You'll put me in the trash.

A pup puts me in a hole.

What am I? (I'm a bone!)

I'm tall and thin.

You'll see a flag and rope on me.

What am I? (I'm a pole!)

Name ______________________

Words with Long *o*

Spelling Words				
home	hope	rose	woke	those
bone	hose	joke	rode	stone

High-Frequency Words
there
together

Read about Fluff and Puff. **Write** the missing list words.

Fluff and Puff live by a big **1.** ____________. One day Pup dug for a **2.** ____________. Pup **3.** ____________ Fluff and Puff. He entered their **4.** ____________. Now **5.** ____________ bunnies needed a new home. They had little **6.** ____________. Puff **7.** ____________ on Fluff's back as they looked. Then Pup poked up over a **8.** ____________ bush. Pup pointed over **9.** ____________. "I found a perfect home. You can live by the bush **10.** ____________."

Home Activity Your child used spelling words and high-frequency words in a story. Ask your child to write his or her own story, using some of the words.

Name ______________________________

Proper Nouns: Days, Months, Holidays

Tell about a picnic, a fair, or a party.
Use the name of a month or holiday from the box.

February	October	Valentine's Day
May	November	Fourth of July
July	December	Thanksgiving

Home Activity Your child learned how to use days, months, and holidays in writing. Write these names on paper: *tuesday, april, memorial day.* Have your child explain what is wrong and write the names correctly.

Name ______________________________

Words with Long *o*

Write the words.

1. ______________ 2. ______________

3. ______________ 4. ______________

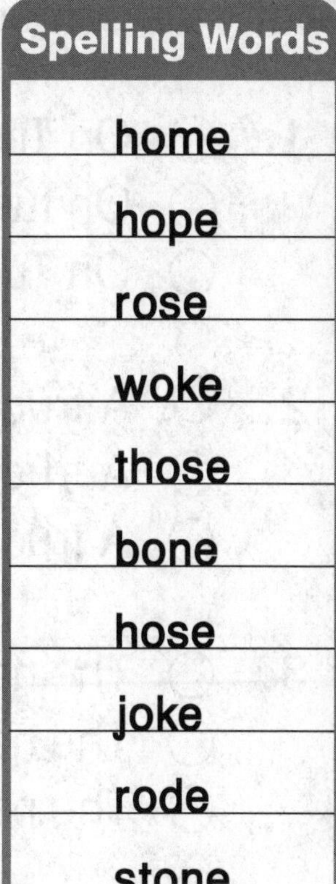

Spelling Words
home
hope
rose
woke
those
bone
hose
joke
rode
stone

Write the missing letters. **Write** the list word.

5. h __ p __ ______________
6. th __ __ __ ______________
7. __ __ d __ ______________
8. j __ __ __ ______________
9. h __ s __ ______________
10. w __ k __ ______________

hope
woke
those
joke
rode
hose

Home Activity Your child has been learning to spell words with long *o*. Have your child think of and write words that rhyme with *nose* or *cone*.

Name ______________________________

Proper Nouns: Days, Months, Holidays

Mark the sentence that uses the day, month, or holiday correctly.

1. ◯ On Tuesday we collect cans.
   ◯ On tuesday we collect cans.
   ◯ On TuesDay we collect cans.

2. ◯ A truck picks up the cans on friday.
   ◯ A truck picks up the cans on Friday.
   ◯ A truck picks up the cans on FRiday.

3. ◯ The neighbors plant a garden in june.
   ◯ The neighbors plant a garden in JUne.
   ◯ The neighbors plant a garden in June.

4. ◯ In august they pick the vegetables.
   ◯ In August they pick the vegetables.
   ◯ In AuGust they pick the vegetables.

5. ◯ On memorial Day our town has a parade.
   ◯ On Memorial day our town has a parade.
   ◯ On Memorial Day our town has a parade.

6. ◯ We watch fireworks on the Fourth of July.
   ◯ We watch fireworks on the fourth of July.
   ◯ We watch fireworks on the Fourth of july.

Home Activity Your child prepared for taking tests on days, months, and holidays. Together look through a newspaper or magazine. Have your child find and circle any days, months, and holidays that he or she finds.

Name ______________________________

Circle the word for each picture.

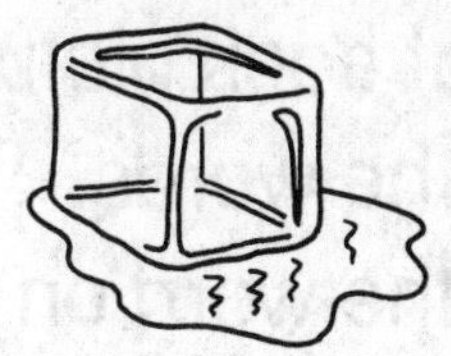

1.

mule mile

2.

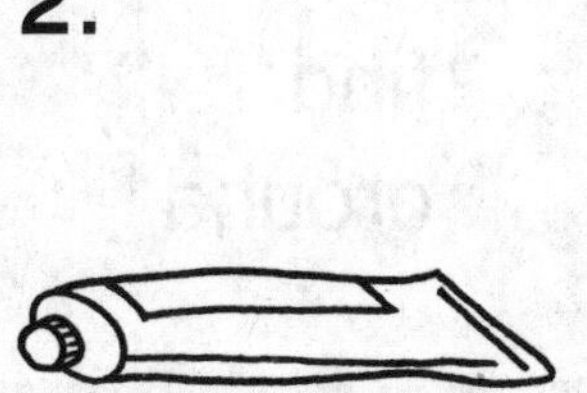

tub tube

3.

cub cube

4.

Pete pet

5.

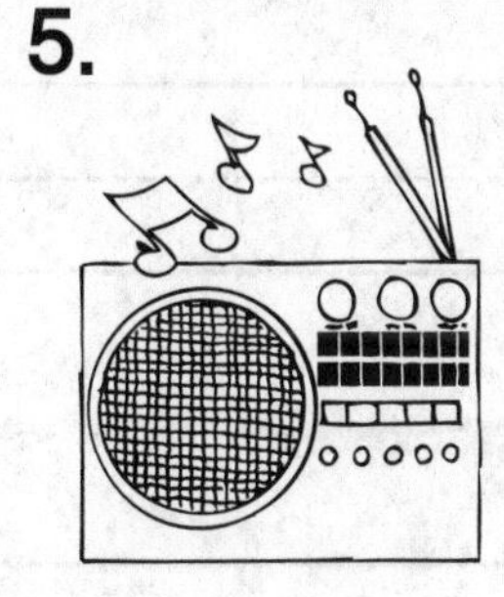

tug tune

6.

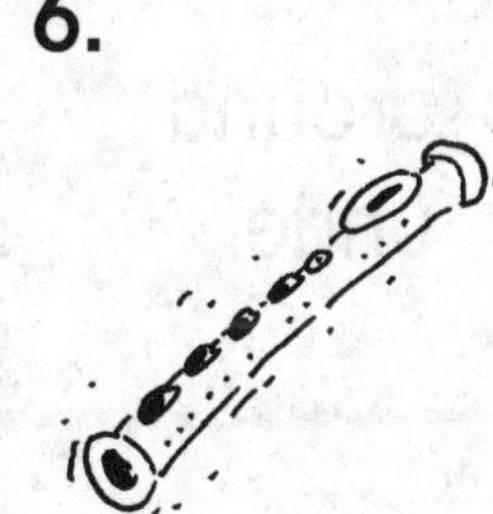

flat flute

7.

tub tube

8.

hug huge

Find the word that has the same **long u** sound as .
Mark the ⬭ to show your answer.

9. ⬭ rut
⬭ rid
⬭ rule

10. ⬭ cut
⬭ cute
⬭ cup

Home Activity Your child practiced reading words with the long *u* sound spelled *u – e*, such as *cube*. Write words from this page in a list. Say each word. Have your child point to the word and read it.

Name ______________________

Look at each picture.
Read the words.
Write the word on the line that best fits the picture.

1. 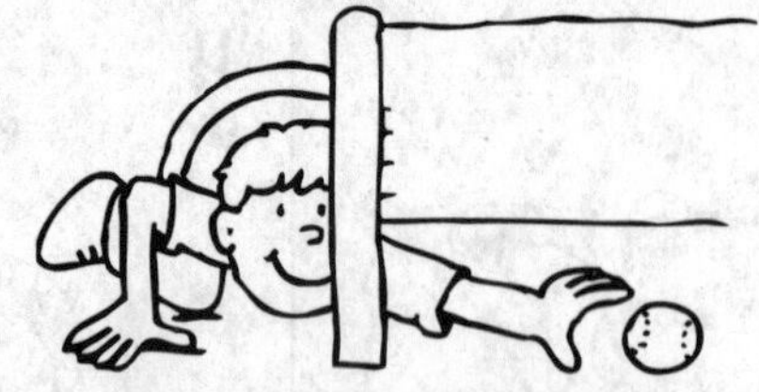
find
around
____

2. 
water
food
____

3. 
around
under
____

4. 
grow
find
____

5. 
water
under
____

6. 
food
water
____

School + Home **Home Activity** Your child identified and read the words *around*, *find*, *food*, *grow*, *under*, and *water*. Make up clues for the words on this page. Ask your child to identify the words. Challenge your child to think of some clues too.

Name ______________________________

Look at this book cover.
Circle or **write** your answers.

1. Who wrote this book? ______________________

2. What do you think this book will be about?

real dogs   silly dogs   a real trip

3. What do you think this book will be like?

funny   sad   full of facts

4. Why do you think the writer wrote this book?

to tell facts about dogs   to make you sad   to make you laugh

5. Would you want to read this book? Why or why not?

____

____

Home Activity Your child learned to tell what a book might be about by figuring out why it was written. As you read various materials with your child, have your child tell you what he or she thinks each is about and why the author wrote it.

Name ______________________________

Writing • Description

Oh Deer!

Deer live in woods and fields. They eat all kinds of plants. Deer love apples. They eat apples that fall on the ground. In the winter they eat leaves. They nibble on branches. They use their paws to dig snow. Then they eat the nuts and plants they find. I like watching deer. They are beautiful.

Key Features of a Description

- It tells about real people or things.
- It uses descriptive words.

Name ______________________________

Pick a word from the box to finish each sentence.
Add -ed to each word. **Write** it on the line.

call	**walk**	**sniff**	**jump**	**rest**

1. They ________________ rope together.

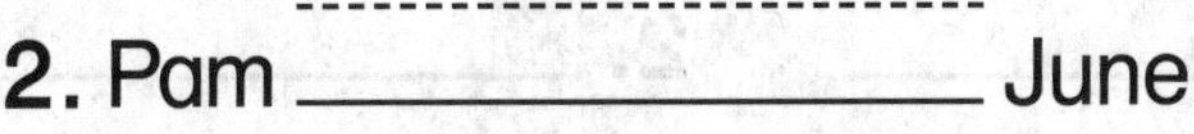

2. Pam ________________ June.

3. They ________________ to the park.

4. They ________________ in the shade.

5. They ________________ the flowers.

Home Activity Your child practiced writing words ending in *-ed*, such as *patched*. Ask your child to read each word and use it in a sentence.

Name ______________________________

Words with Long *u*

Spelling Words				
huge	June	rule	tube	use
cube	cute	flute	rude	mule

Write the list word that names the picture.
Write a list word that rhymes.

1. ____________ 2. ____________

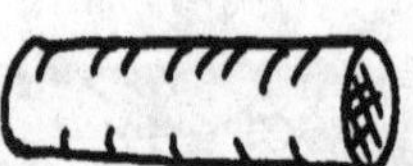

3. ____________ 4. ____________

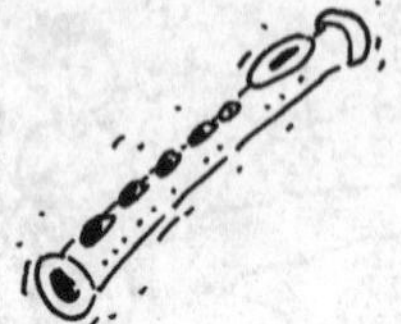

5. ____________ 6. ____________

Read the meaning. **Write** the list word.

June
use
rude
huge

7. very big ____________
8. not polite ____________
9. a month ____________
10. to work with something ____________

Home Activity Your child spelled words with the long *u* vowel sound. Ask your child to name the two letters that occur in every word. (*u* and *e*)

Name ______________________________

Singular and Plural Nouns

Many nouns add **-s** to mean more than one.

tree 

trees 

Draw a line from the noun to the correct picture.
Say a sentence for each plural noun.

1. bug bugs	2. rocks rock
3. plants plant	4. log logs

Home Activity Your child learned about plural nouns. Write the words *desk, lamp, chair, table,* and *cup*. Have your child add -s to each word to make it mean more than one.

Name ___________________________

Idea Web

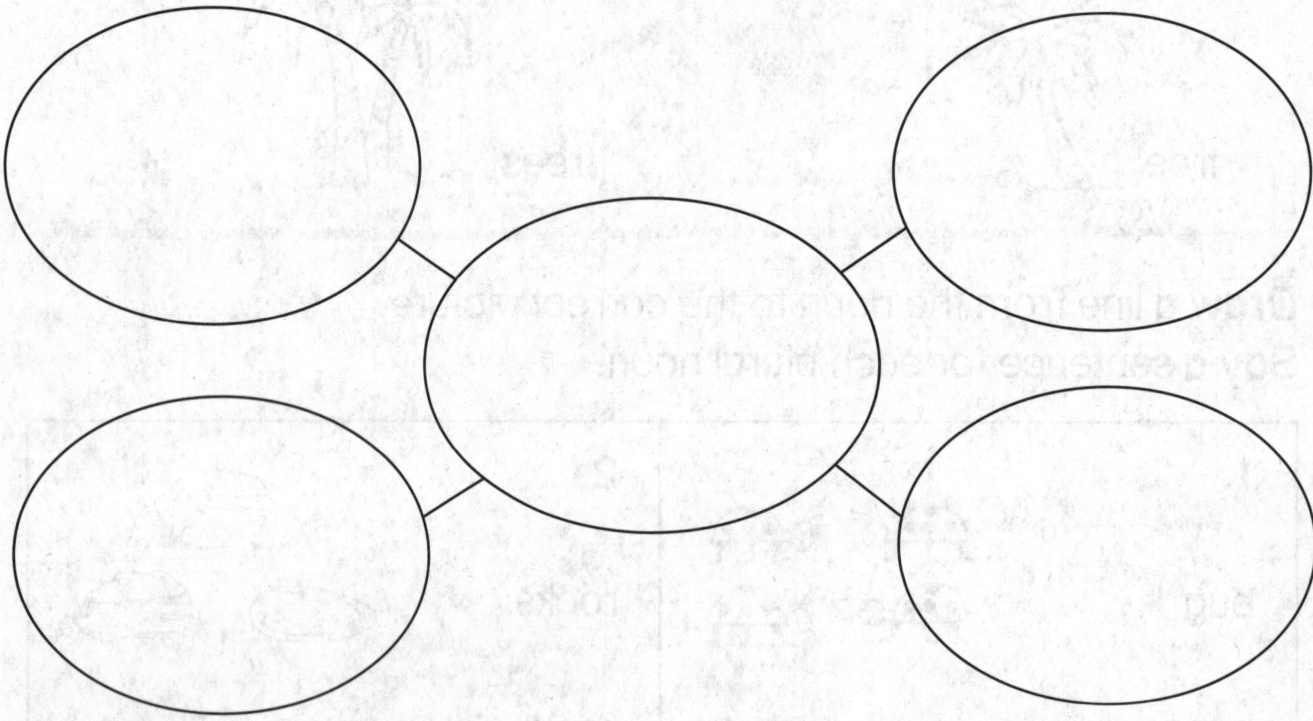

School + Home **Home Activity** Your child is learning how to describe animals in writing. Ask your child to describe things that one kind of animal does.

Name ______________________

D d

Copy the words. Write the letters the correct size.

Duke	____________	Dan	____________
dusted	____________	use	____________
hushed	____________	these	____________
Deke	____________	rushed	____________
theme	____________	rocked	____________
eve	____________	dashed	____________

Did you write all of your letters the correct size? Yes No

Home Activity Your child practiced writing words with *Dd*, long *u*, long *e*, and words that end in *-ed*. Help your child find, read, and copy words from a favorite book.

Name ______________________

Read each index. **Answer** the questions.

1. What can you read about on page 10? ______________

2. What page can you find out about vines? ______________

Look at the words. **Place** them in the ABC order.

3. Where does **penguin** go?

fox ______________ lion   lion ______________ zebra

4. Where does **cactus** go?

blossom ______________ flower   flower ______________ tree

5. Where does **bird** go?

lion ______________ zebra   ant ______________ fox

Home Activity Your child learned how to use alphabetical order to find information in an index. Ask your child to help you prepare a food-shopping list. Have your child alphabetize the list.

In June the gate broke.

Duke handed Pete a wire.

Duke helped fix the gate!

Decodable Story *Duke the Mule*
Target Skill Long *u*, Long *e*; Inflected Ending *-ed*

Name ______________________

Duke the Mule

Long u/ Long e		Inflected Ending *-ed*		High-Frequency Words	
Pete	mule	yelled	jumped	a	he
cute	cube	handed	helped	is	was
Duke				the	now

Pete has a cute pet.

His pet is Duke the mule.

Duke had a trick when he was small.

Pete yelled "Jump!"

Then Duke jumped past the cube.

Now Duke is big.

He walks places. He takes naps.

But Duke still has tricks.

Name ______________________

Words with Long *u*

Pick the word that finishes each sentence.
Write it on the line.

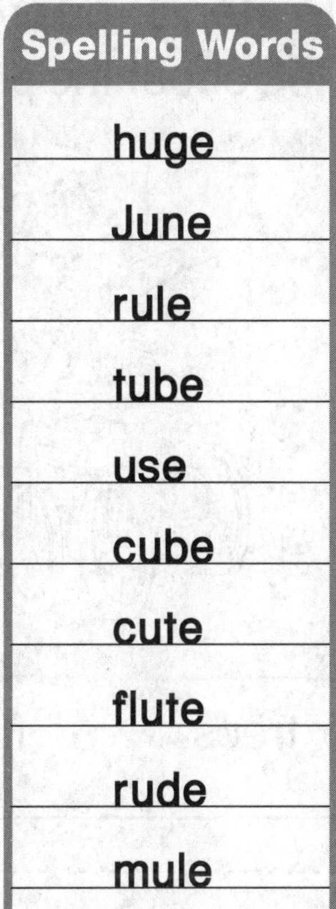

1. Put an ice ______________ in the glass.
2. I got to pet the ______________ .
3. You can ______________ my pen.
4. School is out in ______________ .
5. What a ______________ kitten!
6. Is there a ______________ about that?
7. This apple is ______________ !
8. Let's roll the ball down the ______________ .
9. Fill the glass with ______________ .
10. The bug is ______________ the rock.

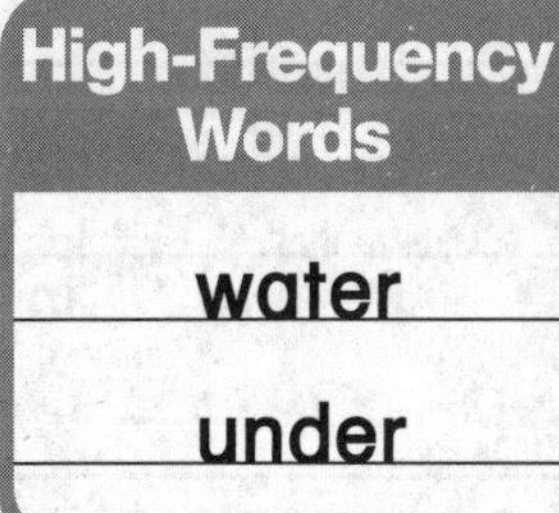

Home Activity Your child completed sentences by spelling words with long *u*. Write ___*u*___*e* and have your child fill in the blanks to spell a word.

Name ___________________________

Singular and Plural Nouns

Pretend you are in this park.
Tell about the plants and animals you see.

trees flowers squirrels birds rabbits

Home Activity Your child learned how to use plural nouns in writing. Read a story together. Ask your child to point out any words he or she sees that mean more than one.

Name ____________________

Words with Long *u*

Spelling Words				
huge	June	rule	tube	use
cube	cute	flute	rude	mule

Read the clue. **Write** the list word in the puzzle.

Across

3. after May

5. a pipe

6. animal

Down

1. a law

2. pretty

4. square box

Circle the word that is spelled correctly.

7. flute flut

8. rude rood

9. huje huge

10. use yuse

School + Home

Home Activity Your child has been learning to spell words with long *u*. Take turns with your child naming and spelling the words.

Name ______________________________

Singular and Plural Nouns

Mark the word that shows more than one.

1. Look at the two frogs.
   - ◯ the
   - ◯ Look
   - ◯ frogs

2. The bird eats the bugs.
   - ◯ bugs
   - ◯ eat
   - ◯ bird

3. The tree has three holes.
   - ◯ has
   - ◯ holes
   - ◯ tree

4. A bear is by the rocks.
   - ◯ bear
   - ◯ rocks
   - ◯ by

5. The squirrel hides the nuts.
   - ◯ nuts
   - ◯ squirrel
   - ◯ The

Home Activity Your child prepared for taking tests on plural nouns. Together look through a newspaper or magazine. Have your child find and circle as many plural nouns as he or she can.

Name ______________________________

Help the bee get home.
Read each word.
Draw a line that goes past only the **long e** words.
Write the **long e** words on the lines.

feet
bed
beet
wet
sheet
we
net
peel
jeep
he
me
jet
Home

1. ____________
2. ____________
3. ____________
4. ____________
5. ____________
6. ____________
7. ____________
8. ____________

Home Activity Your child practiced reading and writing words with the long e sound spelled e and ee, as in *he* and *jeep*. Have your child make a list of words that rhyme with *seed*. Repeat with *jeep*.

Name ______________________________

Read the words in the box.
Pick a word from the box to match each clue.
Write the words in the puzzles.

also	family	new	other	some	their

1. not a lot
2. too

3.

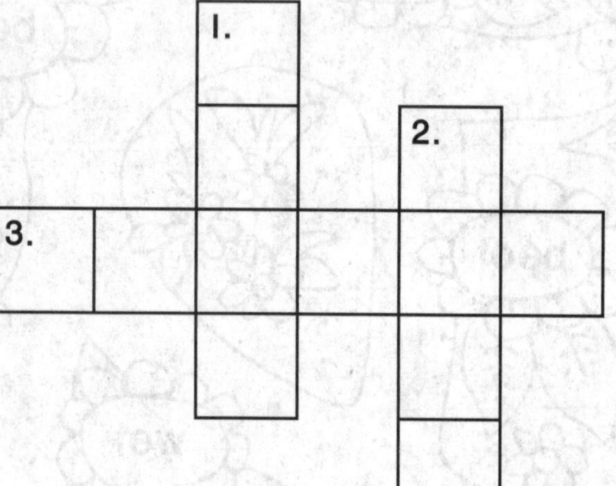

4. not old

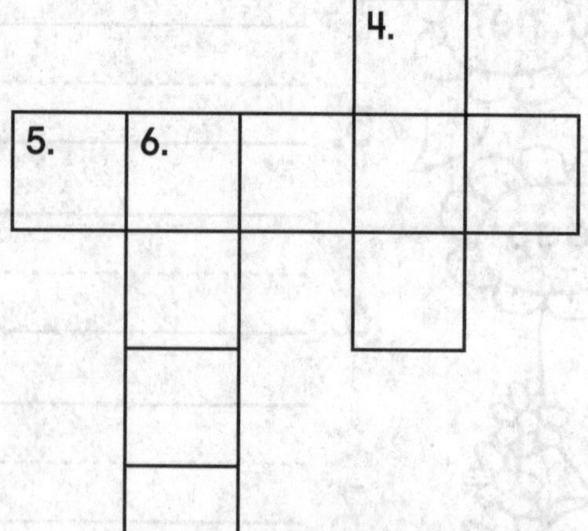

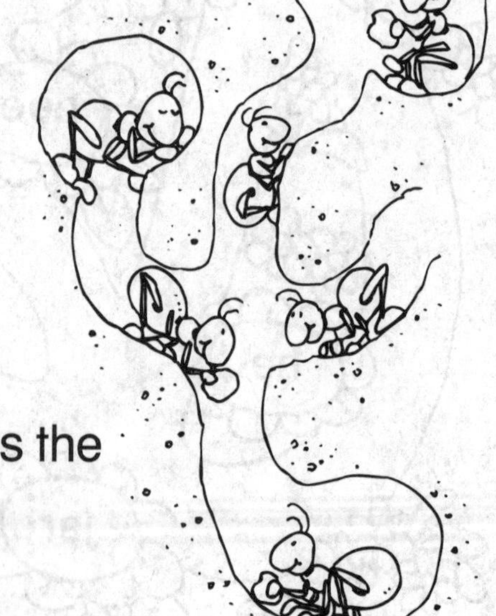

5. It's not this one. It's the ______ one.
6. It's not my food. It's ______ food.

Home Activity Your child identified and read the words *also, family, new, other, some,* and *their*. Help your child to make up a story or poem using these words. Work together to write the story or poem and read it to other family members.

Name ______________________________

Look at both pictures.
Write sentences to tell how the pictures are the same and different.

Dee

Same

1. ______________________________

2. ______________________________

Lee

Different

3. ______________________________

4. ______________________________

5. ______________________________

Home Activity Your child used pictures to tell how two things are alike and different. Point out two objects or two pictures to your child. Encourage your child to tell you how they are the same and how they are different.

Name ___________________________

Writing Prompt: Write a paragraph about how you help your community.

I like to help in my community. I help at the park. On Saturday, I help grown-ups pick up. I help plant flowers in the spring. A bunch of us dress up the park for July 4th. Helping is fun!

Name ______________________________

Circle the word for each picture.

kitten

1.	2.	3.	4.
	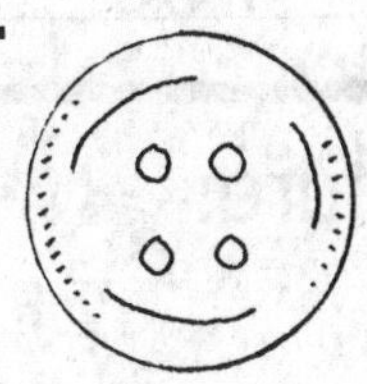		
ramp rabbit	button brake	dinner dent	base basket
5.	6.	7.	8.
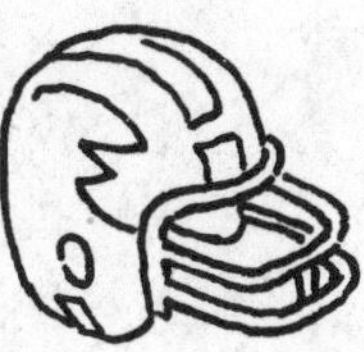			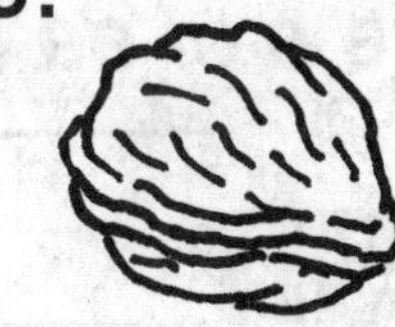
helmet hello	napkin name	mask muffin	wall walnut

Draw a picture for each word.

9. mitten

10. picnic

Home Activity Your child read words with two syllables that have two consonants in the middle, as in *kitten*. Have your child choose five words from the page and use each word in a sentence.

Name ________________________

Words with Long *e*

Spelling Words				
be	feet	he	see	we
green	me	she	tree	week

Write the list word that names the picture.

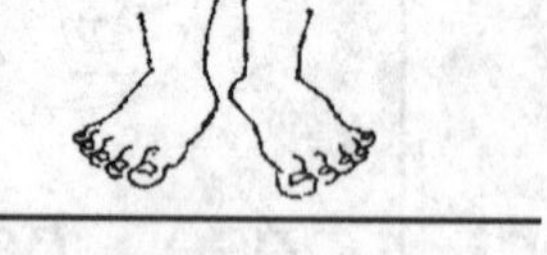

1. ____________ 2. ____________

Write *e* or *ee* to finish the word. **Write** the word.

3. sh____ ____________

4. h____ ____________

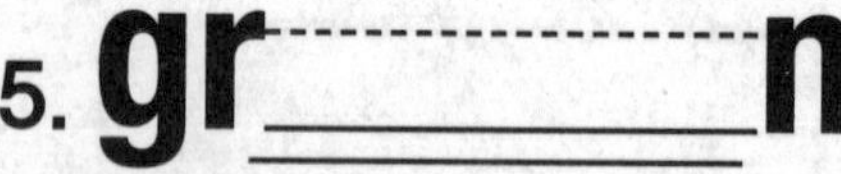

5. gr____n ____________

6. m____ ____________

7. s____ ____________

8. w____k ____________

9. w____ ____________

10. b____ ____________

Home Activity Your child spelled words with the long *e* vowel sound. Ask your child to identify two different ways the sound is spelled in the list words. (*e* and *ee*)

Name ______________________

Nouns in Sentences

A **noun** names a person, a place, an animal, or a thing. A noun can be in more than one place in a sentence.

Bees live in a **hive.**

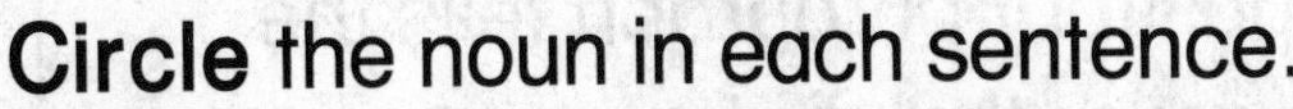

Circle the noun in each sentence.
Draw and **color** a picture for each noun.
Say a sentence about your picture.

1. The sun is warm.

2. Look at the bee.

3. Where is the flower?

Home Activity Your child learned about nouns in sentences. Read a story together. Point to a sentence and have your child point to the nouns in the sentence. Continue with other sentences.

Name ________________________________

Expository Paragraph

Top-Score Response

Focus/Ideas	A good expository paragraph tells important ideas about the main topic.
Organization	A good expository paragraph tells the ideas in an order that makes sense.
Voice	A good expository paragraph shows that you are interested in your topic.
Word Choice	A good expository paragraph uses words that describe.
Sentences	A good expository paragraph has sentences that are different lengths.
Conventions	A good expository paragraph has a noun in every sentence.

Home Activity Your child is learning to write a paragraph about a topic such as insects. Ask your child to tell what kinds of insects live together in groups.

Name ______________________

B b

Copy the words. Leave the correct space between the letters.

Bee ______________________ be ______________________

seed ______________________ see ______________________

beet ______________________ being ______________________

he ______________________ cheek ______________________

she ______________________ wheel ______________________

weep ______________________ seem ______________________

deep ______________________ beef ______________________

Did you leave the correct space between your letters? 

Home Activity Your child practiced writing words with *Bb* and the long *e* sound as in *bee*. Have your child choose the long *e* words that begin with *b* and write them again.

Name ________________________________

Answer the questions.

1. You are reading about bees this week. **Write** three other insects you would like to know more about.

______________ ______________ ______________

2. **Circle** the insect you want to know more about. **Write** two questions.

____

____

3. **Circle** where you would find more information.

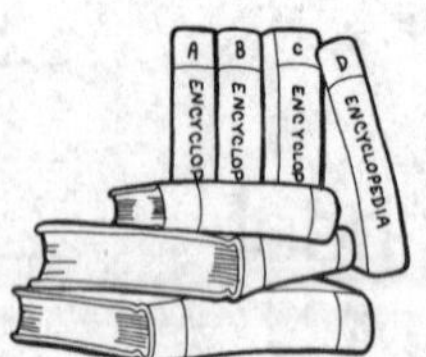

globe **encyclopedia** **computer**

Home Activity Your child learned how to identify a topic and ask questions about the topic. Have a discussion with your child about which insects he or she would like to learn about. If possible, visit your local library to find books or other sources of reference about the topic.

Lee picked beets in six weeks.

"See the basket?" asked Lee.

"We'll get beets for lunch!"

Decodable Story *Seeds*
Target Skills Long *e*, VC/CV Words

Name ______________________

Seeds

Long *e: e, ee*		VC/CV words	High-Frequency Words
he	needed	happen	to
be	weeds	problems	the
Lee	keep	insects	for
beet	weeks	basket	what
beets	see		watered
seeds	we'll		

Lee had seeds.

He needed to plant the seeds.

"What will the seeds be?" he asked.

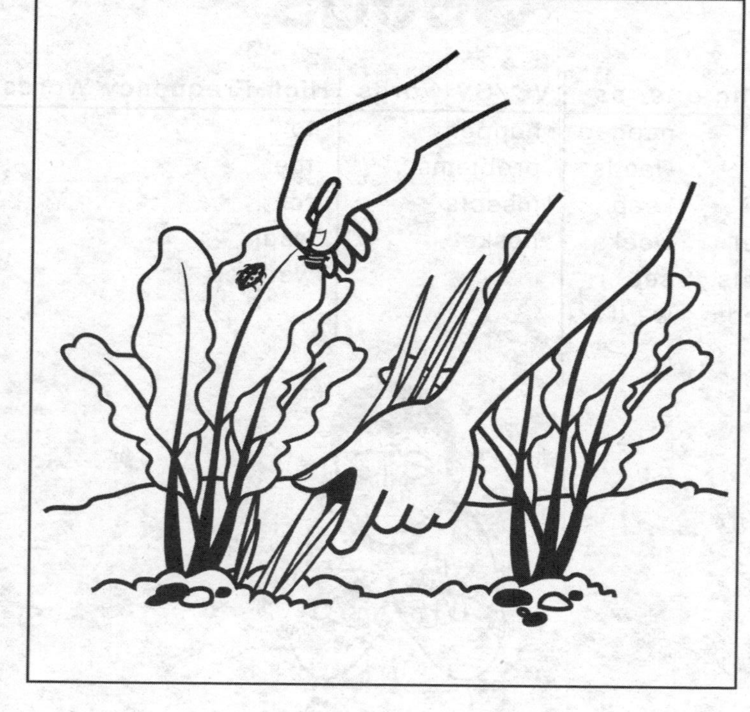

Lee had problems.

Weeds came in.

Lee had to keep insects off.

Lee dug holes for the seeds.

He watered the seeds.

"What will happen?" he asked.

Name ______________________

Words with Long e

Spelling Words				
be	feet	he	see	we
green	me	she	tree	week

High-Frequency Words
some
family

Read the story. **Write** the missing list words.

1. Dad helped ______________ build a house for the birds.

2. A bird came the next ______________ .

3. Soon ______________ laid some eggs.

4. Dad held me up to ______________ them.

5. There were three ______________ eggs.

6. I asked if ______________ could take one inside.

7. Dad said that would not ______________ wise.

8. I knew ______________ was right.

9. Soon there will be ______________ birds.

10. Now a bird ______________ lives in the tree.

Home Activity Your child used spelling words to complete a story. Ask your child to use some of the list words in a story about an event in his or her life.

Name ____________________

Nouns in Sentences

Bees are like a family.
Bees have special jobs.
Do people in your family have special jobs?
Write about the jobs.

Home Activity Your child learned how to use nouns when writing sentences. Take turns with your child telling about jobs that you do at home. Have your child identify any nouns either of you uses in your sentences.

Name ______________________________

Words with Long e

Spelling Words				
be	feet	he	see	we
green	me	she	tree	week

Read the clue. **Write** the list word in the puzzle.

Down

1. seven days
2. large plant

Across

3. the color of grass
4. what you stand on

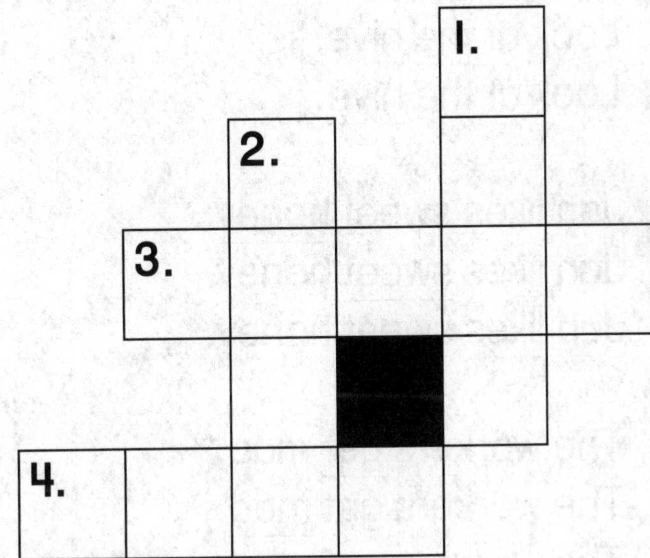

Circle the word that is spelled correctly. **Write** it.

5. b be ______________
6. we whe ______________
7. he hee ______________
8. mee me ______________
9. se see ______________
10. she shee ______________

Home Activity Your child has been learning to spell words with long *e*. Draw a tree and have your child write words with long *e* in the branches.

Name ________________________________

Nouns in Sentences

Mark the sentence that has a line under the noun.

1. ◯ The bees wake up.
   ◯ The bees wake up.
   ◯ The bees wake up.

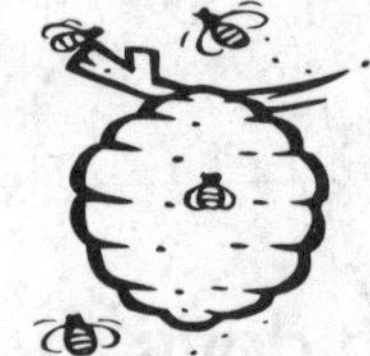

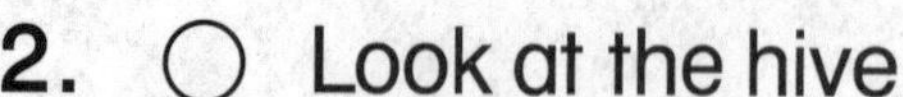

2. ◯ Look at the hive.
   ◯ Look at the hive.
   ◯ Look at the hive.

3. ◯ Jan likes sweet honey.
   ◯ Jan likes sweet honey.
   ◯ Jan likes sweet honey.

4. ◯ The workers get mad.
   ◯ The workers get mad.
   ◯ The workers get mad.

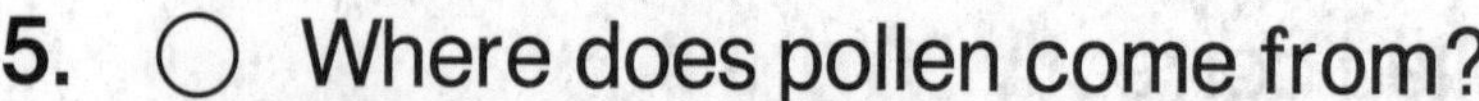

5. ◯ Where does pollen come from?
   ◯ Where does pollen come from?
   ◯ Where does pollen come from?

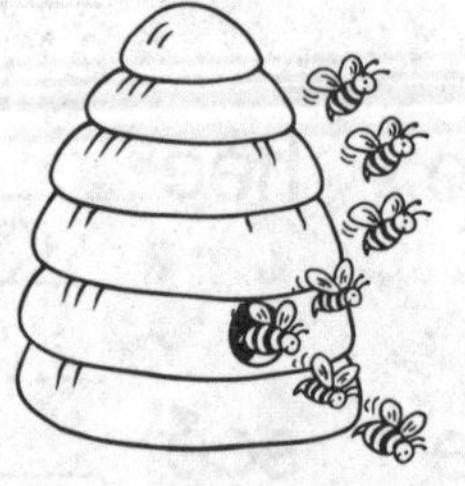

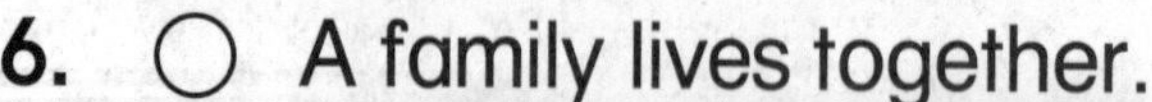

6. ◯ A family lives together.
   ◯ A family lives together.
   ◯ A family lives together.

Home Activity Your child prepared for taking tests on nouns in sentences. Together read a simple newspaper or magazine article. Have your child circle as many nouns as he or she can find.

Name ______________________________

fry baby

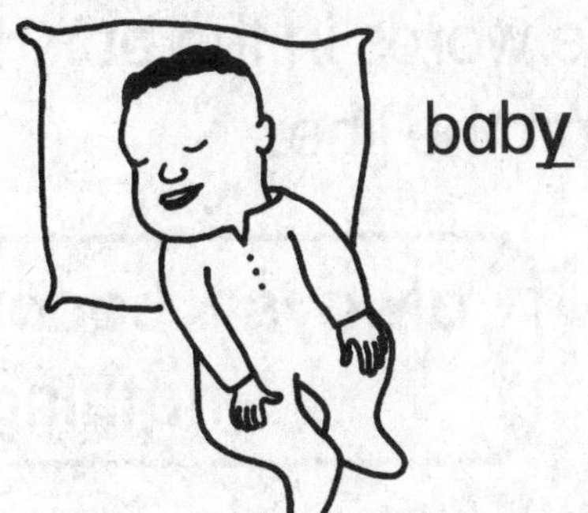

Circle the word for each picture.

1. puppy put
2. flop fly
3. muddy meet
4. bunny ball
5. crib cry
6. sit city
7. sky skate
8. had happy

Circle the word to finish each sentence. **Write** it on the line.

9. I didn't eat breakfast and I was very ______________.
hungry money

10. After a day at the beach, my bathing suit was not ______________.
dry my

Home Activity Your child practiced reading words with the vowel sounds of *y* heard in *fry* or *baby*. Work with your child to put the above answers into two word lists—one of words in which *y* represents the long e sound (*baby*) and one in which it represents the long *i* sound (*fry*).

Name ______________________

Read the words in the box. **Pick** a word to finish each sentence. **Write** it on the line.

always	becomes	day	everything
nothing	stays	things	

1. Jazzy likes to play all ______________ .

2. ______________ can stop him!

3. He gets into ______________ .

4. He ______________ makes a mess.

5. Jazzy ______________ in my room.

6. He hides ______________ under the bed.

7. He rests when he ______________ sleepy.

Home Activity This week your child identified and read the words *always, becomes, day, everything, nothing, stays,* and *things*. Use paper bag puppets to act out a scene using these new words.

Name ___________________________

Read the story. **Look** at the pictures.
Write 1, 2, 3 to show the right order.

1. It was a sunny day.
Tim saw a slide.
Tim went up the slide.
Tim came down the slide.

2. **Read** the story.
Write a sentence that tells what might happen next.
Then **draw** a picture.

Polly planted a seed.
The seed grew into a plant.

____

Home Activity Your child learned about the order in which events happen in a story. As you read stories with your child, have your child tell you what parts of the story are important and the order in which they happen.

Name ______________________________

Writing • Realistic Story

The Slide

Beth and Dave liked the park. They liked the big slide. They ran to the park. The big slide was gone!

"Wow!" Beth said. "Look at the new red slide over there!" Dave ran to it.

"It is a tube slide!" They slid down the new slide. They went zig and then zag. They liked it better than the old slide.

Key Features of a Realistic Story

- Characters and events seem real.
- The setting is like a real place.
- The story has a beginning, middle, and end.

Name ____________________

Circle a word to finish each sentence.
Write it on the line.

He Hi

1. "__________," Luke said.

Hi He

2. __________ is little.

No Nod

3. __________ one can see him.

so see

4. She is __________ big.

bed be

5. He will grow to __________ big too.

Home Activity Your child practiced reading words with the long vowel pattern heard in *me, hi,* and *go*. Work with your child to make a list of words with the long *e* sound spelled *e* and the long *o* sound spelled *o*.

Name ________________________

Words with Vowel Sounds of *y*

Spelling Words				
my	by	try	sunny	handy
fly	cry	lucky	silly	puppy

Write five list words that rhyme with **why.**

1. ____________ 2. ____________ 3. ____________

4. ____________ 5. ____________

Write the missing word.

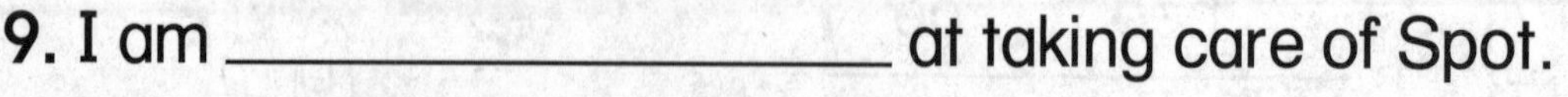

sunny silly lucky handy puppy

6. I have a ____________ named Spot.

7. Spot likes ____________ days.

8. My pup acts ____________ .

9. I am ____________ at taking care of Spot.

10. I am ____________ to have a pup.

Home Activity Your child spelled words in which the long *e* or long *i* sound is spelled *y*. Ask your child to name the letter that is in every list word (*y*) and pronounce its sound (long *e* as in *puppy* or long *i* as in *fly*).

Name ______________________________

Action Verbs

A **verb** tells what someone or something does.

The girl **jumps.**

The boy **walks.**

Underline the verb in each sentence.
Say a sentence using each verb.

1. The plant grows in the sun.

2. Benny helps Ms. Torres.

3. Mr. Gray works in the neighborhood.

4. Benny wishes for a place to play.

5. Nai Nai plays by the slide.

6. Mom walks down the hall.

Home Activity Your child learned about verbs. Read a story together. Point to a sentence and have your child point to the verb in the sentence. Continue with other sentences.

Name ____________________

Story Chart

Title ____________________

Characters

Settings

Beginning

Middle

End of Story

Home Activity Your child can plan and then write a brief story. Have him or her tell what happens in the story.

Name ______________________________

Y y

Copy the words. Write the letters from left to right.

Yancy ____________	sky ____________
baby ____________	foggy ____________
why ____________	dusty ____________
fly ____________	fry ____________
silly ____________	funny ____________
happy ____________	hilly ____________
shy ____________	cry ____________

Did you write your letters from left to right? **Yes** **No**

Home Activity Your child practiced writing words with *Yy*. Have your child copy the following sentence as neatly as he or she can. *Why is the street hilly, bumpy, and rocky?*

Name ______________________________

Jan is presenting a report about playgrounds.
Help her gather information.

builder | librarian | children

1. **Circle** who could help Jan find books about playgrounds.

2. **Put a diamond** around who could tell Jan how much it costs to build a playground.

3. **Put a box** around who could help Jan find out which playground toys are the most fun.

4. **Ask** two classmates which playground toy is their favorite. Write their answers.

______________________________ ______________________________

5. **Share** the information you gathered with your class.

Home Activity Your child learned about interviewing people as sources of information. Talk with your child about the people you rely on when you need information or answers. Ask you child to write two interview questions to ask a member of your family or community.

"Try my muffin," said Molly.

"It is fluffy and yummy."

"No," said Jody. "It is tiny!"

Decodable Story *I'll Try It!*
Target Skills Vowel Sounds of *y*, Syllable Pattern CV

Name ______________________

I'll Try It!

Vowel sounds of *y*:		Syllable Pattern CV		High-Frequency Words
my	bumpy	hi	hello	said
try	Katy	tiny	Bo	the
Jody	picky	we	no	is
funny	Molly	me		to
mushy	fluffy	be		
yucky	yummy	so		

"Hi!" said Jody.

"Hello!" said the kids.

"We got muffins at the shop."

"My muffin tastes funny.

It is so mushy," said Bo.

"Hand it to me. I'll try it!" Jody yelled.

"My muffin is yucky.

It is bumpy," said Katy.

"Don't be so picky," Jody said. "I'll try it!"

Name ______________________

Words with Vowel Sounds of *y*

Spelling Words				
my	by	try	sunny	handy
fly	cry	lucky	silly	puppy

High-Frequency Words
things
always

Fill in the circle. **Write** the word.

1. Look at ○ **fly** ○ **my** ○ **handy** bike. ____________
2. Today is a ○ **sunny** ○ **try** ○ **by** day. ____________
3. Did you ○ **silly** ○ **puppy** ○ **cry**? ____________
4. The song is ○ **sunny** ○ **silly** ○ **my**. ____________
5. She was ○ **lucky** ○ **my** ○ **fly**. ____________
6. I ○ **try** ○ **lucky** ○ **sunny** very hard. ____________
7. Bats can ○ **silly** ○ **fly** ○ **my**. ____________
8. Do you have a ○ **puppy** ○ **cry** ○ **lucky**? ____________
9. I see many ○ **sunny** ○ **fly** ○ **things**. ____________
10. We ○ **lucky** ○ **fly** ○ **always** ride the bus. ____________

Home Activity Your child wrote spelling words to complete sentences. Read a sentence from this page. Ask your child to spell the list word.

Name ______________________________

Action Verbs

Write about things you do every day.
Use action verbs from the box or your own words.
Say several sentences and identify the verb.

eat	go	read
sleep	play	talk

____

____

____

____

____

Home Activity Your child learned how to use verbs in writing. Take turns with your child telling about things that you do every day. Have your child identify any action verbs either of you uses in your sentences.

Name ______________________

Words with Vowel Sounds of *y*

Write the letter **y.** Then write the word.

Spelling Words
my
by
try
sunny
handy
fly
cry
lucky
silly
puppy

1. **fl**______ ______________
2. **pupp**______ ______________
3. **cr**______ ______________
4. **hand**______ ______________
5. **sunn**______ ______________
6. **sill**______ ______________
7. **luck**______ ______________

Circle the words that rhyme with **fly. Write** the words.

sunny try handy silly by my

8. ______________ 9. ______________ 10. ______________

Home Activity Your child has been learning to spell words in which the long *e* or long *i* sound is spelled *y*. Have your child underline list words with a long *i* sound and circle list words with a long *e* sound.

Name ___________________________

Action Verbs

Mark the sentence that has a line under the verb.

1. ◯ Benny helps Mr. Gray.
   ◯ Benny helps Mr. Gray.
   ◯ Benny helps Mr. Gray.

2. ◯ Mr. Gray lives in the neighborhood.
   ◯ Mr. Gray lives in the neighborhood.
   ◯ Mr. Gray lives in the neighborhood.

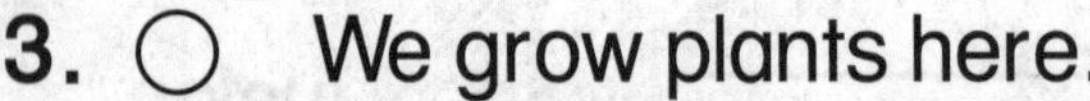

3. ◯ We grow plants here.
   ◯ We grow plants here.
   ◯ We grow plants here.

4. ◯ Nai Nai walks to the meeting.
   ◯ Nai Nai walks to the meeting.
   ◯ Nai Nai walks to the meeting.

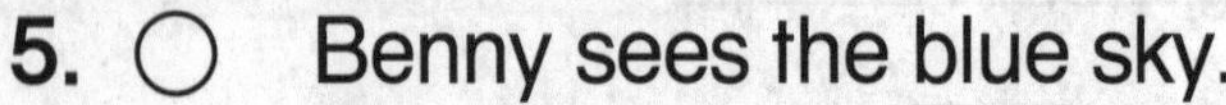

5. ◯ Benny sees the blue sky.
   ◯ Benny sees the blue sky.
   ◯ Benny sees the blue sky.

6. ◯ Ms. Torres likes this place.
   ◯ Ms. Torres likes this place.
   ◯ Ms. Torres likes this place.

Home Activity Your child prepared for taking tests on verbs. Together read a short, simple newspaper or magazine article. Have your child circle as many action verbs as he or she can find.

Name ___________________________

ri<u>ng</u>

ba<u>nk</u>

Circle the word for each picture.

1.  sink sing	2.  skunk skate	3. 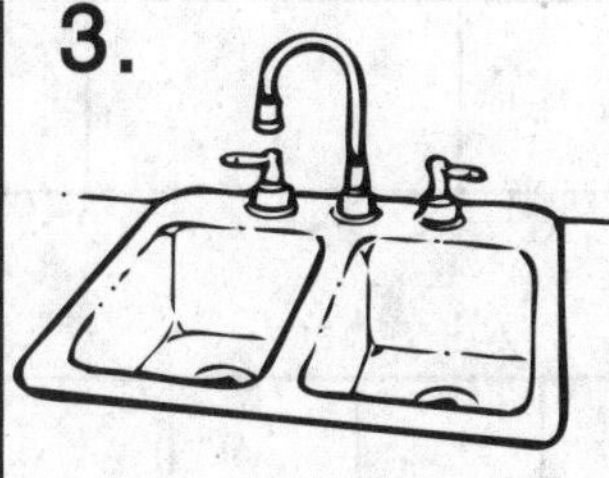 sink side	4.  kink king
5.  wink wing	6.  trunk truck	7. 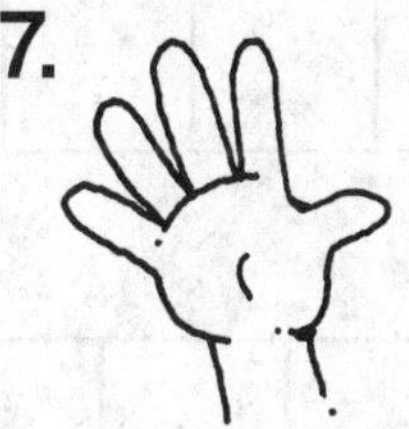 hand hang	8.  swim swing

Write the letters **ng** or **nk** to finish the words for each sentence.

9. Please b r i ___ ___ me a d r i ___ ___.

10. T h a ___ ___ you for the pretty r i ___ ___ .

11. I heard the horn h o ___ ___ .

Home Activity Your child read words that end with *ng* and *nk*. Say one of the words with *ng* or *nk* on this page and ask your child to say a word that rhymes with it. Then have your child say a word for you to rhyme.

Name ______________________________

Read the words in the box.
Write a word to finish each sentence.

any	enough	ever	
every	own	sure	were

1. Do we have ☐☐☐☐☐☐ food?

2. Yes, I am ☐☐☐☐ we do.

3. Is ☐☐☐☐☐ place set?

4. Yes, they ☐☐☐☐ set last night.

5. Do you need ☐☐☐ flowers?

6. No, I have my ☐☐☐ .

7. This will be the best day ☐☐☐☐ !

Home Activity This week your child identified and read the words *any, enough, ever, every, own, sure,* and *were*. Help your child make up a short story using some of these words. Then help your child to write down the sentences and draw a picture to go with his or her story.

Name ______________________________

Read the stories.
Circle the answer to each question.

Hens

Many hens are white.

But hens can also be red or black.

Some hens can fly a little.

Hens will roll in dust.

A hen can be a pet.

Pigs

Some pigs are pink.

But there are black pigs too.

A pig can be a pet.

Pigs will roll in the mud.

They do this when they are hot.

---

1. Which animal can fly?	hen	pig
2. Which animal rolls in mud?	hen	pig
3. Which animal can be black?	hen and pig	just hen
4. Which animal can be pink?	hen and pig	just pig
5. Which animal can be a pet?	hen and pig	just pig

Home Activity Your child compared and contrasted information in two stories. Have your child choose two birds and tell how the birds are alike and different.

Name ________________________________

Writing · Comments About a Story

What I Like About Ruby

I like when Ruby does not eat at first. Sometimes I don't want to eat. I know how she feels. My favorite part is when Ruby flies really high and far. That sounds like fun!

Key Features of Comments About a Story

- comments respond to the story
- tell the writer's opinion or what the writer thinks and feels

Name ________________________________

Pick a word from the box to finish each compound word.
Write it on the line.
Draw a line to the picture it matches.

ball	cakes	pole	set

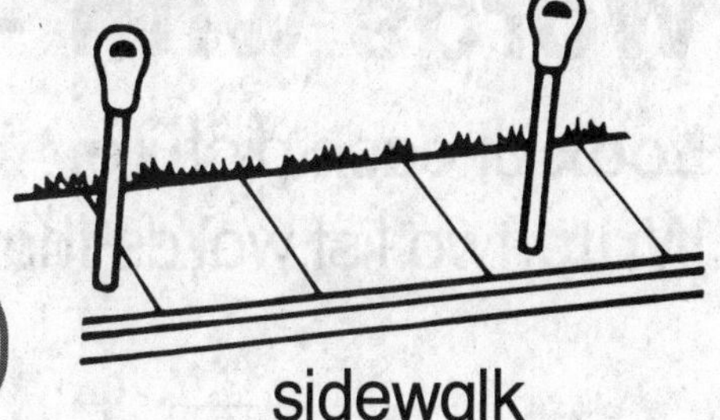

1. pan ____________

2. sun ____________

3. flag ____________

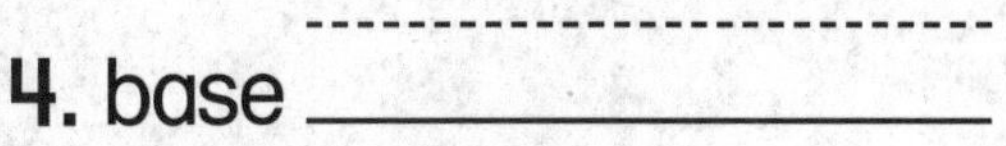

4. base ____________

Find the compound word.
Mark the ⬭ to show your answer.

5. ⬭ sandy
   ⬭ sandman
   ⬭ sanding

6. ⬭ napkin
   ⬭ happen
   ⬭ dishpan

Home Activity Your child read compound words—words formed by joining two or more other words. Walk around your house with your child and find things you see that are compound words *(toothbrush, hairbrush, bathtub)*. Say each word and have your child identify the two words used to make the compound word.

Name ______________________

Words with *-ng*, *-nk*

Look at each picture.
Write two list words that rhyme.

Spelling Words

- bring
- trunk
- pink
- bank
- sang
- wing
- rink
- blank
- rang
- sunk

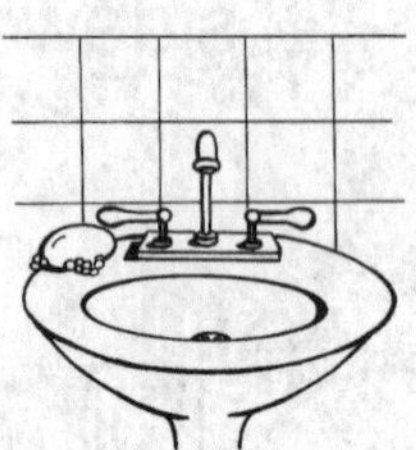
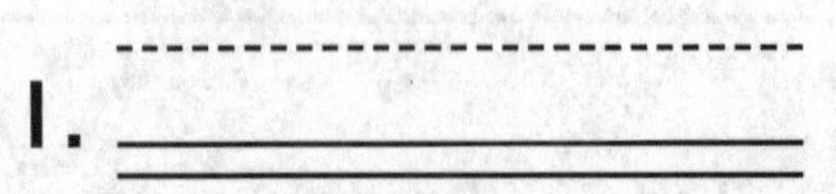
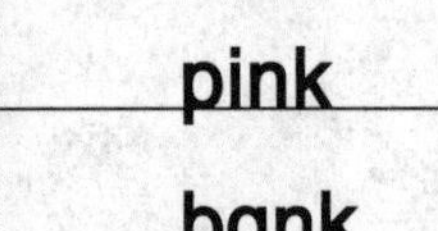

1. ______________________
2. ______________________

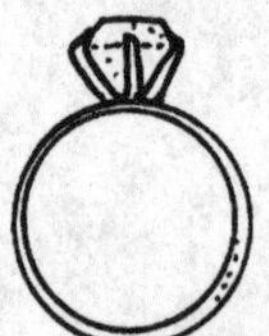

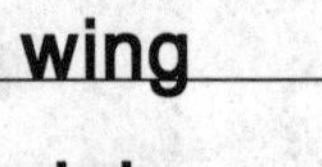

3. ______________________
4. ______________________

5. ______________________
6. ______________________

Read the clue. **Write** the word.

7. You keep money in it. 7. ______________________

8. You did it to a bell. 8. ______________________

9. You did it to a song. 9. ______________________

10. You can write a word to fill it. 10. ______________________

Home Activity Your child spelled words ending in *-ng* and *-nk*. Have your child identify and spell each list word that ends with *-nk*.

Name ______________________

Verbs That Add -*s*

A **verb** can tell what one person, animal, or thing does. Add **-s** to show what is being done now.

Ruby **grows** bigger.

Ruby **spreads** her wings.

Complete each sentence.
Write the correct word on the line.
Say a sentence using each verb you wrote.

1. Pam ______________________ a book.
(reads, read)

2. Ned ______________________ a cake.
(bake, bakes)

3. José ______________________ a bike.
(rides, ride)

4. Tina ______________________ her shoes.
(tie, ties)

Home Activity Your child learned about verbs that add -*s*. Write the words *swim, run, walk, jump,* and *dance* on paper. Have your child add an -*s* to each word and then act out the word.

Name ______________________________

Comments and Feelings

I Like When Ruby . . .	I Feel . . .	Because . . .

Home Activity Your child can express ideas about a story. Ask your child's opinion about the story of Ruby the duck.

Name ______________________

K k

Copy the words. Write the letters from left to right.

King ______ bring ______

long ______ dunk ______

honk ______ thank ______

think ______ Kang ______

tank ______ wing ______

sang ______ clank ______

bank ______ link ______

Did you write your letters from left to right? 

No

Home Activity Your child practiced writing words with *Kk* and words that end in *-nk* or *-ng*. Have your child write words that rhyme with *think*.

Name ______________________________

Find these words in the Glossary of your student book.
Draw a picture to show what each word means.

1. feather	2. mother
3. night	4. rain
5. father	6. flew

Home Activity Your child learned how to use a glossary to look up the meaning of words. Find a glossary in a book at home or at the library and work with your child to look up other words.

"I will sing with them," said the king.

"I will sing a long song.

Then I will be happy!"

Decodable Story *The King Sings a Song*
Target Skills Consonant Patterns *-ng* and *-nk,* Compound Words

The King Sings a Song

Consonant Patterns *ng* and *nk*		Compound Words		High-Frequency Words	
think	king	upset	anything	a	do
pink	sing	inside	baseball	I	said
thanks	song	himself	hilltop	of	the
honk	long	cannot	rosebuds	to	

A king felt upset.

He sat inside by himself.

"I cannot think of anything to do," he said.

"Get the baseball," said the queen.

"We can toss it on the hilltop."

"No, thanks," said the king.

"Take a walk," said the princess.

"See the rosebuds. Pet the pink pigs.

The geese will honk a song."

Name ______________________

Words with *-ng, -nk*

Spelling Words				
bring	trunk	pink	bank	sang
wing	rink	blank	rang	sunk

High-Frequency Words
every
sure

Write the missing **ng** or **nk**. **Write** the word.

1. Did you skate at the **ri**______? ______________
2. Put the bag in the **tru**______. ______________
3. The bell **ra**______. ______________
4. The boat has **su**______. ______________
5. We clapped as he **sa**______. ______________
6. I have a piggy **ba**______. ______________
7. The bird hurt its **wi**______. ______________
8. Did you paint it **pi**______? ______________

Write a high-frequency word to fit each clue.

9. no doubt ______________ 10. all ______________

Home Activity Your child wrote spelling words to complete sentences. Have your child say and spell the list words with *-ng*.

Name ________________________________

Verbs That Add *-s*

Look at the picture.
Write a verb to finish each sentence.
Remember to add **-s** to each verb.
Add more words to the sentence if you want.

The girl ________________________________.

The boy ________________________________.

The dad ________________________________.

The mom ________________________________.

Choose other verbs. **Say** a sentence for each verb.

Home Activity Your child learned how to use verbs that add *-s* in writing. Write these sentence frames on paper: *Dan* ____. *Anna* ____. Have your child write verbs that add *-s* to each sentence frame to make as many sentences as possible.

Name ______________________

Words with *-ng*, *-nk*

Unscramble the letters to make a list word.
Write the word.

Spelling Words
bring
trunk
pink
bank
sang
wing
rink
blank
rang
sunk

1. k i n p 1. ______________
2. r n g a 2. ______________
3. g n i w 3. ______________
4. n r i k 4. ______________
5. r t n k u 5. ______________

Write three list words that begin like  .

6. ______________ 7. ______________ 8. ______________

Write two list words that begin like  .

9. ______________ 10. ______________

Home Activity Your child has been learning to spell words with *-ng* or *-nk*. Have your child spell a list word and use it in a sentence.

Name ______________________________

Verbs That Add *-s*

Mark the sentence that is correct.

1. ○ Amy plays a song.
   ○ Amys plays a song.
   ○ Amy plays a songs.

2. ○ Johns writes his name.
   ○ John writes his name.
   ○ John writes hiss name.

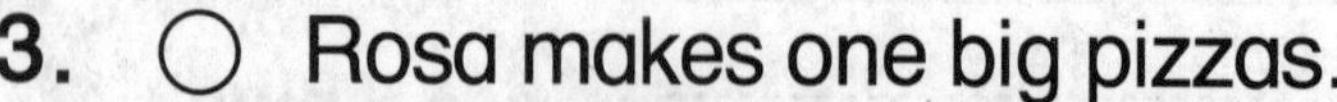

3. ○ Rosa makes one big pizzas.
   ○ Rosa makes one bigs pizza.
   ○ Rosa makes one big pizza.

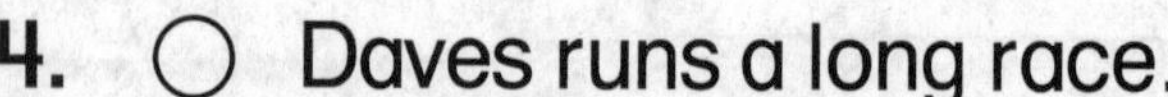

4. ○ Daves runs a long race.
   ○ Dave runs a long race.
   ○ Dave runs a longs race.

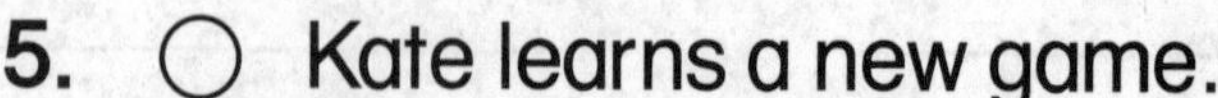

5. ○ Kate learns a new game.
   ○ Kates learns a new game.
   ○ Kate learns a new games.

6. ○ Sam spells a hards word.
   ○ Sam spells a hard words.
   ○ Sam spells a hard word.

Home Activity Your child prepared for taking tests on verbs that add *-s*. Together read a short, simple newspaper or magazine article. Have your child find and circle as many verbs that end in *-s* as possible.

Name ______________________________

Greg fix<u>es</u> the bench<u>es</u>.

Add the ending.
Write the new word on the line.

Word		Ending	New Word
1. mix	+	-es	
2. brush	+	-es	
3. glass	+	-es	
4. catch	+	-es	
5. dress	+	-es	
6. bus	+	-es	
7. dish	+	-es	
8. fox	+	-es	
9. nut	+	-s	
10. patch	+	-es	

School + Home

Home Activity Your child added *-es* to verbs and nouns. Have your child use each new word in a sentence.

Name ______________________

Read the words in the box.
Pick a word to finish each sentence.
Write it on the line.

away	**car**	**friends**	**house**	**our**	**school**	**very**

1. This is our new ______________.

2. It is by my ______________.

3. It is ______________ nice.

4. We go with our ______________.

5. They come in a ______________.

6. My mom will walk ______________. I will stay.

7. ______________ teacher is inside.

Home Activity This week your child identified and read the words *away, car, friends, house, our, school,* and *very*. Use sock puppets to act out a new story using the words. Help your child write down the story you create.

Name ______________________

Read the story.
Follow the directions.

Kate has a pet bird called Bing.

Her bird is green and red.

A bird is the best pet of all pets.

Bing plays with a bell.

Bing likes to talk.

1. Write two facts about the story.

____

____

2. Write the sentence from the story that is an opinion. **Explain** your answer.

____

____

Home Activity Your child has learned about fact and opinion. Discuss the difference between a fact and an opinion. A fact can be proven to be true; an opinion cannot be proven to be true. Have your child tell a fact and an opinion about his or her favorite food.

Name ______________________________

Writing Prompt: Write a summary of your favorite story.

Ruby in Her Own Time is my favorite story. Ruby takes longer to do things than her brothers and sisters. She eats later. She swims later. But she flies farthest first. She leaves home. Then she comes back. She brings her new family.

Name ______________________________

Circle the word for each picture.

storm

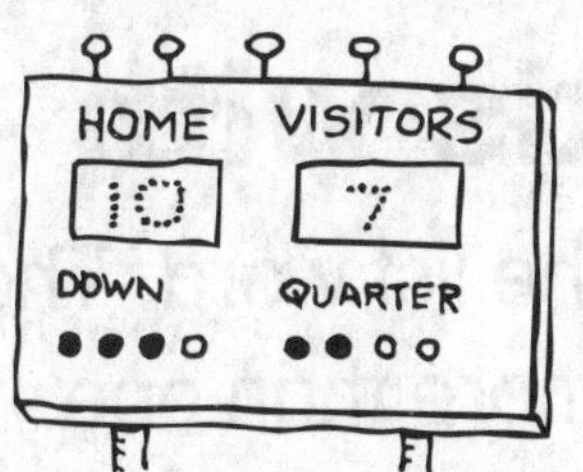

score

1.
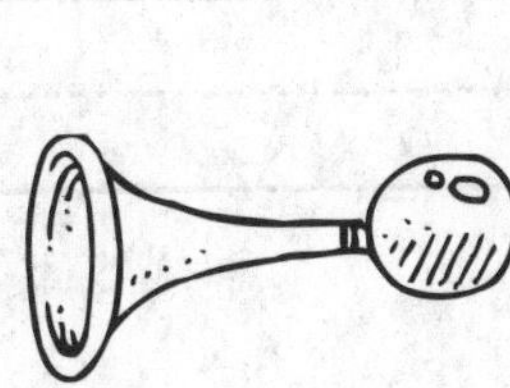
fork flick

2.

hen horn

3.

core conk

4.

store stock

5.
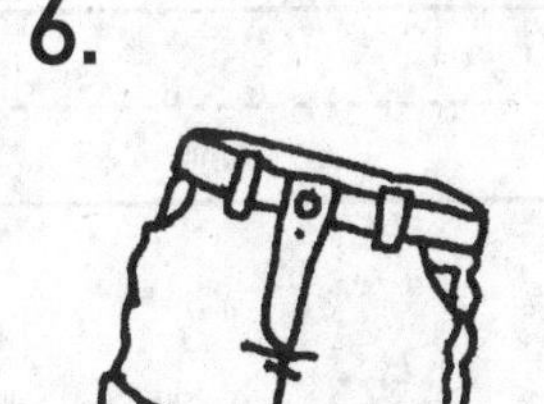
con corn

6.

shorts shots

7.
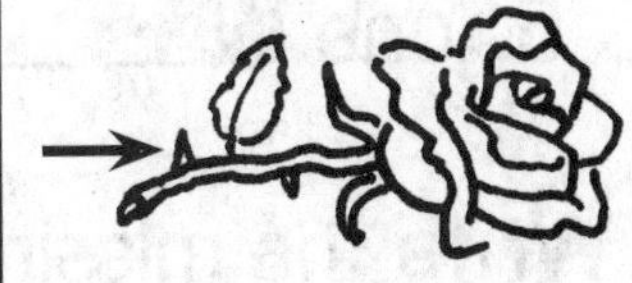
port pot

8.
thorn tone

Find the word that has the same middle sound as .
Mark the ⬭ to show your answer.

9. ⬭ porch
⬭ poke
⬭ pole

10. ⬭ such
⬭ shut
⬭ shore

Home Activity Your child read words with *or* as in *storm* and *ore* as in *score*. Help your child make up a story using words with this vowel sound, such as *snore, horn, popcorn,* and *short*. Then have your child illustrate his or her story.

Name ________________________

Words with -es

Finish the list word. Then **write** the word that means more than one.

Spelling Words
fix
fixes
class
classes
wish
wishes
kiss
kisses
bus
buses

1. one **b**________ 2. three ________

3. one **k**________ 4. three ________

5. one **w**________ 6. three ________

Write the missing word.

classes
fix
fixes
class

7. My ________ has ten boys.

8. Sam ________ clocks.

9. Do the music ________ meet here?

10. Can you ________ my bike?

Home Activity Your child spelled words that end with *-es*. Say a list word that does not end with *-es*. Ask your child to add *-es* and spell the new word.

Name ______________________

Verbs That Do Not Add *-s*

Do not add ***-s*** to a verb that tells what two or more people, animals, or things do now.

Meg and Jen **want** a new pet.

Circle the verb that shows more than one.
Say a sentence for each verb you wrote.

1. Meg and Jen (find, finds) some pets.
2. The pets (likes, like) to eat.
3. Pet stores (sell, sells) many pets.

Circle the correct verb. **Write** the verb on the line.

4. The girls ______________________ many pets.
   (see, sees)

5. The pets ______________________ to see us.
   (runs, run)

Home Activity Your child learned about verbs that do not add -*s*. Write this sentence beginning: *The children* ___. Then act out a verb, such as *swim, run, walk, jump,* and *dance*. Have your child say the verb to finish the sentence.

Read Together

Name ___________________________

Writing Rubric Summary

Top-Score Response

Focus/Ideas	A good summary tells important information.
Organization	A good summary tells the ideas in the correct order.
Voice	A good summary shows that you understand the ideas.
Word Choice	A good summary uses words that describe and show time order.
Sentences	A good summary uses complete sentences.
Conventions	A good summary uses subjects and verbs that go together.

Home Activity Your child is learning how to write a short summary of a story. Read a short story together, and ask you child to briefly retell what happens in the story.

Name ______________________

R r

Copy the words. Write the letters the correct size.

Rory

shore

for

corn

store

more

chore

short

storm

sore

born

fort

torn

fork

Did you write all of your letters the correct size? Yes No

Home Activity Your child practiced writing words with *Rr*, *or*, and *ore*. Have your child read and write any five words from the list one more time.

Name ______________________________

Read Alex's chart with facts he has gathered.
Help him revise his topic.

Facts About	
Mammals	**Reptiles**
have hair on their bodies babies born alive bears, cats, whales, people	have dry skin and no hair alligators, crocodiles, turtles, snakes

1. Alex's topic is "Facts about Mammals and Reptiles." Does he have the right information to write about that topic? Why or why not?

____

____

2. What additional fact about reptiles might Alex want to find?

____

____

3. Alex wants to revise his topic. Use Alex's chart to choose the topic.

How mammals and reptiles are alike and different

How mammals and reptiles live

4. Why is that a better topic for Alex?

____

____

Home Activity Your child learned how to review and revise topics. Choose a topic that is of interest to your child. Ask your child to share some facts about this topic with you. Then, using a reference source such as a computer or encyclopedia, read with your child about the topic. Have your child revise his or her list based on the results of your research.

Funny Fox snored. Elf got a horn.

"I will grant this last wish.

No more snores!" said Elf.

Decodable Story *Six Wishes*
Target Skills Endings *-es;* Plural *-es; r*-controlled *or, ore*

Name ________________

Six Wishes

Ending *-es* and plural *-es*		*r*-controlled *or* and *ore*		High-Frequency Words	
fetches	foxes	porch	chores	a	said
hatches	buses	for	snored	the	of
wishes	boxes	horn	snores	I	is
		more			

Elf sat on the porch.

"I will grant six wishes," said Elf.

"This will be fun," said the foxes.

Franny Fox wished for a pet that fetches.

"Can I get a hen that hatches fancy eggs?" asked Freddy Fox.

Sleepy Fox wished for buses.

Winky Fox wished for boxes of dishes.

"My wish is no more chores," said Franky Fox.

Name ______________________

Words with -es

Spelling Words				
fix	fixes	class	classes	wish
wishes	kiss	kisses	bus	buses

High-Frequency Words
friends
very

Read about a wish. **Write** the missing list words.

1. I ______________ I could visit my aunt.
2. I would go by ______________.
3. I might need to ride on two or three ______________.
4. My aunt ______________ hair in her shop.
5. She would ______________ my hair.
6. She teaches art ______________, too.
7. I could go to a ______________.
8. I would give my aunt a big ______________.
9. She would give me a ______________ big kiss.
10. I hope my ______________ meet her.

Home Activity Your child wrote spelling words to complete a story. Ask your child to write about a wish, using some of the list words.

Name ____________________

Verbs That Do Not Add *-s*

Pretend you see two new girls at school.
Write about what you do.
Write about what they do.
Begin your sentences with we and they.
Include a sentence that ends with an exclamation point. (!)

Home Activity Your child learned how to use verbs that do not add *-s* in writing. Point to pictures that show more than one person, animal, or thing. Ask: *What do the (children, birds, etc.) do?* Have your child write the answer to the question.

Name ______________________

Words with -es

Read the clues. **Write** the list words.

Spelling Words
fix
fixes
class
classes
wish
wishes
kiss
kisses
bus
buses

1. It rhymes with **Gus**. ______________________

2. It rhymes with **glass**. ______________________

3. It rhymes with **fishes**. ______________________

4. It rhymes with **dish**. ______________________

5. It rhymes with **mix**. ______________________

6. It rhymes with **miss**. ______________________

Add -es. Write the new word in the puzzle.

Down
7. bus
8. fix

Across
9. kiss
10. class

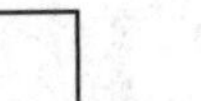

7.
8.
9.
10.

Home Activity Your child has been learning to add -*es* to words. Have your child write a list word that ends with -*es*. Then have your child cross out -*es* to make a different list word.

Name ______________________________

Verbs That Do Not Add -s

Mark the sentence that is correct.

1. ○ Ann and Pat walks to a pet store.
   ○ Ann walk to a pet store.
   ○ Ann and Pat walk to a pet store.

2. ○ The girls like their new pets.
   ○ The girls likes their new pets.
   ○ The girl like their new pets.

3. ○ Their pet live in a box.
   ○ Their pets live in a box.
   ○ Their pets lives in a box.

4. ○ Ben and Vic talk to the girls.
   ○ Ben talk to the girls.
   ○ Ben and Vic talks to the girls.

5. ○ The boy tell about the new pet.
   ○ The boys tell about the new pet.
   ○ The boys tells about the new pet.

6. ○ Pat like the mice.
   ○ Ann and Pat likes the mice.
   ○ Ann and Pat like the mice.

Choose other verbs. **Say** a sentence with each verb.

Home Activity Your child prepared for taking tests on verbs that do not add *-s*. Together read a paragraph from a newspaper or magazine article. Have your child find and circle verbs that do not end in *-s*.

Name ______________________________

Dan is mop**ping** up the mess.
The mess is mop**ped** up.

Add -ed and **-ing** to each word.
Write the new words on the lines.

	Add -ed	Add -ing
1. nap		
2. pat		
3. nod		
4. jog		
5. wag		
6. stop		
7. pet		
8. drop		
9. clap		
10. plan		

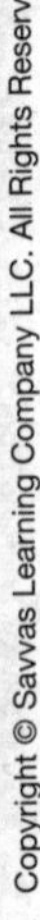

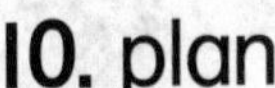

School + Home **Home Activity** Your child practiced writing words that end in *-ed* and *-ing*. Together with your child make up a story using the words above.

Name ________________________

Circle a word to finish each sentence.
Write it on the line.

how few

1. We have a ____________ to take back.

afraid read

2. We ____________ them all and came for new ones.

again few

3. Can we get some ____________ ?

soon how

4. We can read ____________ to plant flowers.

afraid few

5. I am ____________ this is not the best one.

afraid soon

6. My mom will be here ____________ .

Home Activity This week your child identified and read the words *afraid, again, few, how, read,* and *soon.* Make some flash cards and have your child practice reading the words.

Name ______________________________

Read the story.
Circle or write the answer to each question.

Skunks are always black and white.

Some skunks are black with white spots.

Skunks eat at sunset.

Skunks are good at digging.

They dig to find bugs to eat.

---

1. What is this story about?

bugs   skunks   sunsets

2. Why do you think the writer wrote this story? Explain your answer.

to make you laugh   to make you sad   to tell facts

____

____

3. What are two things the story tells about skunks?

____

____

____

____

Home Activity Your child read an informational story and figured out why it was written. Read a funny story with your child and talk about why the author wrote it.

Name ______________________________

Writing • Lists

Things That Helped

Toad planted the seeds in the ground.

Toad let the seeds get rain.

Things That Did Not Help

Toad told the seeds to grow.

Toad read a story to the seeds.

Key Features of a List

- has words or sentences written one below the other
- can have a heading

Name ______________________________

Circle the word for each picture.

farm

1.
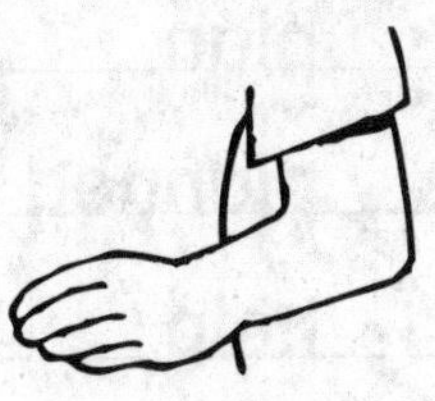
arm am

2.

band barn

3.

core car

4.

far jam

5.

duck dark

6.

party patty

7.

cart cork

8.

cord card

Find the word that rhymes with ☆.
Mark the ⬭ to show your answer.

9. ⬭ form
⬭ far
⬭ for

10. ⬭ tar
⬭ torn
⬭ trap

Home Activity Your child read words with *ar* as in *farm*. Help your child make up a story about a car trip. Encourage your child to use words with *ar* that have the same vowel sound as *car*.

Name ______________________

Words with *-ed*

Write the list word to finish the chart.

	Base Word	-ed Word
1.	______	**asked**
2.	**drop**	______
3.	______	**helped**
4.	**plan**	______

Spelling Words
ask
asked
plan
planned
help
helped
drop
dropped
call
called

Read the clues. **Write** the list word.

It rhymes with 
It starts with **pl.**

5. ______________

It rhymes with  
It starts with **c.**

6. ______________

It rhymes with
It starts with **dr.**

7. ______________

Write the list word that tells what happened in the past.

8. We can ask for paper. We ______________ for paper.

9. I will call my friends. I ______________ my friends.

10. He can help. He ______________.

Home Activity Your child spelled words that do and do not end with *-ed*. Say a list word that does not end with *-ed*. Have your child say and spell the corresponding *-ed* word.

Name ____________________

Verbs for Past and for Future

A verb can tell what happened in the past. Some verbs that tell about the past end with **-ed.** A verb can tell what happens in the future. It can begin with **will.**

Frog **walked.** (past) Frog **will walk.** (future)

Read each word in the box. **Write** the word under *The Past* if it tells about the past. **Write** the word under *The Future* if it tells about the future. **Say** each verb you wrote in a sentence.

will tell	liked	jumped
helped	will play	will ask

The Past	The Future
1. ____________	4. ____________
2. ____________	5. ____________
3. ____________	6. ____________

Home Activity Your child learned about verbs for the past and for the future. Write the words *talk, laugh,* and *yell* on paper. Have your child add *-ed* or *will* to make a verb for the past and a verb for the future.

Name ____________________

Idea Web

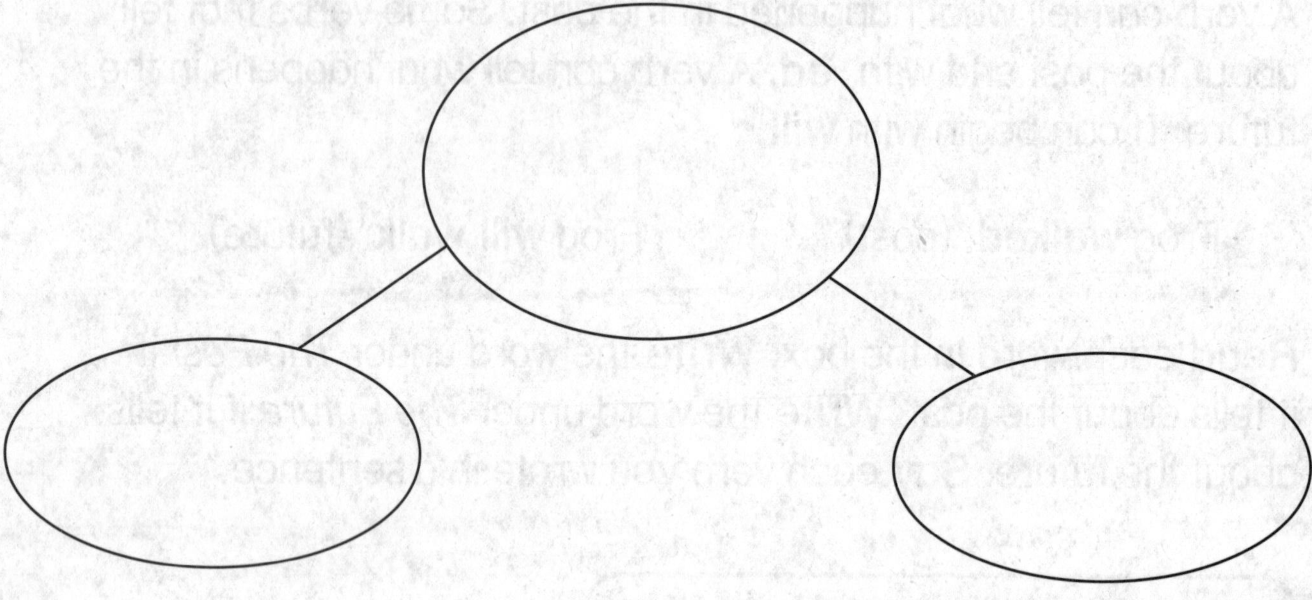

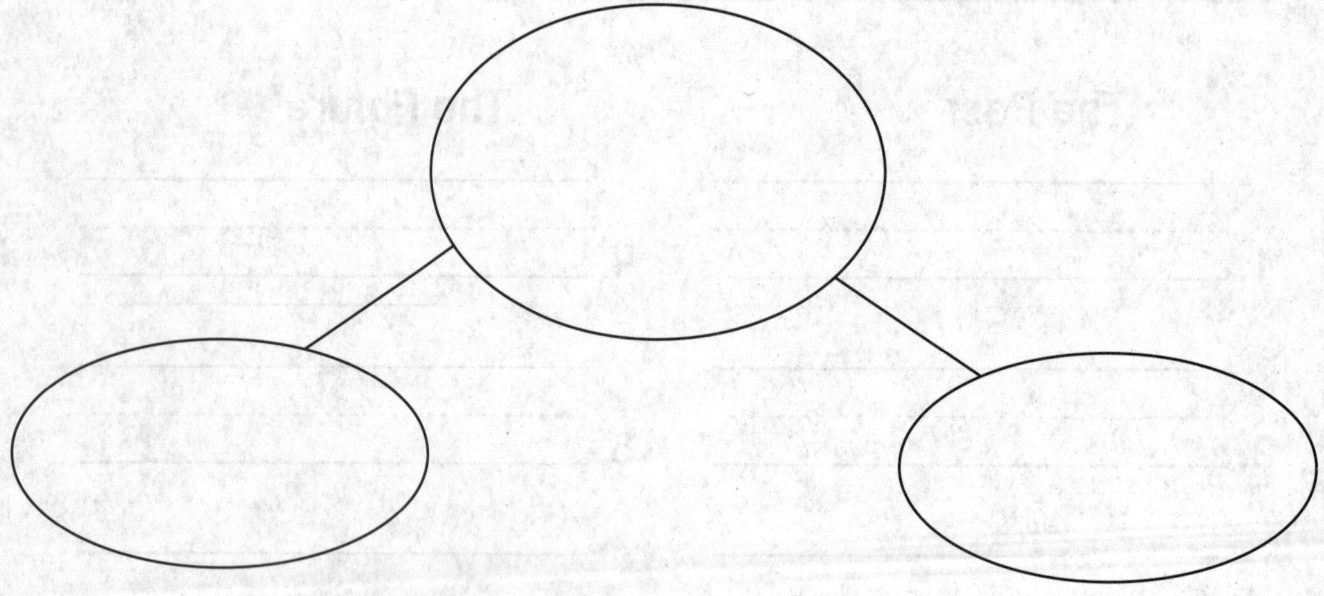

Home Activity Your child can write about the actions of characters in stories. Share a memory about a story you have heard or read with your child and why characters did things.

Name ______________________________

C c

Copy the words. Leave the correct space between your letters.

Carl	________	Cal	________
car	________	cape	________
barn	________	harm	________
start	________	jar	________
chart	________	star	________
part	________	bark	________
card	________	dark	________

Did you leave the correct space between your letters?  Yes  No

Home Activity Your child practiced writing words with *Cc* and *ar*. Have your child find three words from the list that rhyme with *far* and write them one more time. (*car, jar, star*)

Name ___________________________

We use our eyes to gather information.
Look at the storm. **Write** what you see.

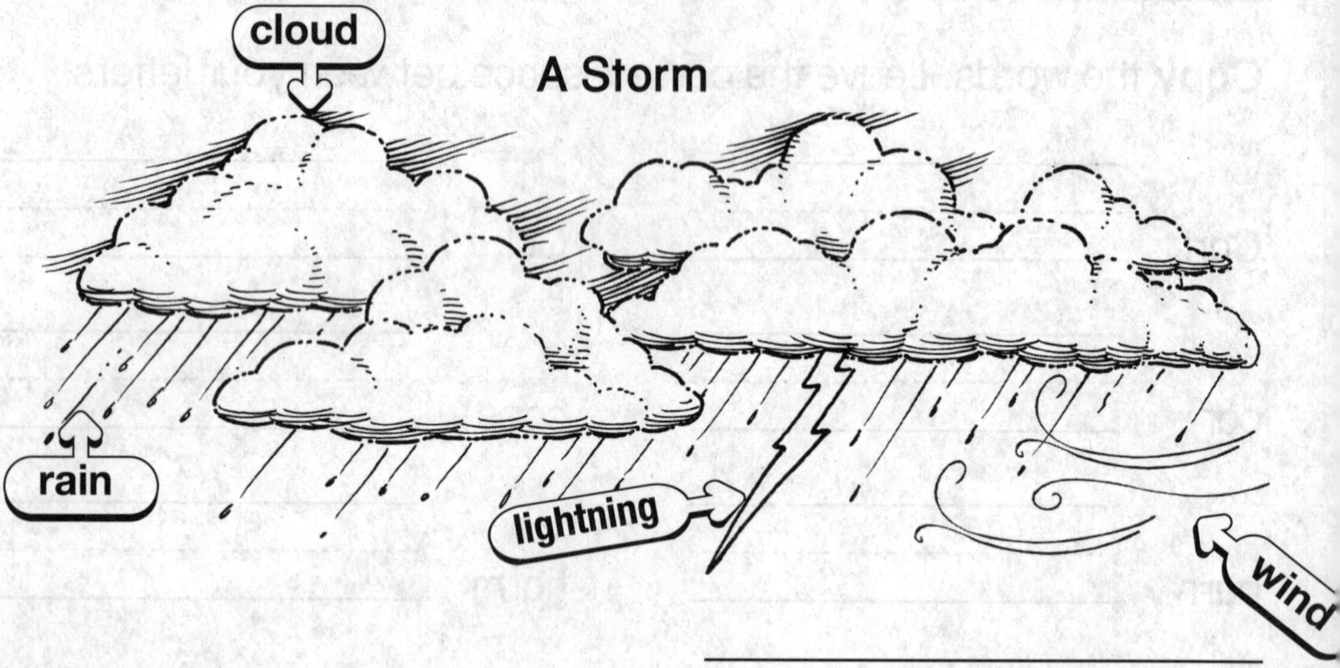

A Storm

1. Where does the rain come from? ___________

2. How many bolts of lightning do you see? ___________

3. Do you see a cloud? Circle a cloud.

4. Think about what you know about storms. What part makes you wet? ___________

5. Ask a local expert, such as a weather reporter, questions about storms. Write the answer.

____

Home Activity Your child made observations from a natural source and recorded those observations. As you interact with your child this week, point out what can be observed in our homes and in nature.

"I'm not quitting," Arty yelled to Dad.

"Marny is getting in the cart."

This time he had a happy bark!

Decodable Story *The Cart*
Target Skills Adding Endings, *r*-controlled *ar*

Name ______________________

The Cart

Adding endings-double final consonants		*r*-controlled *ar*		High-Frequency Words	
humming	grabbed	Arty	started	a	said
running	stepped	cart	Marny	I	to
quitting	stopped	park	barked	the	is
getting	hugged	yard	bark		
begged					

Dad made Arty a black cart.

"Can I drive at the park?" begged Arty.

"No. Drive in the yard," said Dad.

Arty began humming.

He grabbed the wheel and stepped on the gas.

The cart started!

Marny the dog began running beside Arty.

He barked a sad bark.

Arty stopped the cart and hugged Marny.

Name ______________________

Words with *-ed*

Spelling Words				
ask	asked	plan	planned	help
helped	drop	dropped	call	called

High-Frequency Words
again
soon

Write the missing list words.

1. He ______________ if I could come.
2. We have not ______________ a trip.
3. She ______________ a pen.
4. Has your mom ______________ you back home?
5. Jack ______________ clean.
6. Did you ______________ your dog?
7. I will ______________ for more.
8. Tom likes to ______________ and run.
9. Liz will have a plan ______________ .
10. I jogged on the path ______________ .

Home Activity Your child wrote words that end with *-ed* and their base words. Ask your child to find two words in which the final consonant was doubled before adding *-ed* (*plan/planned, jog/jogged*).

Name ______________________________

Verbs for Past and for Future

In the past you were a baby.
Tell about things you did then.

Now you are in first grade.
Tell about things you will do in the future.

Say the verbs you wrote. **Use** each verb in a sentence.

Home Activity Your child learned about verbs for the past and for the future. With your child, look through a family photo album. Talk about what you were doing then using verbs for the past. Talk about what you might be doing in the future.

Name ______________________________

Words with *-ed*

Spelling Words
ask
asked
plan
planned
help
helped
drop
dropped
call
called

Read the base word. **Write** the **-ed** word in the puzzle.

Across

2. drop **4.** call

5. help

Down

1. ask

3. plan

Circle the word that is spelled correctly.

6. plan plann **7.** asc ask

8. cal call **9.** help halp

10. drop dropp

Home Activity Your child has been learning to add *-ed* to base words. Have your child write a list word that ends with *-ed*. Then have your child cross out the ending (*-ed* or consonant + *-ed*) to find the base word.

Name ______________________________

Verbs for Past and for Future

Mark the sentence that is correct.

1. ○ Last week Frog planted seeds in the garden.
   ○ Last week Frog plants seeds in the garden.
   ○ Last week Frog plant seeds in the garden.

2. ○ Soon Toad plant seeds.
   ○ Soon Toad will plant seeds.
   ○ Soon Toad planted seeds.

3. ○ Tomorrow the seeds will start to grow.
   ○ Tomorrow the seeds started to grow.
   ○ Tomorrow the seeds start to grow.

4. ○ Yesterday Frog will shout at Toad.
   ○ Yesterday Frog shouted at Toad.
   ○ Yesterday Frog shouts at Toad.

5. ○ Last week the sun shined.
   ○ Last week the sun shine.
   ○ Last week the sun shines.

6. ○ Tomorrow Toad looks at his garden.
   ○ Tomorrow Toad looked at his garden.
   ○ Tomorrow Toad will look at his garden.

Say sentences using verbs for the past and for the future.

Home Activity Your child prepared for taking tests on verbs for the past and for the future. Together read part of a newspaper or magazine article. Have your child find verbs that tell about the past or the future.

Name ___________________________

her

bird

surf

Circle the word for each picture.

1.

short shirt

2.

clerk click

3.

curl chill

4.

barn burn

5.
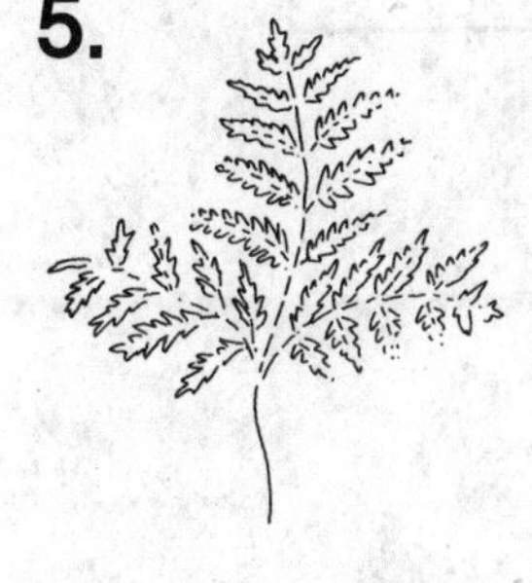
fern fan

6.

skirt skit

7.

fist first

8.

stir store

Find the word that has the same vowel sound as .
Mark the  to show your answer.

9. ⬭ hard
⬭ hut
⬭ hurt

10. ⬭ torn
⬭ turn
⬭ tune

Home Activity Your child read words spelled with *er, ir,* and *ur* that have the same vowel sound as *bird*. Help your child make up rhymes using words with this vowel sound spelled *er, ir, ur*. For example, *You can't wear that shirt. It is covered in dirt!*

Name ____________________

Read the words in the box.
Pick a word to finish each sentence.
Write the words in the puzzles.

push visit wait

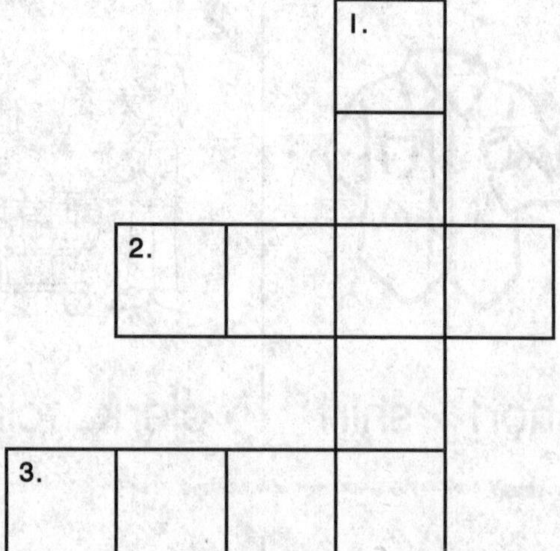

1. We'll __________ our friends soon.
2. They will __________ us on the swings.
3. I can not __________ !

done know

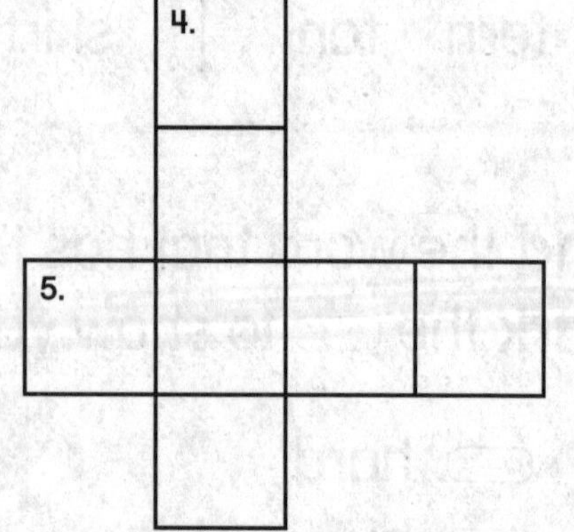

4. I __________ we will do well!
5. We will try to win. We will be happy when we are __________ .

Home Activity Your child identified and read the words *done, know, push, visit,* and *wait.* Write the words on a sheet of paper. Give your child a clue for each word. Then have him or her guess the word and point to it.

Name ______________________________

Read the story.
Follow the directions.

Hand drums are fun to play.

You don't use sticks.

You tap on the top of the drum with your hands.

In the past, people made hand drums from trees.

They made the tops of the drums with animal skins.

1. **Write** two facts from the story.

____

____

____

____

2. **Write** the sentence from the story that is an opinion.

____

____

Home Activity Your child has learned about fact and opinion. Review the difference between a fact and an opinion. A fact can be proven to be true; an opinion cannot be proven to be true. Have your child tell a fact and an opinion about one of the seasons of the year.

Name ______________________________

Writing • Captions and Pictures

The bird is yellow in summer.

Now the bird is brown. It changed color in winter.

Key Features of Captions and Pictures

- Captions tell about what pictures show.
- Many captions are sentences.

Name ______________________________

Pick a word from the box that means the same as each pair of words. **Write** it on the line.

She is tall.
She's tall.

he's	**it's**	**I've**	**that's**	**they're**
they've	**we're**	**we've**	**you're**	**you've**

1. I + have ______________

2. we + are ______________

3. it + is ______________

4. that + is ______________

5. you + have ______________

6. they + have ______________

7. we + have ______________

8. he + is ______________

9. they + are ______________

10. you + are ______________

Home Activity Your child practiced making contractions with *'s, 've,* and *'re.* Read each contraction on this page aloud. Challenge your child to use each one in a sentence. Then work together to write each sentence.

Name ____________________

Words with *er, ir, ur*

Spelling Words				
her	first	bird	girl	burn
were	shirt	fur	hurt	sir

Read the clues. **Write** the list word.

It starts like (fan). It rhymes with **bur.**

1. ____________

It starts like (shell). It rhymes with **dirt.**

2. ____________

It starts like (bed). It rhymes with **turn.**

3. ____________

Write the list word that means the opposite.

4. last ____________

5. boy ____________

6. heal ____________

7. him ____________

Write the missing list word.

sir	were	bird

8. We saw a ____________ .

9. May I help you, ____________ ?

10. We ____________ at a pond.

Home Activity Your child spelled words with *er, ir,* and *ur*. Have your child circle these letter combinations in the list words.

Name ______________________

Verbs: *Am, Is, Are, Was, Were*

The words **am, is,** and **are** tell about now. Use **am** or **is** to tell about one. Use **are** to tell about more than one.

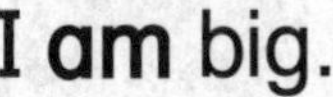

I am big. **It is** little. They **are** tiny.

The words **was** and **were** tell about the past. Use **was** to tell about one. Use **were** to tell about more than one.

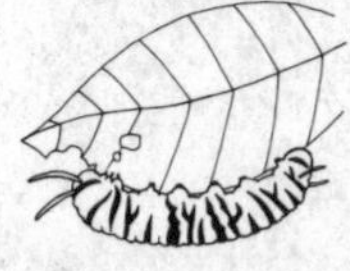
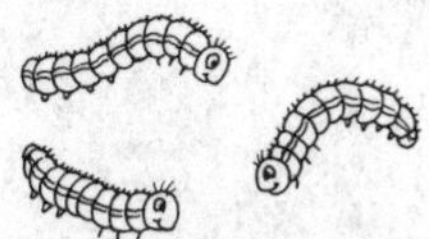

It **was** hungry. They **were** hungry.

Circle the verb in each sentence. **Write Now** if the sentence tells about now. **Write Past** if the sentence tells about the past.

1. I was an egg. ______________

2. I am a caterpillar. ______________

3. They are caterpillars. ______________

4. They were eggs. ______________

5. The change is amazing. ______________

Home Activity Your child learned about *am, is, are, was,* and *were*. Read a story with your child. Have your child point out the verbs *am, is, are, was,* and *were* in the story and tell whether the sentence tells about now or the past.

Name ______________________________

Picture Plan

Picture 1

Caption: ______________________________

Picture 2

Caption: ______________________________

School + Home

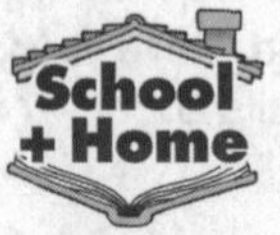

Home Activity Your child is writing captions. Together, look at pictures in children's books and read captions.

Name ______________________

V v

An apostrophe takes the place of missing letters.

→ ' ve

Copy the words. Write the letters from left to right.

Val	Van
I've	hive
vine	we've
you've	vest
five	Vicky
haven't	dive
could've	they've

Did you write your letters from left to right? **Yes** **No**

Home Activity Your child practiced writing words with *Vv* and contractions with *'ve.* Say the words that form some contractions on this page, and have your child write the contractions one more time: *I have (I've); you have (you've); we have (we've); they have (they've); could have (could've).*

Name ______________________________

We use our eyes to gather information.
Look at the park. **Write** what you see.

1. What is the man doing? ______________________________

2. Do you see things that fly? **Circle** them.

3. How many people do you see in the park? ______________

4. **Write** two questions that you would ask the people in the park.

____

____

School + Home

Home Activity Your child made observations from a natural source and recorded those observations. As you interact with your child this week, point out what can be observed in our homes and in nature.

Fern and Kurt grinned.

"We're glad to help.

Then you'll get to play a game with us!"

Decodable Story *Helping Mom*
Target Skills *r*-controlled *er, ir, ur;* Contractions

Name ______________________

Helping Mom

r-controlled *er, ir, ur*		Contractions	High-Frequency Words	
Fern	bird	I've	said	to
her	stir	I'll	the	play
shirts	fur	can't	I	
skirts	Kurt	we're	you	
dirty	burn	you'll	is	

"I've got sixteen jobs on my list," said Mom.

"I'll need all the help I can get."

"Fern, will you hang up these shirts and skirts?" asked Mom.

"Will you brush the dog? Her fur is dirty."

"Kurt, will you feed the bird?" asked Mom.

"Will you stir the gumbo? We can't let it burn."

Name ____________________

Words with *er, ir, ur*

Circle the word that is spelled correctly. **Write** it.

1. I like your ____.
   shert shirt shurt
2. I knew where you ____.
   were wir wure
3. Meet the new ____.
   gerl girl gurl
4. Let the candle ____.
   bern birn burn
5. Judy said, "Yes, ____."
   ser sir sur
6. Look at the ____.
   berd bird burd
7. Can I be ____?
   ferst first furst
8. His dog has black ____.
   fer fure fur
9. Are you ____?
   dun dune done
10. Let's ____ our friends.
    visit visot visat

Spelling Words
her
first
bird
girl
burn
were
shirt
fur
hurt
sir

High-Frequency Words
visit
done

Home Activity Your child used spelling words in sentences. Help your child make up a new sentence for each spelling word.

Name ______________________________

Verbs: *Am, Is, Are, Was, Were*

Look at the picture.
Tell about what you see.
Use am, is, are, was, or **were.**

Read the question. **Change** the words to write the answer.
Is that a bird?

Home Activity Your child learned how to use *am, is, are, was,* and *were* in writing. Write these sentence frames on paper: *Today I ___ happy. Now he ___ happy. Yesterday she ___ happy. Now they ___ happy. Yesterday we ___ happy.* Have your child complete the sentences with *am, is, are, was,* and *were.*

Name ____________________

Words with *er, ir, ur*

Spelling Words				
her	first	bird	girl	burn
were	shirt	fur	hurt	sir

Use this code. **Write** the words.

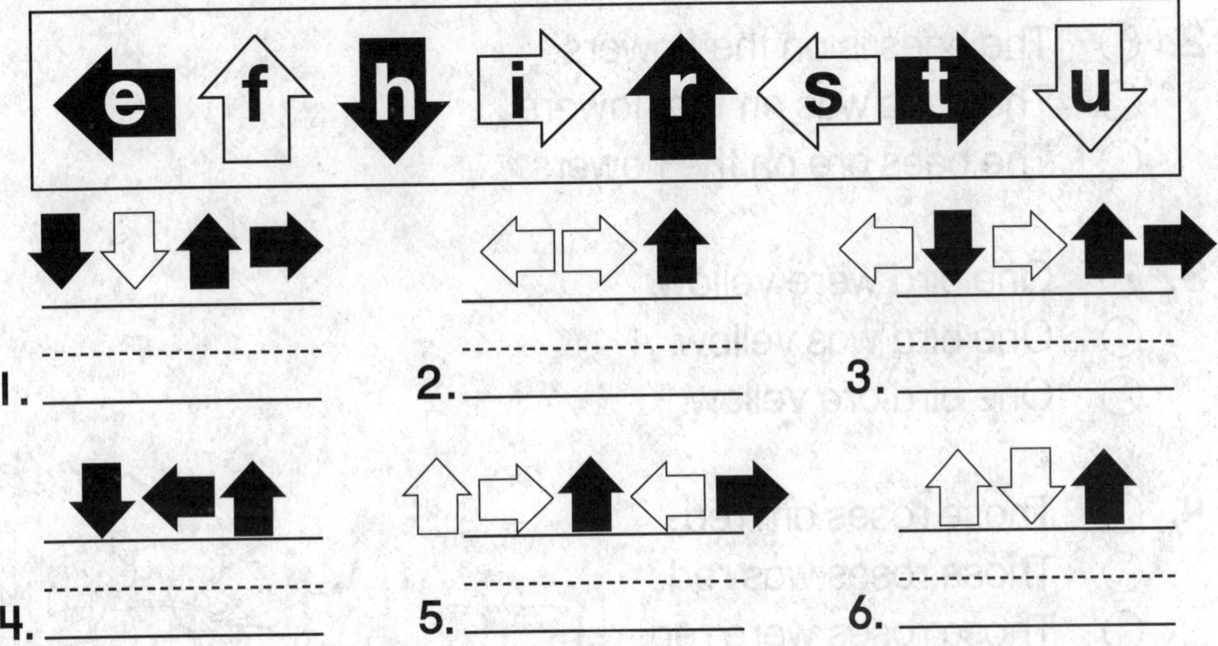

1. ____________________
2. ____________________
3. ____________________
4. ____________________
5. ____________________
6. ____________________

Draw a line through the word that does not match.
Then **write** the word that matches.

7. were where were ____________________
8. bird bird bid ____________________
9. grill girl girl ____________________
10. burn turn burn ____________________

Home Activity Your child has been learning to spell words with *er, ir,* and *ur*. Write a list word, but replace the letter before *r* with a blank (b__rd). Ask your child to correctly fill in the blank.

Name ____________________

Verbs: *Am, Is, Are, Was, Were*

Mark the sentence that is correct.

1. ○ The caterpillar is in the tree.
   ○ The caterpillar am in the tree.
   ○ The caterpillar are in the tree.

2. ○ The bees is on the flowers.
   ○ The bees was on the flowers.
   ○ The bees are on the flowers.

3. ○ One bird were yellow.
   ○ One bird was yellow.
   ○ One bird are yellow.

4. ○ Those roses am red.
   ○ Those roses was red.
   ○ Those roses were red.

5. ○ I am next to the butterfly.
   ○ I are next to the butterfly.
   ○ I is next to the butterfly.

6. ○ We am happy in the trees.
   ○ We are happy in the trees.
   ○ We was happy in the trees.

Home Activity Your child prepared for taking tests on *am, is, are, was,* and *were*. Together read part of a newspaper or magazine article. Have your child circle the verbs *am, is, are, was,* and *were*.

Name ______________________________

Circle the word for each picture.

small smaller smallest

1. 

faster fastest

2. 

bigger biggest

3. 

taller tallest

4. 

sweeter sweetest

5.

thicker thickest

6. 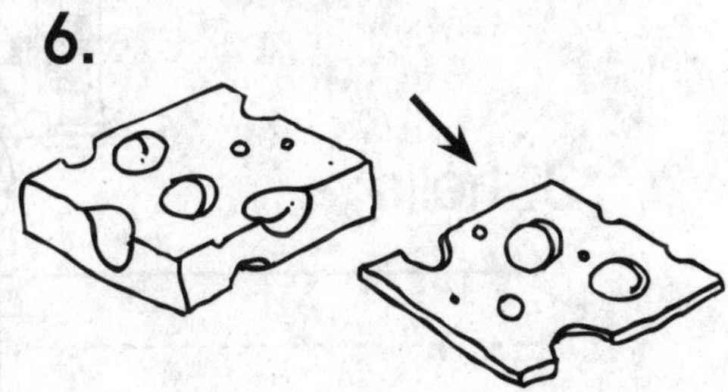

thinner thinnest

Write -er or **-est** to finish the word in each sentence.

7. The little bird has the few ________ eggs.

8. The little bird has a long ________ tail than the big bird.

Home Activity Your child identified the comparative endings *-er* and *-est* as in *smaller* and *smallest*. Discuss the sizes, shapes, and colors of animals. Have your child compare the animals using *-er* when comparing two and *-est* when comparing more than two.

Name ______________________

Read the words in the box.
Pick a word that is the opposite of each word below.
Write it on the line.

before good-bye right won't

1. after ____________

2. will ____________

3. hello ____________

4. wrong ____________

Pick a word from the box to finish each sentence.
Write it on the line. **Remember** to use capital letters.

oh does

5. ____________ a bear start its long sleep in the spring?

6. ____________, no. It sleeps when the days start to get cold.

Home Activity Your child identified and read the words *before, good-bye, right,* and *won't*. Write the opposite of these words on cards and mix them up. Have your child match the words that are opposites and then read the pairs. Then have him or her write two sentences using *does* and *oh*.

Name ______________________________

Read the story.
Circle the answer to each question.

Zak has a puppy with the name Sparky.

Zak is sitting on his bed.

Sparky puts his nose under the bed.

1. Why do you think Sparky puts his nose under the bed?

Sparky wants to get up on the bed.

Sparky wants something under the bed.

Zak finds a ball under the bed.

Sparky starts barking!

2. Why do you think Sparky starts barking?

Sparky wants to play with the ball.

Sparky wants Zak to pet him.

Then Zak starts to go outside.

Sparky jumps up and down!

3. Why do you think Sparky jumps up and down?

Sparky likes to jump up and down.

Sparky wants to play outside with Zak.

Home Activity Your child drew conclusions about a story. Reread the story with your child. Have your child tell you what he or she already knew about dogs that helped him or her draw conclusions.

Name ___________________________

Writing • Play Scene

A Friendly Phone Call

Goose: Hello?

Raccoon: Hi, Goose! How are you?

Squirrel: We wish you were here!

Goose: I miss my friends. But I can't stand the cold.

Raccoon: It sure is cold here. We went ice skating.

Goose: I went fishing today.

Squirrel: When will you come home?

Goose: I will be back in spring.

Raccoon: We can't wait!

Squirrel: 'Bye, Goose.

Key Features of a Play Scene

- is written to be acted for an audience
- characters have lines to say

Name ________________________

Read each word in the box. **Pick** a word from the box to finish each sentence. **Write** it on the line. **Read** each completed sentence.

fudge	hedge	judge	ledge	smudge

bad**ge**

1. Mom made ____________ for us to eat.

2. She set it on the ____________.

3. Did it fall into the ____________?

4. Look, there's a ____________ on Bear's face.

5. The ____________ thinks Bear ate it too.

Home Activity Your child learned to read words that end with *-dge* that have the sound heard in *judge*. Have your child make a list of words that rhyme with *judge*.

Name ______________________

Words with *-er, -est*

Spelling Words				
bigger	biggest	faster	fastest	taller
tallest	shorter	shortest	sadder	saddest

Look at the pictures. **Write** list words that end with **-er** and **-est**.

short 1. ______________ 2. ______________

fast 3. ______________ 4. ______________

big 5. ______________ 6. ______________

Write a list word that rhymes with the underlined word.

7. This plant is smaller than that ______________ one.

8. The forest has the smallest and the ______________ trees.

9. His face grew ______________ as he put away the ladder.

10. This is the ______________ and the maddest he's ever been.

Home Activity Your child spelled words that end with *-er* and *-est*. Say a base word, such as *big*. Ask your child to say and spell the *-er* and *-est* words *(bigger, biggest)*.

Name ______________________________

Contractions with *Not*

A **contraction** is a short way to put two words together. A **verb** and the word **not** can be put together to make a contraction. An **apostrophe (')** is used in place of the letter **o** in **not**.

are + not = aren't
did + not = didn't
do + not = don't
does + not = doesn't
has + not = hasn't
is + not = isn't
was + not = wasn't
were + not = weren't

Circle the contraction in each sentence.

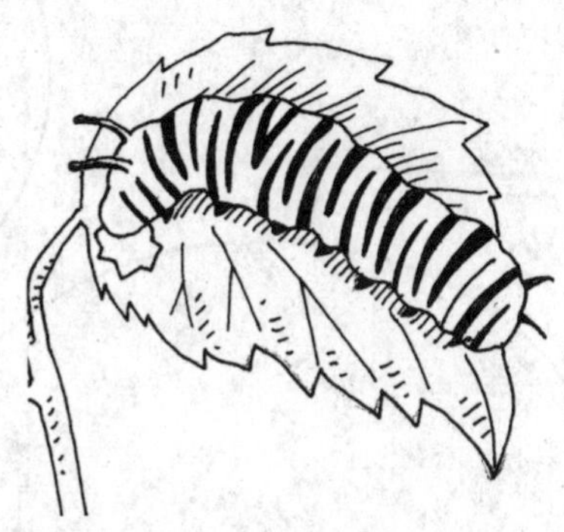

1. The animals don't have much time.
2. Caterpillar doesn't come out until spring.
3. Goose isn't staying for the winter.

Write the contraction for the underlined words.

4. The leaves <u>are not</u> on the trees. ______________
5. Raccoon <u>was not</u> leaving the forest. ______________

School + Home **Home Activity** Your child learned about contractions with *not*. Read a story with your child. Have your child look for contractions with *not* and tell the two words that were put together to make each contraction.

Name ______________________________

Idea Web

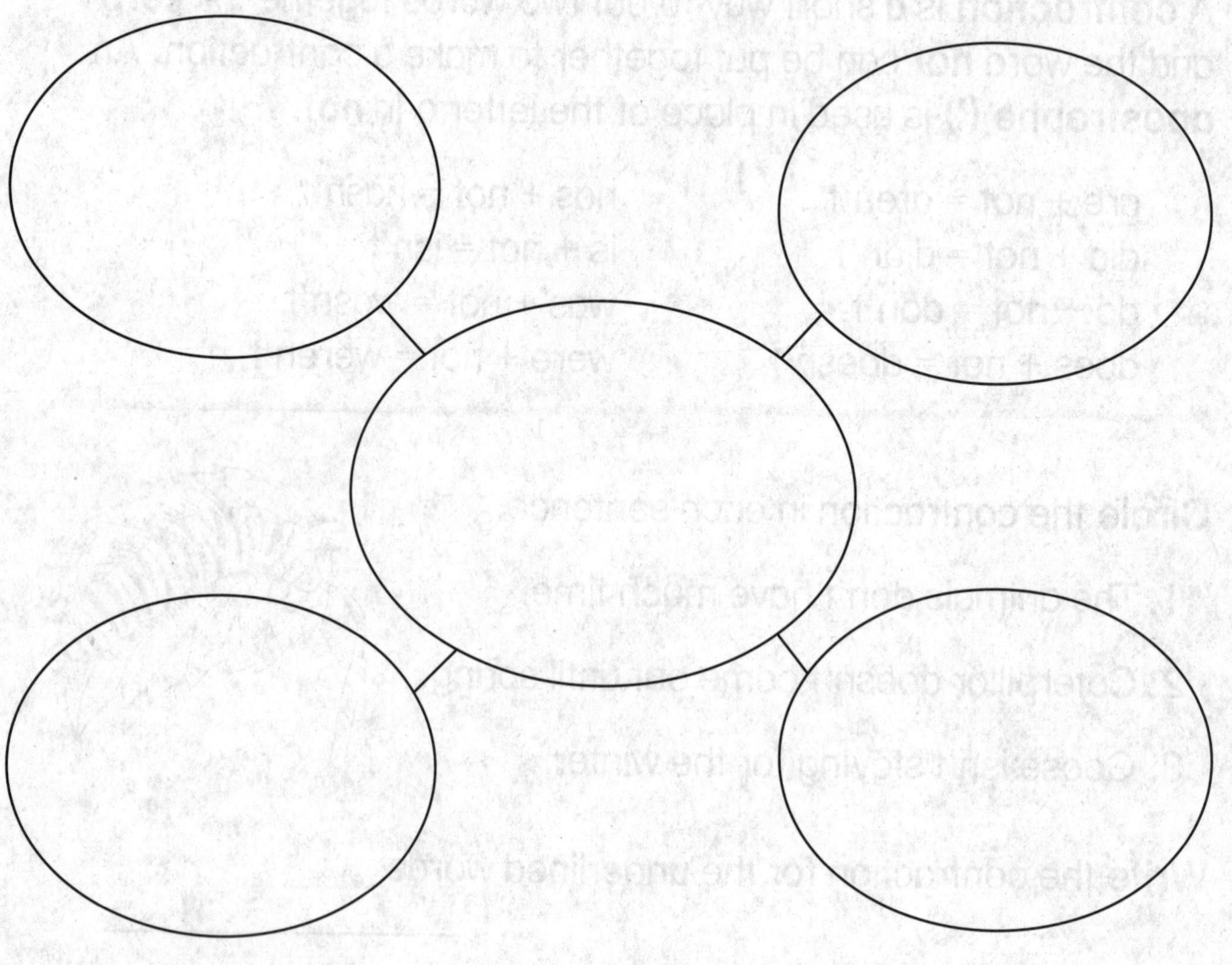

School + Home **Home Activity** Your child has ideas for a play scene. Have him or her explain how actors in a play perform a story.

Name ______________________

J j

Copy the words. Write your letters the correct size.

Jack	______	Jill	______
Jake	______	jar	______
just	______	jelly	______
judge	______	jog	______
jam	______	Jon	______
wedge	______	lodge	______
jiffy	______	Jane	______

Did you write your letters the correct size? Yes No

Home Activity Your child practiced writing words with *Jj* and *dge*. Have your child choose some words from the chart and use those words in a sentence.

Name ______________________________

Luke asked his classmates what animals they like the most. Help Luke complete the picture graph.

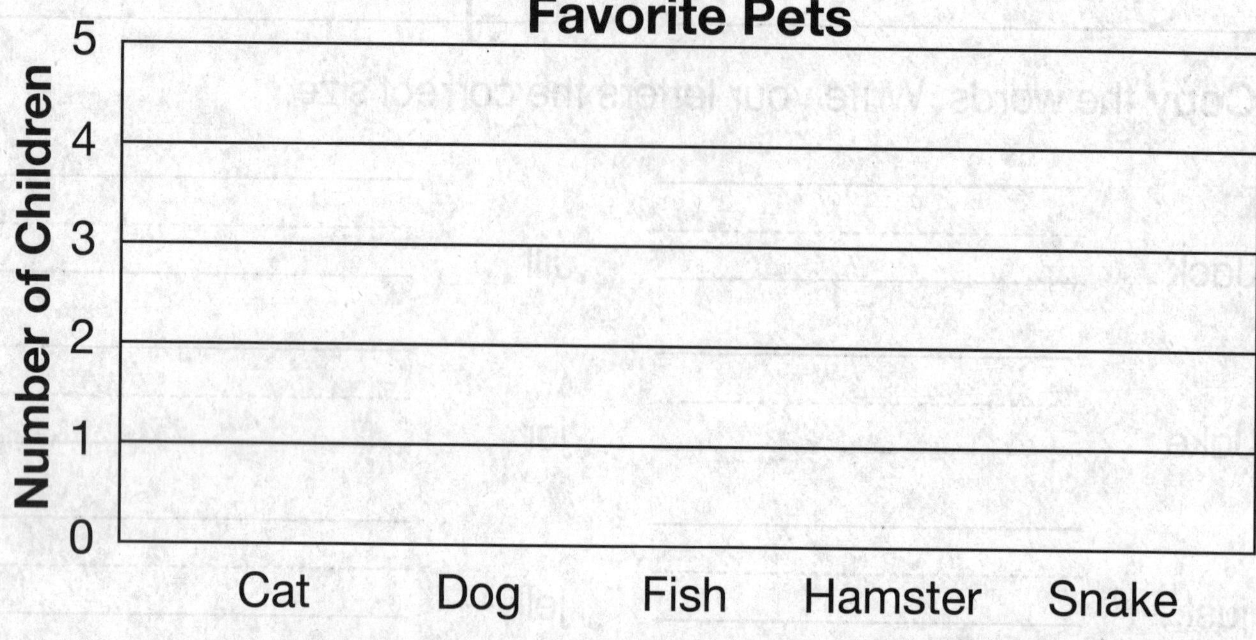

1. Five classmates like cats the most. **Draw** five cats on the picture graph.

2. Five classmates like dogs the most. **Draw** five dogs on the picture graph.

3. Three classmates like fish the most. **Draw** three fish on the picture graph.

4. Four classmates like hamsters the most. **Draw** four hamsters on the picture graph.

5. Two classmates like snakes the most. **Draw** two snakes on the picture graph.

Home Activity Your child learned to read and complete a picture graph. Together, make a picture graph that shows information about your favorite animals and that of your friends and family.

"My fudge is darkest," said Jess.

"My pencil is sharpest."

"You're not the judge anymore!" said Bart.

Decodable Story *The Contest*
Target Skill Comparative Endings *-er* and *-est,* Consonant Pattern *-dge*

Name ______________________

The Contest

Comparative Endings *-er* and *-est*		Consonant Pattern *-dge*	High-Frequency Words	
bigger	hardest	judge	have	the
harder	darkest	edge	a	is
biggest	sharpest	fudge	said	

"Let's have a contest," said Bart.

"Jess will be the judge.

Sit on the edge, Jess."

"My plant is big," said Bart.

"My plant is bigger than that plant," said Sandy.

"Mine is the biggest," said Jess.

"See this hard trick?" said Bart.

"My trick is harder," said Sandy.

"My trick is the hardest yet," said Jess.

Name ______________________

Words with *-er, -est*

Spelling Words				
bigger	biggest	faster	fastest	taller
tallest	shorter	shortest	sadder	saddest

High-Frequency Words
good-bye
before

Add *-er* or *-est*. Write the list word.

1. Tad is the tall___ boy in our class. ______________
2. The fast___ runner will win the race. ______________
3. My bat is short___ than yours. ______________
4. I need some bigg___ shoes. ______________
5. That is the sadd___ clown I've ever seen. ______________
6. You walk fast___ than I do. ______________
7. The story made her feel even sadd___. ______________
8. This is the world's bigg___ pizza. ______________

Write a word that is the opposite of each word.

9. after ______________ 10. hello ______________

Home Activity Your child wrote spelling words to complete sentences. Help your child make up a new sentence for each spelling word.

Name ______________________________

Contractions with *Not*

Write a sentence about each season.
Use a contraction with *not* in each sentence.

Winter

____

Spring

____

Summer

____

Fall

____

Home Activity Your child learned how to use contractions with *not* in writing. Write these sentences on paper: *He does not like winter. They do not like summer. She is not sad in the fall. We are not cold in the spring.* Have your child write the sentences using contractions with *not*.

Name ____________________

Words with *-er, -est*

Spelling Words				
bigger	biggest	faster	fastest	taller
tallest	shorter	shortest	sadder	saddest

Finish the list words.

1. ta_ _ _r
2. sh_ _ _ _r
3. ta_ _ _s_
4. sh_ _ _ _s_
5. s_ _d_ _
6. b_ _ _ _ _t
7. b_ _ _e_
8. s_ _ _ _s_

Write the missing words.

Froggy

Hopper

9. Hopper is ____________________ than Froggy.

10. Hopper is ____________________.

fastest
faster

Home Activity Your child has been learning to spell words ending in *-er* and *-est*. Play a game with your child by tossing a coin onto this page. Read the list word that is closest to where the coin lands and have your child spell it. Take turns.

Name ____________________________

Contractions with *Not*

Mark the sentence that spells the contraction correctly.

1. ○ Days aren't long in the winter.
   ○ Days arent long in the winter.
   ○ Days are'nt long in the winter.

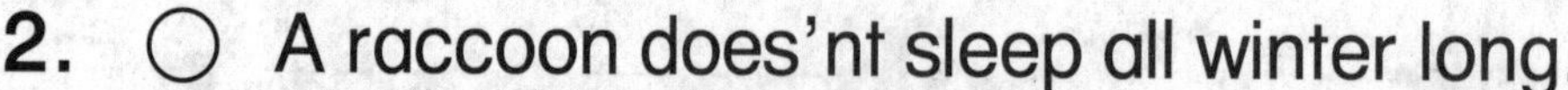

2. ○ A raccoon does'nt sleep all winter long.
   ○ A raccoon doesnt sleep all winter long.
   ○ A raccoon doesn't sleep all winter long.

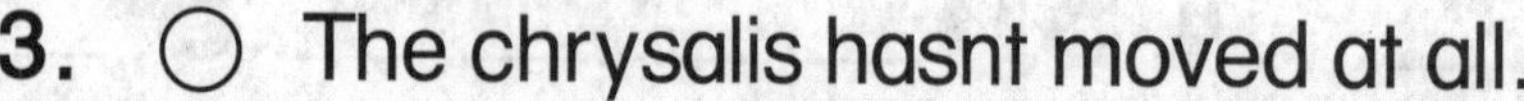

3. ○ The chrysalis hasnt moved at all.
   ○ The chrysalis hasn't moved at all.
   ○ The chrysalis has'nt moved at all.

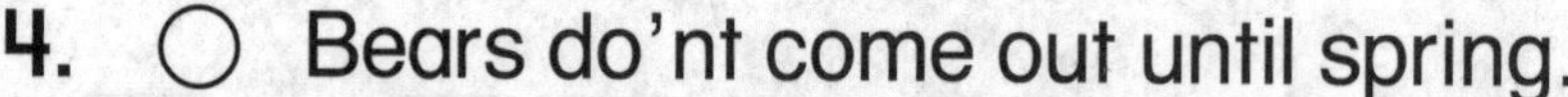

4. ○ Bears do'nt come out until spring.
   ○ Bears dont come out until spring.
   ○ Bears don't come out until spring.

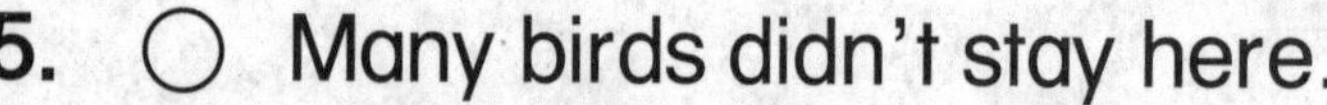

5. ○ Many birds didn't stay here.
   ○ Many birds did'nt stay here.
   ○ Many birds didnt stay here.

6. ○ The fat bear was'nt hungry.
   ○ The fat bear wasn't hungry.
   ○ The fat bear wasnt hungry.

Home Activity Your child prepared for taking tests on contractions with *not*. Together read part of a short newspaper or magazine article. Take turns with your child circling contractions with *not*. Ask your child what two words make up each contraction.

Name ______________________________

Circle the word for each picture.

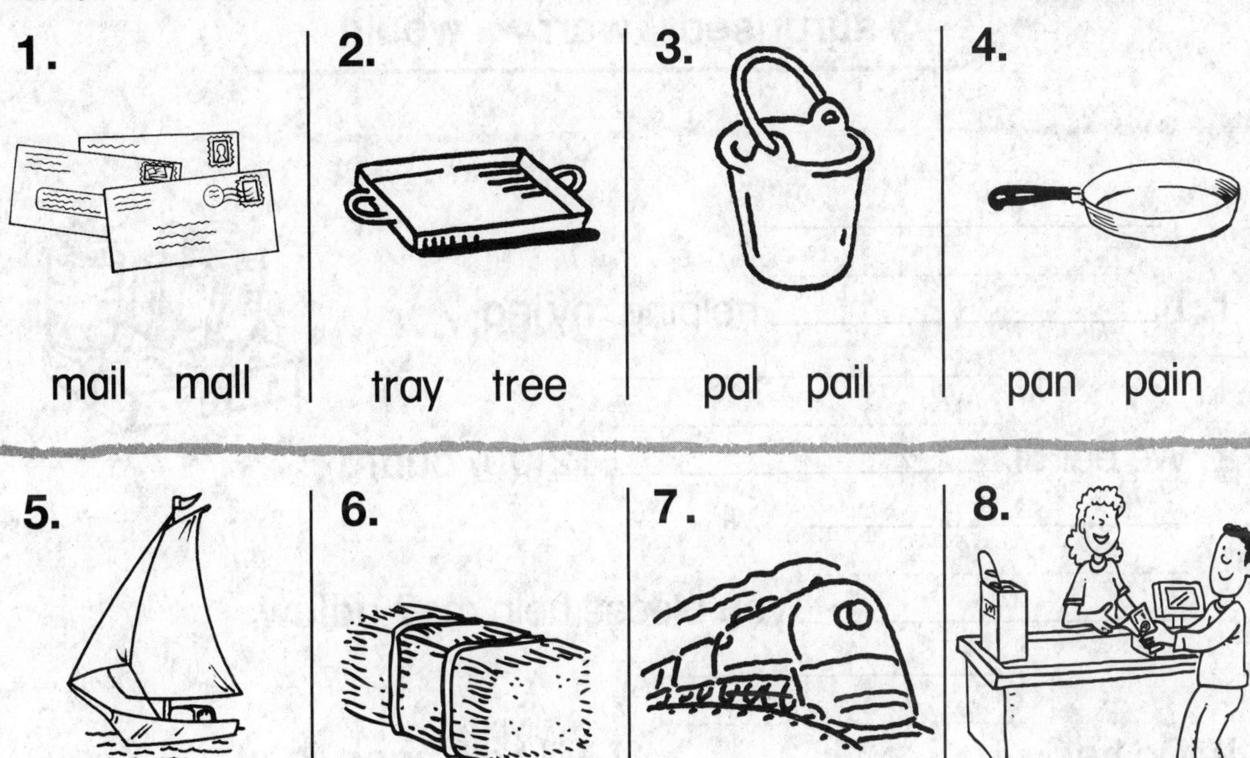

1. mail mall
2. tray tree
3. pal pail
4. pan pain
5. sell sail
6. he hay
7. train trap
8. page pay

Find the word that has the same **long a** sound as .
Mark the ⬭ to show your answer.

9. ⬭ clip
   ⬭ clap
   ⬭ clay

10. ⬭ man
    ⬭ main
    ⬭ mine

Home Activity Your child read words in which the long *a* sound is spelled *ai* and *ay*, as in *rain* and *hay*. Ask your child to name a rhyming word for each long *a* word on this page.

Name ______________________

Read the words in the box.
Pick a word to complete each sentence.
Look at the scrambled letters for a hint.
Write the word on the line.

about enjoy gives surprise surprised worry would

1. I ______________ helping. **nyjeo**

2. We eat at ______________ 12:00. **buato**

3. ______________ you please help me? **odluw**

4. Do not ______________. I will help. **woryr**

5. When we jump up, she will be ______________. **sipresrud**

6. Dad ______________ us gifts. **ivseg**

7. The gifts are always a big ______________. **rrpsiues**

Home Activity Your child identified and read the words *about, enjoy, gives, surprise, surprised, worry,* and *would*. Ask your child to use these words to create a puppet show with paper bag puppets. Record the script on paper and have your child practice reading it aloud.

Name ______________________________

Look at the picture.
Circle the sentence that tells about the picture.

1. 

Dad is happy about his new shed from Jen.

Jen is happy about her tree house from Dad.

2.

They planted a garden.

Flowers grow in gardens.

3. 

We are singing in the play.

The class sets up for a play.

4.

Tom is good at running.

Tom is a good friend.

Write a sentence about the picture.

5. 

____

____

Home Activity Your child drew conclusions from pictures. Look at a story with your child. Cover up the words with paper. Invite your child to tell you about the story using only the illustrations.

Name ____________________

Writing • Friendly Letter

Dear Ken,

It is almost your birthday!
What gift do you hope to get?
Do you want it to be a surprise?
Mom will take me to your party.
I will bring your gift then.
I hope you will like it.

Your friend,
Jill

Key Features of a Friendly Letter

- The letter is written to someone the writer knows.
- The letter has a polite greeting and closing.

Name ___________________

Write each word correctly.
Use 's or **'** at the end of each word.

Meg's hat

1. Janes drum = ___________ drum

2. dogs bone = ___________ bone

3. Moms cup = ___________ cup

4. babys crib = ___________ crib

5. pets beds = ___________ beds

Pick a word from the box to match each picture.
Write it on the line.

girls'	Matt's

6. ___________ lunch

7. ___________ games

Home Activity Your child wrote words that show ownership. Point out objects in your home that are owned by one or more persons in the family. Ask your child to use a possessive to tell you who owns each object *(Mike's pen)*.

Name ____________________

Words with *ai, ay*

Spelling Words				
train	way	tail	play	day
may	rain	gray	mail	afraid

Write the words in ABC order.

tail afraid way may gray day

1. ____________________
2. ____________________
3. ____________________
4. ____________________
5. ____________________
6. ____________________

Draw a line from the word to its picture. **Write** the word.

mail

rain

train

play

7. ____________________
8. ____________________
9. ____________________
10. ____________________

Home Activity Your child spelled words with the long *a* sound spelled *ai* and *ay*. Have your child circle *ai* and *ay* in the spelling words.

Name ______________________________

Adjectives

An **adjective** tells about a person, place, animal, or thing.

happy woman

big city

loud dog

nice present

Circle the adjective. **Write** the adjective on the line.
Say a sentence for each adjective.

1. heavy piñata  ____________________

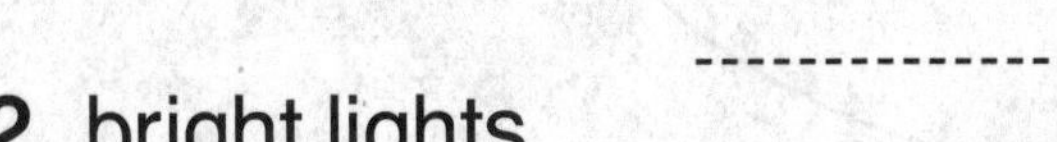
2. bright lights ____________________

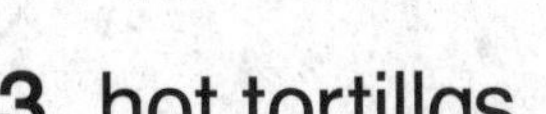
3. hot tortillas ____________________

4. good friends ____________________

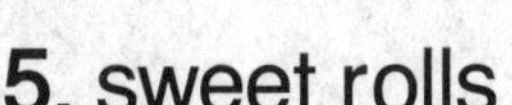
5. sweet rolls ____________________

Home Activity Your child learned about adjectives. Read a story with your child. Point to a sentence and ask your child to identify any adjectives in the sentence. Continue with other sentences.

Name ______________________________

Web

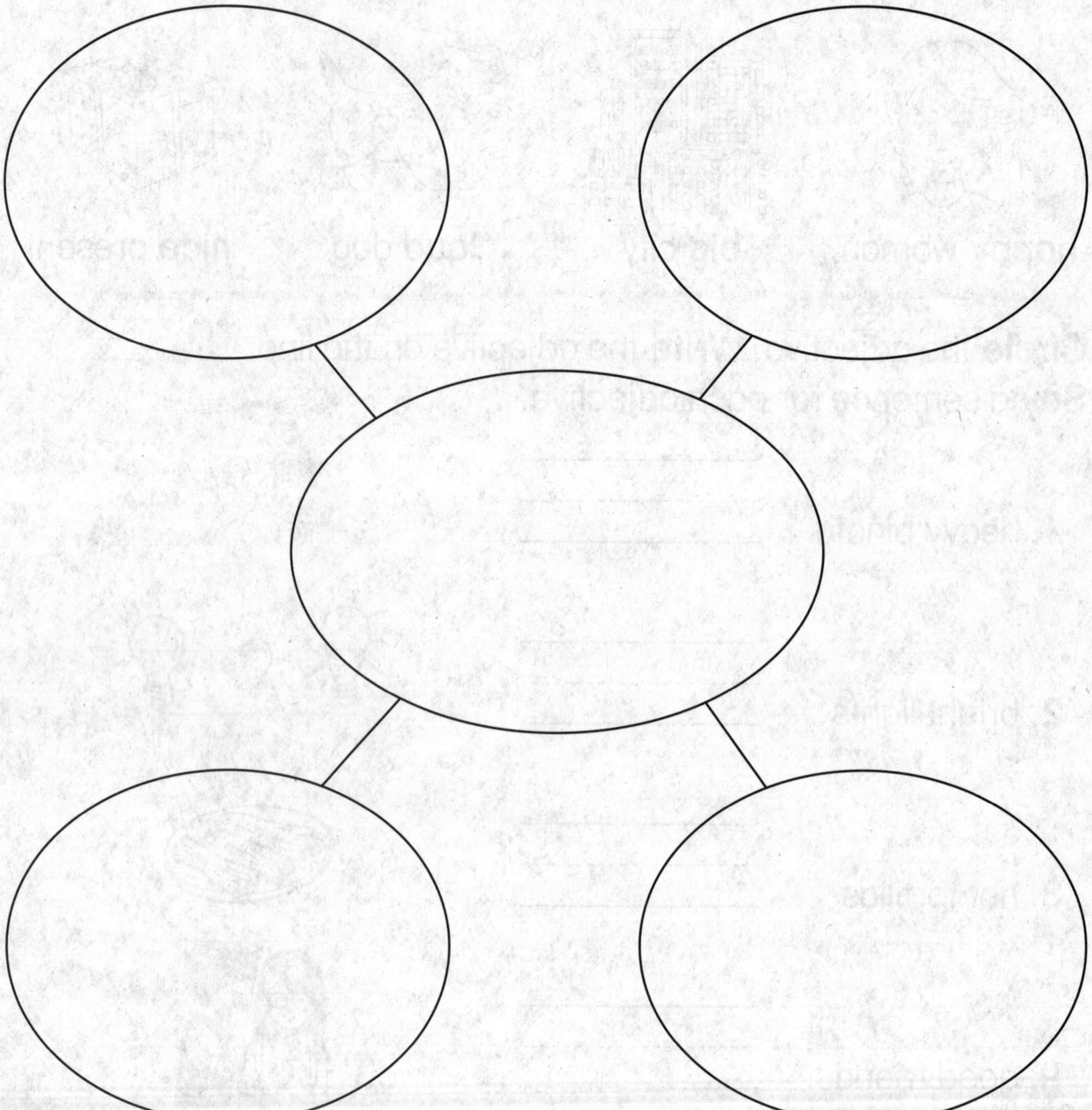

Home Activity Your child is learning more about writing a letter. Have your child plan a letter to a relative.

Name ______________________

M m

Copy the words. Write the letters the correct size.

Meg	______	March	______
main	______	mail	______
May	______	stay	______
maid	______	chain	______
play	______	fail	______
rain	______	paid	______
Max	______	way	______

Did you write all of your letters the correct size?  **Yes** **No**

Home Activity Your child practiced writing words with *Mm, ai,* and *ay*. Have your child read and copy the following sentence as neatly as he or she can. *Meg may stay and play in the rain.*

Name ______________________

Find out about foods people make for celebrations.

chef **classmates**

1. Who would you interview to find out foods that different families eat at celebrations?

2. Who would you interview to find out how to make some of those foods?

3. Write questions you would ask a local expert, such as a chef, about how to make food for a celebration.

4. Interview a local expert using the questions you created. Share what you learned with your class.

Home Activity Your child learned about gathering information by interviewing people. Talk with your child about special traditions your family has for different celebrations. Ask you child to write two interview questions to ask a member of your family about the celebrations and traditions.

What do quails say?

One quail's call is *bob . . . WHITE!*

You may see a bobwhite someday!

Decodable Story *Quails*
Target Skills Vowel Digraphs *ai, ay;* Singular and Plural Possessives

Name ______________________

Quails

Vowel Digraphs *ai, ay*		Singular and Plural Possessives	High-Frequency Words	
quails	stay	birds'	are	what
main	say	farmers'	their	do
trail	may	quail's	is	one
raid	someday		the	you
gray			many	a
			live	

Quails are small, plump birds.

Quails can fly, but their main home is on land.

Many quails are tan, gray, and white.

The birds' spots and stripes help them hide.

They run up the trail when foxes raid.

Quails can live on farmers' farms.

They like seeds and insects.

Farmers hope the quails will stay!

Name ______________________

Words with *ai, ay*

Spelling Words				
train	way	tail	play	day
may	rain	gray	mail	afraid

High-Frequency Words
about
would

Read about a dog. **Write** the missing list words.

1. I have a ______________ dog.
2. He is ______________ of storms.
3. He hides when it starts to ______________ .
4. He barks when he hears a ______________ .
5. Could he learn a ______________ to play catch?
6. Could he fetch the ______________ ?
7. I think he ______________ learn.
8. Look at him wag his ______________ .
9. I think he ______________ like to play.
10. Let's think ______________ training another day.

Home Activity Your child wrote spelling words to complete a story about a dog. Have your child make up a story using some of the list words.

Name ______________________

Adjectives

Write an adjective from the box to complete each sentence.

green	sharp	soft

1. Gina's cat has ____________ fur.

2. The cat has ____________ eyes.

3. Look at the cat's ____________ claws.

Tell about something you like.
Use adjectives to describe it.

____

____

____

Choose other adjectives. **Say** a sentence for each adjective.

Home Activity Your child learned how to use adjectives in writing. Take turns with your child describing what you are wearing. Have your child identify any adjectives either of you uses in your descriptions.

Name ______________________________

Words with *ai, ay*

Spelling Words				
train	way	tail	play	day
may	rain	gray	mail	afraid

Underline the words that rhyme. **Write** the words.

Whose tail is on the mail?

1. ____________

2. ____________

Is there a train in the rain?

3. ____________

4. ____________

When may we play?

5. ____________

6. ____________

Circle the word that is spelled correctly.

7. gray gra

8. day dai

9. afrayd afraid

10. waye way

Home Activity Your child has been learning to spell words with the long *a* sound spelled *ai* and *ay*. Help your child think of and spell words that rhyme with some of the list words.

Name ______________________

Adjectives

Mark the sentence that has a line under the adjective.

1. ○ Grandmother reads a <u>funny</u> book.
   ○ Grandmother <u>reads</u> a funny book.
   ○ <u>Grandmother</u> reads a funny book.

2. ○ Mama <u>gave</u> Francisco a big hug.
   ○ Mama gave Francisco a <u>big</u> hug.
   ○ Mama gave Francisco a big <u>hug</u>.

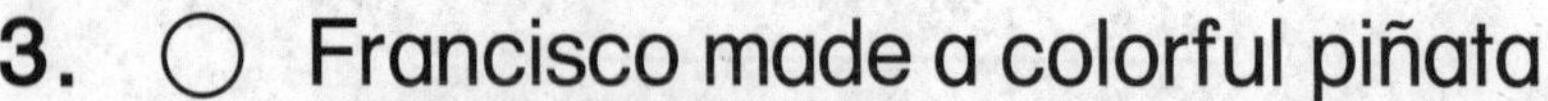

3. ○ Francisco <u>made</u> a colorful piñata.
   ○ <u>Francisco</u> made a colorful piñata.
   ○ Francisco made a <u>colorful</u> piñata.

4. ○ Everyone <u>ate</u> the fresh tortillas.
   ○ Everyone ate the fresh <u>tortillas</u>.
   ○ Everyone ate the <u>fresh</u> tortillas.

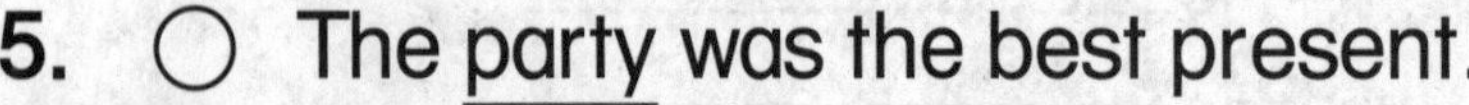

5. ○ The <u>party</u> was the best present.
   ○ The party was the <u>best</u> present.
   ○ The party was the best <u>present</u>.

6. ○ Papa played a <u>long</u> song.
   ○ Papa <u>played</u> a long song.
   ○ <u>Papa</u> played a long song.

Choose other adjectives. **Say** a sentence for each adjective.

Home Activity Your child prepared for taking tests on adjectives. Together read a short, simple newspaper or magazine article. Have your child circle as many adjectives as he or she can find.

Name ______________________________

Circle the word for each picture.

1\.

head herd

2\.

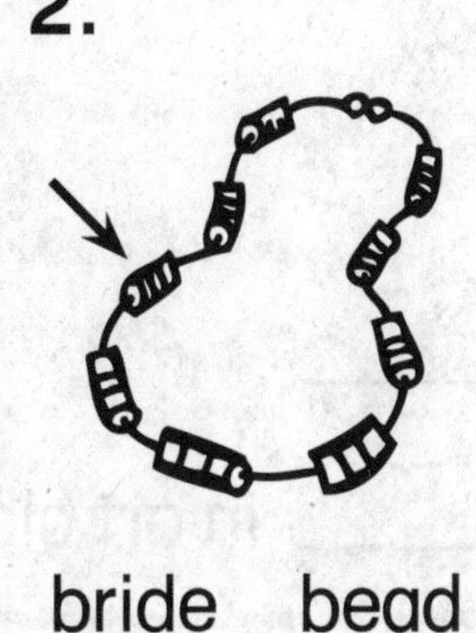

bride bead

3\.

sail seal

4\.

berry bread

5\.

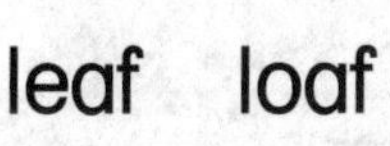

leaf loaf

6\.

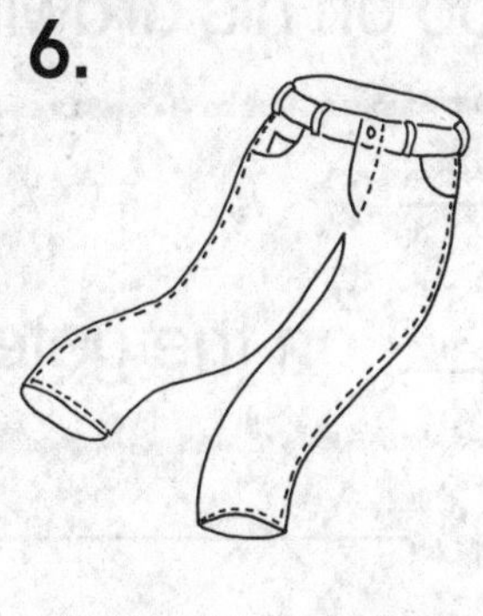

jeans jars

7\.

bake beak

8\.

clean clang

Circle the words that finish each sentence.

9. Please/Place pass the peas/bees.

10. I spread/spent the jam on the cracker.

11. I read /rang my book at the beach/birch yesterday.

Home Activity Your child read words in which both short *e* and long *e* sounds are spelled *ea*. Ask your child to think of rhyming words for the words on this page. Write word and review the spelling together.

Name ______________________________

Read the words in the box.
Pick a word to complete each sentence.
Write the word on the line.

draw	colors	over	
drew	great	sign	show

1. Each day I like to ______________ in art class.

2. Ted did a ______________ job on his drawing!

3. I can read the ______________ on the gate.

4. I think red and blue are the best ______________.

5. The map will ______________ us the way to go.

6. The frogs jump ______________ the rocks.

7. Last week I ______________ a dog in art class.

Home Activity Your child identified and read the words *draw, colors, over, drew, great, sign,* and *show*. Have your child read each word again and make up a new sentence for each word.

Name ____________________

Read the story.
Follow the directions.

One day, Penny and her mom went to East Mall. Mom wanted to get jeans for Penny. East Mall was a big mall. Penny and her mom spent a long time walking from store to store. Soon Penny wanted to go home. But her mom wanted to go to one more store. At last, they got jeans for Penny. Then they headed home. Penny went into the house first. She saw paper chains everywhere! She saw a cake. Then her friends came running and yelled, "Surprise, Penny!"

1. Circle the sentence that is the big idea of the story.

Penny and her mom walked around a big mall.

Penny's friends gave her a surprise birthday party.

2. Circle why you think Mom spent a long time at the mall.

She wanted Penny's friends to get to the house before Penny.

On that day, she wanted to spend a lot of time with Penny.

3. Write a title for this story

____

____

Home Activity Your child identified the theme—the big idea—of a story. Reread the story with your child. Help your child identify the sentences in the story that helped him or her tell the big idea.

Name ________________________________

Writing • Invitation

Dear Emma,

My older brother plays soccer. He will give a free soccer lesson to kids. Please come to the lesson. It will be at my house on April 20 at 3:00 P.M. I hope you will come.

Your friend,
Kat

Key Features of an Invitation

- An invitation asks someone to an event, using polite words.
- An invitation tells important information about the event.

Name ______________________

Add -ed to each word.
Write the new word on the line.

fr**ied**

1. dry ______ **2.** cry ______ **3.** spy ______

4. worry ______ **5.** try ______ **6.** copy ______

Add -er and **-est** to each word.
Write the new word on the lines.

	Add -er	Add -est
7. silly		
8. funny		
9. happy		
10. easy		

Home Activity Your child practiced adding endings to words where the spelling changed from *y* to *i* before adding *-ed*, *-er*, or *-est*. Use the words above to make up a story with your child.

Name ________________________

Words with *ea*

Spelling Words				
eat	sea	each	team	please
dream	treat	beach	clean	lean

Write two list words that rhyme with the picture.

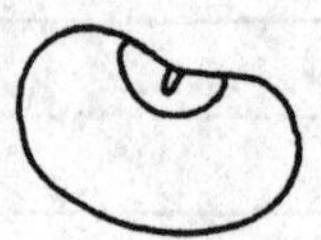

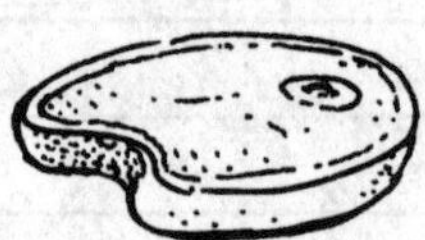

1. ________________
2. ________________
3. ________________
4. ________________
5. ________________
6. ________________

Write the missing words.

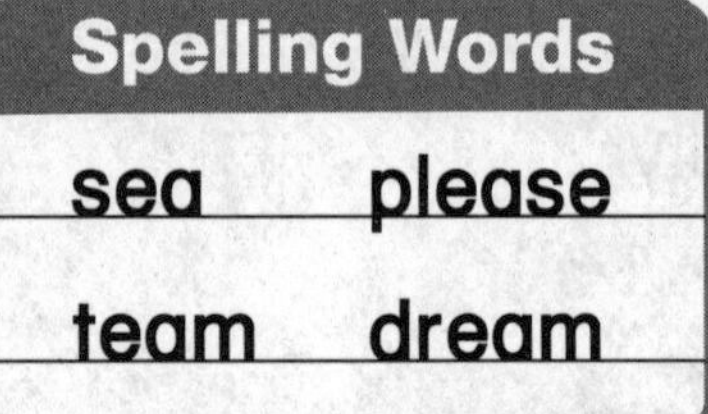

Spelling Words	
sea	please
team	dream

7. My ________________ won!
8. I ________________ about trips.
9. I love the ________________ .
10. Can we ________________ go there?

Home Activity Your child spelled words with the long *e* sound spelled *ea*. Ask your child to name the two letters that appear in every spelling word (*ea*).

Name ______________________________

Adjectives for Colors and Shapes

Some **adjectives** name colors.

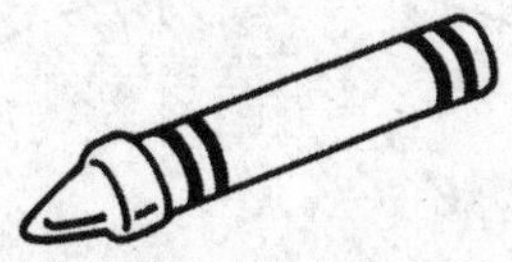

white crayon

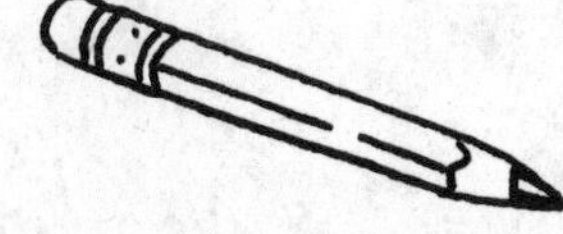

black pencil

Some **adjectives** name shapes.

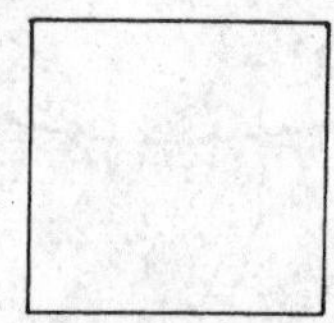

square paper

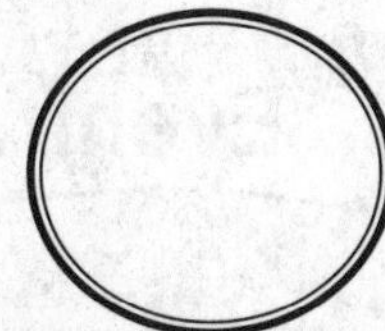

round frame

Circle the adjective in each sentence that names a color or shape.
Say a sentence for each adjective.

1. Roz has blue markers.

2. Gert has green markers.

3. Roz draws round circles.

4. Gert draws square boxes.

5. Roz adds brown dots.

6. Gert makes yellow lines.

Home Activity Your child learned about adjectives for colors and shapes. Point to objects around your home and have your child describe the objects using adjectives that name colors and shapes.

Name ___________________________

Web

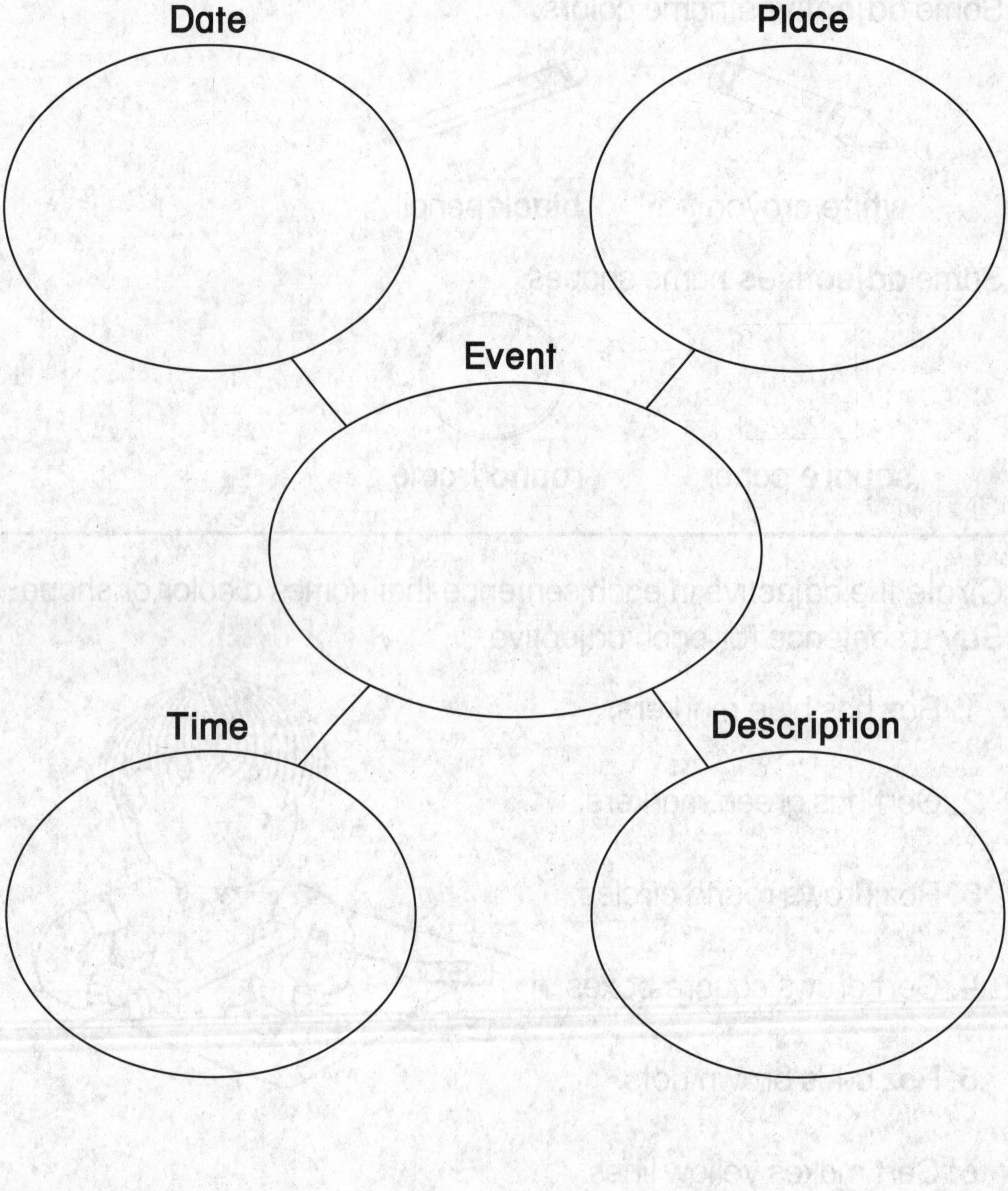

Date

Place

Event

Time

Description

Home Activity Your child is learning about invitations. Share ideas about how people invite family members to events.

Name ______________________

L l

Copy the words. Leave the correct space between your letters.

Len	bead
lean	Leah
leap	leaf
plea	sea
seal	beam
clean	seat
leak	heap

Did you leave the correct space between your letters?  

Home Activity Your child practiced writing words with *Ll* and *ea*. Have your child choose one word with *ea* and write as many rhyming words as he or she can from words on the list and not on the list.

Name ____________________________

Jordan asked her classmates which story is their favorite. Help Jordan complete the chart.

Favorite Stories	
Goldilocks	
The Three Little Pigs	
Little Red Riding Hood	
The Tortoise and the Hare	
The Billy Goats Gruff	

卌 = 5

Make tally marks on the chart to show what Jordan learned.

1. Five classmates like **Goldilocks** the most.
2. Four classmates like **The Three Little Pigs** the most.
3. Three classmates like **Little Red Riding Hood** the most.
4. Two classmates like **The Tortoise and the Hare** the most.
5. Six classmates like **The Three Billy Goats Gruff** the most.
6. Present Jordan's results to your class by acting out the story that her classmates liked the most.

Home Activity Your child used a chart to find information, answer questions, and convey results of research. Together, make a chart showing chores that each family member does at home. Ask your child to fill in the chart as chores are completed.

"This is a treat!" said Beth.

"But I must leave after the meal."

"No . . . after we clean up!" said Neal.

Decodable Story *Bread*
Target Skills Vowel Digraph *ea;* Adding Endings: Changing *y* to *i*

Name ____________________

Bread

Vowel Digraph *ea*		Adding Endings: Change *y* to *i*	High-Frequency Words	
bread	yeast	babies	a	I
eat	treat	ladies	your	the
feast	leave	dried	are	is
wheat	meal	fried	you	
read	clean	tried	about	
beat			said	

"Babies like it! Ladies like it!

Eat it with jelly!

It's a feast in your belly!" sang Neal.

"Are you singing about bread?" asked Beth.

"Yes!" said Neal. "I'm mixing wheat bread.

Will you help me?"

"I've never tried that before," said Beth.

"But I can read the card.

I'll beat in the yeast."

Name ______________________

Words with *ea*

Spelling Words				
eat	sea	each	team	please
dream	treat	beach	clean	lean

High-Frequency Words
colors
sign

Write the missing letters. **Write** the word.

1. Is it time to **ea**___ ? ______
2. Let's go to the ___**ea**___ ___ . ______
3. I can ___ ___**ea**___ the porch. ______
4. Don't ___**ea**___ over too far. ______
5. I had a ___ ___**ea**___ last night. ______
6. Will you ___ ___**ea**___ ___ sit? ______
7. Fish live in the ___**ea**. ______
8. My ___**ea**___ lost! ______
9. **Write** a word that rhymes with **fine**. ______
10. Blue, green, and red are ______.

Home Activity Your child wrote spelling words to complete sentences. Read a sentence on this page and have your child spell the list word.

Name ______________________________

Adjectives for Colors and Shapes

Color the boxes and circles.

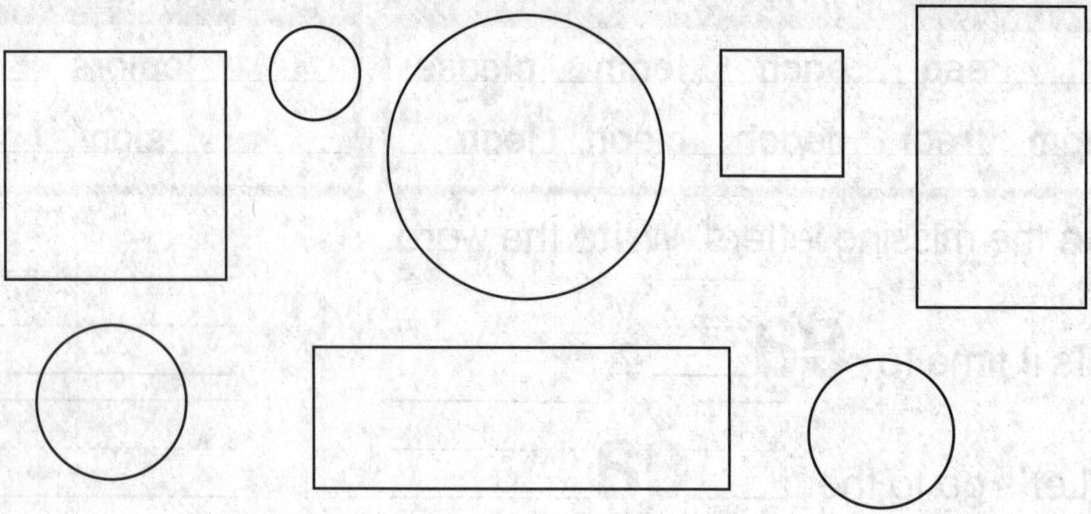

Write about the picture.
Use color and shape words.

Choose other adjectives. **Say** a sentence for each adjective.

Home Activity Your child learned how to use adjectives for colors and shapes in writing. Write this sentence frame on paper: *The* ___ *animal runs.* Have your child write color adjectives in the sentence frame to make as many sentences as possible.

Name ____________________

Words with *ea*

Write list words in the puzzle.

Across
2. chew food
4. not dirty

Down
1. sandy shore
3. ocean
5. thin

Spelling Words
eat
sea
each
team
please
dream
treat
beach
clean
lean

Draw lines through all the *i*'s and *k*'s. **Write** the word that is left.

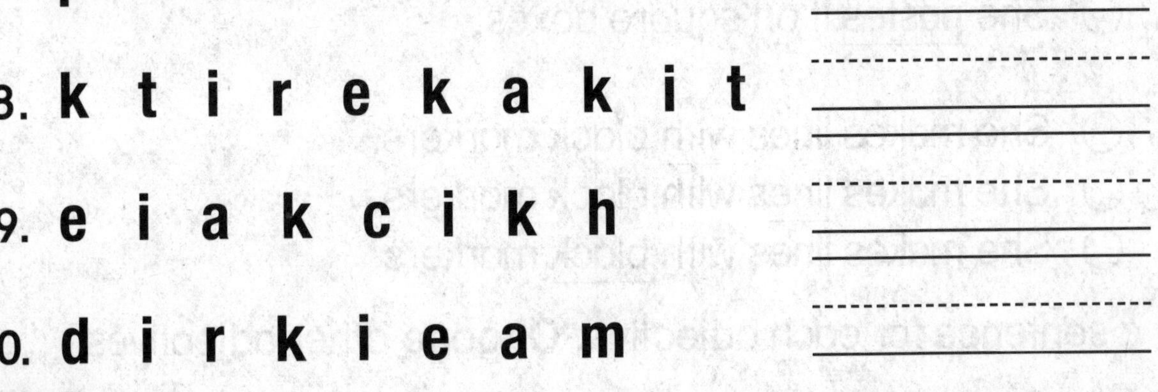

6. t i e k a k m i ____________
7. p l i e a k k s i e ____________
8. k t i r e k a k i t ____________
9. e i a k c i k h ____________
10. d i r k i e a m ____________

Home Activity Your child has been learning to spell words with the long *e* sound spelled *ea*. Have your child identify and spell the three words he or she found most difficult.

Name ______________________________

Adjectives for Colors and Shapes

Mark the sentence that has a line under the adjective.

1. ◯ Will Cindy draw yellow flowers?
   ◯ Will Cindy draw yellow flowers?
   ◯ Will Cindy draw yellow flowers?

2. ◯ She makes round shapes.
   ◯ She makes round shapes.
   ◯ She makes round shapes.

3. ◯ She adds green stems.
   ◯ She adds green stems.
   ◯ She adds green stems.

4. ◯ Cindy cuts brown paper.
   ◯ Cindy cuts brown paper.
   ◯ Cindy cuts brown paper.

5. ◯ She pastes it on square boxes.
   ◯ She pastes it on square boxes.
   ◯ She pastes it on square boxes.

6. ◯ She makes lines with black markers.
   ◯ She makes lines with black markers.
   ◯ She makes lines with black markers.

Say a sentence for each adjective. **Choose** other adjectives.

Home Activity Your child prepared for taking tests on adjectives for colors and shapes. Together read a favorite book. Have your child point out adjectives that name colors and shapes.

Name ______________________________

Circle the word for each picture.

toad

blow

1. snap snow

2. road rod

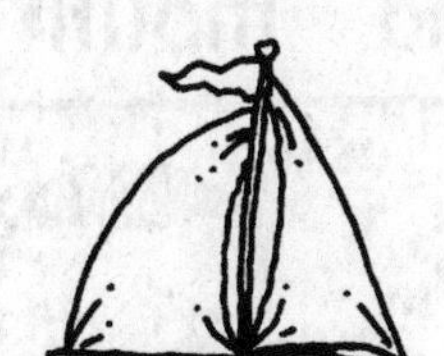

3. boat beat

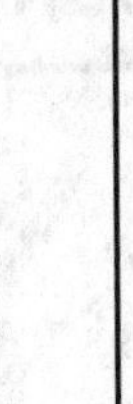

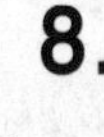

4. sap soap

5. bee bow

6. coat cot

7. ray row

8. leaf loaf

Write the letters that finish the words in each sentence.

9. The g ________ t drank from the b ________ l.

10. They looked high and l ________ but they could not find the r ________ d.

Home Activity Your child created and read words in which the long *o* sound is spelled *oa* and *ow*, as in *toad* and *blow*. Together, list as many words as possible with the long *o* sound in their names. Then ask your child to sort the words by their spellings.

Name ______________________________

Read the words in the box.
Pick a word to finish each sentence.
Write it in the puzzle.

found	**mouth**	**once**	**took**	**wild**

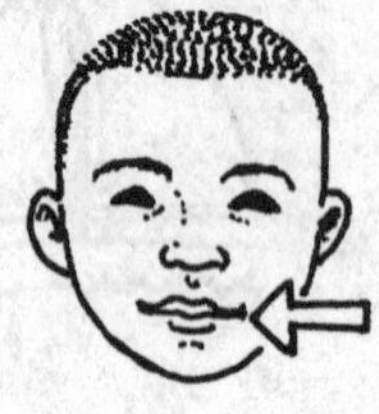

1\. You talk with your ______.

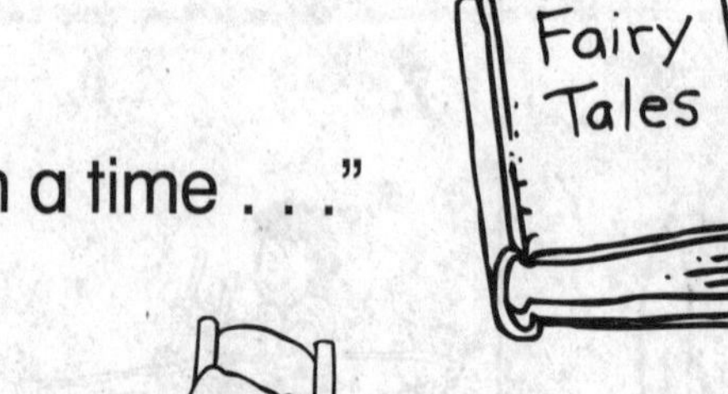

2\. "______ upon a time . . ."

3\. not lost

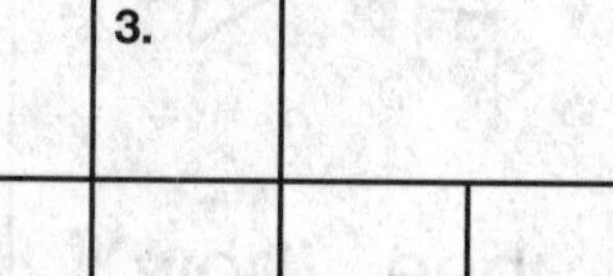

4\. He ______ three bites of his cake.

5\. A raccoon is a ______ animal.

Home Activity Your child identified and read the words *found, mouth, once, took,* and *wild*. Ask your child to write and illustrate a fairy tale about a boy or girl who finds a wild animal. Encourage your child to use the new words and help him or her with spelling if necessary.

Name ______________________

Read the details.

On Friday, Michael and his father are going on vacation. They will drive the family car to Mount Rushmore. Mount Rushmore is in South Dakota. It is a mountain with the faces of four American presidents carved into it. Michael and his father will camp nearby. They will have a lot of fun.

Circle the details that are from the story you just read.

1. Michael and his father are going on vacation.

Michael and his father will fly.

Mount Rushmore is in North Dakota.

Michael and his father will camp.

Michael and his father will drive.

Write two facts about the story.

2.

Home Activity Your child has learned to identify facts and details from a story. Read a story with your child and point out facts and details.

Name ______________________________

Writing • Descriptive Poem

The Farm

We hop on the big yellow school bus.

To the farm it takes us.

Cows, pigs, and sheep we see!

But the best part of all

is watching the farmer haul

huge bales of hay

to the barn where the animals stay.

Key Features of a Descriptive Poem

- Most descriptive poems are shorter than a story.
- Lines in a descriptive poem can either rhyme or not rhyme.

Name ____________________

Circle the word for each picture.

1. 
stub
scrub

2. 
splash
slash

3. 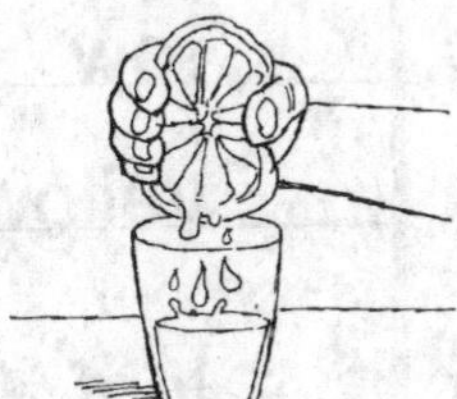
squeeze
sneeze

4. 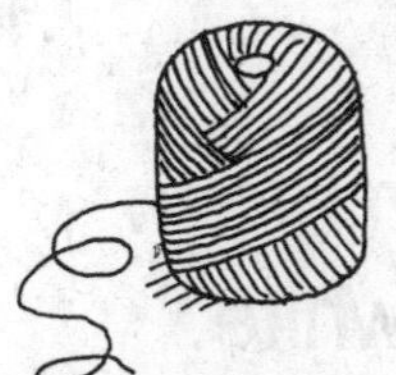
sting
string

5. 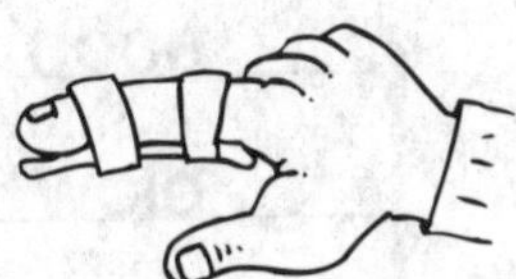
lint
splint

6. 
spring
sing

7. 
those
three

8. 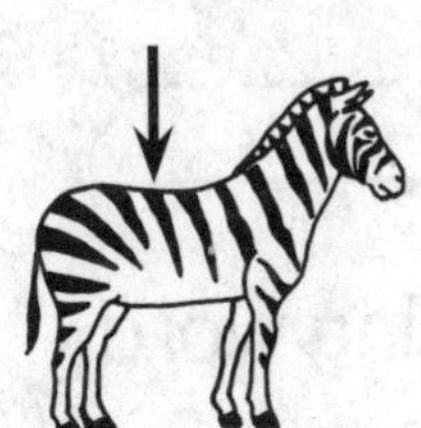
stripe
ripe

Write the letters that finish the words in each sentence.

9. She ______ e w the ball ______ o u g h the ______ e e n door.

10. I had a sore ______ o a t .

Home Activity Your child created and read words that begin with three-letter consonant blends. Have your child draw pictures of *screen, spray, squint,* and *street*. Have him or her label each picture with the word.

Name ____________________

Words with *oa, ow*

Read the clues. **Write** the word.

Spelling Words
boat
road
snow
row
yellow
loaf
coat
soap
blow
pillow

It rhymes with **willow**.
You sleep on it.

1. ____________________

It rhymes with **goat**.
It goes in water.

2. ____________________

It rhymes with **mow**.
It's cold and white.

3. ____________________

It rhymes with **fellow**.
It's a color.

4. ____________________

It rhymes with **load**.
Cars go on it.

5. ____________________

It rhymes with **goat**.
You wear it.

6. ____________________

Write the missing word.

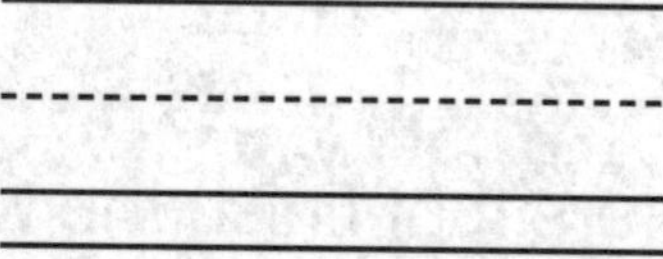

7. I like to ____ bubbles. ____________________

8. Did you ____ the boat? ____________________

9. I got ____ in my eyes. ____________________

10. The ____ of bread is warm. ____________________

Home Activity Your child spelled words with the long *o* vowel sound spelled *oa* and *ow*. Have your child underline *oa* and *ow* in the spelling words.

Name ____________________

Adjectives for Sizes

Some **adjectives** describe size. Words such as **big, small, long,** and **short** describe size.

small bird

big bird

Circle each adjective that describes size.
Say a sentence for each adjective.

1. big bus

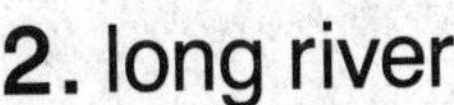

2. long river

3. little fish

4. short stripes

5. tall window

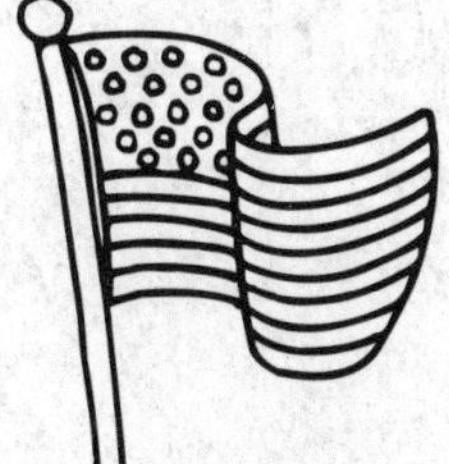

6. huge flag

Home Activity Your child learned about adjectives for sizes. Point to objects around your home. Ask your child if the object is big or small (tall or short, long or short). Have your child answer using the adjective in a sentence.

Name ______________________________

Writing • Poem

A Place and What You See

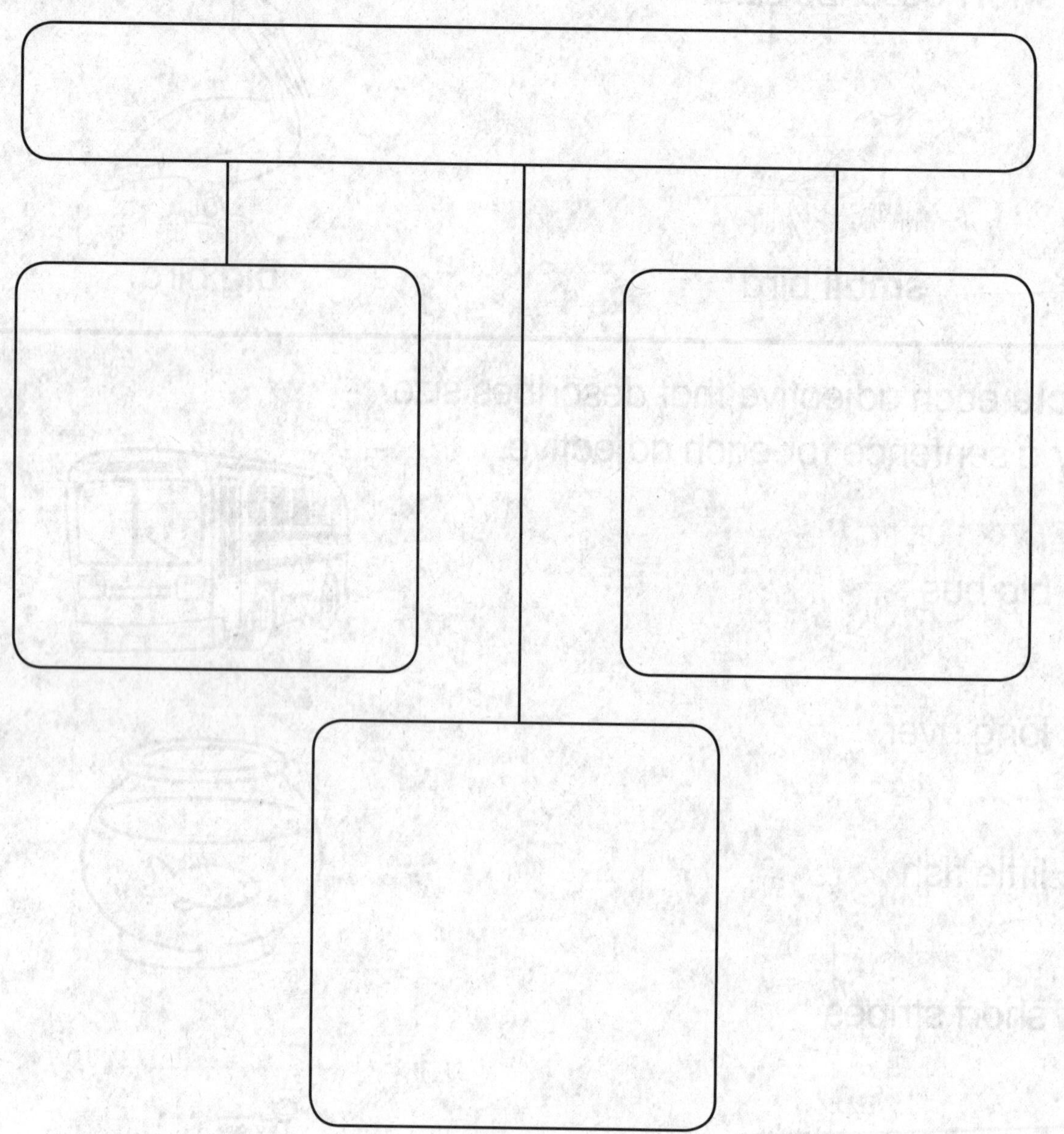

Home Activity Your child can plan a poem that describes a place. Look at pictures of a place with your child. Describe it.

Name ______________________

F f

Copy the words. Write the letters from left to right.

Flo	Fred
float	goat
boat	grow
flow	foam
loaf	throat
road	blow
moan	slow

Did you write all of your letters from left to right? Yes No

Home Activity Your child practiced writing words with *Ff, ow,* and *oa*. Have your child read and write any five words from the list one more time.

Name ______________________________

Ray asked his friends about their favorite American treasures. Help Ray complete the bar graph.

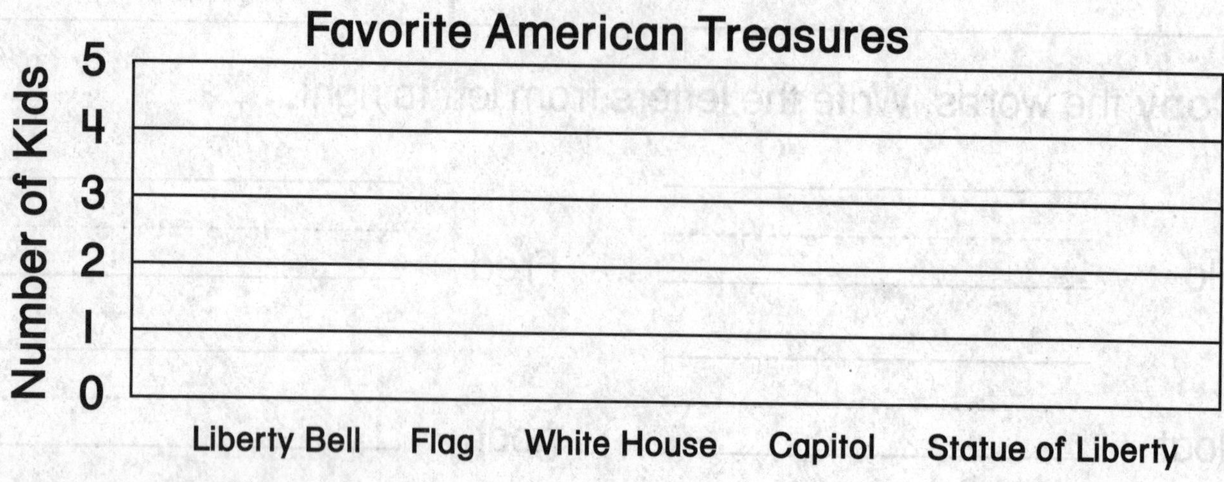

Make bars on the graph to show what Ray learned.

1. Three friends like the Liberty Bell the most.
2. Four friends like the American Flag the most.
3. Two friends like the White House the most.
4. One friend likes the Capitol the most.
5. Five friends like the Statue of Liberty the most.
6. Present Ray's results to your class by dramatizing the American treasure that his friends liked the most.

Home Activity Your child learned how to make and read a bar graph. Help your child poll family members and friends about their favorite places to visit. Make a bar graph to record the results.

Spring is a thrill!

Spring is the best season on my street . . . until summer, that is!

Decodable Story *It's Spring!*
Target Skills Vowel Digraphs *oa, ow;* 3-Letter Consonant Blends, Including *thr, spl*

Name ____________________

It's Spring!

Vowel Digraphs *oa, ow*			3-Letter Consonant Blends, Including *thr, spl*		High-Frequency Words	
toad	snow	show	spring	thrill	the	a
croaks	crow	throw	splash	street	what	your
boat	flowers	yellow	sprout		do	out
goat	row		stream		you	is
oats	grow		stretch		to	

The snow went away. It's spring!

The crow flies. The toad croaks.

The fish splash. The flowers sprout.

What do you like to do in spring?

You can row a boat up the stream.

You can grow a rose.

You can throw a ball to a pal.

You can feed oats to the goat.

You can stretch out on the grass.

Name ____________________

Words with *oa, ow*

Spelling Words				
boat	road	snow	row	yellow
loaf	coat	soap	blow	pillow

High-Frequency Words
wild
once

Write the missing list word.

1. Lemons are ____________.
2. Wash with ____________.
3. Would you like to ride in our ____________?
4. I sleep on a soft ____________.
5. Wear your ____________.
6. He will ____________ the boat.
7. Please buy a ____________ of bread.
8. Is it cold enough to ____________?
9. I took this road ____________.
10. The monkey is a ____________ animal.

Home Activity Your child wrote spelling words to complete sentences. Ask your child to create a sentence using one or two of the spelling words.

Name ______________________________

Adjectives for Sizes

Write about something you like that is very big.
It might be an animal, a place, or a thing.
Use adjectives to tell about it.

Write about something you like that is very small.
It might be an animal, a place, or a thing.
Use adjectives to tell about it. **Say** the adjectives you used.

Home Activity Your child learned how to use adjectives for sizes in writing. Point to pictures that show big, small, long, short, and tall things, one at a time. Ask: *What size is the ___?* Have your child answer the question.

Name ___________________________

Words with *oa, ow*

Spelling Words				
boat	road	snow	row	yellow
loaf	coat	soap	blow	pillow

Write the list word that belongs in the group.

blanket sheet

1. ___________

rain sleet

2. ___________

blue red

3. ___________

street highway

4. ___________

jacket sweater

5. ___________

ship ocean liner

6. ___________

Circle the word that matches. **Write** it.

7. row   bow row   ___________

8. loaf   load loaf   ___________

9. blow   blow flow   ___________

10. soap   soak soap   ___________

Home Activity Your child has been learning words with the long *o* vowel sound spelled *oa* and *ow*. Give clues about a word. Can your child guess and spell the word?

Adjectives for Sizes

Mark the sentence that has a line under the adjective.

1. ○ We saw a big bus.
   ○ We saw a big bus.
   ○ We saw a big bus.

2. ○ Look at the huge house.
   ○ Look at the huge house.
   ○ Look at the huge house.

3. ○ A long river flows by the road.
   ○ A long river flows by the road.
   ○ A long river flows by the road.

4. ○ The bird has a small fish.
   ○ The bird has a small fish.
   ○ The bird has a small fish.

5. ○ The fish has a short tail.
   ○ The fish has a short tail.
   ○ The fish has a short tail.

6. ○ A little bird was in the sky.
   ○ A little bird was in the sky.
   ○ A little bird was in the sky.

Choose other adjectives. **Say** a sentence for each adjective.

Home Activity Your child prepared for taking tests on adjectives for sizes. Together read a favorite storybook. Have your child find adjectives for sizes.

Name ______________________________

Circle the word for each picture.

1.	2.	3.	4.
night note	sit lie	tie tea	fit fight

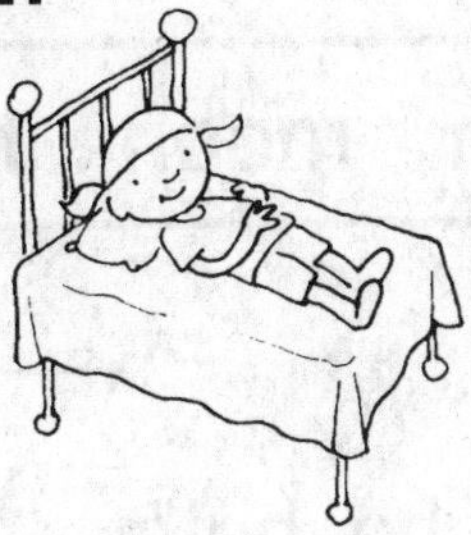

5.	6.	7.	8.
pit pie	hay high	sit sight	tight toad

Read the sentences.
Circle the words that have the **long i** sound spelled **ie** and **igh**.
Underline the words that have the **long e** sound spelled **ie**.

9. I would like another piece of birthday cake.

10. He believes that he is right.

11. I am sorry that I lied to you.

Home Activity Your child practiced reading words in which the long *i* sound is spelled *igh* and *ie* as in *light* and *pie*, and words in which the long *e* sound is spelled *ie*. Encourage your child to create a poem, nonsense rhyme, or song using *igh* and *ie* words.

Name ______________________________

Read the words in the box.
Pick a word to match each clue.
Write it on the line.

above	eight	laugh	moon	touch

1.  "Ha, ha, ha!" ______________

2. 8 five, six, seven, ______________

3.  not below ______________

4.  feel ______________

5.  stars, planets, ______________

Home Activity Your child identified and read the words *above, eight, laugh, moon,* and *touch*. Act out clues for each word and have your child guess which word you picked.

Name ______________________

Read the story.

Nina and Anna are best friends. On Sunday, they will go to camp for one week. They will sleep in a tent. They will meet other girls. They will go swimming. At night they can watch the moon and the stars. Nina and Anna will have a good time.

Read the details. **Circle** the details that are from the story.

They will sleep in tents.

They will go swimming.

They will look for shells.

Camp is a long way from their home.

At night they will watch the moon and the stars.

Write two facts about the story.

Home Activity Your child has learned to identify facts and details from a story. Read a story with your child and ask your child to name one detail and one fact from the story.

Name ______________________________

Writing Prompt: Write a story about a child who rides a horse.

Riley's Ride

Riley went with her family to the fair. There were horses there. Could she ride one? Riley's mom paid for a ride. Riley got to ride a horse. She picked a black and white horse. They went in circles around the field. It was fun!

Name ______________________________

Circle the word for each picture.

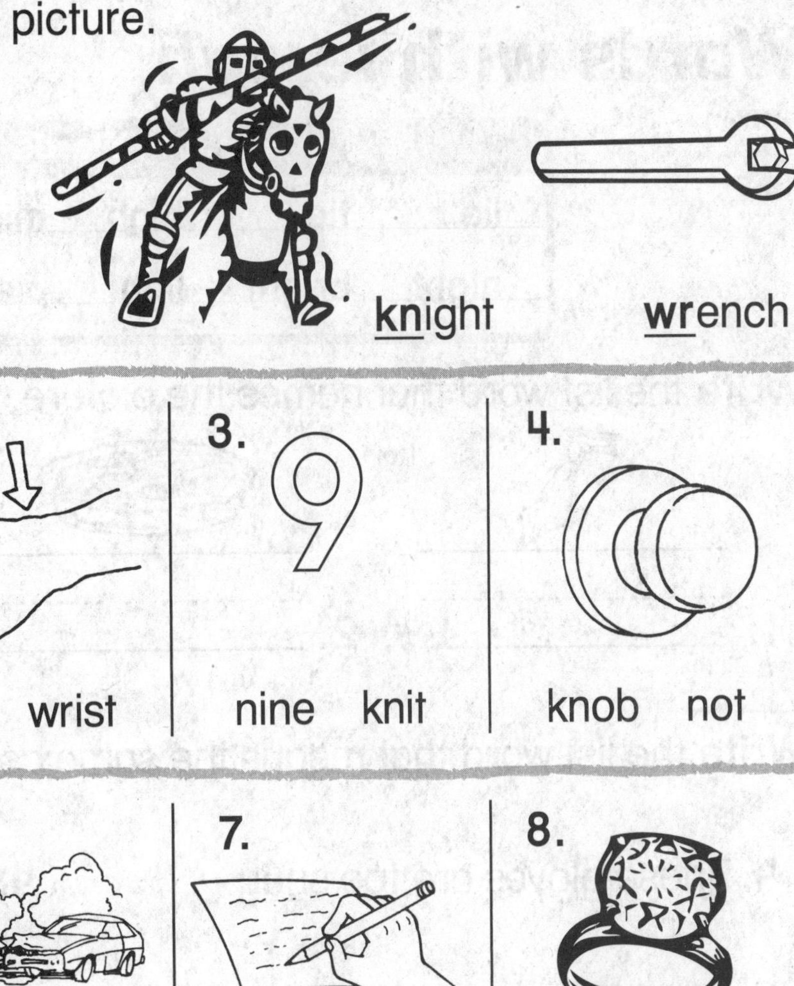

1.	2.	3.	4.
		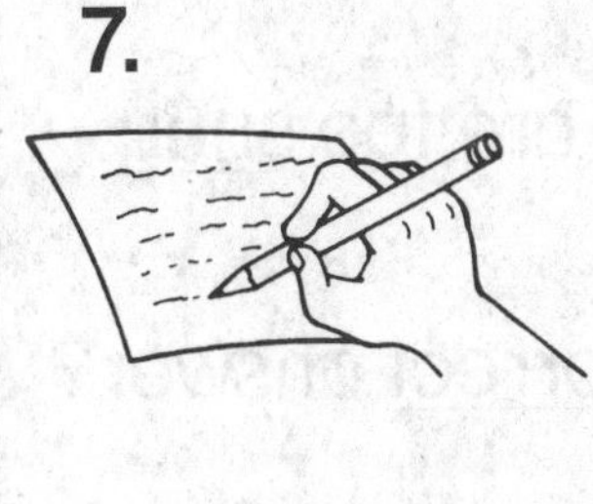	
knife night	rest wrist	nine knit	knob not

5.	6.	7.	8.
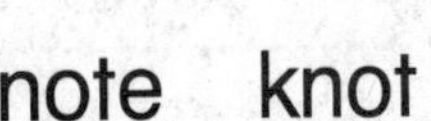			
note knot	wreck rack	white write	ring wrong

Find the word that has the same beginning sound as the picture.
Mark the ⬭ to show your answer.

9. ⬭ wren
⬭ when
⬭ went

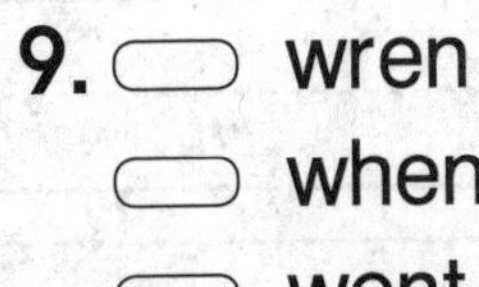

10. ⬭ sneak
⬭ kite
⬭ knock

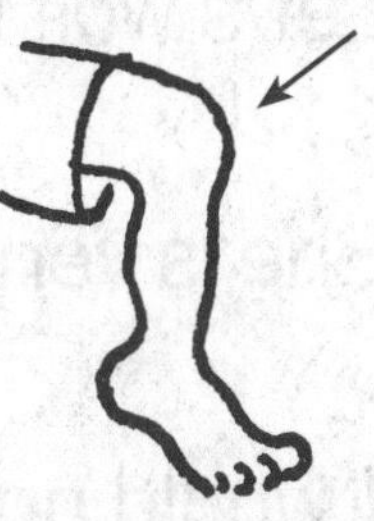

Home Activity Your child read words that begin with *kn* as in *knight* and *wr* as in *wrench*. Have your child copy all the words from the page that begin with *kn* and *wr* and ask him or her to circle the silent letter in each word.

Name ______________________

Words with *ie, igh*

Spelling Words				
lie	tie	high	might	right
night	bright	light	pie	tight

Write the list word that names the picture.

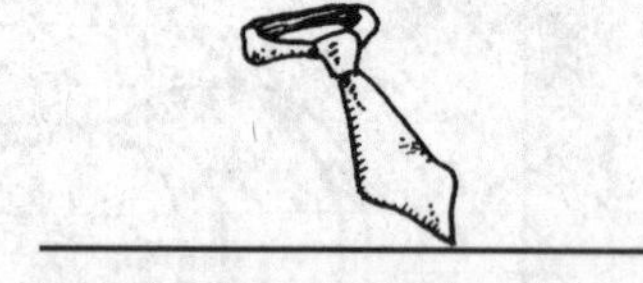

1. ______ 2. ______ 3. ______

Write the list word that means the same as the underlined word.

4. These gloves are too snug. 4. ______

5. What is the correct answer? 5. ______

6. The wall is tall. 6. ______

7. We pulled with all our strength. 7. ______

8. Let's wait until evening. 8. ______

9. She is very smart. 9. ______

10. I would not tell a fib. 10. ______

Home Activity Your child spelled words with the long *i* sound spelled *ie* and *igh*. Have your child circle *ie* and igh in the spelling words.

Name ______________________________

Adjectives for What Kind

An **adjective** can tell what kind.

warm day

pretty flowers

Write the adjective that tells what kind.
Say a sentence for each adjective.

1. loud cattle ______________________

2. happy cows ______________________

3. hot sun ______________________

4. bright lights ______________________

5. tall tree ______________________

6. dark skies ______________________

Home Activity Your child learned about adjectives for what kind. Write *hot, cold, dry* in one list and the nouns *snow, sun, socks* in another list. Ask your child to combine the adjectives and nouns (*hot sun, cold snow, dry socks*).

Name ______________________________

Read Together

Realistic Story

Top Score Response

Focus/Ideas	A good realistic story clearly tells what characters do.
Organization	A good realistic story has a beginning, middle, and end.
Voice	A good realistic story shows the writer's and characters' feelings.
Word Choice	A good realistic story uses words that describe characters, setting, and events.
Sentences	A good realistic story has different kinds of sentences that are clear and complete.
Conventions	A good realistic story uses adjectives that tell what kind.

Home Activity Your child is writing a story about children at a ranch. Share ideas about ranches in stories, movies, or experience.

Name ______________________________

Z z

Copy the words. Write your letters the correct size.

Zeke ______________ high ______________

buzz ______________ fizz ______________

tie ______________ fried ______________

sigh ______________ fuzz ______________

cried ______________ lie ______________

flies ______________ Zena ______________

sight ______________ light ______________

Did you write all of your letters the correct size? **Yes** 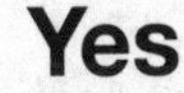 **No**

Home Activity Your child practiced writing words with *Zz, ie,* and *igh*. Have your child find three words from the list that rhyme with *sigh* and write them one more time. *(high, tie, lie)*

Name ______________________

Read the guide words.
Write the word from the box that you would find on that page.

tag bed hand hot cat

1. hat hunt

____

2. bag box

____

3. book cut

____

4. sack tend

____

dog feed gone lip mint

5. let lock

____

6. day duck

____

7. gas gust

____

8. man mole

____

Home Activity Your child learned about using alphabetical order and guide words in a dictionary. Look through a children's dictionary with your child. Make a game of finding new words by using the guide words at the top of each page.

Carl didn't know what to do.

Then he got a wrench instead.

He wrapped it. Dad liked it!

Decodable Story *The Gift*
Target Skills Vowel Digraphs *ie, igh;* Consonant Patterns *kn, wr*

Name ____________________

The Gift

Vowel Digraphs *ie, igh*		Consonant Patterns *kn, wr*		High-Frequency Words	
brief	might	knee	wrench	a	were
chief	right	kneeled	wrapped	the	is
necktie	bright	knot		was	what
ties	tight	know		to	do
tie	sighed	wrong		said	too
night					

Carl went on a brief shopping trip.

The chief reason was to get a gift.

His dad's birthday party was that night.

"Dad might like a necktie," said Carl.

The ties were right by his knee.

Carl kneeled to see.

Carl tried on a bright red tie.

He made the knot too tight.

"This is all wrong!" he sighed.

Name ______________________

Words with *ie, igh*

Spelling Words				
lie	tie	high	might	right
night	bright	light	pie	tight

High-Frequency Words
above
laugh

Write a list word to finish the sentence.

1. You are **r**____. 1. ______
2. Turn on the **l**____. 2. ______
3. I love to eat **p**____! 3. ______
4. Will you wear a **t**____? 4. ______
5. The roof is **h**____. 5. ______
6. It's a cold **n**____. 6. ______
7. The stars are **b**____. 7. ______
8. My belt is too **t**____. 8. ______
9. Do not **l**____ at us. 9. ______
10. The sign is **a**____ the school. 10. ______

Home Activity Your child wrote spelling words to complete sentences. Help your child use the list words in new sentences.

Name ______________________

Adjectives for What Kind

Write about something your family does on a holiday.
Use adjectives such as *loud*, *tasty*, or *cold* to tell about it.

Choose other adjectives. **Say** a sentence for each adjective.

Home Activity Your child learned how to use adjectives for what kind in writing. With your child, look through a family photo album. Talk about what you see in photos using adjectives that tell what kind.

Name ______________________

Words with *ie, igh*

Draw a line through three rhyming list words in a row. **Write** the words.

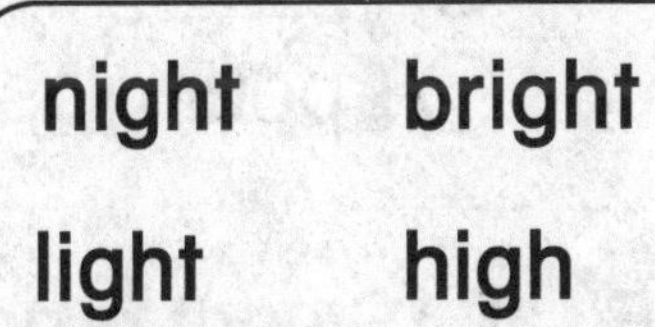

might	read	lie
row	tie	tight
pie	loaf	road

pie	right	coat
sled	tight	low
blue	might	high

1. ______________
2. ______________
3. ______________
4. ______________
5. ______________
6. ______________

Spelling Words

lie
tie
high
might
right
night
bright
light
pie
tight

Write the missing words.

night bright
light high

7. It is up ______________ .
8. It looks ______________ .
9. You see it at ______________ .
10. It looks like a ______________ .

Home Activity Your child has been learning to spell words with the long *i* sound spelled *ie* and *igh*. Say a list word. Ask your child how the long *i* sound is spelled (*ie* or *igh*).

Name ____________________

Adjectives for What Kind

Mark the sentence that has a line under the adjective.

1. ○ Dinner on Sunday is a great meal.
   ○ Dinner on Sunday is a great meal.
   ○ Dinner on Sunday is a great meal.

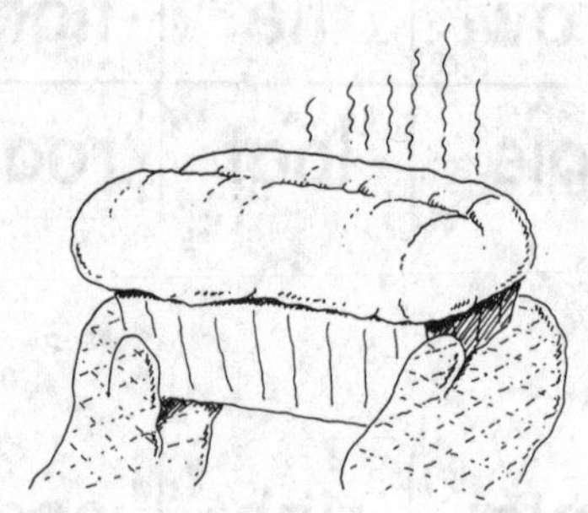

2. ○ A ranch hand bakes fresh bread.
   ○ A ranch hand bakes fresh bread.
   ○ A ranch hand bakes fresh bread.

3. ○ Another ranch hand makes spicy stew.
   ○ Another ranch hand makes spicy stew.
   ○ Another ranch hand makes spicy stew.

4. ○ I pour glasses of cold milk.
   ○ I pour glasses of cold milk.
   ○ I pour glasses of cold milk.

5. ○ Sweet oranges are our dessert.
   ○ Sweet oranges are our dessert.
   ○ Sweet oranges are our dessert.

6. ○ We wash the dirty dishes together.
   ○ We wash the dirty dishes together.
   ○ We wash the dirty dishes together.

Choose other adjectives. **Say** a sentence for each adjective.

Home Activity Your child prepared for taking tests on adjectives for what kind. Together read a short, simple newspaper or magazine article. Have your child circle adjectives that tell what kind.

Name ___________________________

Pick a word from the box to finish each compound word.
Write it on the line.
Draw a line to the picture it matches.

flashlight

boat	man	paper	watch

1. news ______________

2. row ______________

3. wrist ______________

4. snow ______________

Find the compound word.
Mark the ⬭ to show your answer.

5. ⬭ raining
   ⬭ rainy
   ⬭ raincoat

6. ⬭ popcorn
   ⬭ puppy
   ⬭ popping

7. ⬭ mitten
   ⬭ marching
   ⬭ backpack

8. ⬭ balloon
   ⬭ daydream
   ⬭ broken

Home Activity Your child read compound words—words formed by joining two or more words. Have your child tell what two words make up these compound words: *rainbow, snowflake, peanut, baseball, backpack.*

Name ______________________________

Read the words in the box.
Pick a word to finish each sentence.
Write it on the line.

picture	remember	room	stood	thought	would

1. Mom took a ____________________ of my friends and me.

2. We ____________________ by a tree.

3. I ____________________ the picture was wonderful.

4. I will hang the picture in my ____________________ .

5. It will help me ____________________ my friends.

Home Activity Your child learned to identify and read the words *picture, remember, room, stood,* and *thought.* Write each word on a small piece of paper. Say each word. Have your child put the words in the order in which you read them and then repeat the words in a different order.

Name ___________________________

Read the story.
Underline the answer to each question.

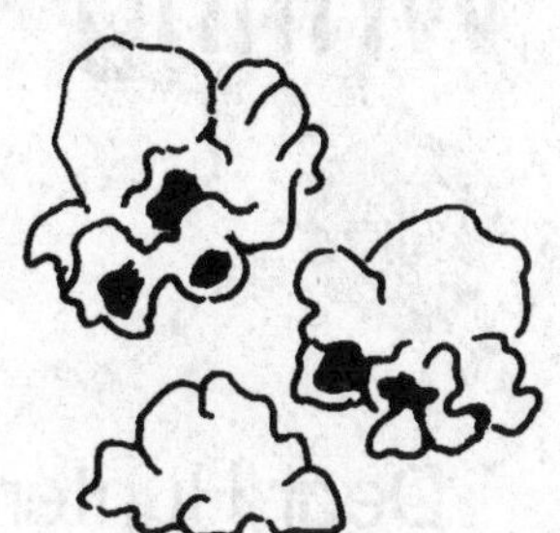

Popcorn is a very old food. People in many lands planted popcorn. They found out something about this corn. Heat would make it pop! Other corns would not pop. The popped corn looked like snowflakes. Some people wore strings of it around their necks or on their heads. These people also ate the popped corn. Other people ate popcorn in a bowl with milk.

1. What is the story all about?

popcorn snowflakes

2. What is the big idea of the story?

Long ago, people found many uses for popcorn.

People can wear strings of popped popcorn.

3. Why do you think some people wore strings of popcorn?

They liked the color of the popped corn.

They liked the snowflake shape of the popped corn.

Home Activity Your child identified the theme—the big idea—of a story. Reread the story with your child. Have your child underline the sentences in the story that helped him or her tell the big idea.

Name ______________________________

Writing • Thank-You Note

Dear Hunter,

Thank you for sharing your basketball with me.
I had fun playing two games with you.

Your friend,
Cody

Key Features of a Thank-You Note

- A thank-you note thanks someone for doing something nice.
- It tells how the writer feels.

Home Activity Your child is learning about writing a thank-you note. Discuss ways of expressing thanks.

Name ______________________

Circle the word for each picture.

1. 
blew black

2. flow flew

3. glue glow

4. chick chew

5. 
sit suit

6. 
stew stop

7. joke juice

8. 
news nose

Read the words in the box.
Pick a word to finish each sentence.

bruise	**drew**	**true**

9. It is ______________ that I love ice cream.

10. He has a ______________ on his leg.

11. My sister ______________ this picture.

Home Activity Your child practiced reading words with *ew, ue,* and *ui* as in *blew, glue,* and *suit.* Work with your child to make up silly rhyming pairs that contain this vowel sound and these spellings, such as *blue stew* or *fruit suit.*

Name ______________________

Compound Words

Write the list word that names the picture.

Spelling Words
backpack
outside
baseball
herself
flashlight
bluebird
lunchbox
suitcase
inside
brainstorm

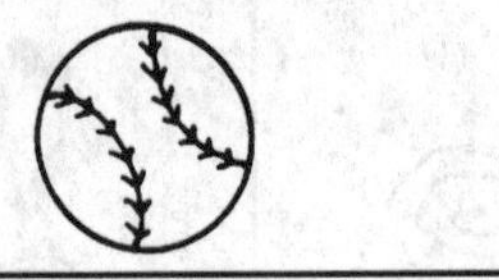

1. ______________________

2. ______________________

3. ______________________

4. ______________________

5. ______________________

6. ______________________

Write the last part of the compound word.
Write the compound word.

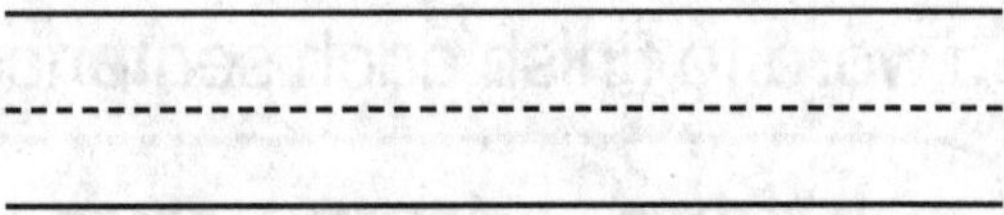

7. in ______________ ______________________

8. her ______________ ______________________

9. brain ______________ ______________________

10. out ______________ ______________________

Home Activity Your child spelled compound words. Have your child name the two words in each compound word.

Name ______________________________

Adjectives for How Many and Articles

Some **adjectives** tell how many. The adjectives **a, an,** and **the** are called **articles**.

three dogs

the baby

Draw lines to match the words to the pictures.
Say each adjective in a sentence.

1. two cribs

2. four chairs

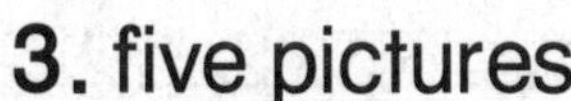

3. five pictures

4. three boys

5. a house

Home Activity Your child learned about adjectives for how many. Read a counting story with your child. Have your child point out the adjectives that tell how many and use his or her fingers to show how many each adjective describes.

Name ______________________

Letter Format

Dear ______________________ ,

______________________ ,

Name ______________________________

1 2 3 4 5

Trace and **write** the numbers.

1

2

3

4

5

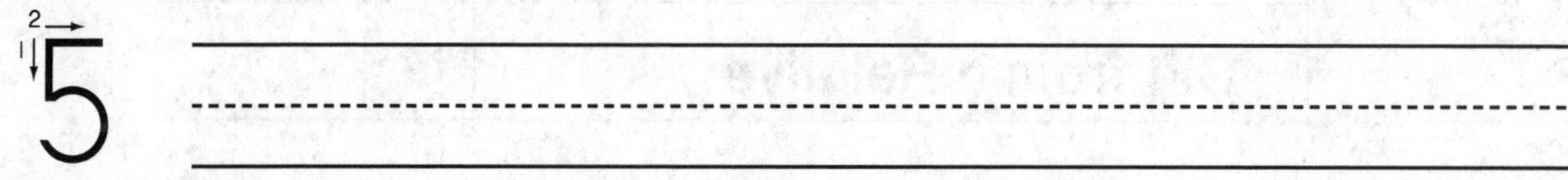

Circle your best number in each line.

Copy the sentence. Leave the correct space between words.

Sue has a new blue suit.

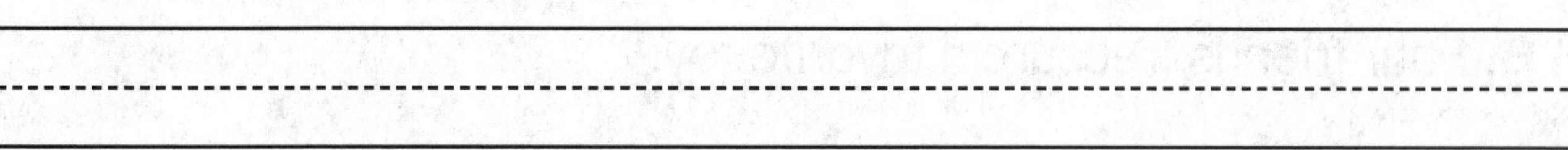

Home Activity Your child practiced writing numbers 1, 2, 3, 4, 5 and sentences with words with *ew, ui,* and *eu.* Have your child practice writing the numbers one more time. Then write the following words on a sheet of paper and have your child rewrite them to make a sentence: *knew, I, was, it,* and *true. (I knew it was true.)*

Name ______________________________

Alan sent this e-mail to his friends.
Help Alan record what he learned.

From: Alan
Subject: Your favorite treasure
Date: April 4

I want to find out your favorite treasure.

Please tell me what your favorite treasure is.

Favorite Treasures	
Stuffed Animal	
Blanket	
Favorite Toy	
Gift from a Relative	

卌 = 5

Make tally marks to show what Alan learned.

1. Five friends treasure a stuffed animal.
2. Three friends treasure a blanket.
3. Four friends treasure a favorite toy.
4. Seven friends treasure a gift from a relative.

Home Activity Your child learned how to write, send, and reply to an e-mail. If possible, help your child compose and send an e-mail to a family member.

"Time for math!" said Miss Drew.

"I must quit daydreaming," Sue said to herself.

"But a cruise might be fun . . ."

Decodable Story *Sue's Daydream*
Target Skills Compound Words; Vowel Digraphs *ue, ew, ui*

Sue's Daydream

Compound Words		Vowel Digraphs ***ue, ew, ui***		High-Frequency Words	
daydream	sunlight	Sue	crew	was	I
daydreaming	inside	true	Drew	a	to
onto	popcorn	blue	juice	the	
suitcase	everyone	new	cruise	they	
into	herself	flew		said	

Sue was in reading class,

but she wasn't reading.

It's true—Sue was daydreaming!

She got onto a plane with her new suitcase.

The plane flew off into the blue sky.

Sunlight streamed in.

The crew inside was nice.

"We've got juice and popcorn for everyone," they said.

Name ______________________________

Compound Words

Spelling Words				
backpack	outside	baseball	herself	flashlight
bluebird	lunchbox	suitcase	inside	brainstorm

Read about some good friends. **Write** the missing list words.

High-Frequency Words
remember
picture

1. Ellie and I went **o**____________________.
2. Ellie had a **f**____________________.
3. We saw **b**____________________ feathers.
4. We looked **i**____________________ a hollow tree.
5. Next, we played **b**____________________.
6. Then we got a snack out of my **l**____________________.
7. We got juice out of Ellie's **b**____________________.
8. Ellie drank three boxes of juice by **h**____________________.
9. I still **p**____________________ Ellie and the juice.
10. It is fun to **r**____________________ her.

Home Activity Your child used spelling words to complete a story about friends. Ask your child to tell about a friend, using some of the list words.

Name ______________________

Adjectives for How Many and Articles

Look at the picture. **Complete** each sentence with an adjective from the box. **Say** a sentence for each article.

a two three

1. There are ______________ people in this family.

2. There are ______________ children.

3. There is ______________ man.

Write about the people in your family.
Use adjectives that tell how many.

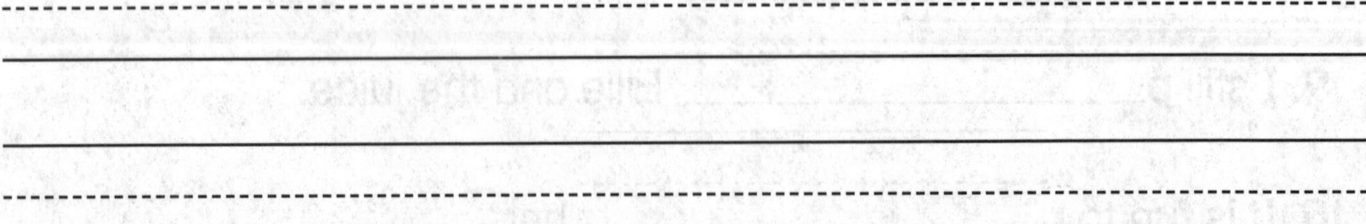

Home Activity Your child learned how to use adjectives for how many in writing. Place groups of one, two, three, four, and five pennies on a table and have your child write sentences about the groups using adjectives that tell how many.

Name ______________________________

Compound Words

Connect two parts to make a list word.
Write the compound word.

Spelling Words
backpack
outside
baseball
herself
flashlight
bluebird
lunchbox
suitcase
inside
brainstorm

1. in   storm   1. ____________
2. her   side   2. ____________
3. brain   light   3. ____________
4. flash   self   4. ____________
5. suit   bird   5. ____________
6. blue   case   6. ____________

Circle the word that is spelled correctly.

7. lunchbox   lonchbox
8. owtside   outside
9. backpack   back pack
10. basball   baseball

School + Home

Home Activity Your child has been learning to spell compound words. Help your child brainstorm other compound words.

Name ____________________

Adjectives for How Many and Articles

Mark the sentence that has a line under the adjective.

1. ◯ There are <u>ten</u> families in the park.
   ◯ There are ten <u>families</u> in the park.
   ◯ There are ten families in the <u>park</u>.

2. ◯ Four brothers <u>throw</u> a football.
   ◯ Four brothers throw a <u>football</u>.
   ◯ <u>Four</u> brothers throw a football.

3. ◯ I see three <u>fathers</u> on a bench.
   ◯ I see <u>three</u> fathers on a bench.
   ◯ I <u>see</u> three fathers on a bench.

4. ◯ Where <u>are</u> my two sisters?
   ◯ Where are my two <u>sisters</u>?
   ◯ Where are my <u>two</u> sisters?

5. ◯ <u>Six</u> children play tag on the grass.
   ◯ Six children <u>play</u> tag on the grass.
   ◯ Six children play tag on the <u>grass</u>.

6. ◯ There are five <u>mothers</u> with babies.
   ◯ There are <u>five</u> mothers with babies.
   ◯ There are five mothers with <u>babies</u>.

Choose other adjectives. **Say** a sentence for each adjective.

Home Activity Your child prepared for taking tests on adjectives for how many. Together read a short, simple newspaper or magazine article. Have your child circle adjectives that tell how many.

Name ______________________________

Add -ly or **-ful** to the word in ( ).
Write the new word on the line.

nice + -ly = nice<u>ly</u>

(play)

____

1. The dog is ______________________ .

(slow)

____

2. The dog walked ______________________ .

(quick)

____

3. Then it ran ______________________ !

(safe)

____

4. The dog got home ______________________ .

(thank)

____

5. Miss Moon was ______________________ .

Home Activity Your child added *-ly* and *-ful* to words. Ask your child to give you instructions using words with the *-ly* suffix, such as *Clap loudly; Talk softly; Walk quickly*. Follow the instructions. Then have your child write simple sentences using *playful* and *thankful*.

Name ______________________

Read the words in the box.
Pick a word to match each clue.
Write it on the line.

across	because	dance	only	opened	shoes	told

1\.

____

2\.

____

3\.

____

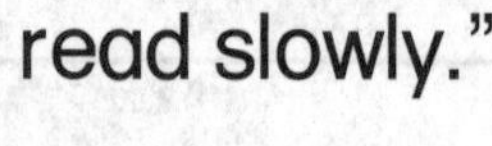

4\. She said, "I ______ you to read slowly."

____

5\. The plant grows ______ it has water.

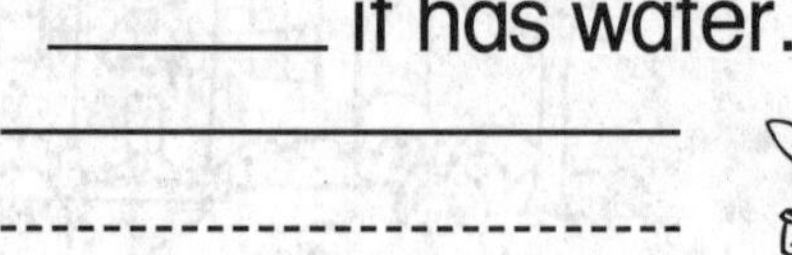

____

6\. Mom said, "______ one treat!"

____

7\.

____

Home Activity Your child learned to read the words *across, because, dance, only, opened, shoes,* and *told.* Make up more clues for the words on this page. Ask your child to identify the words. Challenge your child to think of some clues.

Name ______________________________

Draw a line to match what happens with why it happens.

What Happens | **Why It Happens**

1. 

2. 

3. 

4. 

5. 

Home Activity Your child learned about what happens (effect) and why it happens (cause). While watching a sporting event, such as a soccer game or swim meet, invite your child to identify what happens and why.

Name ______________________________

Writing • Directions

How to Make a Drum

First, get a coffee can with a plastic lid.

Next, color a piece of paper.

Wrap it around the coffee can.

Then give it to your friend.

See who can drum the loudest!

Key Features of Directions

- Directions give details about how to do something.
- Directions should be clear and easy to understand.

Home Activity Your child is learning to write simple directions for how to do something. Share an activity at home and discuss how to do it.

Name ______________________

Circle the word for each picture.

1\.

zoo zip

2\.

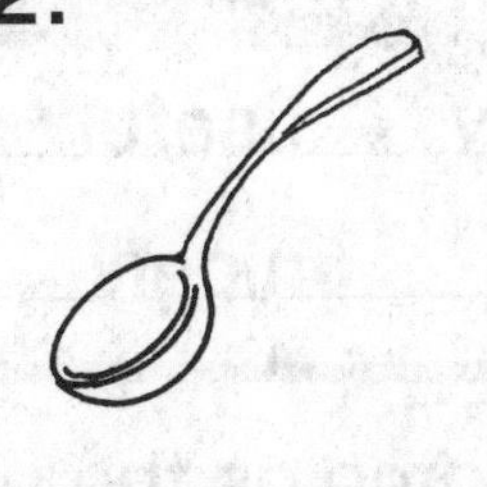

span spoon

3\.

pal pool

4\.

stool stale

5\.

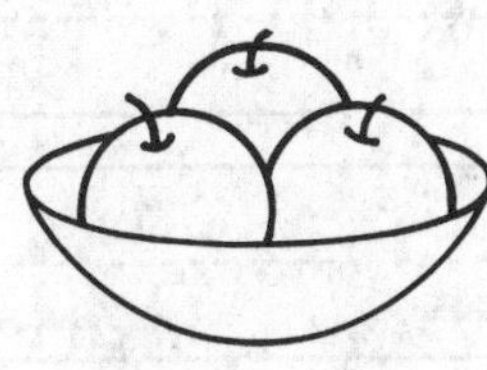

fruit fool

6\.

gaze goose

7\.

boot bait

8\.

spool spill

Pick a word to finish each sentence.
Write the word in the sentence.

9\. The ______________ blocked the cars on the road.
moose mouse

10\. I dropped my ______________ on the floor.
farm food

11\. I used a ______________ to clean up the mess.
boot broom

Home Activity Your child practiced reading and creating words with *oo* as in *moon*. Write the *oo* words from this page on scraps of paper. Have your child pick a word and use it in a sentence.

Name ______________________

Words with Suffixes *-ly, -ful*

Spelling Words				
slowly	careful	quickly	useful	painful
playful	sadly	gladly	nicely	wonderful

Write the list word that means the same as the underlined words.

1. She said good-bye in a sad way. 1. ______
2. We had a very good time. 2. ______
3. Be alert when playing ball. 3. ______
4. The twins play in a nice way. 4. ______
5. Her foot was full of pain. 5. ______
6. I will be happy to help. 6. ______
7. The hamsters are full of play. 7. ______
8. Drive in a slow way. 8. ______
9. My pen is still full of use. 9. ______
10. He finished his work in a fast way. 10. ______

School + Home

Home Activity Your child spelled words with the suffixes *-ly* and *-ful.* Ask your child to explain what each suffix means. (Suffix *-ly* means "in a ___ way." Suffix *-ful* means "full of ___.")

Name ______________________________

Adjectives That Compare

Add **-er** to an adjective to compare two persons, places, or things.

The cat is **smaller** than the dog.

Add **-est** to an adjective to compare three or more persons, places, or things.

The mouse is **smallest** of the three.

Circle the adjectives that compare two things.
Underline the adjectives that compare three or more things.

1. Mrs. Hopper is taller than Henry.
2. Henry's father is tallest of the three.
3. Mudge is smarter than that dog.
4. Mudge is the smartest dog of all.
5. Henry's mother is older than Henry.
6. Mrs. Hopper is the oldest of the three.

Home Activity Your child learned about adjectives that compare. Read a story with your child. Have your child look for adjectives that compare and tell what things are being compared.

Name ______________________________

Sequence

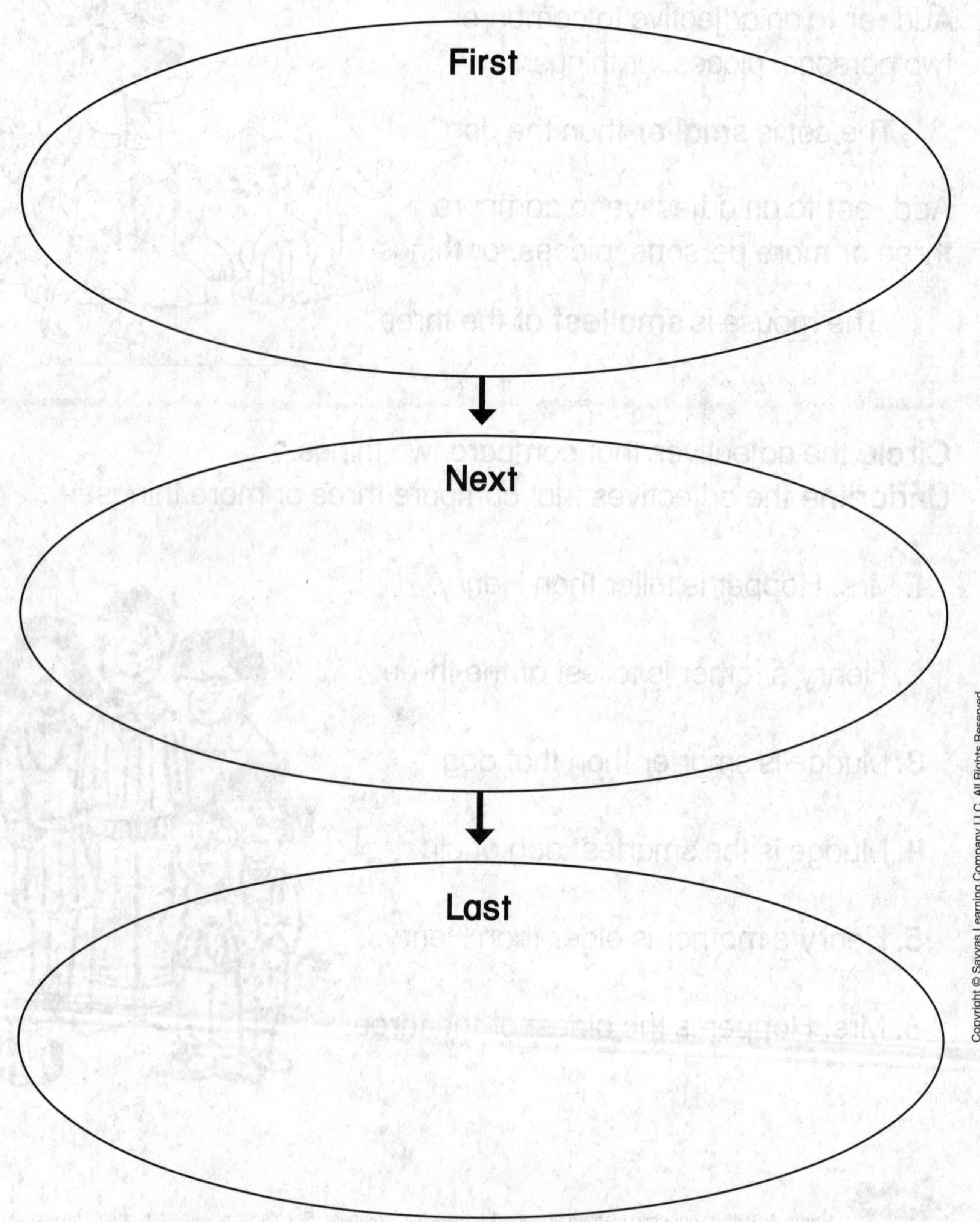

Name ________________________________

6 7 8 9 10

Trace and **write** the numbers.

6 ________________________________

7 ________________________________

8 ________________________________

9 ________________________________

10 ________________________________

Circle your best number in each line.

Copy the sentence. Leave the correct space between words.

You can not be too helpful.

____

Home Activity Your child practiced writing numbers 6, 7, 8, 9, 10 and sentences with words with *-ly, -ful,* and *oo.* Have your child practice writing the numbers one more time. Then write the following words on a sheet of paper and have your child read and rewrite them as neatly as possible: *skillful, softly, broom.*

Name ______________________________

Put each group of last names in ABC order.
Write the names on the lines.

Turza Taylor Terry Till

1. ________________

2. ________________

3. ________________

4. ________________

Lin Lewis Lopez Lance

5. ________________

6. ________________

7. ________________

8. ________________

Turn to the glossary on page 231 of your Unit 4 Student Edition. What is the second word in ABC Order on the page?

9. ________________

School + Home

Home Activity Your child learned to use alphabetical order to find names in a phone book. The next time you need a phone number, ask your child to help you find the information.

You'll likely visit a zoo someday.

Will you go soon?

Will you help at a zoo too?

Decodable Story *Helping at a Zoo*
Target Skills Suffixes *-ly, -ful;* Vowel Sound in *moon: oo*

Name ______________________

Helping at a Zoo

Suffixes *-ly, -ful*	Vowel Sound in *moon*: *oo*		High-Frequency Words	
mainly	zoo	cool	a	some
quickly	bloom	soon	many	visit
likely	food	too	people	you
playful	broom			
painful	booth			

Many people help at a zoo.

Some mainly help flowers bloom.

Some get food for everyone.

Some helpers use a broom all day.

Some helpers sell treats in a booth.

Some helpers keep playful hippos cool.

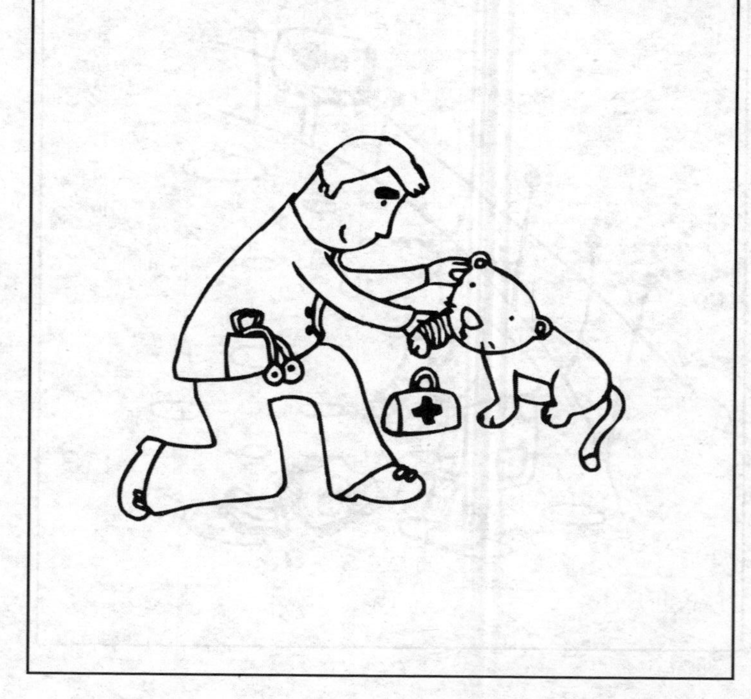

A vet helps at a zoo.

A cub might get a painful cut.

A vet quickly helps its cut heal.

Name ____________________

Words with Suffixes *-ly, -ful*

Spelling Words				
slowly	careful	quickly	useful	painful
playful	sadly	gladly	nicely	wonderful

High-Frequency Words
because
across

Write the suffix *-ly* or *-ful*. **Write** the word.

1. I went glad________ . ________

2. The swimmers were care________ . ________

3. It is a wonder________ party. ________

4. A cell phone is very use________ . ________

5. Mia plays nice________ . ________

6. We quick________ shut the door. ________

7. That's a play________ kitten. ________

8. Cook the stew slow________ . ________

Write the words to complete this sentence.

I went 9. ________________ the street 10. ________________ I saw my friend.

Home Activity Your child used spelling words to complete sentences. Read a sentence and have your child spell the list word.

Name ______________________________

Adjectives That Compare

Write about three special friends.
Use words from the box or your own adjectives that compare.

oldest	shorter	quieter	faster	tallest

Home Activity Your child learned how to use adjectives that compare in writing. Talk about neighbors or family friends with your child. Together write sentences that compare two or more of these people. Use an adjective with *-er* or *-est* in each sentence.

Name ______________________________

Words with Suffixes *-ly, -ful*

Spelling Words				
slowly	careful	quickly	useful	painful
playful	sadly	gladly	nicely	wonderful

Circle the word that is spelled correctly.

1. sadly sady
2. galadly gladly
3. quickly quikly
4. wondrful wonderful

Write the list words in the puzzle.

Across

7. in a nice way
9. in a slow way
10. full of use

Down

5. full of pain
6. full of play
8. not careless

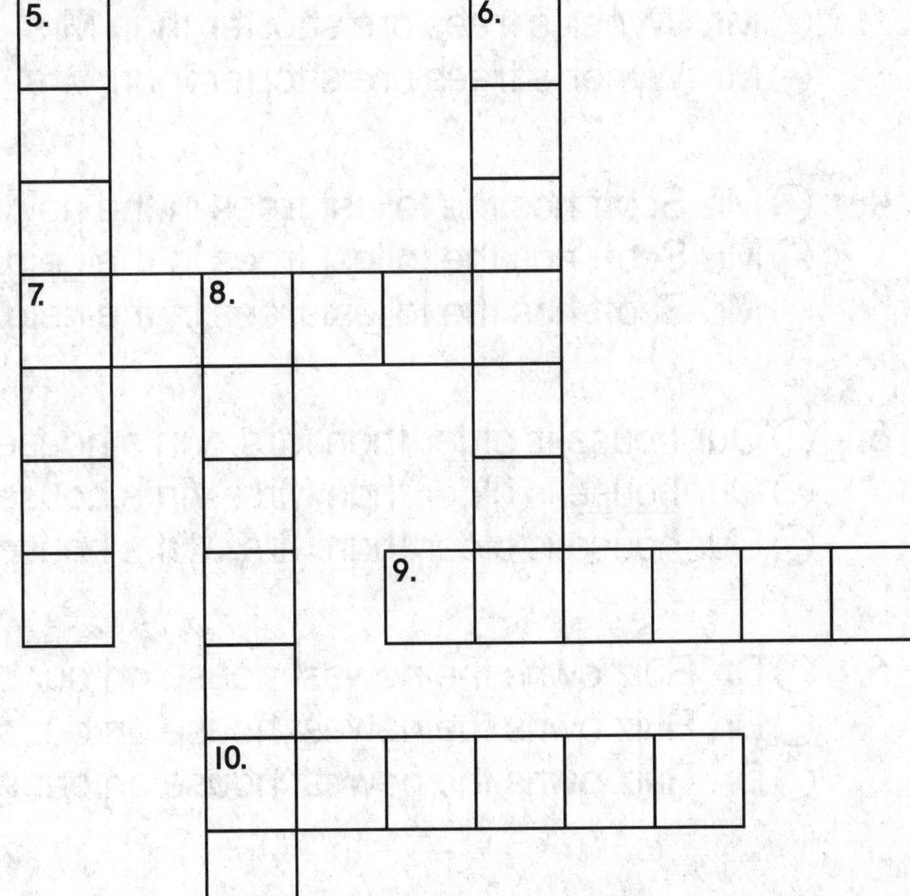

Home Activity Your child has been learning to spell words with the suffixes *-ly* and *-ful*. Say a base word. Ask your child to add *-ly* or *-ful* and say and spell the new word.

Name ______________________

Adjectives That Compare

Mark the sentence that has a line under the adjective.

1. ◯ Ms. Feld's lawn is <u>greener</u> than Mrs. Ho's lawn.
   ◯ Ms. Feld's <u>lawn</u> is greener than Mrs. Ho's lawn.
   ◯ Ms. Feld's lawn <u>is</u> greener than Mrs. Ho's lawn.

2. ◯ <u>Mr. Jones</u> has the brownest lawn of all.
   ◯ Mr. Jones <u>has</u> the brownest lawn of all.
   ◯ Mr. Jones has the <u>brownest</u> lawn of all.

3. ◯ Mr. Wyner's <u>trees</u> are shorter than Mrs. Garcia's trees.
   ◯ Mr. Wyner's trees are <u>shorter</u> than Mrs. Garcia's trees.
   ◯ Mr. Wyner's trees <u>are</u> shorter than Mrs. Garcia's trees.

4. ◯ Mr. Scott has the tallest <u>trees</u> in the neighborhood.
   ◯ Mr. Scott has the tallest trees in the <u>neighborhood</u>.
   ◯ Mr. Scott has the <u>tallest</u> trees in the neighborhood.

5. ◯ Our house is <u>older</u> than Mrs. Vin's house.
   ◯ Our <u>house</u> is older than Mrs. Vin's house.
   ◯ Our house is older <u>than</u> Mrs. Vin's house.

6. ◯ <u>Dr. Ruiz</u> owns the newest house on our street.
   ◯ Dr. Ruiz owns the <u>newest</u> house on our street.
   ◯ Dr. Ruiz owns the newest house on our <u>street.</u>

Home Activity Your child prepared for taking tests on adjectives that compare. With your child, look through a newspaper or magazine article. Help your child circle adjectives that compare. Then discuss what each adjective is comparing.

Name ______________________________

Pick a word from the box to match each picture.
Write it on the line.

cr<u>ow</u>n

cloud	clown	flower	house

1.  ____________________

2. 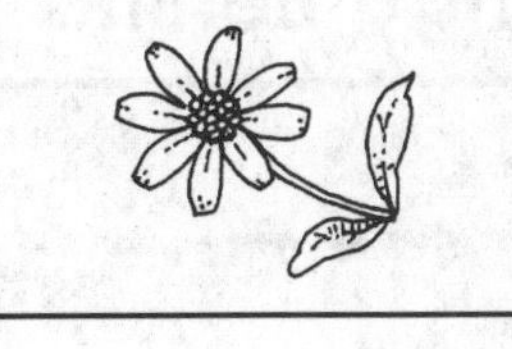 ____________________

3.  ____________________

4.  ____________________

Unscramble the letters to make a word.

uodl ________________ wtno ________________ tuo ________________

Pick a word to finish each sentence. **Write** it on the line.

5. The opposite of *in* is ________________.

6. The radio was too ________________.

7. I like to shop in ________________.

Home Activity Your child read and wrote words with *ow* that have the vowel sound heard in *crown*. Encourage your child to make a list of other words with *ow* that rhyme with *cow* and *brown*.

Name ______________________________

Read the words in the box.
Pick a word to finish each sentence. **Write** it on the line.
Remember to use a capital letter at the beginning of a sentence.

along	behind	eyes	never	pulling	toward

1. The dogs walked ______________ the wall.

2. The dogs stopped ______________ the puddle.

3. Mom is ______________ the boy away.

4. ______________ pet a dog you do not know well.

5. The puppy ran ______________ its mother.

6. Its ______________ were happy and bright.

Home Activity Your child learned to identify and read the words *along, behind, eyes, never, pulling,* and *toward*. Ask your child to make up a puppet show using this week's words. Write out the script that your child dictates. Use paper bags or stick puppets to act it out.

Name ______________________________

Read the story.
Write the answer to each question.

Many weeks ago, Tony and Dad planted daisy seeds. They planted the seeds in a sunny part of a garden. Soon daisy plants were growing in the garden. The plants grew very tall with many daisies. One night it rained hard. Tony went out to the garden the next day. He felt so sad. All the plants were bent down. Then Dad came with sticks and string. He tied the plants to the sticks. Soon the plants were standing up!

1. Who are the characters in the story?

____

2. Where does the story happen?

____

3. Why did Tony feel sad?

____

4. Why did Dad tie the plants to sticks?

____

5. How do you think Tony feels at the end of the story?

____

Home Activity Your child identified the characters, setting, and the problem and solution in a story. Together read a story that has an obvious problem and solution. Pause as you read to ask your child how the characters feel and why they feel that way.

Name ______________________________

Writing • Animal Fantasy

Cleaning Up

Bob and Sue were squirrels. They liked to play in the lot behind the hardware store. One day, a kid threw trash. Sue got angry.

Sue complained, "All this littering has to stop."

Bob said, "Yes. Let's get people to help clean."

Bob and Sue made signs for a cleanup on Saturday. They climbed trees and hung up the signs. On Saturday, many people showed up. No one knew who had the great idea to clean the lot. But everyone was glad to help. Now Bob and Sue have a great place to play!

Key Features of an Animal Fantasy

- characters are animals
- characters do things that real animals can't do

Name ______________________________

Circle the word for each picture.

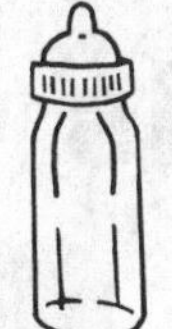

bott<u>le</u>

1.	2.	3.	4.
	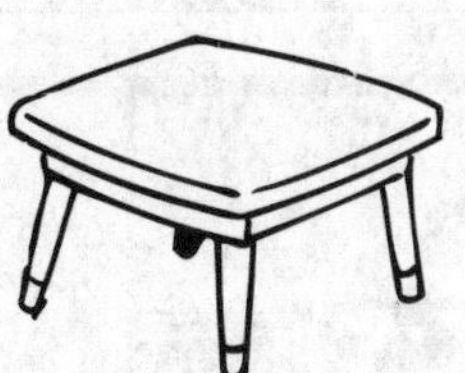	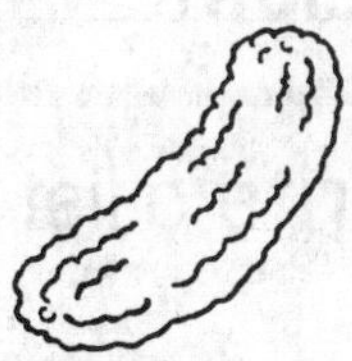	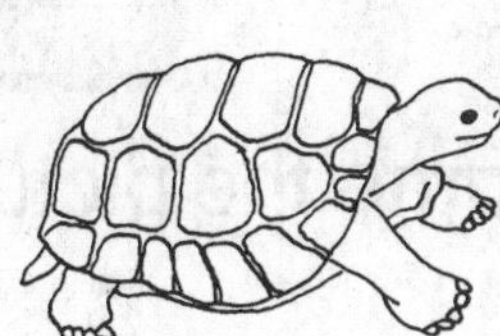
cattle canned	tabbed table	picking pickle	turtle turned

5.	6.	7.	8.
	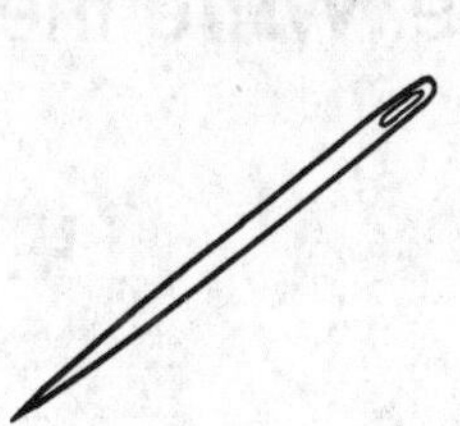 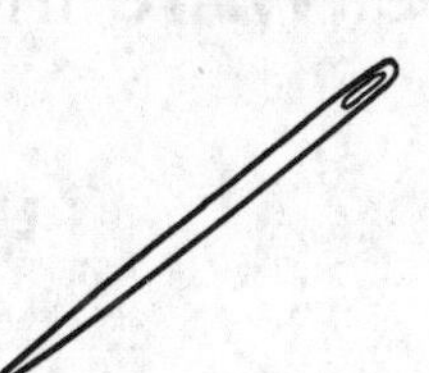	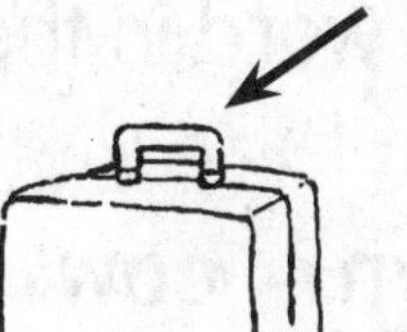	
candle candy	needy needle	handy handle	saddle sadder

Find the word that has the same ending sound as .
Mark the ⬭ to show your answer.

9. ⬭ litter
⬭ lightly
⬭ little

10. ⬭ purple
⬭ purred
⬭ purest

Home Activity Your child read two-syllable words with *-le* in the second syllable. Have your child fold a sheet of paper into four boxes, choose four of the words he or she circled, find a rhyming word for that word, and draw pictures of the rhyming word. Ask your child to label each picture.

Name ______________________

Words with *ow*

Spelling Words				
how	town	down	now	brown
cow	clown	frown	crowd	growl

Name the picture. **Write** a list word.

1. ______________ 2. ______________ 3. ______________

Circle the correct word in the phrase. **Write** the word.

4. up and **down** **cow** 4. ______________

5. a **brown** **frown** cow 5. ______________

6. **town** **how** about that 6. ______________

7. lost in the **crowd** **down** 7. ______________

8. the **brown** **growl** of the lion 8. ______________

9. **clown** **now** and then 9. ______________

10. wipe off that **frown** **down** 10. ______________

Home Activity Your child spelled words with the vowel sound in *how*. Ask your child to name two letters common to all the spelling words. (*ow*)

Name ______________________________

Imperative Sentences

An **imperative sentence** is a **command** sentence that tells someone to do something. It begins with a **capital letter.** It ends with a **period (.)**.

Go to the garden**.**

Please watch the dog**.**

Underline each sentence that is a command.

1. Are you thirsty?

2. Pour a glass of milk.

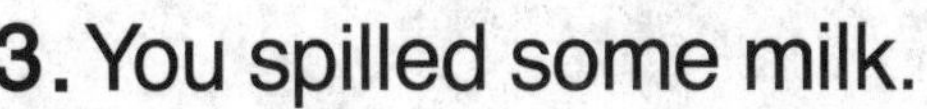

3. You spilled some milk.

4. Please wipe up the milk.

5. Let me help you.

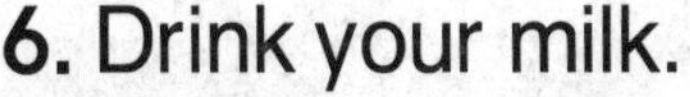

6. Drink your milk.

Home Activity Your child learned about commands. Explain how to play a game to your child. Have your child say "Command" each time he or she hears you use a command.

Name ______________________________

Story Map

Characters	Setting

Events

Beginning

Middle

End

Home Activity Your child is writing a story with animal characters. Together make up or remember a story about animal characters.

Name ___________________________

11 12 13 14 15

Trace and **write** the numbers.

11

12

13

14

15

Circle your best number in each line.

Copy the sentence. Leave the correct space between words.

The cow is in the stable.

Home Activity Your child practiced writing numbers 11, 12, 13, 14, 15 and sentences with words with *ou*, *ow*, and *-le*. Have your child practice writing the numbers one more time. Then have your child read and rewrite the sentence from above.

Name ______________________

When does a problem have a clever solution?

Step 1—Think about problems that you have to solve.

1. Write two or three problems.

____

____

Step 2—Choose a topic.

2. Write the problem that you want to try to solve.

____

Step 3—Formulate research questions.

3. Write two questions about the problem that you want to solve.

____

____

4. What sources of information could you use to help answer your questions about the problem?

____

Home Activity Your child learned how to generate topic ideas, formulate research questions, and choose reference sources. Talk to your child about problems around your home that need to be solved and help your child develop solutions.

Then Miss Mingle got Chow a treat.

"Nibble this," she said with a chuckle.

"Now we'll all feel better!"

Decodable Story *Chow*
Target Skills Diphthongs *ow* and *ou*, Final Syllable *-le*

Name ________

Chow

Diphthongs *ow* and *ou*			Final Syllable *-le*	High-Frequency Words
Chow	town	ground	little	was
how	growl	around	beagle	a
bow	stout	grouch	tumble	said
now	hound	sound	Mingle	I
howl	proud	loud	puddle	the
scowled	found		nibble	to
			chuckle	is

Chow was a stout little beagle.

"See how my hound can tumble and bow?" said Miss Mingle. "I am proud!"

Chow found a puddle on the ground.

He splashed mud all around.

"Now I am a grouch!" said Miss Mingle.

Chow started to howl.

"That sound is too loud," Miss Mingle scowled.

"Everyone in town will growl!"

Name ______________________________

Words with *ow*

Spelling Words				
how	town	down	now	brown
cow	clown	frown	crowd	growl

High-Frequency Words
eyes
never

Write the missing list word.

1. We saw him milk a ____________________ .

2. Don't get lost in the ____________________ .

3. Her hair is ____________________ .

4. Do you know ____________________ to skate?

5. I heard the dog ____________________ .

6. We have a park in our ____________________ .

7. Let's go ____________________ the slide.

8. The best time is ____________________ .

9. I closed my ____________________ .

10. I will ____________________ stop laughing.

Home Activity Your child wrote spelling words to complete sentences. Have your child spell a list word and use it in a sentence.

Name ___________________________

Imperative Sentences

Pam has a problem with her cat.
What should Pam do?
Tell what Pam should do.
Write about your ideas.
Use commands.

Home Activity Your child learned how to use commands in writing. Ask your child to write about how to make a sandwich. Then have your child underline commands he or she used.

Name ______________________

Words with *ow*

Spelling Words				
how	town	down	now	brown
cow	clown	frown	crowd	growl

Unscramble the letters. **Write** the list word.

1. l o c n w 1. ____________
2. w o h 2. ____________
3. b n r o w 3. ____________
4. w l g r o 4. ____________
5. o w c 5. ____________
6. n t w o 6. ____________
7. o n w 7. ____________

Write the missing words.

8. The ____________ had to wait in a long line.

9. There was no place to sit ____________ .

10. Everyone began to ____________ .

Home Activity Your child has been learning to spell words with the vowel sound in *how*. Give clues about a word. Ask your child to guess and spell the word.

Name ______________________________

Imperative Sentences

Mark the sentence that has a command.

1. ○ Look in the newspaper.
   ○ Will you look in the newspaper?
   ○ Ben looks in the newspaper.

2. ○ Meg will find the answer.
   ○ Find the answer.
   ○ Did she find the answer?

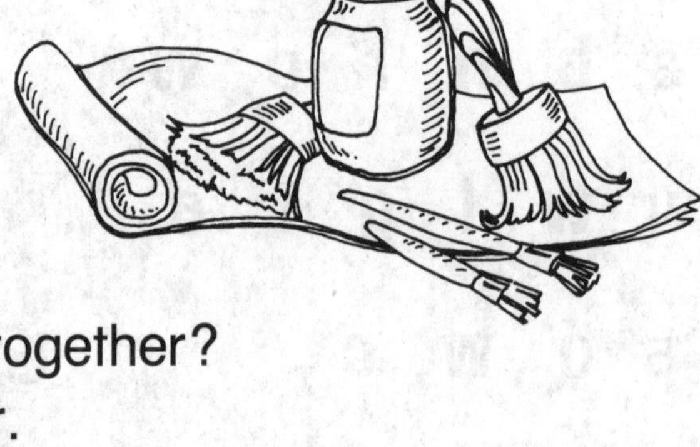

3. ○ Cam left the key here.
   ○ Where is the key?
   ○ Please find the key.

4. ○ Will the glue hold the pieces together?
   ○ I will glue the pieces together.
   ○ Glue the pieces together.

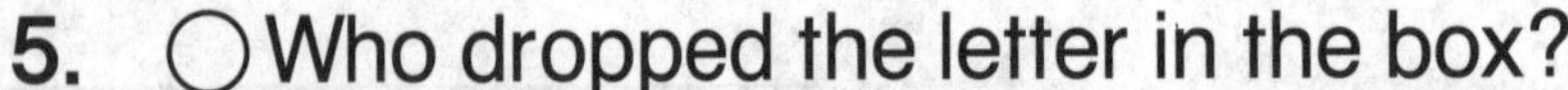

5. ○ Who dropped the letter in the box?
   ○ Please drop the letter in the box.
   ○ Ann dropped the letter in the box.

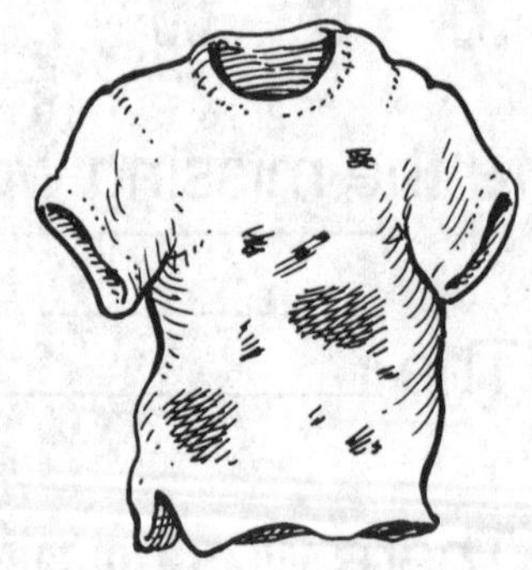

6. ○ Look at this dirty shirt.
   ○ This shirt is dirty.
   ○ Why is this shirt dirty?

Home Activity Your child prepared for taking tests on commands. Together read a favorite story. Have your child point out commands, questions, and statements in the story.

Name ______________________

Write a word from the box to match each picture.

couch	cow	flour
snowman	towel	rowboat

1. ______

2.  ______

3.  ______

4. 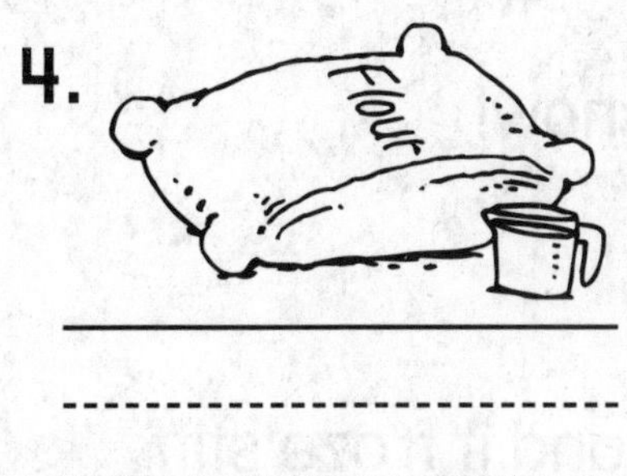

______

5.  ______

6. 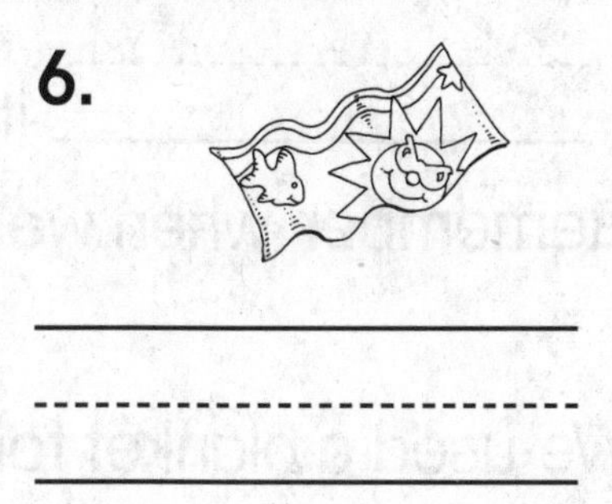 ______

Write the word to finish each sentence. **Remember** to use capital letters at the beginning of a sentence.

7. ______ does your garden grow? **how** **have**

8. Can I come to play at your ______? **toy** **house**

9. I like to ______ bubbles. **blue** **blow**

10. I went ______ to take a walk. **outside** **inside**

Home Activity Your child read and wrote words with vowel patterns *ou* as in *couch,* and *ow* as in *cow* and *snow*. Encourage your child to make a list of words that rhyme with these vowel patterns.

Name ______________________________

Read the words in the box.
Pick a word to finish each sentence.
Write it on the line.

door loved should wood

Dear Jack,

I had such a good time at your house last week.

I ________________ it when we played in the snow!
Remember when we made an igloo?

We used a blanket for the ________________, and it froze stiff.

You ________________ come to my house!
It is very warm here even in the winter.

My dad and I are going to paint the ________________ rail.

Your friend,

Sam

Home Activity Your child learned to identify and read the words *door, loved, should,* and *wood*. Ask your child to write a story that uses each word and read it aloud.

Name ______________________________

Read the story.
Write an answer to each question.

Jean painted a picture of a vase with roses in it. Some of the roses were red. Some were yellow roses. The vase was blue. Jean took her picture to an art show. A man hung Jean's picture on a wall. Many people came to the show to see the pictures. Then Jean saw a blue tag on her picture. The man handed Jean the blue tag. All the people clapped.

1. Why do you think the people clapped?

2. What do you think the blue tag means?

3. What do you think Jean will do next?

Home Activity Your child used what he or she already knew about a situation to draw conclusions about an event. Reread the story with your child. Have your child tell you what he or she already knew about art shows that helped him or her draw conclusions about the story.

Name ____________________________

Writing • Letter to a Character

Dear Mr. Wolf,

I have read a lot of books where you always seem to show up and cause trouble. It makes me angry to see you blow the pigs' houses down. What did they ever do to you?

It makes me sad to see you scare Little Red Riding Hood. She is just trying to get through the woods to see her grandma.

So, please Mr. Wolf, try to be nice and stop scaring people and ruining their homes.

Thank you,
Patrick

Key Features of a Letter to a Character

- describes feelings or opinions to a story character
- includes a friendly greeting and closing

Name ______________________________

Circle the word for each picture.

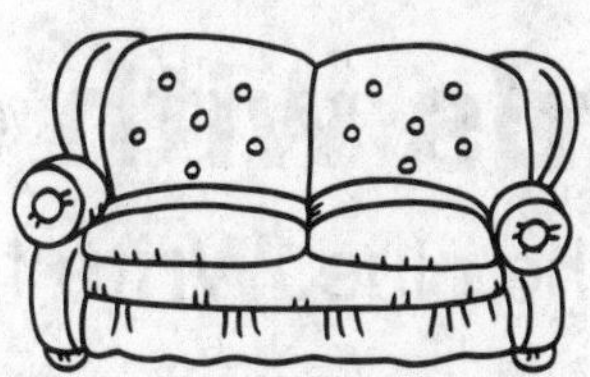

sofa

1.

lesson lemon

2.

pillow pilot

3.

bacon basket

4.

wagging wagon

5.

river rigged

6.

cabin cab

7.

timber tiger

8.

came camel

Draw a picture for each word.

9. spider

10. baby

School + Home

Home Activity Your child read words with two syllables that have one consonant in the middle. Have your child choose five words from the page and use each word in a sentence.

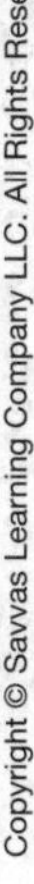

Name ______________________

Words with *ou*

Read the clue. **Write** the list word.

Spelling Words
mouth
house
found
our
out
cloud
ouch
shout
round
count

It starts with **h**, and it rhymes with **mouse**.

1. ______________

It starts with **cl**, and it rhymes with **loud**.

2. ______________

It starts with **sh,** and it rhymes with **pout.**

3. ______________

It starts with **o,** and it rhymes with **couch.**

4. ______________

Write the missing list word.

5. Look at ______________ pups.

6. We ______________ them last week.

7. Can you ______________ them?

8. One pup wants to get ______________ .

9. He put a ball in his ______________ .

10. The ball is ______________ .

Home Activity Your child spelled words with the vowel sound in *out*. Ask your child to name two letters common to all the spelling words. (*ou*)

Name ______________________________

Pronouns

A **pronoun** is a word that takes the place of a noun or nouns. The words **he, she, it, we, you,** and **they** are pronouns.

People see the bird.	**They** see the bird.
Jake helps the bird.	**He** helps the bird.

Circle the pronoun in each sentence.
Say a sentence for each pronoun.

1. We need to feed the birds.

2. They like to eat.

3. He likes the wild bird.

4. It can fly away.

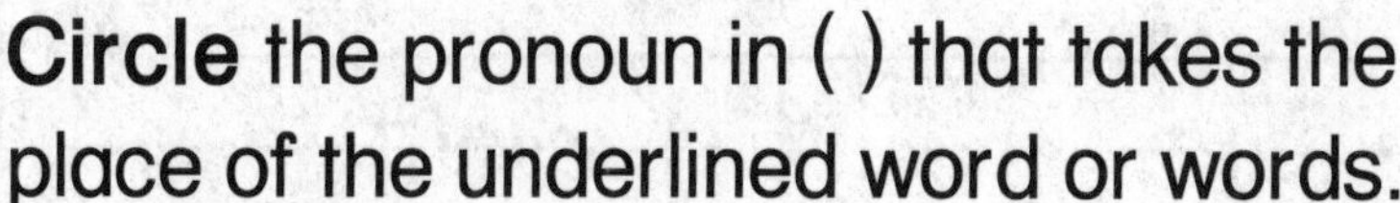

Circle the pronoun in ( ) that takes the place of the underlined word or words.

5. This bird is little. (She, It)

6. Mole and I went to the forest. (He, We)

7. Mole gets food for the bird. (He, They)

8. Mole and Grandad let the bird go. (They, You)

Home Activity Your child learned about pronouns. Write *he, she, it, we, you,* and *they* in a list. Point to each word and ask your child to use it in a sentence.

Name ____________________

Letter Format

Dear ____________________,

Home Activity Your child can express opinions about a story. Discuss a book you both have liked.

Name ______________________________

16 17 18 19 20

Trace and **write** the numbers.

16 ______________________________

17 ______________________________

18 ______________________________

19 ______________________________

20 ______________________________

Copy the sentence. Leave the correct space between words.

The baby camel is cute.

____

Did you leave the correct space between your words? Yes No

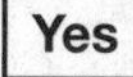

Home Activity Your child practiced writing numbers *16, 17, 18, 19, 20* and words with short and long vowels. Have your child practice writing the numbers one more time. Then have your child read and rewrite the sentence from above.

Name ______________________________

Read the numbered words in each list.
Match each numbered word with the guide words that show where you would find the word in a dictionary.
Draw a line from the numbered word to its guide words.

1. mouth	**A.** part/plant
2. picture	**B.** gerbil/goose
3. give	**C.** mouse/much

4. dance	**D.** damp/date
5. because	**E.** clam/cube
6. color	**F.** bark/beep

7. present	**G.** name/nice
8. draw	**H.** dish/duck
9. never	**I.** porch/price

Home Activity Your child learned about using alphabetical order and guide words in a dictionary. Help your child look up other words in a dictionary at home.

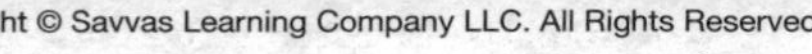

Dad and Toby missed their house in town.

But Dad liked his new job,and Toby liked his shiny new closet!

Decodable Story *A New Home*
Target Skills Vowel Patterns *ow* (how, show), *ou*; Syllables V/CV and VC/V

Name ______________________

A New Home

Vowel Patterns *ow* (how)(show), *ou*			Syllables V/CV and VC/V		High-Frequency Words	
brown	windows	found	Toby's	city	a	is
now	throw	house	tiny	models	I	of
down	yellow	out	begin	comics	the	to
town	pillow		baby	closet	said	their
			label			

Toby's dad got a new job.

"I found a brown house in the city," he said.

"It is tiny, but it has lots of windows."

"I'll begin to pack right now," said Toby.

"I'll throw out my yellow baby pillow,

but I'll pack my models and comics!"

"I'll label the boxes," said Dad.

"We'll take them down to the truck."

Name ______________________________

Words with *ou*

Spelling Words				
mouth	house	found	our	out
cloud	ouch	shout	round	count

High-Frequency Words
loved
should

Read about finding bugs. **Write** the missing list words.

1. We ____________ some bugs.
2. They are ____________ .
3. Let's ____________ them.
4. One got in my ____________ .
5. Did you ____________ ?
6. I said ____________ .
7. I spit it ____________ .
8. Look at that ____________ !
9. The bugs ____________ not be here.
10. No one ____________ these bugs.

Home Activity Your child used spelling words and high-frequency words to complete sentences. Read a sentence on this page. Have your child spell the list word.

Name ___________________________

Pronouns

Look at the picture.
Write about what the people are doing.
Use pronouns.

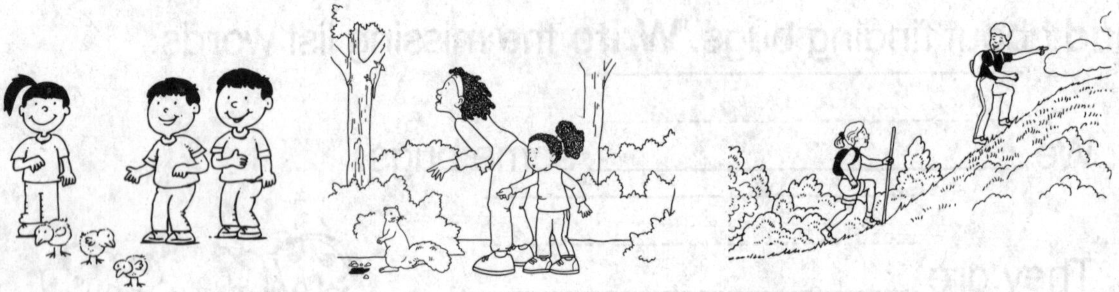

Find other pronouns. **Say** a sentence for each pronoun.

Home Activity Your child learned how to use pronouns in writing. With your child, look through a family photo album. Talk about what you see in the photos, using pronouns instead of names.

Name ____________________

Words with *ou*

Spelling Words				
mouth	house	found	our	out
cloud	ouch	shout	round	count

Write the words in the puzzle.

1. _ o u _ _
2. o u _
3. o u _ _
4. _ _ o u _

cloud
ouch
out
mouth

Connect the matching list words.

5. found
6. round
7. our
8. house
9. shout
10. count

found
house
count
shout
our
round

Home Activity Your child has been learning to spell words with the vowel sound in *out*. Draw a big butterfly. Have your child write the list words on the wings.

Name ______________________________

Pronouns

Mark the pronoun that can replace each underlined word or words.

1. Birds can fly.
   - ◯ **A** He
   - ◯ **B** It
   - ◯ **C** They

2. A mole is an animal.
   - ◯ **A** It
   - ◯ **B** She
   - ◯ **C** You

3. Mole and I feed the bird.
   - ◯ **A** It
   - ◯ **B** We
   - ◯ **C** She

4. Ann plays with the bird.
   - ◯ **A** She
   - ◯ **B** They
   - ◯ **C** We

5. Rob makes a nest.
   - ◯ **A** They
   - ◯ **B** He
   - ◯ **C** It

Say a sentence for each pronoun.

Home Activity Your child prepared for taking tests on pronouns. Together look through a newspaper or magazine article. Take turns finding and circling the pronouns *he, she, it, we, you*, and *they*.

Name ______________________

Circle the word for each picture.

1\. had hood

2\. 

cook coat

3\. hook hard

4\. 

wide wood

5\. 

bake book

6\. look lock

7\. 

store stood

8\. 

brook brake

Read the words in the box.
Circle the words that have the same vowel sound as 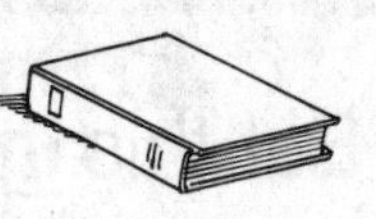 .
Pick one of these words to finish each sentence.

take	foot	took	soon	goat	tool	good

9\. He ______________ a picture of the lake.

10\. That was a ______________ joke.

11\. My ______________ hurts.

Home Activity Your child read and wrote words with *oo* that have the vowel sound heard in *foot*. Encourage your child to make lists that sort the words into those that rhyme with *took* and those that rhyme with *good*.

Name ______________________________

Read the sentence. **Unscramble** the letters. **Write** the word on the line. **Remember** to use a capital letter at the beginning of a sentence.

among another instead none

1. I will have **ahernot**.

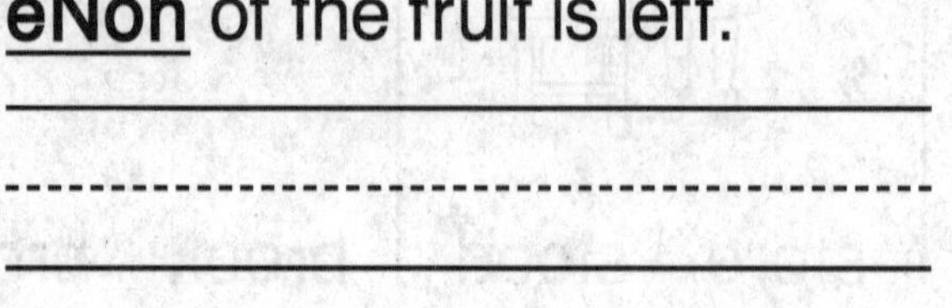

2. **eNon** of the fruit is left.

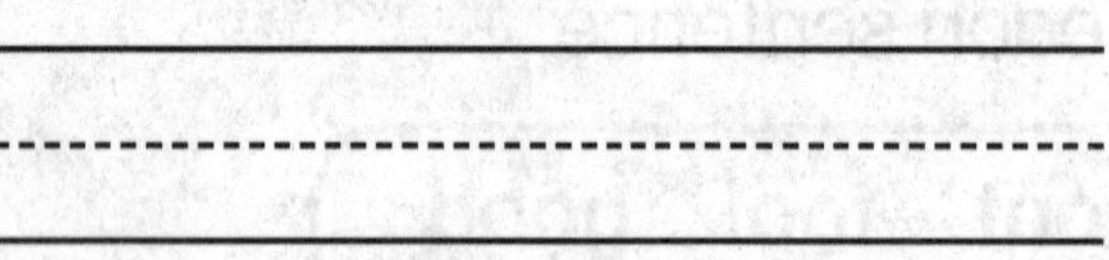

3. Eat this **ineadst**.

4. He likes to nap **angmo** his dogs.

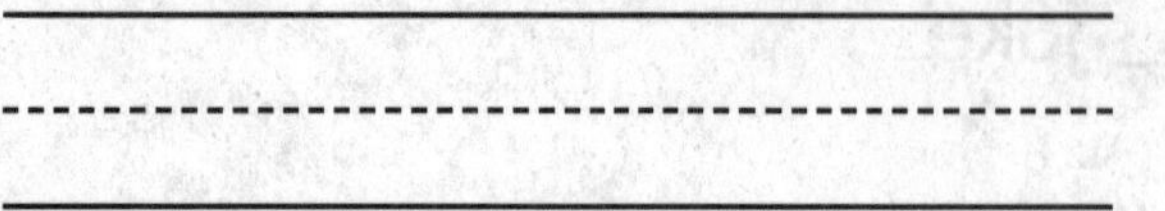

Home Activity Your child learned to identify and read the words *among, another, instead,* and *none*. Write sentences such as these: *Is there another towel like this one? Try this one instead. None of the pie is left.* Leave a blank where the word should be, and have your child fill it in.

Name ______________________________

Read the story. **Look** at the pictures.

Circle the answer to each question.

Chick and Spot are friends. They do not fight. They like to play games. Sometimes, they chase each other around the yard. I laugh when I watch them play.

1. Who is big? Spot Chick

2. Who is small? Spot Chick

3. Who can bark? Spot Chick

4. Who is standing? Spot Chick

5. Who has wings? Spot Chick

6. **Draw** two cats that look the same.

7. **Draw** two cats that do not look the same.

Home Activity Your child compared and contrasted characters in a story. As you read stories with your child, have him or her compare the characters in the stories.

Name ______________________________

Writing • Questions

Animals in Africa

What animals can I see in Africa?

When do giraffes sleep?

How much does an elephant weigh?

A male elephant weighs about 12,000 pounds. A female elephant weighs about 7,000 pounds.

Key Features of Questions

- Many *start* with the words **who, what, where, when,** or **how.**
- Questions end with a question mark.

Name ___________________________

Add -s, -ed, or **-ing** to the word in ( ).
Write the new word on the line.

(hope + -s)

1. Jean _______________ to grow corn.

(slope + -ing)

2. She plants seeds on the _______________ hill.

(care + -ed)

3. Jean _______________ for the plants.

(taste + -ed)

4. Jean _______________ the corn.

(smile + -ing)

5. She is _______________ .

Home Activity Your child added *-s*, *-ed*, or *-ing* to verbs that end in *e*. Write *hope, slope, care, taste,* and *smile* on a sheet of paper. Ask your child to tell the rule about adding *-s*, *-ed*, or *-ing* to each word. Then write the new words.

Name ______________________

Words with *oo*

Circle the words in the box that rhyme. **Write** them.

foot	took
look	pool

1. ______________
2. ______________

foot	moon
book	noon

3. ______________
4. ______________

Spelling Words
book
moon
took
food
look
pool
zoo
noon
good
foot

Write a word that often goes with the list word.

5. bad 5. ______________
6. hand 6. ______________
7. drink 7. ______________

Write the missing list word.

8. Greg wants to read a ______________.
9. Ann wants to swim at the ______________.
10. Joe wants to feed deer at the ______________.

Home Activity Your child spelled words with the vowel sounds in *book* and *moon*. Ask your child to pronounce each list word and identify the vowel sound.

Name ______________________

Pronouns *I* and *Me*

The pronouns I and **me** take the place of your name. Use I in the subject of a sentence. Use **me** after an action verb. Always write I with a capital letter.

Dot calls **me.** I talk to her.

When you talk about yourself and another person, name yourself last.

Jabber and I talk on the phone. Dot calls Jabber and **me.**

Write **I** or **me** to complete each sentence.

1. ____________ see an acorn.

2. It gives ____________ an idea.

3. ____________ take the acorn home.

4. Dot and ____________ paint it.

5. See Dot and ____________ hide the acorn.

Home Activity Your child learned about using *I* and *me*. Take turns telling about ways you use the telephone. Use *I* and *me* as you talk.

Name ______________________________

Topics for Questions

Questions

1. ______________________________

2. ______________________________

3. ______________________________

Home Activity Your child can write questions and answers. Talk with your child about questions that interest each of you.

Name ______________________________

Copy the **sentences.** Leave the correct space between words.

1. We hoped mom baked.

2. I am taking this book.

3. They smiled at us.

4. He is judging a contest.

5. We liked making juice.

Did you leave the correct space between your words? Yes No

Home Activity Your child practiced writing sentences with words with added endings such as *-ed* and *-ing*. Write these words on a sheet of paper: *hide, ride, shine*. Have your child copy each word and then drop the *e* and add *-ing* to write the new word.

Name ___________________________

Read the article. **Write** the answers.

Acorns

Acorns are nuts. They are the fruit of the **oak** tree. They fall to the ground in the FALL.

Who Eats Acorns

- Squirrels
- Mice
- Birds

The squirrel often buries his acorns. He eats them in the WINTER.

1. What is the title of the article? ___________________________

2. Use the picture to write a sentence about squirrels.

____

3. Write a heading from the article. ___________________________

4. Which words are all capitals? ___________________________

Home Activity Your child learned about text features. Look through nonfiction books with your child. Have your child point out text features, such as titles, subheads, and words that are all capitals or are in italics or boldface.

"We're piling in the car and riding downtown," said Dad, waving at the kids.

"I know just the place to go!"

Decodable Story *Going for a Drive*
Target Skills Vowel Sound in *foot: oo;* Drop Final *e* to Add Endings

Name ____________________

Going for a Drive

Vowel Sound in *foot: oo*	Drop Final *e* to Add Endings		High-Frequency Words	
stood	smiling	saving	was	what
good	driving	piling	a	to
shook	taking	riding	said	I
cookies	baking	waving	their	go
cookbook	writing		the	
look				

Dad was smiling. He stood up.

"It's a good day for driving," he said.

"I'm taking everyone with me. Let's go!"

Lacy and Mike shook their heads.

"We're baking cookies, but we can't find the cookbook."

Jon and Margo shook their heads.

"We're writing about saving the whales, but we don't know what to look up."

Name ______________________

Words with *oo*

Spelling Words					High-Frequency Words
book	moon	took	food	look	instead
pool	zoo	noon	good	foot	another

Choose a word to finish the sentence.
Fill in the circle. **Write** the word.

1. I ○ **took** ○ **look** ○ **foot** a sack lunch. ______
2. Read the ○ **took** ○ **zoo** ○ **book**. ______
3. My ○ **foot** ○ **noon** ○ **took** got wet. ______
4. We need more ○ **noon** ○ **food** ○ **look**. ______
5. Bears are at the ○ **zoo** ○ **moon** ○ **foot**. ______
6. That is ○ **look** ○ **good** ○ **took** news. ______
7. We swim in the ○ **noon** ○ **foot** ○ **pool**. ______
8. The ○ **look** ○ **took** ○ **moon** is bright. ______

Write the word that matches each clue.

9. in- ______ 10. an- ______

Home Activity Your child wrote spelling words and high-frequency words to complete sentences. Have your child create a sentence using three or more list words.

Name ______________________

Pronouns *I* and *Me*

Answer the question.
Change the words to write the answer.

Can I solve the mystery?

Write sentences about a mystery you solved.
Use I and **me.**

Home Activity Your child learned how to use *I* and *me* in writing. Have your child read aloud the sentences he or she wrote on this page. Ask your child to point out the *I*'s and *me*'s.

Name ______________________________

Words with *oo*

Write the missing letters.

1. ______oo______

2. ______oo______

3. ______oo______

4. ______oo______

Spelling Words

- book
- moon
- took
- food
- look
- pool
- zoo
- noon
- good
- foot

Write the list words in the puzzle.

Across

6. 12:00
8. you eat this
10. see

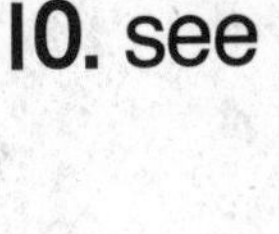

Down

5. not bad
7. opposite of **gave**
9. animals live there

Home Activity Your child has been learning to spell words with the vowel sounds in *book* and *moon*. Write *oo* and pronounce a list word. Have your child add letters to spell the word. Continue with other list words.

Name ____________________

Pronouns *I* and *Me*

Mark the letter of the word or words that complete each sentence.

1. ____ saw a squirrel.
   - ○ Dad and me
   - ○ Dad and I
   - ○ Me

2. ____ found an acorn.
   - ○ Me
   - ○ Dad and me
   - ○ I

3. Jabber asks ____ for clues.
   - ○ Dot and me
   - ○ Dot and I
   - ○ I

4. ____ put the acorn in a hole.
   - ○ Dot and me
   - ○ Me
   - ○ Dot and I

5. It was clever of ____ to solve the mystery.
   - ○ I
   - ○ me
   - ○ me and I

Home Activity Your child prepared for taking tests on using *I* and *me*. Ask your child to read the sentences on this page and to say the word or words that complete each sentence as he or she reads it.

Name ______________________

Circle the word for each picture.

 toy  soil

1.  coins canes

2.  bay boy

3.  boil bail

4.  joy jay

5.  boil book

6.  all oil

7.  foil fail

8.  round royal

Pick a word to finish each sentence. **Write** the word in the sentence.

9. May I ______________ you for lunch? (jolly, join)

10. My favorite ______________ is a racing car. (tray, toy)

11. The meat will ______________ in the hot sun. (spoil, spool)

Home Activity Your child read and wrote words with *oi* and *oy* as heard in *toy* and *soil*. Have your child sort the *oi* and *oy* words on this page and make two lists. Then have him or her read the words aloud.

Name ______________________________

Read the words in the box.
Pick a word to finish each sentence.
Write it in the puzzle.

against goes heavy kinds today

1. We push the umbrella ______ the wind.

2. The rain ______ into our shoes.

3. We play all ______ of games in the big puddles!

4. Rain this ______ does not happen often.

5. We will need dry socks ______!

Home Activity Your child learned to read the words *against, goes, heavy, kinds,* and *today*. Ask your child to use the words in a silly song. Write the words of the song and invite him or her to illustrate it.

Name ______________________

Read the story.
Circle the sentence that tells what the story is all about.
Draw a picture of what the story is about.

1. The ground felt soft under my feet. The trees were tall and green. The air was warm. I liked hiking in the forest.

2.

Read the title of the story.
Circle a detail that might be in the story.
Draw a picture of that detail.

3. Title: The Party
Jen and Fran sang "Happy Birthday."
Jen and Fran have bikes.
Jen and Fran like school.

4.

School + Home

Home Activity Your child learned about the main idea and details of a story. As you read stories with your child, have your child tell you what the story is all about. Have your child tell you details from the story.

Name ______________________

Writing • Advertisement

You Need a Computer!

Everyone needs a computer!
A computer can help you find information.
You can find facts about your favorite animal.
A computer can help you stay in touch.
You can use it to send an e-mail to a friend.
You can use a computer to buy things.
You can even use it to watch a movie.
Buy a computer today!

Key Features of an Advertisement

- An advertisement promotes a product or a service.
- An advertisement describes the product or service.

Name ___________________________

Write a word from the box to match each picture.

baker	sailor	painter	teacher

1. 

2. 

3. 

4. 

Draw a picture of each word.

5. driver

6. actor

Home Activity Your child read and wrote words that end in *-er* and *-or* as in *worker* and *actor.* Write each word on a slip of paper. Have your child choose a slip and act out the word for you to guess.

Name ___________________________

Words with *oi, oy*

Spelling Words				
oil	soil	voice	point	boy
boil	coin	oink	toy	join

Circle the rhyming words in each row. **Write** them.

toy oil boil 1. __________ 2. __________

coin join boil 3. __________ 4. __________

toy soil boy 5. __________ 6. __________

Read the sentence. **Write** a list word that means the same as the underlined word.

7. Do you hear the big pig squeal? 7. __________

8. The farmer's sound is loud. 8. __________

9. The post has a sharp end. 9. __________

10. The ground is very muddy. 10. __________

Home Activity Your child spelled words with the vowel sound in *boy* spelled *oi* and *oy*. Ask your child to pronounce each list word, spell it, and then check the spelling.

Name ____________________

More About Pronouns

A **pronoun** can take the place of some words in a sentence. **I, you, he, she, it, we,** and **they** are used in the **naming part** of a sentence. **Me, you, him, her, it, us,** and **them** are used in the **action part** of a sentence.

Ben likes **machines. He** makes **them**.

Write the pronoun in ( ) that can take the place of the underlined word or words.

1. Sara uses a lever. (Him, She) ____________

2. Pulleys are all around. (They, Them) ____________

3. Ben helps Sara. (He, Him) ____________

4. Sara sees the machines. (She, Her) ____________

5. Sara likes the machines. (them, they) ____________

6. I like Ben's machine. (her, it) ____________

Home Activity Your child learned more about pronouns. Ask your child to make up new sentences using the pronouns he or she wrote on this page.

Name ___________________________________

Web B

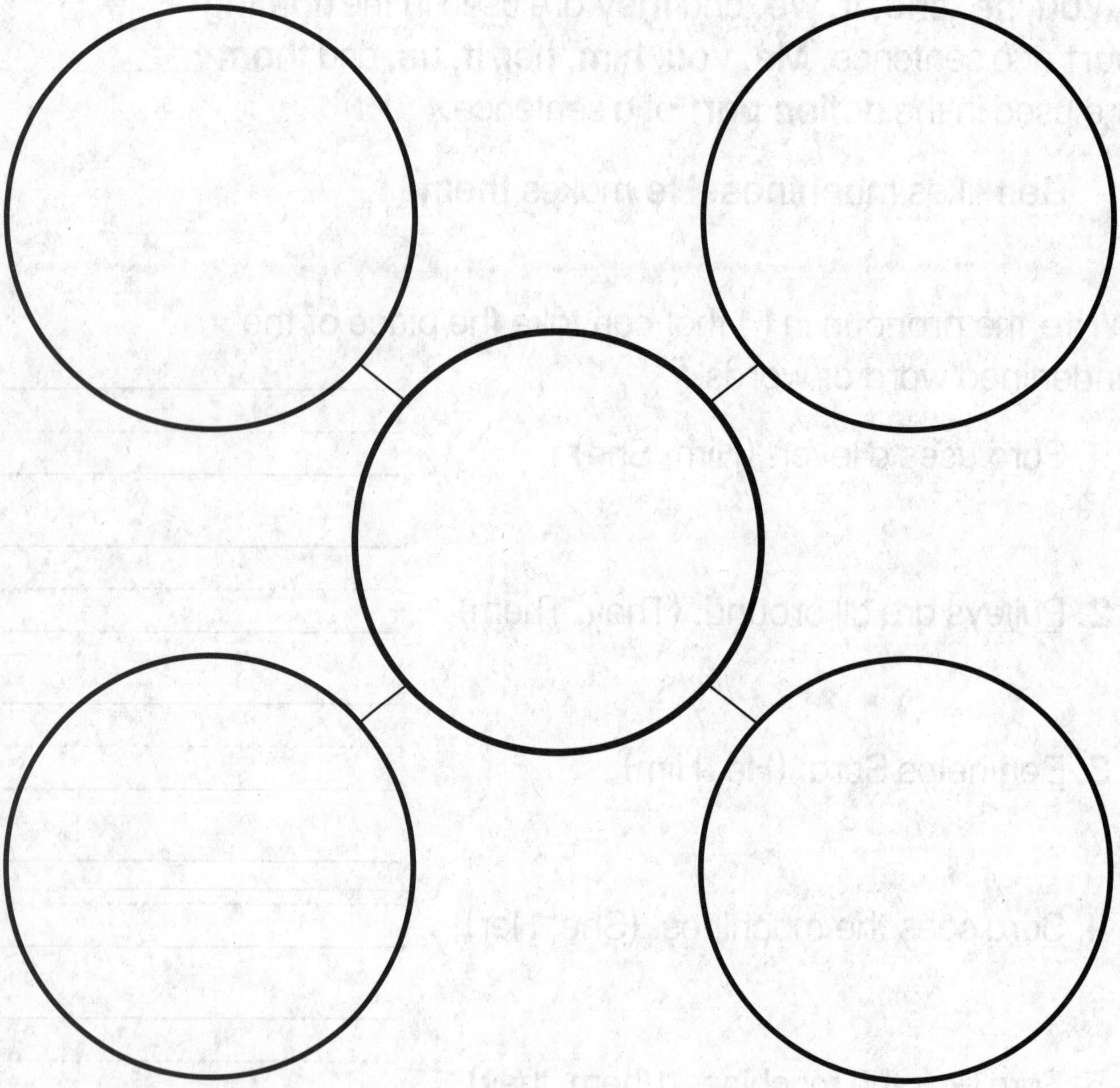

Home Activity Your child can write about topics such as machines. Discuss machines in your home and good ways to use them.

Name ______________________________

Copy the **sentences.** Leave the correct space between words.

1. The boy is noisy.

2. We lost the coin.

3. I did enjoy it.

4. Roy is a good baker.

5. My dad is a sailor.

Did you leave the correct space between your words? Yes 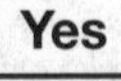 No

School + Home **Home Activity** Your child practiced writing sentences with words with *oy, oi, er,* and *or*. Write these words on a sheet of paper: *boil, corn, Mother, will, the*. Have your child rewrite the words to make a sentence. (*Mother will boil the corn.*)

Name ______________________________

Amy asked her friends which invention they liked the most. Help Amy complete the picture graph.

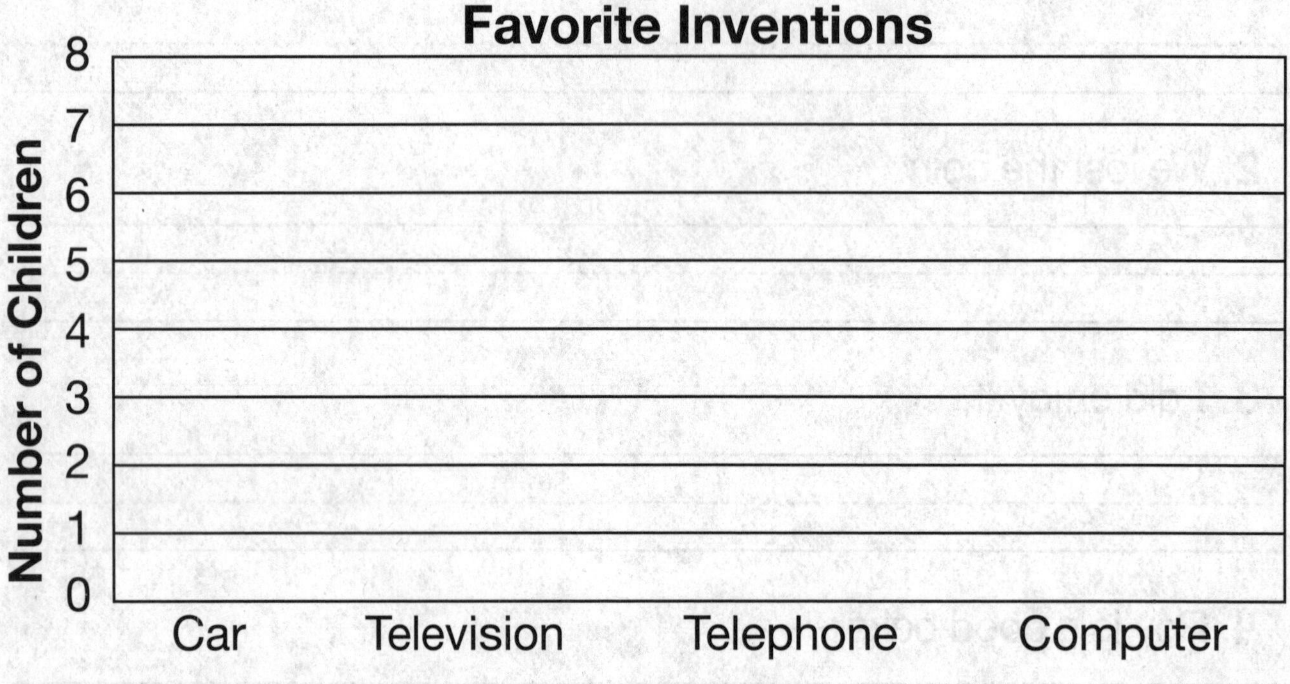

1. Eight friends like cars the most. **Draw** eight cars on the picture graph.
2. Seven friends like television the most. **Draw** seven televisions on the picture graph.
3. Three friends like telephones the most. **Draw** three telephones on the picture graph.
4. Five friends like computers the most. **Draw** five computers on the picture graph.
5. Present Amy's results to your class by acting out the creation of the invention that her classmates liked most.

Home Activity Your child learned to make a picture graph. Together, make a picture graph that shows information about your family, such as favorite foods or favorite hobbies of each family member.

You are good at many things.

Try new things.

Keep doing the things that bring you joy!

Decodable Story *What Are You?*
Target Skills Diphthongs *oi, oy;* Suffixes *-er, -or*

Name ____________________

What Are You?

Diphthongs *oi, oy*	Suffixes *-er, -or*		High-Frequency Words
soil	reader	singer	a
coins	writer	actor	are
boy	talker	baker	you
toy	dreamer	maker	do
joy	runner	farmer	the
	skater	banker	many

You're a boy or girl.

You're a reader and writer.

You're a talker and dreamer.

Are you a fast runner or skater?

Are you a good singer or actor?

Are you a baker or toy maker?

Do you like the soil?

Do you collect coins?

Will you be a farmer or a banker?

Name ______________________

Words with *oi, oy*

Spelling Words				
oil	soil	voice	point	boy
boil	coin	oink	toy	join

High-Frequency Words
heavy
against

Circle a word to finish the sentence. **Write** the word.

1. Cover the seeds with **soil** **toy**. ______
2. He put a **voice** **coin** in his bank. ______
3. I will **boil** **point** to the answer. ______
4. Is this wagon your **soil** **toy**? ______
5. The pigs began to **oink** **coin**. ______
6. Did you **voice** **join** the club? ______
7. I saw a **boy** **oil** in the hall. ______
8. She spoke in a soft **coin** **voice**. ______
9. Put the bike **against** **heavy** the wall. ______
10. The rock was so **against** **heavy**. ______

Home Activity Your child wrote spelling words and high-frequency words to complete sentences. Have your child identify and spell the five list words that are most difficult for him or her.

Name ______________________________

More About Pronouns

Imagine you are using a machine.
Write about what happens.
Use the pronouns **it, he, him, she, her, I, me, we,** or **us.**

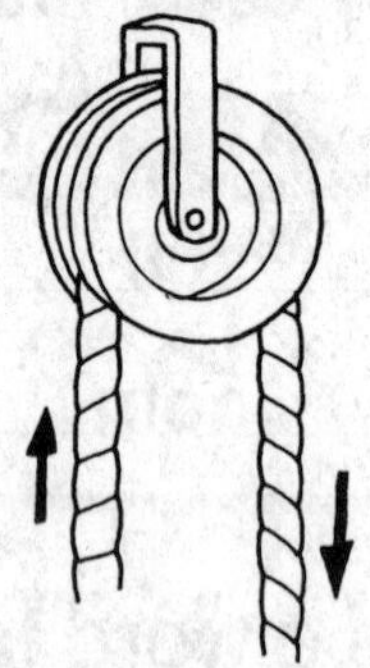

Home Activity Your child learned how to use pronouns in writing. Take turns with your child writing sentences using the pronouns listed on this page.

Name ______________________________

Words with *oi, oy*

Spelling Words				
oil	soil	voice	point	boy
boil	coin	oink	toy	join

Write these words in ABC order.

soil
voice
point
toy

1. ______________ 2. ______________

3. ______________ 4. ______________

Use this code. **Write** the words.

5. ______________ 6. ______________ 7. ______________

8. ______________ 9. ______________ 10. ______________

Home Activity Your child has been learning to spell words with the vowel sound in *boy* spelled *oi* and *oy*. Help your child brainstorm other words with *oi* and *oy*.

Name ______________________________

More About Pronouns

Mark the pronoun that can replace the underlined word or words.

1. The young girl has many ideas.
   - ○ She
   - ○ Them
   - ○ We

2. Her mother asks Sara about her plan.
   - ○ he
   - ○ she
   - ○ her

3. Sara sees a big mess.
   - ○ her
   - ○ it
   - ○ you

4. Sara's friends help her clean.
   - ○ Them
   - ○ He
   - ○ They

5. Her plan surprises the neighbors.
   - ○ them
   - ○ they
   - ○ we

Home Activity Your child prepared for taking tests on pronouns. Read aloud a favorite storybook to your child. Ask your child to say "Stop" each time he or she hears a pronoun and to identify the pronoun.

Name ______________________________

Circle the word for each picture.

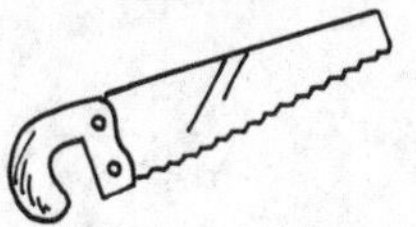

saw

auto

1. 

pail paw

2. 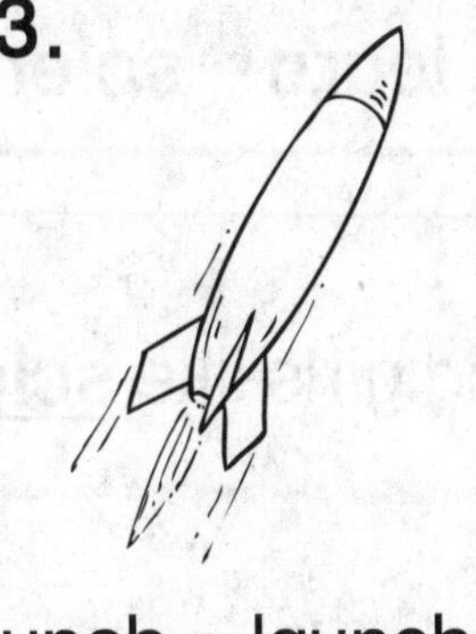

yawn yard

3. 

lunch launch

4. stray straw

5. 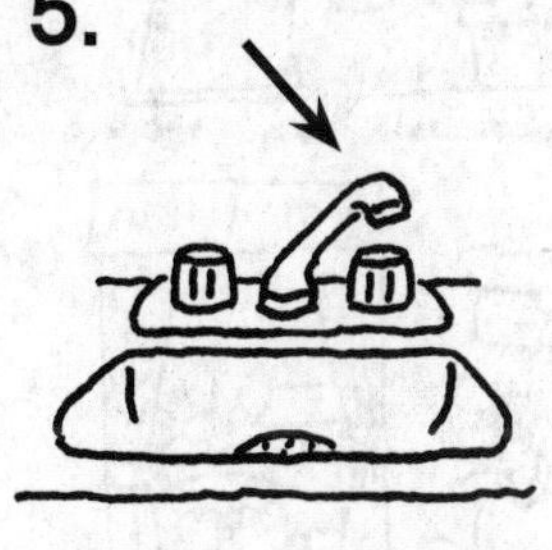

false faucet

6. 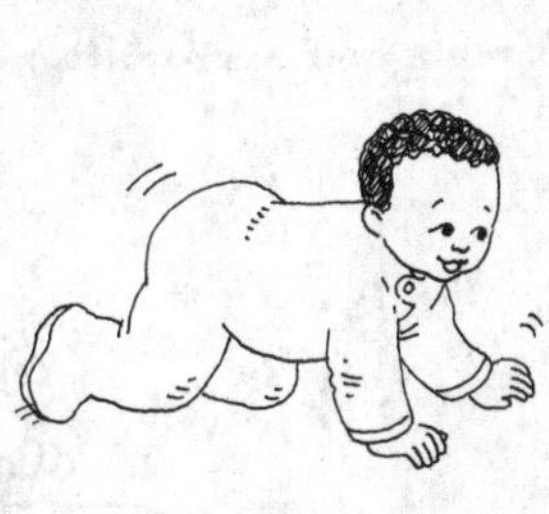

crawl call

7. 

lane lawn

8. 

laundry landed

Pick a word to finish each sentence. **Circle** the word.
Write the word in the sentence.

9. I like pasta with ______________ .

sauce sash

10. The bear used his ______________ to open the bag.

clay claw

Home Activity Your child read words with the vowel sounds *aw* and *au* as heard in *saw* and *auto*. Have your child make silly rhyming sentences using words that rhyme with *saw*. Example: *The cat can draw with her paw*.

Name ______________________

Read the sentence.
Unscramble the letters.
Write the word on the line.

built	early	learn	science	through

1. Many boys and girls like **sciceen**. ______________

2. We **lnear** about plants. ______________

3. We get up **earyl** to see the sun rise. ______________

4. We **uiltb** a little car! ______________

5. We look **ourghth** the glass. ______________

Home Activity Your child learned to identify and read the words *built, early, learn, science,* and *through.* Find children's books about famous scientists and mathematicians. Read them together and challenge your child to find the words in the text.

Name ________________________________

Read the story. **Follow** the directions.

Mr. Lee's class is going on a trip. First they all get on the bus. It is going to be a fun day. Then the class gets off the bus at Rock Park Zoo. Rock Park Zoo is a big zoo. Next the class walks to the snake house.

1. **Circle** words in the story that help you know the order of events.
2. **Write 1, 2, 3** to show the order of story events.

The class gets on the bus. ________

The class walks to the snake house. ________

The class gets off the bus ________

3. **Draw** a picture of what might happen next. Then **retell** the story in correct order.

Home Activity Your child identified order words and used them to put story events in the correct order. Have your child use order words to tell you what he or she does in the morning.

Name ______________________________

Writing Prompt: Think about something great that happened to you. Now write an autobiography that tells about it.

The Best Day

Last year I was with Mom in a store. A lady asked me to be in a TV ad for the store. I happily said yes. The next day, Mom took me to the store. The lady was there. She told me what to do. She said I should act normally. We practiced for the ad. Then we quickly taped it. The ad was on TV! Soon my family and friends saw it.

Name ________________________________

Circle the word that names each picture.

1. 

platter painter painting

2. 

toyshop trays toolbox

3. 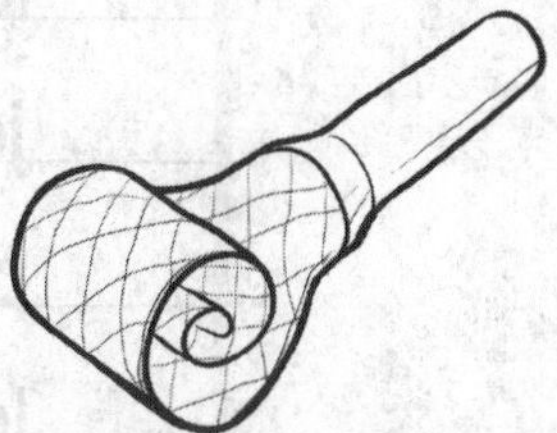

nose nothing noisemaker

4. 

another awning author

Write the word from the box to finish each sentence.

oatmeal	endpoint	football	boyhood

5. A bowl of hot ____________________ is good for you.

6. I like to play ____________________.

7. He had a great ____________________.

8. A dot at the end of a line is an ____________________.

Home Activity Your child read compound words with vowel diphthongs (*oi*, *oy*) and vowel digraphs (*oa*). Have your child read the following words aloud and then make up a sentence for each: *football*, *boyhood*, and *oatmeal*.

Name ________________________

Words with *aw*

Write a list word that belongs in the group.

Spelling Words
saw
draw
crawl
straw
law
jaw
paw
lawn
yawn
hawk

1. jay, eagle, ________________
2. hammer, sandpaper, ________________
3. skull, ribs, ________________
4. skip, walk, ________________
5. paint, sketch, ________________
6. rule, order, ________________

Write the missing word.

7. I sat on the ________________ .
8. My dog sat on some ________________ .
9. He put his ________________ on my leg.
10. We both began to ________________ .

Home Activity Your child spelled words with the vowel sound in *saw*. Have your child name the two letters common to all the spelling words (*aw*).

Name ______________________________

Adverbs

I learned a song **today.**
Today tells when.

Aleck worked on his invention **downstairs.**
Downstairs tells where.

Circle the adverb in each sentence that tells when or where.
Say a new sentence for each adverb.

1. Aleck got sick often.
2. Aleck went away to get better.
3. I built my invention yesterday.
4. I thought a lot about it before.
5. I got a good idea recently.
6. I will work on it next.

Home Activity Your child learned about adverbs that tell when and where. With your child, make a list of all the adverbs you can think of that tell when and where.

Read Together

Name ______________________________

Autobiography

Top-Score Response

Focus/Ideas	A good autobiography tells about real events in the author's life.
Organization	A good autobiography is told in time order.
Voice	A good autobiography tells how the author feels about the events.
Word Choice	A good autobiography uses words that tell how, when, or where events happened.
Sentences	A good autobiography uses sentences that work together to tell the writer's ideas.
Conventions	A good autobiography uses words like **I** and **me**.

Home Activity Your child is learning how writers tell events in their own lives. Have your child tell you about an event from his or her life.

Name ______________________________

Copy the **sentences.** Leave the correct space between words.

1. Laura has a new shawl.

2. We saw the vault.

3. Maureen made sauce.

4. I saw a drawing.

5. The baby can crawl.

Did you leave the correct space between your words? Yes No

Home Activity Your child practiced writing sentences with words with *aw* and *au*. Have your child choose one sentence to copy on a separate sheet of paper.

Name ______________________

Look at the Web page.
Answer the questions.

car television oven

1. Which button would you click on to look at the page you looked at before this one? ______________________

2. Which picture would you click on to make a paper copy of the information on this page? ______________________

3. What is the address of this page?

____

4. What is the title of this page? ______________________

5. What would you do to learn more about ovens?

____

Home Activity Your child learned about using a Web page to find information. When you and your child are online, discuss how to navigate the Web.

Paul had a blue ox named Babe.

Babe ate thirty bales of straw for a snack.

What other tall tales do people tell?

Decodable Story *Paul Bunyan*
Target Skills Vowel Sound *aw, au;* Syllable Patterns: Digraphs and Diphthongs

Name ______________________

Paul Bunyan

Vowel Sound *aw, au*		Syllable Patterns: Digraphs and Diphthongs		High Frequency Words	
Paul	sawed	boyhood	sailboats	a	of
yawned	Paul's	football	oatmeal	was	other
dawn	straw		seacoast	as	do
				the	

People tell tall tales about Paul Bunyan.

Paul had quite a boyhood.

His room was as big as ten football fields.

Paul liked to look at the seacoast.

When Paul yawned, he slurped the sailboats right out of the sea.

Paul ate nine bathtubs of oatmeal each dawn.

Then Paul and his dad sawed wood.

Paul was a hard worker.

Name ______________________________

Words with *aw*

Spelling Words				
saw	draw	crawl	straw	law
jaw	paw	lawn	yawn	hawk

High-Frequency Words
science
through

Write the missing list word.

1. The ____ says to wear seatbelts.
2. The baby is learning to ____.
3. Did you mow the ____?
4. Look at that ____ fly.
5. My ____ is sore.
6. Let's ____ a picture.
7. We ____ a snake.
8. My cat has one white ____.
9. Sue drank ____ a straw.
10. I like to study ____.

Home Activity Your child wrote spelling words and high-frequency words to complete sentences. Help your child make silly sentences by substituting other list words in the sentences. For example: The **hawk** says to wear seatbelts.

Name ________________________________

Adverbs

Write about a time you built or made something.
Use **adverbs** to tell when and where.
Read your story aloud to the class.

Choose other adverbs. **Say** a sentence for each adverb.

Home Activity Your child learned how to use adverbs in writing. Have your child read aloud the story he or she wrote on this page. Ask your child to point out the adverbs.

Name ______________________

Words with *aw*

Spelling Words				
saw	draw	crawl	straw	law
jaw	paw	lawn	yawn	hawk

Draw lines through all the **p**'s and **o**'s.
Write the word that is left.

1. **h o a p w p k o** 1. ______
2. **l o o a p w p n** 2. ______
3. **p c o r p a w p l** 3. ______
4. **y o a p w p p n o** 4. ______

Write six list words that rhyme with **thaw**.

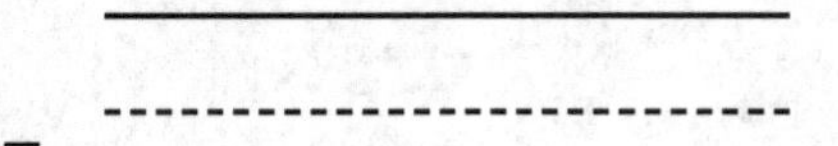

5. ______ 6. ______

7. ______ 8. ______

9. ______ 10. ______

Home Activity Your child has been learning to spell words with the vowel sound in *saw*. Help your child use the list words to make more word puzzles similar to those at the top of this page.

Name ______________________________

Adverbs

Fill in the circle by the adverb that tells when or where.

1. Maya and I built our invention yesterday.
- ◯ Maya
- ◯ built
- ◯ yesterday

2. We made it upstairs in my room.
- ◯ We
- ◯ upstairs
- ◯ my

3. We had to start over often.
- ◯ had
- ◯ start
- ◯ often

4. Soon, we figured it out.
- ◯ Soon
- ◯ figured
- ◯ out

5. Next, we showed our parents.
- ◯ Next
- ◯ we
- ◯ parents

Home Activity Your child prepared for taking tests on adverbs that tell when and where. Read aloud a favorite story to your child. Have your child listen for adverbs that tell when and where.

Name ______________________

Add re- or **un-** to the word in ( ).
Write the new word on the line.

re- + do = **re**do
un- + clear = **un**clear

(build)

1. Mr. Ford will ______________ the car.

(happy)

2. He is ______________ with the color.

(paint)

3. He will ______________ it.

(fills)

4. He ______________ the car with gas.

(lock)

5. Don't forget to ______________ the door!

Home Activity Your child added the prefixes *un-* and *re-* to words. Ask your child to think of other words to which *un-* and *re-* can be added. Have him or her list the words and use them in sentences.

Name ______________________

Pick a word from the box to finish each sentence.
Write it on the line.

poor	answered
different	carry

1. The soil was so ______________ that nothing grew.

2. I ______________ all the questions about my garden.

3. All of the flowers were ______________ colors.

4. I have to ______________ the garden tools to the backyard.

Pick two words from the box.
Write your own sentences using each word.

5. ______________________________

6. ______________________________

7. ______________________________

8. ______________________________

Home Activity Your child learned to read and identify the words *answered, carry, different*, and *poor*. Encourage your child to make up a story that uses these words and draw pictures to illustrate the story.

Name ______________________________

Read the story. **Answer** the questions.

This story is a folktale. It was passed along by the native people in the Philippines.

The Stars and the Moon

Long ago, the sky was close to the ground. A woman wanted to pound rice with her hammer. Before she started, she took off her beads from her neck. She took off the comb in her hair. She hung them both on the sky. Each time she raised her hammer, it would hit the sky. One time her hammer struck the sky so hard that the sky began to rise. It went up so far she lost her beads and comb. They never came back. The comb became the moon. The beads became the stars.

1. What is the big idea of the story?

____

____

2. How did the woman change the sky and the ground?

____

____

3. How do you know this is a folktale?

____

____

Home Activity Your child has learned about themes in stories. As you read stories with your child, discuss the big ideas in the stories.

Name ______________________________

Writing • Poem

My Piggy Bank

"Milk's all gone,"
said my older brother Sean.
He threw the jug in the trash can,
but I took it out and ran
right to the sink to wash it clean.
Then I used a marker to paint it green.
Now the jug's my very own piggy bank.
For that I have my brother Sean to thank.

Key Features of a Poem

- Many poems are shorter than a story.
- The lines in a poem often end with rhyming words.

Name ______________________________

Circle the word for each picture.

post

gold

rind

wild

1. 
fold fell

2. 
kite kind

3. 
child chilled

4. 
mast most

5. 
cold call

6. 
fin find

7. 
wind went

8. 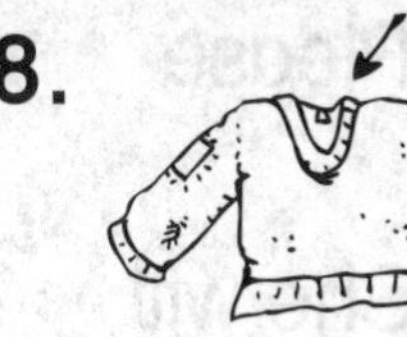

old all

Circle the word to finish each sentence.

9. I told / tied my baby sister a story.

10. I can't fine / find my pencil.

Home Activity Your child read words with the long *o* sound as in *post* and *gold* and the long *i* sound as in *rind* and *wild*. Use each word in a sentence with your child.

Name ______________________

Words with Prefixes *un-, re-*

Spelling Words				
unhappy	refill	untie	undo	repay
unkind	undress	retell	reopen	rewind

Circle a word to finish the sentence. **Write** it.

1. Will you **unkind** **untie** my ribbon? ______________

2. She looks **unhappy** **repay**. ______________

3. Please **refill** **reopen** the book. ______________

4. She will **repay** **unhappy** you. ______________

5. Please **retell** **undress** that story. ______________

6. I will **retell** **undress** the doll. ______________

7. Please **rewind** **undo** the movie. ______________

8. Can you **repay** **undo** this knot? ______________

9. He is **rewind** **unkind** to the dog. ______________

10. He will **retell** **refill** the glasses. ______________

Home Activity Your child spelled words to complete sentences. Read a sentence on this page. Ask your child to identify the word with the prefix *re-* or *un-* and spell it.

Name ______________________________

Prepositions and Prepositional Phrases

A **preposition** is the first word in a group of words called a **prepositional phrase.**

Preposition	Momoko sat <u>on</u> the steps.
Prepositional Phrase	Momoko sat <u>on the steps</u>.

Circle the preposition in each sentence.
Say a new sentence using each preposition.

1. Susie read a book about gardens.
2. Susie wanted a garden in her yard.
3. She started working before school.
4. She planted flowers after school.

Write the prepositional phrase in the sentence.
Say other prepositional phrases that could replace it.

5. I got a good idea in the morning.

____

Home Activity Your child learned about prepositions. Read an article to your child. Have him or her identify prepositional phrases from the article.

Name ______________________

Sequence

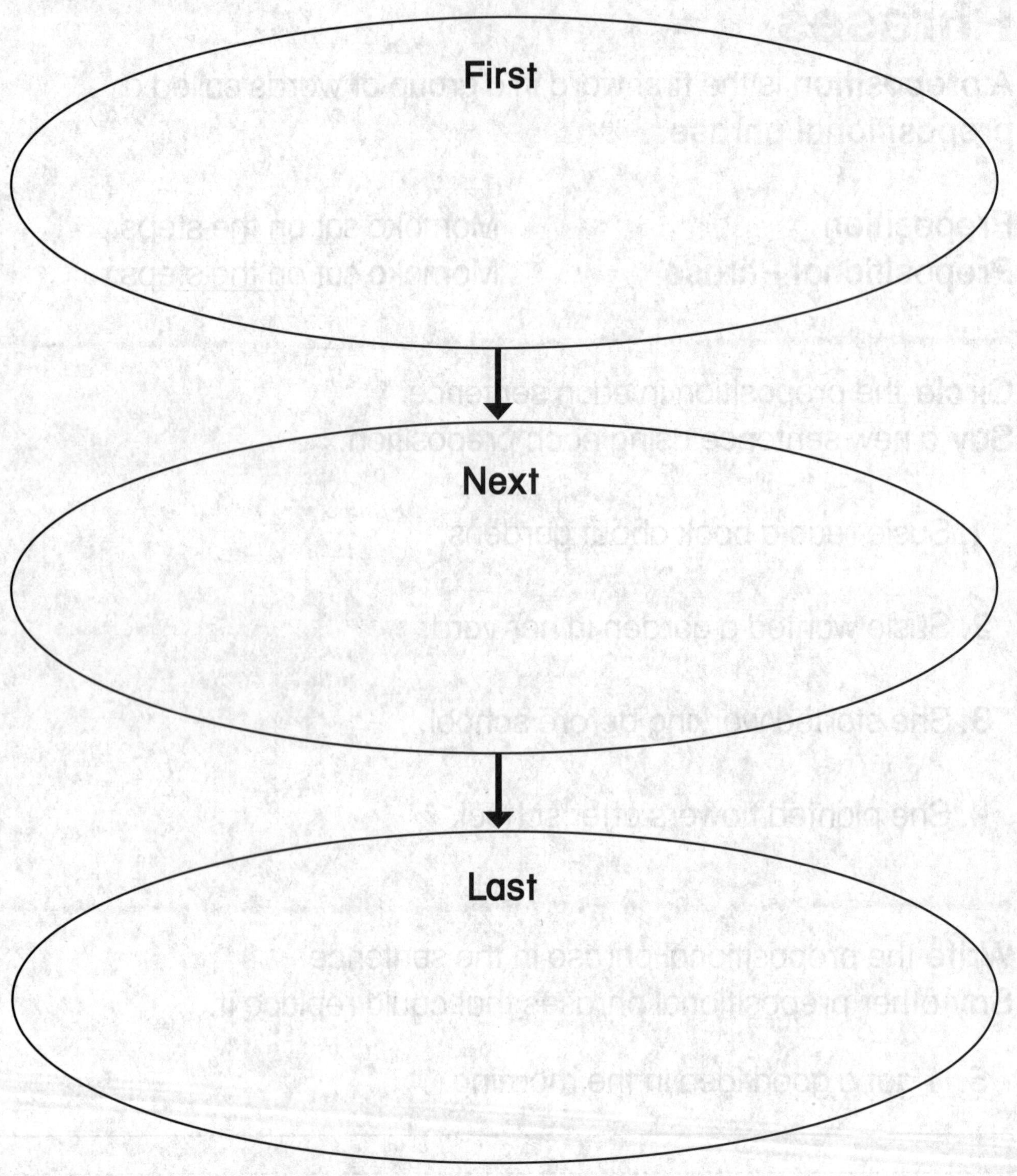

School + Home

Home Activity Your child has planned a poem. Play a word game by making up phrases that rhyme with household words, such as *bed* (sleepy head) or *book* (take a look).

Name ______________________________

Copy the **sentences.** Leave the correct space between words.

1. Please unfold the paper.

2. He will unlock the safe.

3. The store will reopen.

4. Rewrite your name.

5. Let's unload the box.

Did you leave the correct space between your words? 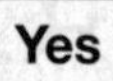 Yes 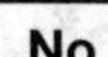 No

Home Activity Your child practiced writing sentences using words that begin with *un-* and *re-*. Write the following words on a sheet of paper and have your child read and rewrite them as neatly as possible: *rejoin, remake, unseen, unkind.*

Name ______________________________

Look at the picture.
Read the introduction.
Write what each character will say.
Present the play.

One day, a boy walked into town. He was hungry. He had a pot and a stone. He decided to make stone soup.

Stone Soup: The Play

Boy: I am going to make stone soup, but I need vegetables.

____

Farmer: ______________________________

Woman: Here are some onions.

Young Girl: Here are some tomatoes.

____

Young Boy: ______________________________

Mule: Here is some water.

Boy: The soup is ready. Please have some.

Everyone: By working together, everyone enjoyed the soup.

Home Activity Your child learned how to write a script. Together with your child, think of a favorite folktale, fairy tale, or other story that you enjoy. Work together to write a script based on the characters of the story. If possible, cast the characters and present the play as a family.

Jess folded her arms.

"It's unwise to stay sad," she said. "Let's restart your day and have some fun!"

Decodable Story *Quincy's Bad Day*
Target Skills Prefixes *un-* and *re-*; Long *o* and Long *i*

Name ____________________

Quincy's Bad Day

Prefixes *un-* and *re-*	Long *o* and Long *i*		High-Frequency Words	
unhappy	told	wild	you	the
unlocked	sold	kind	I	to
unwise	old	find	said	your
replace	folded		a	some
restart	most			

"You look most unhappy," Jess told Quincy.

"I AM unhappy," Quincy said.

"Why?" asked Jess with a kind smile.

"First, Dad sold my old bike.

"I hope I can replace it."

"Then, the dog went wild.

He ran out the unlocked gate.

I didn't find him until just now."

Name ____________________

Words with Prefixes *un-*, *re-*

Spelling Words					High-Frequency Words
unhappy	refill	untie	undo	repay	different
unkind	undress	retell	reopen	rewind	carry

Write the prefix **un-** or **re-**. **Write** the list word.

1. Dad will ________tell the joke. ____________
2. I can ________tie my shoes. ____________
3. Let's ________do this puzzle. ____________
4. He was ________kind to Sam. ____________
5. She is ________happy. ____________
6. You must ________pay the loan. ____________
7. The men will ________open the crate. ____________
8. Can you ________wind the tape? ____________

Write the word that has the same meaning.

9. not alike ____________ 10. take ____________

Home Activity Your child wrote words with the prefixes *un-* and *re-*. Have your child name the base word in each list word and tell how adding the prefix changes the meaning.

Name ______________________________

Prepositions and Prepositional Phrases

Imagine you are helping build a garden.

Write about what happens. **Use** prepositional phrases.

Choose other prepositions. **Say** a sentence for each preposition.

Home Activity Your child learned how to use prepositions in writing. Take turns with your child writing sentences using prepositional phrases.

Name ______________________

Words with Prefixes *un-*, *re-*

Spelling Words				
unhappy	refill	untie	undo	repay
unkind	undress	retell	reopen	rewind

Read the words in the box.
Add un- or **re-** to make a list word. **Write** it.

pay	tell
wind	fill

1. ______________ 2. ______________

3. ______________ 4. ______________

Find a list word in each row of letters. **Circle** it. **Write** it.

5. r u n t i e s t 5. ______________

6. t h r e o p e n 6. ______________

7. u n k i n d e s 7. ______________

8. x u n d r e s s 8. ______________

9. w i u n d o t s 9. ______________

10. s u n h a p p y 10. ______________

Home Activity Your child has been learning to spell words with the prefixes *un-* and *re-*. Help your child think of other words with these prefixes.

Name ______________________________

Prepositions and Prepositional Phrases

Mark the word in each sentence that is a preposition.

1. The yard was bordered with homes like hers.
   - ○ The
   - ○ yard
   - ○ with

2. Except for old tires, the yard was cold and bare.
   - ○ Except
   - ○ tires
   - ○ the

3. The neighbors watched Momoko from their windows.
   - ○ neighbors
   - ○ from
   - ○ windows

4. Momoko planted the bulbs across the yard.
   - ○ Momoko
   - ○ bulbs
   - ○ across

5. People would sit and visit in the evenings.
   - ○ People
   - ○ sit
   - ○ in

Home Activity Your child prepared for taking tests on prepositions. Read aloud a favorite story to your child. Have your child say "Stop" each time he or she hears a prepositional phrase.

Writing Process Lessons

Name ________________________

Story Chart

Fill out this story chart to help you organize your ideas. **Write** your ideas in sentences.

Title ________________________

Beginning

↓

Middle

↓

End

Name ______________________________

Use Words That Tell How You Feel

Write a word from the box to tell how the writer feels.

Use each word one time. The pictures will help you.

Word Bank
happy
sad
scared
mad

1. My brother took my book.

I feel ______________________.

2. I won a prize.

I feel ______________________.

3. My best friend moved away.

I feel ______________________.

4. A dog growled at me.

I feel ______________________.

Name ______________________________

Adding a Word, Phrase, or Sentence

Read each set of sentences. **Answer** the question.

1. What word did the writer add? Write the word.

   I saw a fish.

   I saw a huge fish.

   ____

2. What phrase did the writer add? Write the phrase.

   The fish swam.

   The fish swam into me.

   ____

3. What sentence did the writer add? Write the sentence.

   Then the fish swam away.

   Then the fish swam away. I laughed.

   ____

Name ______________________________

Self-Evaluation Guide

Check *Yes* or *No* about voice in your story.

	Yes	No
1. I used words that tell feelings or opinions.		
2. I used one or more words that describe.		
3. I used one or more words that show action.		

Answer the questions.

4. What is the best part of your story?

____

____

____

5. What is one thing you would change about this story if you could write it again?

____

____

____

Name ______________________________

Letter Chart

Fill out this letter chart to help you organize your ideas.
Write your ideas in sentences.

Whom is the letter for?

What is the main idea of the letter?

What details support the main idea?

Whom is the letter from?

Name ____________________

Use Correct Letter Form

Write the date, greeting, and closing from the box to complete the letter. **Put** commas in the correct places. **Write** your name at the end.

Yours truly
May 4 2011
Dear Ms. Allen

____

____

You are a good worker. You are always there.

You make sure kids get to school safely.

Thank you.

____

____

Name ______________________________

Deleting a Word, Phrase, or Sentence

Read the sentences. **Follow** the directions.

1. The fire alarm was so so loud!

   Delete, or take out, the word that is not needed. Write the sentence.

2. Juan was scared and afraid.

   Delete the phrase that is not needed. Write the sentence.

3. Juan found out there was no fire. The firefighter said there was no fire.

   Delete one sentence that is not needed. Write the other sentence.

Name ______________________________

Editing 1

Edit these sentences. **Look** for errors in grammar, punctuation, capitalization, and spelling. **Use** proofreading marks to show the corrections.

Proofreading Marks	
Delete (Take out)	ᘐ
Add	^
Spelling	⬭
Uppercase letter	≡
Lowercase letter	/

1. The girls cros the street.

2. They need help

3. Mr. james helps them.

4. The girls is happy.

5. We hav many helpers.

Now you will edit the draft of your letter. Use the rubric from your teacher to check the grammar, punctuation, and spelling in your letter. Then, use your draft to make a final copy of your letter. Finally, you will publish your writing and share it with others.

Name ______________________________

Main Idea and Details Chart

Fill in the chart with the main idea and details for your expository article. **Write** your ideas in sentences.

Main Idea

Detail

Detail

Detail

Name ______________________________

Strong Verbs

Add a strong verb from the box to each sentence.

buzzes	gleams	
bends	paddles	splashes

1. The lake ______________ in the sun.

2. A duck ______________ to shore.

3. Water ______________ on the rocks.

4. The grass ______________ in the wind.

5. A bee ______________ by my ear.

Name ______________________________

Adding or Deleting a Phrase or Sentence

Read the sentence. **Follow** the directions.

1. The birds fly.

   Add a phrase to the sentence. Tell where the birds fly. Write the new sentence.

2. The birds eat grass.

   Add a sentence. Tell why the birds eat grass. Write the new sentence.

3. The autumn leaves are red in the fall.

   Delete the phrase that is not needed. Write the new sentence.

4. There are a lot of trees in the woods. The forest has many trees. Some are tall, and some are short.

   Delete a sentence that is not needed. Write the other sentences.

Name ______________________________

Editing 2

Edit these sentences. **Look** for errors in grammar, punctuation, capitalization, and spelling. **Use** proofreading marks to show the corrections.

Proofreading Marks	
Delete (Take out)	ᘐ
Add	^
Spelling	⬭
Uppercase letter	≡
Lowercase letter	/

1. The beach has big wavs.

2. It is named for a man, will rogers.

3. Is there shells in the sand?

4. The water feels very cold

5. The air smels like salt.

Now you will edit the draft of your expository article. Use the rubric from your teacher to check the grammar, punctuation, and spelling in your expository article. Then, use your draft to make a final copy of your expository article. Finally, you will publish your writing and share it with others.

Name ______________________________

Story Chart

Fill in this story chart to help you organize your ideas.
Write your ideas in sentences.

Title ______________________________

Beginning

↓

Middle

↓

End

Name ______________________

Good Adjectives

Add an adjective from the box to each sentence.

loud	five	
tall	sunny	wild

1. It was a ______________ spring day.

2. Maria heard ______________ quacks.

3. The ______________ ducks had a nest.

4. It was in the ______________ grass.

5. Maria saw ______________ baby ducks.

Name ______________________________

Adding or Deleting a Word or Phrase

Read the sentence. **Follow** the directions.

1. Tim walked.

   Add a phrase to the sentence. Tell where Tim walked. Write the new sentence.

   ____

   ____

2. Tim got a game.

   Add a word to the sentence. Tell more about the game. Write the new sentence.

   ____

   ____

3. Tim and Juan had fun with the fun game.

   Delete a word that is not needed. Draw a line through the word.

4. Tom left his game and forgot it at Juan's house.

   Delete a phrase that is not needed. Draw a line through the phrase.

Name ______________________________

Editing 3

Proofreading Marks	
Delete (Take out)	ᘔ
Add	^
Spelling	⬭
Uppercase letter	≡
Lowercase letter	/

This is part of a realistic story. **Edit** this paragraph. **Look** for errors in grammar, punctuation, capitalization, and spelling. **Use** proofreading marks to show the corrections.

Lee loved too read. Her favorite book was about a girl and her dog. Lee readed it every night. One day the book was lost. Lee looked all over that night she was sad. She could not read her favorite book. She could not slep. Her pillow felt hard. She look under it. There was her book! Lee was so gladd.

Now you will edit the draft of your realistic story. Use the rubric from your teacher to check the grammar, punctuation, and spelling in your realistic story. Then, use your draft to make a final copy of your realistic story. Finally, you will publish your writing and share it with others.

Name ____________________________

K-W-L Chart

Fill out this K-W-L chart to help you organize your ideas. **Write** your ideas in sentences.

What We Know	What We Want to Know	What We Learned

Name ______________________________

Writing Trait: Sentences

• Use all kinds of sentences: statements, questions, commands, and exclamations.
• Use different beginnings. Don't start too many sentences with **the, he,** or **she.**

Write the letter of each sentence next to the word that identifies what kind of sentence it is.

(A) Who is Alexander Graham Bell? **(B)** He invented the telephone. **(C)** That's a wonderful invention! **(D)** Don't forget about his work with deaf people.

1. Statement: ____________ **3.** Command: ____________

2. Question: ____________ **4.** Exclamation: ____________

Rearrange the words in each sentence so it begins with the underlined word. **Write** the paragraph.

Example: She invented a new game last week.
Answer: Last week she invented a new game.

She played the game today. She changed it later. She likes it better now!

____

____

____

____

Name ______________________________

Adding or Deleting a Word or Sentence

Read the sentence. **Follow** the directions.

1. Kate invented a toy.

   Add a word to describe the toy. Write the new sentence.

2. The toy can sing.

   Add a sentence. Tell what else the toy can do. Write both sentences.

3. The first kite was a huge giant leaf.

   Delete a word that is not needed. Draw a line through the word.

4. The first Ferris wheel was 250 feet tall. How tall is the Statue of Liberty? Many people could ride on the Ferris wheel.

   Delete the sentence that does not belong. Draw a line through the sentence.

Name ______________________

Self-Evaluation Guide

Check Yes or **No** about sentences in your report.

	Yes	No
1. I used facts in my research report.		
2. I used different kinds of sentences.		
3. I used different beginnings for my sentences.		

Answer the questions.

4. What is the best part of your report?

5. What is one thing you would change about this report if you could write it again?

Name ______________________________

My Rubric

Title ______________________________

Features of the Writing	4	3	2	1
Content				
Grammar				
Punctuation				
Spelling				

To the Teacher
Use this information to help students use the rubric.
4 = The feature is fully developed in the writing.
3 = The feature is present in the writing, but is not fully developed.
2 = The feature is not clearly present in the writing
1 = The feature is not present in the writing.